HUGH JOHNSON'S

Pocket Encyclopedia of

WINE 1994

A Fireside Book
Published by Simon & Schuster Inc.
New York London Toronto
Sydney Tokyo Singapore

Key to Symbols

r	red
p	rosé
w	white
br	brown
(r)	denotes less important wine
dr	dry (assume wine is dry when dr or sw not indicated)
sw	sweet
s/sw	semi-sweet
sp	sparkling
*	plain, everyday quality
**	above average
***	well known, highly reputed
****	grand, prestigious, expensive
	usually particularly good value in its class
90 91 etc	recommended years which may be currently available
87' etc	vintage regarded as particularly successful for the property in question
85 etc	Years in **bold** should be ready for drinking (the others should be kept). Where both reds and whites are indicated the red is intended unless otherwise stated. **NB** German vintages are codified by a different system. *See* note on page 100.
(89)	provisional rating
DYA	drink the youngest available
NV	Vintage not normally shown on label. In Champagne, means a blend of several vintages for continuity.
SMALL CAPS	properties, areas or terms cross-referred within the section.

See page 5 for extra explanation.
A quick-reference vintage chart appears on page 208.

Fireside
Simon & Schuster Building
Rockefeller Center
1230 Avenue of the Americas
New York, New York 10020

First edition published 1977
Revised editions published 1978, 1979, 1980, 1981, 1982, 1983, 1984, 1985, 1986, 1987, 1988, 1989, 1990, 1991, 1992, 1993

ISBN 0-671-87963-4
Library of Congress Cataloging Data Number 87-640762

Editors Susan Keevil, Anthea Snow
Executive Editor Anne Ryland
Art Director Tim Foster
Production Fiona Wright
Film by Tradespools Ltd, Frome, Somerset
Map origination by Mandarin Offset, Hong Kong
Produced by Mandarin Offset
Printed in Malaysia

Contents

Introduction

Revising this little book every year amounts to a sort of stock-taking of the world's wines. Each year there is even more choice as the 400-odd new in this edition testify. But is there really more diversity?

The answer, I'm afraid, is qualified. The surge of technology that made the '80s so exciting holds dangers for the wines of the '90s. The threat is that modern wines, wherever they come from, will taste more and more alike.

The first reason is the planting of a dismally limited palette of grape varieties: above all Chardonnay and Cabernet. Winemakers like them because they allow them to believe they are emulating the world's best red and white wines (also because they are relatively easy to grow). And marketing folk like them because by now everybody knows their names.

But it is not just grapes that threaten uniformity. It is a set of assumptions about what constitutes a competitive, marketable wine – assumptions propagated and encouraged by the simplistic American habit of 'scoring' wines as though they were boxers.

A typical modern Chardonnay has a certain soft or sweet fruitiness and a distinctive smell and taste of oak. 'French oak' has become a talisman of a certain level of 'quality'. But we are being cheated. The great wines that provide the inspiration are not oak flavoured. Any wine that tastes more of oak than of wine (or indeed more of grapes than wine) should be considered flawed.

The best winemakers look forward. They want to make better use of their land: to find its character in its fruit. Happily the challenge of different grapes shows up more and more in these pages. And so does the merger and shut down of big wineries that let marketing lead them to perdition.

My aim in this book is to squeeze the essence of this ever-changing world of wine into your pocket.

To new readers I must explain that my information is gathered from many sources through innumerable visits and tastings and a perpetual spate of correspondence. The process of revision never stops, whether it involves a change of emphasis or fact, or new vintages, or a new entry. There is constant pressure for inclusion from new producers. Newness itself, however, is not a qualification for entry. Old producers also do newsworthy things.

The book is designed to take the panic out of buying; the panic when faced with a long restaurant wine list or shelf upon mind-numbing shelf of bottles in a store. Your mind goes blank. You fumble for your little book. All you need to establish is what country a wine comes from. Look up the principal words on the label in that country's section. You will find enough potted information to let you judge whether this is the wine you want.

Specifically, you will find information on the type and colour of wine, its status or prestige, whether it is usually good value for money, which vintages are recommendable and which are ready to drink – and often considerably more, about the quantity made, grapes used, ownership and the rest. Thousands of cross-references help you delve further. I can browse for hours...

How to Read an Entry

The top line of most entries consists of the following information:

1 Which part of the country in question the wine comes from.

2 Whether it is red, rosé or white (or brown/amber), dry, sweet or sparkling, or several of these (and which is most important).

3 Its general standing as to quality: a necessarily rough and ready guide based on its current reputation as reflected in its prices.

- ★ plain, everyday quality
- ★★ above average
- ★★★ well-known, highly reputed
- ★★★★ grand, prestigious, expensive

So much is more or less objective. Additionally there is a subjective rating: shading around the stars of any wine which in my experience is usually particularly good within its price range. There are good everyday wines as well as good luxury wines. The shading system helps you find them.

4 Vintage information: which of the recent vintages that *may* still be available can be recommended; of these, which are ready to drink this year, and which will probably improve with keeping. Your first choice for current drinking should be one of the vintage years printed in **bold** type. Buy light-type years for further maturing.

The German vintage information works on a different principle: see the note on page 100.

Acknowledgements

This store of detailed recommendations comes partly from my own notes and partly from those of a great number of kind friends. Without the generous help and cooperation of innumerable winemakers, merchants and critics, I could not attempt it. I particularly want to thank the following for help with research or in the areas of their special knowledge.

Jim Ainsworth
Burton Anderson
Martyn Assirati
Jean-Claude Berrouet
Vicky Bishop
Michael Broadbent MW
Stelios Damianou
Len Evans
Dereck Foster
Rosemary George MW
Howard Goldberg
Garry Grosvenor
Marlies Grosvenor
Grahame Haggart
James Halliday
Russell Hone
Susan Keevil
Andreas Keller
Matt Kramer
Gabriel Lachmann
Tony Laithwaite
David Lake MW
Miles Lambert-Gócs
Christopher Lindlar
Giles MacDonogh
Andreas März
Maggie McNie
Eszter Molnár
Vladimir Moskvan
Christian Moueix
Douglas Murray
Nobuko Nishioka
Jordanis Petridis
Don Philpot
Stuart S Piggott
John Platter
Carlos Read
Jan and Maite Read
Dr Bernard Rhodes
Anne Ryland
Hugh Ryman
Peter A Sichel
Stephen Skelton
Steven Spurrier
Charles Sydney
Bob Thompson
Margarit Todorov
Peter Vinding-Diers
Rebecca Wassermann-Hone
David Wolfe

Grape Varieties

As more and more wine is sold under its grape-variety name, especially in regions and countries with no 'classic' traditions, a knowledge of the flavours and qualities of the most-planted (or rather most-sold) varieties becomes the first weapon in the wine buyer's armoury. Centuries of selection have resulted in each of Europe's traditional wine areas having its favourite variety, or group of varieties. Red burgundy is made of one grape, the Pinot Noir; red Bordeaux of three or four (the proportions at the discretion of the grower). The laws say which grapes must be used, so the labels do not mention them.

But in newer regions the choice of grapes is the growers' most crucial decision. Where they are proud of it, and intend the wine to have the flavour of a particular grape, its variety is the first thing they put on the label. Hence the originally Californian term 'varietal wine' – meaning, in principle, one grape variety.

At least seven varieties – Cabernet, Pinot Noir, Riesling, Sauvignon Blanc, Chardonnay, Gewürztraminer and Muscat – have memorable tastes and smells distinct enough to form international categories of wine. To these you can add Merlot, Syrah, Sémillon, Chenin Blanc, Pinots Blanc and Gris, Sylvaner, Nebbiolo, Sangiovese, Tempranillo...

Further notes on grapes will be found through the book. The following are the best and/or commonest wine grapes. Abbreviations used in the text are in brackets.

Grapes for white wine

Albariño The Spanish name for N Portugal's Alvarinho, newly emerging as excellently fresh and fragrant wine in Galicia.

Aligoté Burgundy's second-rank white grape. Crisp (often sharp) wine, needs drinking in 1–3 years. Perfect for mixing with cassis (blackcurrant liqueur) to make a 'Kir'. Also used in E Europe.

Blanc Fumé Another name for SAUV BL, referring to the reputedly 'smoky' smell of the wine, particularly from the upper Loire (Sancerre and Pouilly). In California the name is often used for oak-aged Sauv Bl and reversed to 'Fumé Blanc'.

Bual Makes top quality sweet madeira wines.

Chardonnay (Chard) The white burgundy grape, one of the grapes of Champagne, and the best white grape of the New World, partly because it is one of the easiest and most forgiving to grow and vinify. All regions are now trying it, mostly aged (or fermented) in oak to reproduce the flavours of burgundy. Australia and California make classics. Those of Italy, Spain, New Zealand, South Africa, New York State, Bulgaria, Chile, Hungary and the Midi are all coming on strong.

Chasselas A prolific early-ripening grape with little aroma, also grown for eating. Best known as Fendant in Switzerland (where it is supreme), Gutedel in Germany.

Chenin Blanc (Chenin Bl) The great white grape of the middle Loire (Vouvray, Layon etc). Wine can be dry or sweet (or very sweet), but always retains plenty of acidity – hence its popularity in California, where it can make fine wine, but is rarely so used. See also Steen.

Clairette A dull, neutral grape formerly widely used in the S of France.

Colombard Slightly fruity, nicely sharp grape, now hugely popular in California, gaining ground in SW France, South Africa etc.

Fendant See Chasselas.

Folle Blanche High acid/little flavour make this ideal for brandy. Called Gros Plant in Brittany, Picpoul in Armagnac. Respectable in California.

Fumé Blanc (Fumé Bl) See Blanc Fumé.

Furmint A grape of great character: the trademark of Hungary both as the principal grape in Tokay and as vivid vigorous table wine with an appley flavour. Called Sipon in Slovenia. Some grown in Austria.

Grechetto or Greco Ancient grape of central and S Italy with vitality and style.

Gewürztraminer, alias Traminer (Gewürz) One of the most pungent grapes, distinctively spicy with aromas like rose petals and grapefruit. Wines are often rich and soft, even when fully dry. Best in Alsace; also good in Germany, E Europe, Australia, California, New Zealand.

Grauburgunder See Pinot Gris.

Grüner Veltliner Austria's favourite. Around Vienna and in the Wachau and Weinviertel (also in Moravia) it can be delicious: light but dry and lively. Drink young.

Italian Riesling Grown in N Italy and all over central E Europe. Much inferior to Rhine RIES, with lower acidity. Alias Welschriesling, Olaszrizling (but no longer legally labelled simply 'Riesling').

Kerner The most successful of a score of recent German varieties, mostly made by crossing RIES x SILVANER (but in this case RIES x (red) Trollinger). Early-ripening flowery (but often too blatant) wine with good acidity. Popular in Pfalz, Rheinhessen etc.

Macabeo The workhorse white grape of N Spain, widespread in Rioja (alias Viura) and in Catalan cava country.

Malvasia Known as Malmsey in Madeira, Malvasia in Italy, Malvoisie in France. Alias Vermentino (esp in Corsica). Also grown in Greece, Spain, W Australia, E Europe. Makes rich brown wines or soft whites, ageing magnificently with superb potential not often realized.

Marsanne Principal white grape (with Roussanne) of the N Rhône (eg St-Joseph, St-Péray, Crozes-Hermitage). Also used to effect in Victoria, California and (as Ermitage Blanc) in the Valais. Soft full wines age well.

Müller-Thurgau (Müller-T) Dominant variety in Germany's Rheinhessen and Pfalz; a cross between RIES and SILVANER. Ripens early to make soft aromatic wines for drinking young. Makes good sweet wines but usually dull, often coarse, dry ones.

Muscadet, alias Melon de Bourgogne Makes light, very dry wines with a seaside tang round Nantes in Brittany. They should not be sharp, but faintly salty and very refreshing. (California 'Pinot Bl' is this grape.)

Muscat (Many varieties; the best is Muscat Blanc à Petits Grains.) Universally grown, easily recognized, pungent grapes, mostly made into perfumed sweet wines, often fortified (as in France's vins doux naturels). Muscat d'Alsace is unusual in being dry.

Muscadelle Adds aroma to many white Bordeaux.

Palomino, alias Listan Makes all the best sherry but poor table wine.

Pedro Ximénez, alias PX Makes very strong wine in Montilla and Málaga. Used in blending sweet sherries. Also grown in Argentina, the Canaries, Australia, California, South Africa.

Pinot Blanc (Pinot Bl) A cousin of PINOT N; not related to CHARD, but with a similar, milder character: light, fresh, fruity, not aromatic; good for eg Italian spumante. Grown in Alsace, N Italy, S Germany, E Europe. Weissburgunder in Germany. See also Muscadet.

Pinot Gris (Pinot Gr) At best makes rather heavy, even 'thick', full-bodied whites with a certain spicy style. Known as Tokay in Alsace, Ruländer or Grauburgunder in Germany, Tocai or Pinot Grigio in Italy and Slovenia (but much thinner wine). Traditional but almost extinct in Burgundy and Champagne.

Pinot Noir (Pinot N) Superlative black grape (See Grapes for red wine) used in Champagne and occasionally elsewhere (eg California, Australia) for making white, sparkling, or very pale pink 'vin gris'.

Riesling (Ries) Germany's great grape, and at present the world's most underrated. Wine of brilliant sweet/acid balance, either dry or sweet, flowery in youth but maturing to subtle oily scents and flavours. Very good (usually dry) in Alsace, Austria, parts of E Europe, Australia (widely grown), California, South Africa. Often called White Johannisberg or Rhine Riesling. Subject to 'noble rot'. Due for a major revival, since (unlike CHARD) it does not need high alcohol for character.

Ruländer German name for PINOT GRIS.

Sauvignon Blanc (Sauv Bl) Makes v distinctive aromatic grassy sometimes smoky-scented wine; can be austere (eg upper Loire) or buxom (in Sauternes blended with SEM, and in parts of California). A brilliant success in New Zealand, vg in NE Italy. Also called Fumé Bl or vice versa.

Scheurebe Spicy-flavoured German RIES x SYLVANER, very successful in Pfalz, esp for Auslesen. Can be weedy in dry wines.

Sémillon (Sém) The grape contributing the lusciousness to great Sauternes; subject to 'noble rot' in the right conditions but increasingly important for Graves and dry white Bordeaux too. Makes soft dry wine of great potential. Traditionally called 'Riesling' in parts of Australia. Old Hunter Valley Sém can be great wine.

Sercial Makes the driest madeira; (where legend says it is really RIESLING!).

Seyval Blanc (Seyval Bl) French-made hybrid of French and American vines. Very hardy and attractively fruity. Popular and reasonably successful in the eastern States and England.

Steen South Africa's most popular white grape: good lively fruity wine. Said to be the CHENIN BL of the Loire.

Silvaner, alias Sylvaner Germany's former workhorse grape: wine rarely better than pleasant except in Franconia where it is savoury and ages admirably, and in Rheinhessen, where it is enjoying a renaissance. Good in the Italian Tyrol and useful in Alsace. Very good (and powerful) as Johannisberg in the Valais, Switzerland.

Tokay See Pinot Gris. Also a table grape in California and a supposedly Hungarian grape in Australia. The wine Tokay is made of FURMINT.

Traminer See Gewürztraminer.

Trebbiano Important but mediocre grape of central Italy, used in Orvieto, Chianti, Soave, etc. Also grown in S France as Ugni Bl, and Cognac as St-Emilion. Thin, neutral wine; really needs blending.

Ugni Blanc (Ugni Bl) See Trebbiano.

Verdejo The grape of Rueda in Castile, potentially fine and long-lived.

Verdelho Madeira grape making excellent medium-sweet wine; in Australia, fresh soft dry wine of great character.

Verdicchio Gives its name to good dry wine in central-eastern Italy.

Vermentino See Malvasia.

Vernaccia Grape grown in central and S Italy and Sardinia for strong smooth lively wine, sometimes inclining towards sherry.

Viognier Rare grape of the Rhône, grown at Condrieu for v fine fragrant wine. Much in vogue in the Midi, California, etc, but still only a trickle.

Viura See Macabeo.

Weissburgunder See Pinot Blanc.

Welschriesling See Italian Riesling.

Grapes for red wine

Aleatico Dark Muscat variety, alias Aglianico, used the length of W Italy for fragrant sweet wines.

Barbera Most popular of many productive grapes of N Italy, esp Piedmont, giving dark, fruity, often sharp wine. Gaining prestige in California.

Brunello S Tuscan form of SANGIOVESE, splendid at Montalcino.

Cabernet Franc, alias Bouchet (Cab F) The lesser of two sorts of Cab grown in Bordeaux but dominant (as 'Bouchet') in St-Emilion. The Cab of the Loire making Chinon, etc, and rosé.

Cabernet Sauvignon (Cab S) Grape of great character: spicy, herby and tannic, with a characteristic 'blackcurrant' aroma. The first grape of the Médoc, also makes most of the best Californian, Australian, S American and E European reds. Its red wine almost always needs ageing and usually benefits from blending with eg MERLOT, CAB F or SYRAH. Makes very aromatic rosé.

Carignan By far the commonest grape of France, covering hundreds of thousands of acres. Prolific with dull but harmless wine. Best from old vines in Corbières. Also common in N Africa, Spain, California.

Cinsaut Common bulk-producing grape of S France; in S Africa crossed with PINOT N to make Pinotage.

Dolcetto Source of soft seductive dry red in Piedmont. Now high fashion.

Gamay The Beaujolais grape: light, very fragrant wines, at their best young. Makes even lighter wine on the Loire, in central France, and in Switzerland and Savoie. Known as 'Napa Gamay' in California.

Gamay Beaujolais Not GAMAY but a poor variety of PINOT N in California.

Grenache, alias Garnacha, Alicante, Cannonau Useful grape for strong fruity but pale wine: good rosé and vin doux naturel. Grown in S France, Spain, California. Usually blended (eg Châteauneuf-du-Pape).

Grignolino Makes one of the good cheap table wines of Piedmont.

Kadarka, alias Gamza Makes healthy sound agreeable reds in Hungary, Bulgaria etc.

Lambrusco Productive grape of the lower Po valley, giving quintessentially Italian, cheerful sweet and fizzy red.

Malbec, alias Cot Minor in Bordeaux, major in Cahors and Argentina. Dark, dense and tannic wine capable of real quality.

Merlot Adaptable grape making the great fragrant and rich wines of Pomerol and (with CAB F) St-Emilion, an important element in Médoc reds, soft and strong in California and Australia, lighter but often good in N Italy, Italian Switzerland, Slovenia, Argentina, etc.

Montepulciano Confusingly, a major central-eastern Italian grape of good quality, as well as a town in Tuscany.

Mourvèdre, alias Mataro Excellent dark aromatic tannic grape used for blending in Provence (especially in Bandol) and the Midi.

Nebbiolo, alias Spanna and Chiavennasca One of Italy's best red grapes; makes Barolo, Barbaresco, Gattinara, Valtellina. Intense, nobly fruity and perfumed wine but very tannic, taking years to mature.

Petit Verdot Excellent but awkward Médoc grape now largely superseded.

Pinot Noir (Pinot N) The glory of Burgundy's Côte d'Or, with scent, flavour, and texture unmatched anywhere. Less happy elsewhere; makes light wines rarely of much distinction in Germany, Switzerland, Austria, Hungary. The great challenge to California and Australia (and recently S Africa). Shows exciting promise in Oregon and the Yarra Valley, Australia.

Pinotage Singular S African grape (PINOT N x CINSAUT). Can be very fruity and age interestingly, but often jammy.

Sangiovese (or Saugioveto) The main red grape of Chianti and much of central Italy. BRUNELLO is the Sangiovese Grosso.

Saperavi Makes good sharp very long-lived wine in Georgia, Ukraine etc. Blends very well with CABERNET.

Spätburgunder German for PINOT N, but a very pale shadow of burgundy.

Syrah, alias Shiraz The best Rhône red grape, with tannic purple peppery wine which can mature superbly. Very important as Shiraz in Australia, increasingly so in the Midi and California.

Tempranillo The pale aromatic fine Rioja grape, called Ull de Lebre in Catalonia, Cencibel in La Mancha. Early ripening.

Zinfandel (Zin) Fruity adaptable grape peculiar to California with blackberry-like, and sometimes metallic, flavour. Can be gloriously lush, but also makes 'blush' white wine.

Wine & Food

Attitudes to matching wine and food range from the slapdash to the near-neurotic. Oddly, it is a subject that has attracted relatively little ink until very recently: it is fertile ground for experiment. Few combinations can be dismissed outright as 'wrong', but generations of experience have produced certain working conventions that certainly do no harm. The following is a list of ideas intended to help you make quick decisions. Any of the groups of recommended wines could be extended almost indefinitely. In general I have stuck to the wines that are widely available, at the same time trying to ring the changes so that the same wines don't come up time and time again – as they tend to do in real life. Remember that in a restaurant that is truly regional (Provençal, Basque, Tuscan, Catalan, Austrian...) there is a ready-made answer – the wine of the region in question.

References to the wines will be found in national sections. The stars refer to the rating system used throughout the book.

Before the meal – aperitifs

The conventional aperitif wines are either sparkling (epitomized by champagne) or fortified (epitomized by sherry). They are still the best, but avoid peanuts, which destroy wine flavours. Olives are also too piquant for most wines; they need sherry or a martini. Eat almonds or walnuts, crisps or cheese straws instead. A glass of white or rosé table wine before eating is presently in vogue. It calls for something light and stimulating, fairly dry but not acid, with a degree of character, such as:

from France Alsace Pinot Blanc, Sylvaner or Riesling; Chablis or a good Aligoté; Muscadet; Sauvignon de Touraine; Graves Blanc; Mâcon Blanc; Crépy; Bugey; Haut-Poitou; Côtes de Gascogne. In Bordeaux the fashion is for a glass of sweet Sauternes, Loupiac or Monbazillac.

from Germany Any Kabinett wine or QbA. Choose a halbtrocken – nearly dry. Or open a mature Spätlese (5–12 yrs old). A great old (eg 76) Auslese can make the finest aperitif of all.

from Italy Pinot Bianco; Soave; Orvieto Secco; Frascati; Gavi; Montecarlo; Greco di Tufo; Vernaccia; Tocai; Lugana; Marsala Vergine.

from Spain Fino or manzanilla sherry, or Montilla (with tapas).

from Portugal Any vinho verde or, better, Alvarinho; Bucelas.

from Eastern Europe Grüner Veltliner; Welschriesling; Riesling; Leanyka; Müller-Thurgau. Tokay Szamarodni is Hungary's esp tasty contribution.

from the USA (California) Riesling; Chenin Blanc; Colombard; Fumé Blanc; Gewürztraminer; or a good 'house blend'. (New York, Oregon) Riesling. (Washington) Sémillon. Please not Chardonnay.

from Australia Barossa, Clare or Coonawarra Riesling; West Australian Verdelho; or a Marsanne from Victoria.

from South Africa Steen is ideal (the KWV labels it Chenin Blanc).

from England Almost any English wine makes a good talking point as an aperitif, especially in the garden in summer. So does New Zealand Sauvignon Blanc.

First courses

Aïoli A thirst-quencher is needed for its garlic heat. Rhône (★→★★), Provence rosé, Frascati, Verdicchio, and marc, too, for courage.

Antipasto in Italy Dry or medium white (★★): Italian (Soave, Pinot Grigio, Greco di Tufo), or light red (Dolcetto, young ★★ Chianti).

Artichoke vinaigrette Young red (★): Bordeaux, Côtes du Rhône; or acidic white: Sauvignon de Touraine.

hollandaise Full-bodied dry or medium white (★ or ★★): Mâcon Blanc, Pfalz, or a California 'house blend'.

Asparagus A difficult flavour for wine, so the wine needs plenty of its own. White burgundy (★★→★★★), Chardonnay, or Jurançon Sec.

Avocado with prawns, crab, etc Dry to medium or slightly sharp white (★★→★★★): Rheingau or Pfalz Kabinett, Sancerre, Pinot Bianco; California or Australian Chard or Sauvignon, Cape Steen, or dry rosé.

vinaigrette Light red (★), or manzanilla sherry.

Bisques Dry white with plenty of body (★★): Pinot Gris, Chardonnay. Fino or dry amontillado sherry, or Montilla.

Boudin (blood sausage) Aligoté.

Bouillabaisse Very dry white (★→★★): Muscadet, Alsace Sylvaner, Entre-Deux-Mers, Pouilly-Fumé, Cassis, Verdicchio, California Blanc Fumé.

Carpaccio beef Seems to work well with the flavour of most wines, including ★★★ reds. Top Tuscan vino da tavola is appropriate.

salmon Chardonnay (★★→★★★), or champagne.

Caviar Champagne (★★★) or iced vodka (or indeed both).

Ceviche California or Australian Chardonnay (★★), NZ Sauvignon Blanc.

Cheese fondue Dry white (★★): Fendant or Johannisberg du Valais, Grüner Veltliner, Alsace Riesling, NZ Sauvignon Blanc.

Clams and chowders Big-scale white (★★), not necessarily bone dry: Pinot Gris, dry Sauternes, Napa Chardonnay, Rhine Spätlese. Or fino sherry.

Consommé Medium-dry sherry (★★→★★★), dry madeira, Marsala Vergine.

Crostini Rustic Tuscan red, Montepulciano d'Abruzzo, Corsican rosé.

Crudités Light red or rosé (★→★★): Côtes du Rhône, Beaujolais, Minervois, Chianti, Zinfandel; or fino sherry.

Dim-Sum White (★★), esp Chard or Riesling Spätlese.

Eggs (See also Soufflés) These present difficulties: they clash with most wines and spoil good ones. So ★→★★ of whatever is going. As a last resort I can bring myself to drink champagne with scrambled eggs.

Escargots White Mâcon-Villages, ★★→★★★ California Chardonnay or Beaujolais-Villages; or ★★ red Rhône.

Fish terrine Rheingau Riesling Spätlese trocken, Chablis, Washington or Australian Sémillon, Sonoma Chardonnay; or fino sherry.

Foie gras White (★★★→★★★★). In Bordeaux they drink Sauternes. Others prefer vintage champagne or a late-harvest Gewürztraminer, or Alsace Pinot Gris. Old dry amontillado can be sublime.

Gazpacho A glass of fino before and after.

Goat's cheese, grilled or fried (warm salad) Chilled Chinon or Saumur-Champigny, Provence rosé.

Grapefruit If you must start a meal with grapefruit try port, madeira or sweet sherry with (or in) it.

Gravlax Akvavit, Grand Cru Chablis, or ★★★ Californian or Australian Chardonnay. Or vintage champagne.

Guacamole California Chardonnay (★★) or Mexican beer.

Haddock, smoked, mousse of A wonderful dish for showing off any stylish full-bodied white, incl Grand Cru Chablis.

Hangtown Fry (oysters, bacon and eggs) NV champagne.

Ham, raw or cured (See also Prosciutto) Lively Spanish or Italian red.

Herrings, raw or pickled Dutch gin (young, not aged) or Scandinavian akvavit, and cold beer.

Hors d'oeuvres (See also Antipasto) Clean fruity sharp white (★→★★): Sancerre or any Sauvignon, Alsace Sylvaner, Muscadet, Cape Steen; or young light red Bordeaux, Rhône or equivalent. Or fino sherry.

Mackerel, smoked An oily wine-destroyer. Manzanilla sherry, or schnapps.

Mayonnaise Adds richness that calls for a contrasting bite in the wine. Côte Chalonnaise whites (eg Rully) are good. Try NZ Sauvignon Blanc, Verdicchio or a Spätlese trocken.

Melon Needs a strong sweet wine (if any): port (★★), Bual madeira, Muscat oloroso sherry or vin doux naturel.

Minestrone Red (★): Grignolino, Chianti, Zinfandel, Shiraz, etc. Or fino.

Mushrooms à la Grecque Greek Verdea or Mantinia, or any hefty dry white, or fresh young red.

Omelettes See Eggs.

Pasta Red or white (★→★★) according to the sauce or trimmings:

cream sauce Orvieto, Frascati, Italian Chardonnay.

meat sauce Chianti, Montepulciano d'Abruzzo, Montefalco d'Arquata.

pesto (basil) sauce Barbera, NZ Sauvignon Blanc.

seafood sauce (vongole, eg) Verdicchio, Soave, Pomino, Sauv Bl.

tomato sauce Barbera, Sicilian or S Italian red, Zinfandel.

Pâté According to constituents and quality:

chicken livers Call for pungent white, a smooth red like a ligh Pomerol, or even amontillado sherry.

with simple pâté A ★★ dry white: Mâcon-Villages, Graves, Fumé Blanc

with duck pâté Chianti Classico.

Pizza Any ★★ dry Italian red or ★★ Rioja, Australian Shiraz or Californi Zinfandel. Or Corbières or Roussillon.

Prawns or shrimps Dry white (★★→★★★): burgundy, Bordeaux, Chard Riesling. ('Cocktail sauce' kills wine, and I suspect, in time, people.)

Prosciutto with melon Full-bodied dry or medium white (★★→★★★) Orvieto, Frascati, Pomino, Fendant, Grüner Veltliner, Alsace o California Gewürztraminer, Australian Riesling, Jurançon Sec.

Quiches Dry white with body (★→★★): Alsace, Graves, Sauvignon, Rheinga dry; or young red (Beaujolais-Villages), according to the ingredients Never a fine-wine dish. (One friend suggests sake.)

Salade niçoise Very dry, ★★, not too light or flowery white or rosé Provençal, Rhône or Corsican; Catalan white; Dão; California Sauv Bl

Salads As a first course, especially with blue cheese dressing, any dry an appetizing white wine. After a main course: no wine.

NB Vinegar in salad dressings destroys the flavour of wine. If yo want salad at a meal with fine wine, dress the salad with wine or little lemon juice instead of vinegar.

Seafood salad Chablis or unoaked Chardonnay.

Salami Very tasty red or rosé (★→★★): Barbera, young Zinfandel, Tavel o Ajaccio rosé, young Bordeaux, Toro, or Chilean Cabernet.

Salmon, smoked A dry but pungent white: fino sherry, Alsace Pinot Gris Chablis Grand Cru, Pfalz Riesling Spätlese, vintage champagne.

Shark's fin soup Add a teaspoon of cognac. Sip amontillado.

Soufflés As show dishes these deserve ★★→★★★ wines.

fish Dry white: burgundy, Bordeaux, Alsace, Chardonnay, etc.

cheese Red burgundy or Bordeaux, Cabernet Sauvignon, etc.

spinach Mâcon-Villages, St-Véran.

Taramasalata A rustic southern white of strong personality; not necessarily Retsina. Fino sherry works well. Try Australian Chardonnay.

Terrine As for pâté, or equivalent red: Mercurey, Beaujolais-Villages, fairly young St-Emilion (★★), California Cab or Zin, Bulgarian or Chilean Cab

Tomato sauce (on anything) The acidity of tomato sauce is no friend to fin wines. Red (★★) will do. Try Chianti. Try skipping tomatoes.

Trout, smoked Sancerre, California or NZ Fumé Blanc. Or Rully.

Vegetable terrine Not a great help to fine wine, but California an Australian Chardonnays make a fashionable marriage.

Fish

Abalone Dry or medium white (★★→★★★): Sauvignon Blanc, Chardonnay Pinot Grigio, Muscadet sur Lie.

Bass, striped or sea Weissburgunder from Baden or Pfalz. Vg for an fine/delicate white.

Beurre blanc, fish with Muscadet sur Lie, a Sauvignon/Sémillon blend, or a German Charta wine.

Carpaccio of salmon or tuna Puligny-Montrachet or top-notch Australian Chardonnay. (See also First courses.)

Cod A good neutral background for fine dry or medium whites: ★★→★★★ Chablis, Meursault, cru classé Graves, German Kabinett, or dry Spätlesen and their equivalents.

Coquilles St Jacques See Scallops.

Crab, cioppino Sauvignon Blanc; but West Coast friends say Zinfandel.

cold, with salad Pfalz Riesling Kabinett or Spätlese, dry California or Australian Riesling, or Viognier from Condrieu.

softshell ★★★ Chardonnay or top quality German Riesling.

Eel, jellied NV champagne or a nice cup of tea.

smoked Either strong or sharp wine: fino sherry, Bourgogne Aligoté. Or schnapps.

Fish and chips, fritto misto (or tempura) Chablis, ★★ white Bordeaux, Sauvignon Blanc, Alsace Riesling, Fiano, Montilla, Koshu, tea...

Fish pie (with creamy sauce) Napa Chardonnay, Pinot Gris d'Alsace.

Haddock Dry white with a certain richness (★★→★★★): Meursault, California or Australian Chardonnay.

Halibut As for Turbot.

Hake Sauvignon Blanc or any freshly fruity white.

Herrings Need a white with some acidity to cut their richness. Bourgogne Aligoté, Gros Plant from Brittany, dry Sauvignon Blanc.

Kippers A good cup of tea, preferably Ceylon (milk, no sugar). Scotch?

Lamproie à la Bordelaise 5-yr-old St-Emilion or Fronsac: ★★→★★★.

Lobster, richly sauced Vintage champagne, fine white burgundy, cru classé Graves, California or Australian Chardonnay, Pfalz Spätlese, Hermitage Blanc.

salad white (★★→★★★★): NV champagne, Alsace Riesling, Chablis Premier Cru, Condrieu, Mosel Spätlese.

Mackerel Hard or sharp white (★★): Sauvignon Blanc from Bergerac or Touraine, Gros Plant, vinho verde, white Rioja. Or Guinness.

Mullet, red A chameleon, adaptable to good whites or reds.

Mussels Gros Plant (★→★★), Muscadet, California 'Chablis'.

stuffed, with garlic See Escargots.

Oysters White (★★→★★★): NV champagne, Chablis or (better) Chablis Premier Cru, Muscadet, white Graves, Sancerre. Or Guinness.

Oyster stew California or Australian Chardonnay.

Perch, Sandre Exquisite fishes for finest wines: Puligny-Montrachet Premiers Crus or noble Mosels. Top Swiss Fendant or Johannisberg.

Salmon, fresh Fine white burgundy (★★★): Puligny- or Chassagne-Montrachet, Meursault, Corton-Charlemagne, Chablis Grand Cru; Condrieu, California, Idaho or Australian Chardonnay, Rheingau Kabinett/Spätlese, California Riesling or equivalent. Young Pinot Noir can be perfect, too.

Sardines, fresh grilled Very dry white (★→★★): vinho verde, Dão, Muscadet.

Sashimi If you are prepared to forego the wasabi, sparkling wines, incl Californian; or California or Australian Chardonnay, Chablis Grand Cru, Rheingau Riesling Halbtrocken. Otherwise, sake or beer.

Scallops An inherently slightly sweet dish, best with medium-dry whites.

in cream sauces German Spätlese (★★★) or a Montrachet.

grilled or fried Hermitage Blanc, Gewürztraminer, Grüner Veltliner, California Chenin Blanc, Riesling or champagne.

Shad White Graves (★★→★★★) or Meursault or Hunter Sémillon.

Shellfish Dry white with plain boiled shellfish, richer wines with richer sauces.

Shrimps, potted Fino sherry, Chablis, Gavi or New York Chardonnay.

Skate with black butter White (★★) with some pungency (eg Alsace Pinot Gr) or a clean straightforward one like Muscadet or Entre-Deux-Mers.

Snapper Serious Sauvignon Blanc country.

Sole, plaice, etc – plain, grilled or fried An ideal accompaniment for fine wines: ★★★→★★★★ white burgundy, or its equivalent.

with sauce Depending on the ingredients: sharp dry wine for tomato sauce, fairly rich for sole véronique, etc.

Sushi Hot wasabi is usually hidden in every piece. German QbA trocken wines or simple Chablis are good enough. Or of course sake.

Swordfish Dry white (★★) of whatever country you are in.

Trout Delicate white wine, eg ★★★ Mosel (esp from the Saar).

smoked A full-flavoured ★★→★★★ white: Gewürztraminer, Alsace Pinot Gris, Rhine Spätlese, Pinot Blanc from Italy or Australian Hunter white.

Tuna, grilled White, red or rosé (★★) of fairly fruity character. NZ Sauvignon Blanc or a top Côtes du Rhône would be fine.

Turbot Fine rich dry white: ★★★ Meursault or its California, Australian or NZ equivalent. Condrieu. Mature Rheingau, Mosel or Nahe Spätlese or Auslese (not trocken).

Meat, poultry, etc

Barbecues Red (★★) with a slight rasp, therefore young: Shiraz, Chianti, Zinfandel, Turkish Buzbag. Bandol for a treat.

Beef, boiled Red (★★): Bordeaux (Bourg or Fronsac), Roussillon, Australian Shiraz. Or good Mâcon-Villages white.

roast An ideal partner for fine red wine: ★★→★★★★ red of any kind.

Beef stew Sturdy red (★★→★★★): Pomerol or St-Emilion, Hermitage, Cornas, Barbera, Shiraz, California/Oregon Pinot Noir, Torres Sangre de Toro.

Beef Stroganoff Suitably dramatic red (★★→★★★): Barolo, Brunello, Valpolicella Amarone, Hermitage, late-harvest Zinfandel – or even Moldovan Negru de Purkar.

Cabbage, stuffed Hungarian Cabernet Franc/Kadarka, Bulgarian Cabernet.

Cajun food Côtes de Brouilly. With gumbo: amontillado or Mexican beer.

Cassoulet Red (★★) from SW France (Madiran, Cahors, Corbières), or Barbera or Zinfandel or Shiraz.

Chicken casserole Lirac, St-Joseph, Crozes-Hermitage.

Kiev Alsace Riesling, Bergerac Rouge.

Chicken/turkey/guinea fowl, roast Virtually any wine, incl very best bottles of dry/medium white and finest old reds (esp burgundy). The meat of fowl can be adapted with sauces to match almost any fine wine (eg coq au vin: red burgundy). Avoid tomato sauces if you want to taste any good bottles.

Chilli con carne Young red (★→★★): Barbera, Beaujolais, Navarra, Zinfandel.

Chinese food: Canton or Peking style Dry to medium-dry white (★★→★★★) – Sauvignon Blanc or (better) Riesling – can be good throughout a Chinese banquet. Dry sparkling (esp cava) is good for cutting the oil. Eschew sweet/sour dishes but try an 88/89 St-Emilion ★★ or St-Estèphe cru bourgeois, or Châteauneuf-du-Pape with duck. I often serve both white and red concurrently with Chinese meals.

Szechuan style Muscadet, Alsace Pinot Blanc or v cold beer.

Choucroute garni Alsace Sylvaner, Pinot Blanc or Riesling.

Cold meats Generally taste better with full-flavoured white wine than red. Mosel Spätlese, Hochheimer are very good. And so is Beaujolais.

Confit d'oie Young tannic red Bordeaux Cru Bourgeois (★★→★★★) helps cut the richness. Alsace Tokay-Pinot Gris or Gewurztraminer matches it.

Coq au vin Red burgundy (★★→★★★★). In an ideal world one bottle of Chambertin in the dish, two on the table.

Corned beef hash Zinfandel, Chianti, Côtes du Rhône red: (★★).

Curry Medium-sweet white (★→★★), very cold: Orvieto abboccato, California Chenin Blanc, Slovenian Traminer, Indian sparkling. Or emphasize the heat with a tannic Barolo or Barbaresco, or deep-flavoured reds such as St-Emilion, Cornas, Shiraz-Cabernet and Valpolicella Amarone.

Duck or goose Rather rich white (★★★): Pfalz Spätlese or Alsace réserve exceptionelle; or ★★★ Bordeaux or burgundy. With oranges or peaches, the Sauternais propose Sauternes, others a top Loire red.

Peking See Chinese food.

wild duck Big-scale red (★★★): Hermitage, Châteauneuf-du-Pape, Cornas, Bandol, California or S African Cabernet, Australian Shiraz.

Frankfurters German (★→★★), New York Riesling, Beaujolais. Or Budweiser.

Game birds: young birds plain roasted The best red wine you can afford.

Older birds in casseroles ★★→★★★ red (Gevrey-Chambertin, Pommard, Grand Cru St-Emilion, Napa Cabernet).

Well-hung game Hermitage, Châteauneuf-du-Pape, Vega Sicilia.

Cold game Mature vintage champagne. See page 18 for more.

Game pie (Hot) Red wine (★★★). **(Cold)** Equivalent white or champagne.

Goulash Strong young red (★★): Zinfandel, Bulgarian Cabernet, Hungarian Kadarka, young Australian Shiraz.

Grouse See Game birds – but push the boat right out.

Ham Fairly fresh red burgundy (★★→★★★): Volnay, Savigny, Beaune; red Loire; slightly sweet German white (Rhine Spätlese); Czech Müller-Thurgau; Tuscan red; lightish Cabernet (eg Chilean).

Hamburger Young red (★→★★): Beaujolais, Corbières or Minervois, Chianti, Zinfandel, Kadarka from Hungary.

Hare Jugged hare calls for ★★→★★★ flavourful red: not-too-old burgundy or Bordeaux, Rhône (eg Gigondas), Bandol, or a fine Rioja reserva. The same for saddle. Australia's Grange Hermitage would be an experience.

Kebabs Vigorous red (★★): Greek Demestica, Turkish Buzbag, Bulgarian or Chilean Cabernet, Zinfandel.

Kidneys Red (★★→★★★): St-Emilion, Cornas, Barbaresco, Rioja, California, Spanish or Australian Cabernet, Portuguese Bairrada.

Lamb, cutlets or chops As for roast lamb, but a little less grand.

roast One of the traditional and best partners for very good red Bordeaux – or its Cabernet equivalents from the New World. In Castile, the partner of the finest old Rioja reservas. See page 18.

Liver Young red (★★→★★★): Beaujolais-Villages, St-Joseph, Médoc, Italian Merlot, Breganze Cabernet, Zinfandel, Oregon Pinot Noir.

Meatballs Red (★★→★★★): Mercurey, Crozes-Hermitage, Madiran, Rubesco, Dão, Bairrada, Zinfandel or Cabernet.

Mixed grill A fairly light, easily swallowable red: ★★ Bordeaux from Bourg, Fronsac or Premières Côtes; Chianti; Bourgogne Passe-Tout-Grains; Chilean Cabernet; or a Cru Beaujolais such as Juliénas.

Moussaka Red or rosé (★→★★): Naoussa from Greece, Chianti, Corbières, Côtes de Provence, Ajaccio or Patrimonio, California 'Burgundy'.

Oxtail or osso bucco Rather rich red (★★→★★★): St-Emilion or Pomerol, Nuits-St-Georges, Barolo or Chianti Classico, Rioja reserva, California or Coonawarra Cabernet; or a dry Riesling Spätlese.

Paella Young (★★) Spanish red, dry white or rosé: Penedès or Rioja.

Partridge, pheasant See Game birds.

Pigeons or squab Red Bordeaux (★★→★★★★), Chianti Classico, California or Australian Cabernet. Silvaner Spätlese from Franconia.

Pork, roast A good rich neutral background to a fairly light red or rich white. It deserves ★★★ treatment. Portugal's famous sucking pig is eaten with Bairrada garrafeira.

Quail As for pigeon.

Rabbit Young Italian red (★→★★★), Chinon, Saumur-Champigny, Rhône rosé.

Ris de veau See Sweetbreads.

Risotto Pinot Gr from Friuli, Gavi, youngish Sém, Dolcetto, or Barbera d'Alba.

with mushrooms Cahors, Madiran, Barbera.

Satay Australian Cabernet-Shiraz or Alsace Pinot Gris or Gewurztraminer.

Sauerkraut Lager or stout. (But see also Choucroute garni.)

Sausages The British banger requires a 2½-yr-old NE Italian Merlot (or a red wine, anyway). See also Frankfurters, Salami.

Shepherd's Pie Rough and ready red (★→★★) seems most appropriate, but no harm would come to a good one.

Spare Ribs Gigondas or St-Joseph, or Australian Shiraz, or Zinfandel.

Steak and kidney pie or pudding Red Rioja reserva or mature ★★→★★★ Bordeaux.

Steak, au poivre A fairly young ★★★ Rhône red or Cabernet.

tartare Vodka or ★★ light young red: Beaujolais, Bergerac, Valpolicella.

with Korean Yuk Whe The world's best, sake.

filet or tournedos Any ★★★ red (but not old wines with béarnaise sauce).

T-bone Reds of similar bone structure (★★→★★★): Barolo, Hermitage, Australian Cabernet or Shiraz.

fiorentina (bistecca) Chianti Classico Riserva or Brunello.

Stews and casseroles A lusty full-flavoured red: young Côtes du Rhône, Corbières, Barbera, Shiraz, Zinfandel, etc.

Sweetbreads These tend to be a grand dish, suggesting a grand wine: Rhine Riesling (★★★) or Franken Silvaner Spätlese, or well-matured Bordeaux or burgundy, depending on the sauce.

Tandoori chicken Sauvignon Blanc, or young ★★ red Bordeaux.

Thai food Ginger and lemon grass call for Gewürztraminer; coconut curries, Hunter Valley Chardonnay. Alsace Pinot Blanc for refreshment.

Tongue Good for any red or white of abundant character, esp Italian.

Tripe Red (★→★★), eg Corbières, Mâcon Rouge; or rather sweet white (eg Liebfraumilch). Better: W Australian 'White Burgundy'.

Veal, roast A good neutral background dish for any fine old red which may have faded with age (eg a Rioja reserva) or a ★★★ German white.

Venison Big-scale red (★★★): Rhône, Bordeaux of a grand vintage; or rather rich white (Pfalz Spätlese or Alsace Tokay-Pinot Gris).

Vitello tonnato Light red (Valpolicella, Beaujolais) served cool.

Wiener Schnitzel Light red (★★→★★★) from the Italian Tyrol (Alto Adige) or the Médoc; Austrian Riesling, Grüner Veltliner or Gumpoldskirchener.

Vegetarian dishes

Bean salad Red Rioja reserva.

Bean stew Bairrada from Portugal, Toro from Spain.

Choucroute (See also Sauerkraut) Alsace Pinot Gris or Sylvaner.

Couscous Young red with a bite: Shiraz, Corbières, Minervois, etc.

Fennel-based dishes Pouilly-Fumé, Beaujolais.

'Meaty' aubergine, lentil or mushroom bakes Corbières, Zinfandel.

Mushrooms (in most contexts) Fleshy red; eg ★★★ Pomerol, California Merlot, Australian Shiraz.

Onion/leek tart Fruity concentrated dry white (★→★★★): Alsace Pinot Gris or Gewurztraminer. Mâcon-Villages of a good vintage, Jurançon, California or Australian Riesling. Or Beaujolais or Loire red.

Peppers or aubergines (eggplant), stuffed Vigorous red (★★): Chianti, Dolcetto, Zinfandel, Bandol, Vacqueyras.

Ratatouille Vigorous young red (★★): Chianti, Zinfandel, Bulgarian, young red Bordeaux or young Côtes du Rhône.

Spinach/pasta bakes Chianti Classico, Crozes-Hermitage, Shiraz.

Cheese

Very strong cheese completely masks the flavour of wine. Only serve fine wine with mild cheeses in peak condition.

Bleu de Bresse, Dolcelatte, Gorgonzola, Stilton or other English blue Need emphatic accompaniment: young ★★→★★★ red wine (Barbera, Dolcetto, Moulin-à-Vent, etc) or Sauternes – or port.

Cream cheeses: Brie, Camembert, Pont-l'Evêque, Bel Paese, etc In their mild state marry with any good wine, red or white. When ripe, resort to Gewürztraminer or Châteauneuf-du-Pape.

English (Scottish, Welsh, Irish) cheeses Can be either mild or strong and acidic. The latter need sweet or strong wine.

Cheddar, Cheshire, Wensleydale, Gloucester, etc If mild: fine burgundy or claret. If mature: good ruby or vintage character (not vintage) port, old dry oloroso sherry, or a very big red (Hermitage, Châteauneuf-du-Pape, Barolo, Barbaresco, etc).

Goat's cheeses White wine (★★→★★★) of marked character, either dry (Sancerre) or sweet (Monbazillac, Sauternes).

Hard Cheese, Parmesan, Gruyère, Emmenthal, old Gouda, Jarlsberg Full-bodied dry whites: Alsace Tokay-Pinot Gris or Vernaccia, or fino or amontillado sherry. But it is worth experimenting with any fine wine: old Gouda ('Mimolette') and Jarlsberg have a sweetness that encourages fine old reds.

Roquefort, Danish Blue So strong-flavoured that only the youngest, biggest or sweetest wines stand a chance. Sauternes is traditional with Roquefort. Only old amontillado or oloroso sherries have the necessary horse-power for Danish Blue.

Desserts

Apple pie or strudel Sweet (★★→★★★) German, Austrian, Hungarian white.

Apples, Cox's Orange Pippins Vintage port (55 60 63 66 70 75 82).

Bread and butter pudding 10-yr-old Barsac from a good château.

Cakes Bual or Malmsey madeira, oloroso or cream sherry.

Cheesecake Sweet white from Vouvray or Anjou, (★★→★★★).

Chocolate cake, mousse, soufflés Bual madeira, Huxelrebe Auslese, California orange Muscat, Beaumes-de-Venise.

Christmas pudding, mince pies Tawny port, cream sherry, Asti Spumante.

Creams, custards and fools Sauternes, Loupiac, Ste-Croix-du-Mont, or Monbazillac: ★★→★★★.

Crème brûlée The most luxurious dish, demanding ★★★→★★★★ Sauternes or Rhine Beerenauslese, or the best madeira or tokay. (With concealed fruit, a more modest sweet wine.)

Crêpes Suzette Sweet champagne or Asti Spumante.

Fruit, fresh Sweet Coteaux du Layon, light sweet or liqueur Muscat.

stewed, ie apricots, pears, etc Sweet Muscatel: Muscat de Beaumes-de-Venise, Moscato di Pantelleria or dessert Tarragona.

Fruit flans (ie peach, raspberry) Sauternes, Monbazillac or sweet Vouvray or Anjou: ★★★.

Fruit salads, orange salad A fine sweet sherry.

Nuts Oloroso sherry, Bual madeira, vintage or tawny port, Vin Santo.

Oranges, caramelized Experiment with old Sauternes.

Pears in red wine A pause before the port.

Pecans See Walnuts.

Raspberries (no cream, little sugar) Excellent with fine reds.

Rice Pudding Liqueur Muscat, Moscatel de Valencia, or Loupiac.

Sorbets, ice-creams Asti Spumante, or (better) Moscato d'Asti Naturale. Or Cointreau.

Strawberries and cream Sauternes (★★★) or similar sweet Bordeaux, or Vouvray Moelleux (1990).

Strawberries, wild (no cream) Serve with ★★★ red Bordeaux poured over them and in your glass.

Summer pudding Fairly young Sauternes of good vintage (82 83 85 86).

Sweet soufflés Sauternes, sweet Vouvray or Coteaux du Layon. Sweet champagne.

Tiramisu Vin Santo, young tawny port, Beaumes-de-Venise.

Trifle Should be sufficiently vibrant with its internal sherry.

Walnuts Nature's match for finest port, madeira, oloroso sherry.

Zabaglione Light gold Marsala.

Food with Wine

With very special bottles the wine sometimes guides the choic of food rather than the usual way round. The followin suggestions are largely based on the gastromic conventions c the wine regions producing these treasures, plus diliger research. They should help bring out the best in your best wines

Red wines

Red Bordeaux and other Cabernet-based wines (very old, light an delicate: eg pre-59, with exceptions such as 45) Leg or rack young lamb, roast with a hint of herbs (not garlic); entrecôt sweetbreads; or cheese soufflé after the meat.

Fully mature great vintages (eg Bordeaux 61, 45) Shoulder or saddle lamb, roast with a touch of garlic, roast ribs or grilled rump of beef.

Mature but still vigorous (eg 70, 66) Shoulder or saddle of lamb (incl kidney with rich sauce, eg béarnaise. Fillet of beef marchand de vin (wi wine and bone-marrow). Avoid Beef Wellington: pastry dulls the palat

Merlot-based Bordeaux (Pomerol, St-Emilion) Beef as above (fillet richest) or venison.

Côte d'Or red burgundy (Consider the weight and texture, which gro lighter/more velvet with age. Also the character: Nuits earth Musigny flowery, great Romanées exotic, Pommard foursquare, et Roast chicken, or better, capon, is safe standard; guinea-fowl slight stronger, then partridge, grouse or woodcock, progressively mor rich/pungent. Hare and venison (chevreuil) are alternatives.

Great old reds The classic burgundian formula is cheese: Epoiss (unfermented). It is a terrible waste of fine old wines.

Vigorous younger burgundy Duck or goose roasted to minimize fat

Great Syrahs: Hermitage, Côte Rôtie, Grange Hermitage, (also Veg Sicilia) Beef, venison; bone-marrow on toast; English cheese (es best farm Cheddar).

Rioja Gran Reserva, Pesquera... Richly flavoured roasts: wild boar, mutto

Barolo, Barbaresco Cheese risotto with white truffles; pasta with gam sauce (eg pappardelle alle lepre); porcini mushrooms; Parmesan.

White wines

Very Good Chablis/White burgundy/Chardonnay White fish simp grilled or meunière with Doria garnish of sautéed cucumber. Dov sole, turbot, Rex sole are best. (Seabass is too delicate; salmon pass but does little for fine wine.)

Supreme white burgundy (Le Montrachet, Corton-Charlemagne) equivalent Graves Roast veal, capon or sweetbreads; richly sauce white fish as above. Or lobster.

Hermitage Blanc, Condrieu, Châteauneuf Blanc Very light pasta scente with herbs and tiny peas or broad beans.

Grand Cru Alsace: Riesling Truite au bleu, smoked salmon or choucrou garni. **Pinot Gris** Roast or grilled veal. **Gewurztraminer** Chees soufflé (Munster cheese). **Vendange Tardive** Tarte Tatin.

Sauternes Simple crisp buttery biscuits (eg Langue-de-Chat), whi peaches, nectarines, strawberries (without cream). Not tropical frui Experiment with cheeses.

Supreme Vouvray moelleux etc Buttery biscuits, apples, apple tart.

Beerenauslese/TBA Biscuits, peaches, greengages.

Finest old amontillado/oloroso Pecan nuts.

Great vintage port or madeira Walnuts or pecans.

Old vintage champagne (not blanc de blancs) As aperitif, or with co partridge, grouse or woodcock.

The 1992 Vintage

Most parts of northern Europe will remember 1992 as the year when, after four drought years, it rained as though it meant it. Some of the rain, as in Bordeaux in August and Provence in September was spectacular – even catastrophic. It came from the west and across the Mediterranean. The general pattern, therefore, is that the further east you go, the more successful the vintage.

Bordeaux suffered rain from flowering time on and off until October, ruining its Merlot crop. St-Emilions and Pomerols are very light, even where bunches on the vine were drastically thinned. At Pétrus and Trotanoy the desperate proprietors even covered the soil with plastic sheeting to keep the rain off. On the other hand some good ripe Cabernet in mid-October gave Médocs much-needed flavour. The crop was huge, and good châteaux drained away hectolitres of excess juice to arrive at well-structured wine.

Burgundy was spared the summer storms and ripened both Pinot Noir and Chardonnay excellently: the red wines are certainly good, the whites ripe and aromatic; some will probably be very good indeed. But further south in Beaujolais the rain diluted a promising crop (the wines are very pretty en primeur), and further south still, the Rhône Valley, much of the Midi and Provence were badly rained-on.

The same weather made the harvest difficult in the port vineyards, in October swept into Rioja and Navarra and put paid to hopes for a great Reserva year, and affected Italy from Piedmont to Sicily. Tuscany had very ripe grapes after a fine summer and perhaps came off best with selective harvesting.

The best wines of the European vintage will come from the sheltered east: Alsace, where it was a normal year, which means fine dry wines and a few sweet ones, and the Rhine, whose harvest, where quantities were kept under control, ranged from very good standard level to superb Auslesen. The Middle Mosel was almost equally fortunate; the Saar, Ruwer and Nahe less so.

Even further east, Franken reports its best vintage since 1979 and Austria, after a rainy June, had a perfect ripening summer for dry whites and reds, though too dry for its sweet botrytis wines. In Eastern Europe generally drought seems to have been a local problem.

California was relieved of its six-year drought by winter rain that enabled the vines to take advantage of a hot summer and ripen an early harvest: probably a very fine one. Then at last, the harvest in, the longed-for rain fell in such quantities that the rivers filled the empty reservoirs.

Meanwhile (or rather six months earlier), Australia has brought in a good vintage in mixed conditions. A belt of rain that interferred with the vintage in South Australia headed off over the Tasman Sea and left Victoria dry and sunny. Prospects for the '93 vintage have also been affected by a good deal of summer rain – but not so's to worry, they say.

France

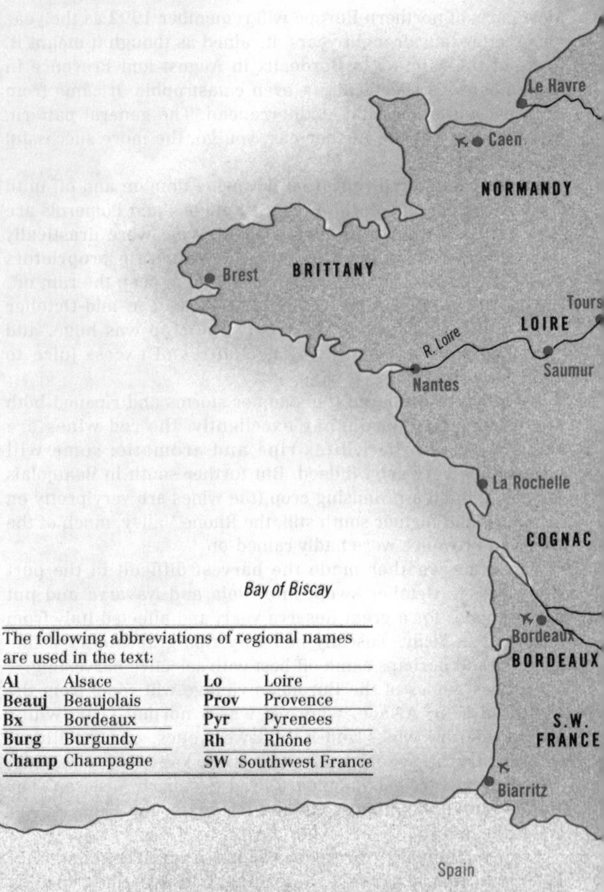

The following abbreviations of regional names are used in the text:

Al	Alsace	**Lo**	Loire
Beauj	Beaujolais	**Prov**	Provence
Bx	Bordeaux	**Pyr**	Pyrenees
Burg	Burgundy	**Rh**	Rhône
Champ	Champagne	**SW**	Southwest France

Every year sees fresh challenges to France's pole position in the wine world. Yet no-one has displaced her by definitively bettering even one of her many kinds of wine and it is hard to imagine that anyone ever will. Tens of thousands of properties make wine of all complexions over a large part of her surface. This is a guide to their names, types and producers: essential information in identifying what is authentic and good of its kind.

All France's best wine regions (producing about 30% of all her wine) have appellations contrôlées, which may apply to a single small vineyard or to a whole large district. The system varies from region to region, with Burgundy on the whole having the smallest and most precise appellations, grouped into larger units by complicated formulae, and Bordeaux the widest and most general, within which it is the particular property ('château')

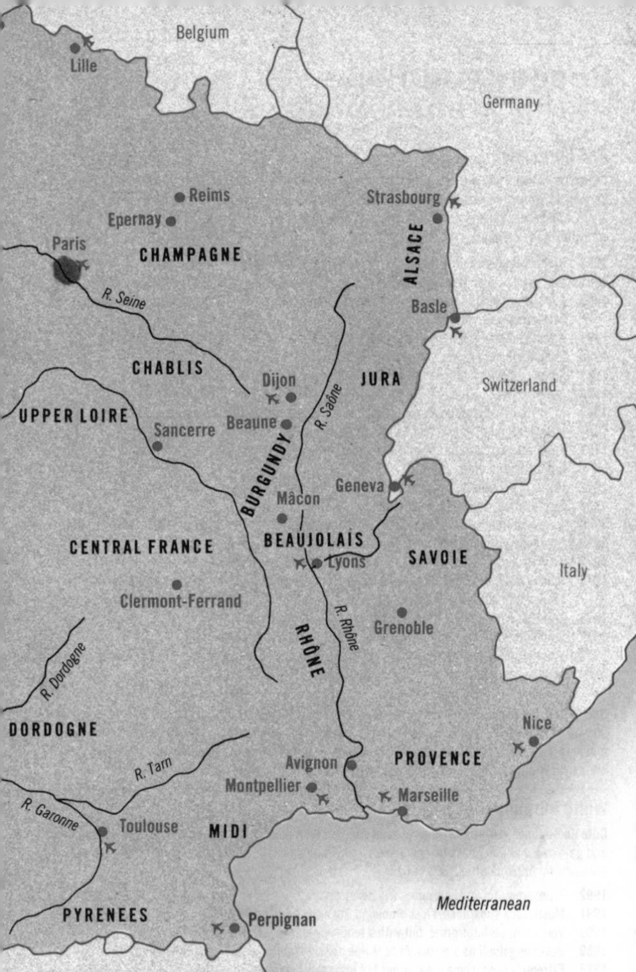

that matters. In between lies an infinity of variations.

An appellation contrôlée is a guarantee of origin, production method, grape varieties and quantities produced, but only partially one of quality. All AC wines are officially tasted, but many of shoddy quality get through the net. The AC therefore is the first thing to look for on a label. But the next is the name of the maker. The best makers' names are a vital ingredient of the pages that follow. Regions without the overall quality and traditions required for an appellation can be ranked as vins délimités de qualité supérieure (VDQS), a shrinking category. Government policy is to promote remaining VDQS regions to AC status, and develop the relatively new and highly successful vins de pays (see page 54). Vins de pays are increasingly worth trying. They include some brilliant originals and often offer France's best value for money.

Recent vintages of the French classics

Red Burgundy

Côte d'Or Côte de Beaune reds generally mature sooner than the bigger wines of the Côte de Nuits. Earliest drinking dates are for lighter commune wines,eg Volnay, Beaune; latest for the biggest wines of eg Chambertin, Romanée. But even the best burgundies are much more attractive young than the equivalent red Bordeaux.

1992 Ripe, plump, pleasing. No great concentration. 1996–2005.
1991 Very good to poor. Depends on date of harvest; before/after rain. Best like 89s.
1990 A great vintage to rival 88: perfect weather compromised only by drought on some slopes and over-production in some v'yds.
1989 A yr of great charm, not necessarily for v long maturing, but will age. Now–2015.
1988 Exceptional quality; a great vintage. 1996–2020?
1987 Small crop with promising ripe fruit flavours esp in Côte de Beaune. Now–2010.
1986 A v mixed bag – aromatic but rather dry: generally lacks flesh. Now–2000.
1985 At best a great vintage. Concentrated wines will be splendid. Now–2010.
1984 Lacks natural ripeness; tends to be dry and/or watery. Now–96.
1983 Powerful, vigorous, tannic and attractive vintage, compromised by rot. The best are splendid, but be careful. Now–2000.
1982 Big vintage, pale but round and charming. Best in Côte de Beaune. Drink soon.
1981 A small crop, ripe but picked in rain.
1980 A wet yr, but attractive wines from best growers who avoided rot. Côte de Nuits best. Drink.
1979 Big, generally good, ripe vintage with weak spots. Drink up.
1978 A small vintage of outstanding quality. The best will live to 2000+.
1976 Hot summer, excellent vintage. As usual great variations, but the best (esp Côte de Beaune) tannic, rich and long-lived – to 2000.
1973 Light wines, but many fruity and delicate. Most are already too old.
1972 Firm and full of character, the best have aged v well. Drink soon.
1971 V powerful and impressive wines, not as long-lasting as they first appeared. Drink.
Older fine vintages: 69, 66, 64, 62, 61, 59 (all mature).

Beaujolais 92: good primeur wines; not keepers. 91: small crop of outstanding wines, Crus excellent. 90 was a lusciously ripe vintage, wonderful en primeur; top Crus will keep. 89 was v fine both short- and long-term. 88 was v attractive with Crus to keep. 87 and 86 wines should be finished. 85 was a wonderful vintage, but generally avoid older wines except possibly some Moulin-à-Vent.

White Burgundy

Côte de Beaune Well-made wines of good vintages with plenty of acidity as well as fruit will improve and gain depth and richness for some years – anything up to 10. Lesser wines from lighter vintages are ready for drinking after 2 or 3 years.

1992 Ripe, aromatic and charming. Will develop.
1991 Mostly lack substance. Frost problems. For early drinking. Now–97.
1990 Very good, perhaps great, but with a tendency to fatness. Now–2000+.
1989 Revealing itself as a model. At best ripe, tense, structured and long. Now–2005.
1988 Extremely good, some great wines but others rather dilute. Now–2000.
1987 Mainly disappointing, though a few exceptions have emerged. Now.
1986 Powerful wines; most with better acidity and balance than 85. Now–97.
1985 V ripe; those that still have balance are ageing v well. Now–2000.
1984 Most lean or hollow. Drink soon.
1983 Potent wines; some exaggerated, some faulty, but the best splendid. To 95.
1982 Fat, tasty but delicate whites of low acidity. Drink up.
1981 A sadly depleted crop with great promise. But time to drink up.
1980 A weak, but not bad, vintage. Should be finished.
1979 Big vintage. Overall good and useful, not great. Drink up.
1978 Vg wines, firm and well-balanced. Keep only the best.
1973 V attractive, now nutty, typical and plentiful. Drink up.
1972 High acidity, but plenty of character. All are now ready to drink.
1971 Great power and style. Top wines are now wonderful. Drink up.

The white wines of the Mâconnais (Pouilly-Fuissé, St-Véran, Mâcon-Villages) follow a similar pattern, but do not last as long. They are more appreciated for their freshness than their richness.

Alsace 92 was a real success; 91 admirable. 90 was the third outstanding vintage in succession. 89 and 88 both made wines of top quality (though rain spoiled some 88s). 87s should be drunk soon and 86s finished. Top 85s and 83s may be drunk or kept.

Chablis Grand Cru Chablis of vintages with both strength and acidity can age superbly for up to 10 years; Premiers Crus proportionately less.

1992 Ripe and charming wines. Now–1999.
1991 Generally better than Côte d'Or. Useful wines. Now–97.
1990 Grands Crus will be magnificent; other wines may lack intensity and acidity. Now–2000.
1989 Excellent vintage of potent character. Now–2000.
1988 Almost a model: great pleasure now in store. Now–98.
1987 Rain at harvest. Wines for the short term. Drink up.
1986 A splendid big vintage. Now–95.
1985 Good but often low-acid wines. The best Grands Crus will age to 95.
1984 A small vintage. Too feeble to last long. Drink up.
1983 Superb vintage if not over-strong. Wonderful Grands Crus now.

Red Bordeaux

Médoc/red Graves For some wines bottle-age is optional: for these it is indispensable. Minor châteaux from light vintages need only 2 or 3 yrs, but even modest wines of great years can improve for 15 or so, and the great châteaux of these years need double that time.

1992 Rain at flowering, in August and at vintage. A huge crop; some fair quality.
1991 Catastrophic frost in April halved crop and rain interrupted vintage. Choose with great care.
1990 A paradox: a drought year with a threat of over-production. Self-discipline was essential. Its results are magnificent. To 2020.
1989 Early spring and splendid summer. The top wines will be classics of the ripe dark kind with elegance and length. Small ch'x are uneven. To 2020.
1988 Generally excellent; ripe, balanced, for long keeping. To 2020.
1987 Much more enjoyable than seemed likely. Not for long keeping. Now or soon.
1986 Another splendid, huge, heatwave harvest. Superior to 85 Pauillac and St-Julien. Now–2020.
1985 Very good vintage, in a heatwave. Some great wines already accessible. Now–2010.
1984 Only fair. Little Merlot but good ripe Cabernet. No charm. Originally overpriced. To 98?
1983 A classic vintage, esp in Margaux: abundant tannin with fruit to balance it. To 2010.
1982 Made in a heatwave. Huge, rich, strong wines which promise a long life but are developing unevenly. Most châteaux are now ready. Now–2010.
1981 Admirable despite rain. Not rich, but balanced and fine. Now–2000.
1980 Small late harvest ripe but rained-on. Some delicious light wines. Drink up.
1979 Abundant harvest of above average quality. Now–2000.
1978 A miracle vintage: magnificent long warm autumn. Some excellent wines. Now–97.
1976 Excessively hot, dry summer; rain just before vintage. Generally vg; now ready.
1975 A v fine vintage, with deep colour, high sugar content and (sometimes excessive) tannin. For long keeping, but begin to drink: some may not improve; many have lost their fruit.
1973 A huge vintage, attractive young but fading fast.
1971 Small crop. Less fruity than 70 and less consistent. All are ready to drink.
1970 Big, excellent vintage with scarcely a failure. Now–2000.
1967 Never seductive, but characterful in its maturity. Drink soon.
1966 A v fine vintage with depth, fruit and tannin. Now.
Older fine vintages: 62, 61, 59, 55, 53, 52, 50, 49, 48, 47, 45, 29, 28.

St-Emilion/Pomerol

1992 Exceptionally dilute but some charming wines to drink quickly.
1991 A sad story. Terrible frost and little chance to recover. Many wines not released.
1990 Another chance to make great wine or a lot of wine. Now–2020.
1989 Large, ripe, early harvest; an overall triumph. To 2020.
1988 Generally excellent; ideal conditions. But some overproduced. Now–2000+.
1987 Some v adequate wines (esp in Pomerol) but for drinking soon.
1986 A prolific vintage; most wines need drinking soon. St-Emilions are generally better.
1985 One of the great yrs, with a long future. To 2010.
1984 A sad story. Most of the crop wiped out in spring. Avoid.
1983 Less impressive than it seemed. Drink soon.
1982 Enormously rich and concentrated wines, most excellent. Now–2000+.
1981 A vg vintage, if not as great as it first seemed. Now–95+.
1980 A poor Merlot yr; v variable quality. Choose carefully. Soon.
1979 A rival to 78, but not developing as well as hoped. Now–95.
1978 Fine wines, but some lack flesh. Drink soon.
1976 V hot, dry summer, but vintage rain. Some excellent. Drink soon.
1975 Most St-Emilions good, the best superb. Pomerol made splendid wine. Now–2000.
1971 On the whole better than Médocs, but now ready.
1970 Beautiful wines with great fruit and strength. V big crop. Now.
Older fine vintages: 67, 66, 64, 61, 59, 53, 52, 49, 47, 45.

Abel-Lepitre Brut NV; Brut 85 86; Cuvée 134 Bl de Blancs 82 83 85 (86-87 blend); Réserve Crémant Bl de Blancs Cuvée 'C' 83 85 86; Rosé 83 85 86 CHAMPAGNE house, also owning GOULET and St-Marceaux. Luxury Cuvées: Prince A de Bourbon-Parme, Cuvée Reserve Abel-Lepitre 85.

Abymes Savoie w ★ DYA Hilly little area nr Chambéry; light mild wine from the Jacquère grape.

Ackerman-Laurance Sparkling METHODE TRADITIONELLE house of the Loire, at SAUMUR, said to be the oldest in the region. Fine CREMANT DE LOIRE.

Ajaccio Corsica r p w ★→★★ 88 89' 90 91 92 The capital of CORSICA. AC for some vg SCIACARELLO reds. Top grower: Peraldi.

Aligoté Second-rank burgundy white grape and its wine. Should be agreeably tart and fruity with considerable local character when young. BOUZERON (AC) makes the best, but don't hesitate to try others from good growers. NB PERNAND-VERGELESSES. Value.

Aloxe-Corton Burg r w ★★→★★★ 78 85 86 87 88' 89 90 91 92 Northernmost village of COTE DE BEAUNE famous for its two GRANDS CRUS: CORTON (red) and CORTON-CHARLEMAGNE (white). Village wines (called Aloxe-Corton) are much lighter but can be good value.

Alsace Al w (r sp) ★★→★★★ 85' 86 88 89 90' 91 92 Aromatic, fruity, often strong, rather Germanic dry white from eastern foothills of Vosges Mountains, bordering the River Rhine. Generally dry but increasingly made sweet (see Vendange Tardive, Sélection des Grains Nobles). Sold by grape variety (Pinot Bl, Ries, GEWURZ, etc). Matures well up to 5, even 10 yrs; GRAND CRU even longer. Also good quality and value CREMANT.

Alsace Grand Cru w ★★★ 83 85 86 88 89' 90 91 92 Appellation restricted to 50 of the best named v'yds (1,400 acres) and noble grapes (Riesling, Pinot Gr ('Tokay'), GEWURZ and MUSCAT).

Ampeau, Robert Exceptional grower and specialist in MEURSAULT; also POMMARD, etc. Perhaps unique in only releasing matured bottles.

André, Pierre Négociant at Ch Corton-André, ALOXE-CORTON with fine 50-acre domaine in CORTON, SAVIGNY, GEVREY-CHAMBERTIN etc. Also owns the down-market REINE PEDAUQUE.

d'Angerville, Marquis Famous burgundy grower with immaculate 30-acre estate in VOLNAY. Top wines: Champans and Clos des Ducs.

Anjou Lo r p w (sw dr sp) ★→★★★ Loire AC embracing wide spectrum of styles. Esp good red (Cab) ANJOU-VILLAGES, strong dry SAVENNIERES, luscious COTEAUX DU LAYON Chenin Bl whites.

Anjou-Coteaux de la Loire Lo w dr sw ★★→★★★ AC for some forceful Chenin Bl whites, incl the notable dry SAVENNIERES.

Anjou-Villages Lo r ★→★★ New AC for reds (mainly Cab F) from less limited zone than SAUMUR-CHAMPIGNY. Potentially juicy and good value.

Appellation Contrôlée (AC or AOC) Government control of origin and production of all the best French wines (see France Introduction).

Apremont Savoie w ★★ DYA One of the best villages of SAVOIE for pale delicate whites, mainly from Jacquère grapes, recently incl CHARD.

Arbin Savoie r ★★ Deep-coloured lively red from Mondeuse grapes, rather like a good Loire Cab. Ideal après-ski wine. Drink at 1–2 yrs.

Arbois Jura r p w (sp) ★★ Various good and original light wines; speciality is VIN JAUNE. On the whole DYA.

l'Ardèche, Coteaux de Central France r p (w) ★→★★ DYA Bargain country reds; best from Syrah, Gamay and recently Cab. Also powerful, almost burgundy-like CHARD 'Grand Ardèche' from LOUIS LATOUR.

Armagnac Region of SW France and its often excellent brandy, a fiery spirit of rustic character. The excellent red of the area is MADIRAN.

Aujoux, J-M Substantial grower/merchant of BEAUJOLAIS. Swiss-owned.

Auxey-Duresses Burg r w ★★→★★★ 78 82 83 85 86 87 88' 89 90 91 92 Second-rank (but v pretty) COTE DE BEAUNE village: affinities with VOLNAY and MEURSAULT. Best estates: Diconne, HOSPICES DE BEAUNE (Cuvée Boillot), LEROY, Prunier. Drink whites in 4–5 years.

Avize Champ ★★★★ One of CHAMPAGNE's best CHARD-growing villages.

Ay Champ ★★★★ One of the best Pinot N-growing villages of CHAMPAGNE.

Ayala NV; Château d'Ay **82 83 85**; Grande Cuvée **82 83 85**; Blanc de Blancs 82 83 Once-famous Aÿ-based old-style CHAMPAGNE concern. Deserves more notice for ripe fresh appley wines.

Bachelet, Denis Brilliant young grower of GEVREY-CHAMBERTIN. Top wine: CHARMES-CHAMBERTIN.

Bahuaut, Donatien Leading Loire-wine merchants and distributors of Ch de la Cassemichère, MUSCADET.

Bandol Prov r p (w) ★★★ **82 83 85' 86 87' 88 89 90 91 92** Little coastal region near Toulon producing Provence's best wines; vigorous tannic reds from the Mourvèdre grape; esp DOM OTT, Dom de Pibarnon, Ch Pradeaux, Mas de la Rouvière, Dom Tempier, Ch Vannières.

Banyuls Pyr br sw ★★ One of the best VINS DOUX NATURELS, made chiefly of Grenache (a Banyuls GRAND CRU is over 75% Grenache, aged for 2+ yrs). Technically a distant relation of port. Best wines are RANCIOS eg from Domaine des Hospices, Dom du Mas Blanc (★★★), at 10–15 yrs old. Also cheap NV wines.

Bar-sur-Aube Champ w (p) ★★★ Important secondary CHAMPAGNE region 100 miles SE of R Marne, Epernay etc. Some good lighter wines and excellent ROSE DES RICEYS.

Barancourt Brut Réserve NV; Rosé NV; Bouzy Brut Grand Cru **81 83 85**; Rosé Grand Cru **85** Grower at Bouzy making full-bodied CHAMPAGNE. Major reorganization in '92; now esp Bouzy Brut and Rosé Grand Cru.

Barsac Bx w sw ★★→★★★★ **70 71 75 76' 78 79' 80 81 82 83' 84 85 86' 88' 89' 90' 91** Neighbour of SAUTERNES with similar superb golden wines, generally less rich and more racy. Top ch'x: CLIMENS, COUTET, DOISY-DAENE, DOISY-VEDRINES.

Barton & Guestier BORDEAUX shipper since 18th C, now owned by Seagram.

Bâtard-Montrachet Burg w ★★★★ **78 79 83 85 86 87 88 89 90 91 92** Larger (55-acre) neighbour of MONTRACHET. Should be v long-lived with intense flavours. Bienvenues-Bâtard-M is a separate adjacent 9-acre GRAND CRU with 15 owners, thus no substantial bottlings and v rare. Top growers incl BOUCHARD PERE, DROUHIN, Gagnard, LOUIS LATOUR, LEFLAIVE, Lequin-Roussot, MOREY, Niellon, RAMONET, SAUZET.

Baumard, Domaine des Leading grower of ANJOU wine, esp SAVENNIERES and COTEAUX DU LAYON (Clos Ste-Catherine).

Baur, Léon Small but vigorous ALSACE family firm at Eguisheim. Esp for Ries: Elisabeth Stumpf. Easily confused with LEON BEYER.

Béarn SW France r p w ★→★★ DYA Wide-spread low-key AC of growing local (Basque country) interest, esp wines from the coop of Sallies de Béarn-Bellocq.

Beaujolais Beauj r (p w) ★ DYA The simple AC of the v big Beaujolais region: light short-lived fruity red from Gamay grapes.

Confusingly, the best wines of the Beaujolais region are not identified as such on their labels by their appellations. They are known simply by the names of their 'crus': Brouilly, Côte de Brouilly, Chénas, Chiroubles, Fleurie, Juliénas, Morgon, Moulin-à-Vent, Regnié, St-Amour. See entries for each of these. The Confrèrie des Compagnons du Beaujolais offers a 'Beaujolais Grumé' label to selected wines from the region with ageing potential.

Beaujolais de l'année The BEAUJOLAIS of the latest vintage, until the next.

Beaujolais Primeur (or Nouveau) Same as above, made in a hurry (often only 4–5 days fermenting) for release at midnight on the third Wednesday in November. Ideally soft, fruity and tempting; often crude, sharp and too alcoholic. BEAUJOLAIS-VILLAGES should be a better bet.

Beaujolais Supérieur Beauj r (w) ★ DYA BEAUJOLAIS of 1% natural alcohol stronger than the 9% minimum. Since sugar is almost always added for strength the difference is trifling.

Beaujolais-Villages Burg r ** **90 91 92** Wines from better (N) half of BEAUJOLAIS; should be much tastier than plain Beaujolais. The 10 (easily) best 'villages' are the 'CRUS': FLEURIE etc (see note on page 25). Of the 30 others the best lie around Beaujeu. Crus cannot be released EN PRIMEUR before December 15th. Best kept until spring (or longer).

Beaumes-de-Venise Rh br (r p) *** DYA Generally France's best dessert MUSCAT, from the S COTES DU RHONE; can be high-flavoured, subtle, lingering (eg Domaine de Coyeux, Domaine Durban, JABOULET). The red and rosé from Ch Redortier and the coop are also good.

Beaune Burg r (w) *** 76 78' 82 83 85' 86 87 88' 89 90 91 92 Middle-rank classic burgundy. Many fine growers. Négociants' CLOS wines (usually PREMIER CRU) are often best; eg DROUHIN'S superb Clos des Mouches, JADOT's Clos des Ursules. Beaune du Château is a (good) BOUCHARD PERE brand. Best v'yds: Bressandes, Fèves, Grèves, Marconnets, Teurons.

Becker, Caves J Proud old family firm at Zellenberg, ALSACE. Classic Ries Hagenschlauf and MUSCAT. Second label: Gaston Beck.

Belesta Leading ROUSSILLON coop of interest for 100% 80-yr-old-vine Carignan: two cuvées, 'Schist' (matures well), 'Granite' (perfumed).

Bellet Prov p r w *** Fashionable much above average local wines from nr Nice. Serious producers: Ch'x de Bellet and Crémat. Pricey.

Bergerac Dordogne r w sw dr ** **86 88 89 90 91 92** Lightweight, often tasty, BORDEAUX-style. Drink young, the white v young. See also Monbazillac, Montravel, Pécharmant. Growers incl Courts-les-Muts, JAUBERTIE, Michel de Montaigne, Ch de Panisseau, Tiregand.

Besserat de Bellefon 'B de B' NV; Cuvée Bl de Blancs; **82 85**; Cuvée des Moines Brut; Rosé **82** 85 Rising CHAMPAGNE house for light wines.

Beyer, Léon Ancient ALSACE family firm at Eguisheim making forceful dry wines that need ageing at least 2–3 yrs, esp Comtes d'Eguisheim. 'Cuvée Particulière' Ries from GRAND CRU Pfersigberg esp fine.

Bichot, Maison Albert One of BEAUNE's biggest growers and merchants. V'yds (Domaine du Clos Frantin is excellent) in CHAMBERTIN, RICHEBOURG, CLOS DE VOUGEOT, etc, and Domaine Long-Depaquit in CHABLIS; also many other brand names.

Billecart-Salmon NV; **85 86**; Rosé NV; Bl de Blancs **83 85**; Grande Cuvée **82** One of the best small CHAMPAGNE houses, founded in 1818, still family-owned. Fresh-flavoured wines incl a v tasty rosé.

Bize, Simon Admirable red burgundy grower with 35 acres at SAVIGNY-LES-BEAUNE. Usually model wines, racy and elegant; fair prices.

Blagny Burg r w **→*** 76 78 82 83 85 86 87 88' 89 90 91 92 Hamlet between MEURSAULT and PULIGNY-MONTRACHET: whites have affinities with both (sold under each AC), reds with VOLNAY (sold as AC Blagny). All need age. Growers incl AMPEAU, Jobard, LATOUR, LEFLAIVE, Matrot, G Thomas.

Blanc de Blancs Any white wine made from white grapes only, esp CHAMPAGNE (usually from red and white). Not an indication of quality.

Blanc de Noirs White (or slightly pink or 'blush') wine from red grapes.

Blanck, Marcel ALSACE grower at Kientzheim, good Pinot Bl, and GRAND CRU Furstentum (GEWURZ, Pinot Gr, Ries).

Blanquette de Limoux Midi w sp ** Good bargain sparkler from nr Carcassonne with long local history. V dry and clean; increasingly tasty as more CHARD is added. Normally NV.

Blaye Bx r w * 88 89 90 91 92 Your daily BORDEAUX from E of the Gironde. PREMIERES COTES DE BLAYE is the AC of the better wines.

Boisset, Jean Claude Dynamic burgundy merchant/grower at NUITS-ST-GEORGES, owns Thomas-Bassot, Lionel Bruck, Pierre Ponnelle, VIENOT. Recently bought BOUCHARD-AINE, JAFELLIN. High commercial standards.

Bollinger NV 'Special Cuvée'; Grande Année **69 70 73 75 76 79 82 83 85** 89; Rosé **81 82 83 85** 89 Top CHAMPAGNE house, at AY. Dry, very full-flavoured style, needs ageing. Luxury wines: RD (**73 75 76 79 81 82**), Vieilles Vignes Françaises (**69 70 75 79 80 81 82 85**) from ungrafted Pinot N vines.

Bonneau du Martray, Domaine The major grower (with 27 acres) of CORTON-CHARLEMAGNE of the highest quality; also red GRAND CRU CORTON. Cellars at PERNAND-VERGELESSES. Whites often outlive reds.

Bonnes-Mares Burg r ★★★★ 66 69 71 76 78' 79 80 82 83 85' 86 87 88' 89 90 91 92 37-acre GRAND CRU between CHAMBOLLE-MUSIGNY and MOREY-ST-DENIS. V sturdy long-lived wines, sometimes (not often) better than CHAMBERTIN. Top growers: DUJAC, Groffier, JADOT, MUGNIER, ROUMIER, DOM DES VAROILLES, DE VOGUE.

Bonnezeaux Lo w sw ★★★ 76' 78 81 83 85 86 88 89' 90' 91 92 Unusual rich tangy wine from Chenin Bl grapes, the best of COTEAUX DU LAYON. Esp Ch de Fesles, Domaine du Petit Val. Ages well.

Bordeaux Bx r w (p) ★ 88 89 90 91 92 (for châteaux see pages 55–75) Basic catch-all AC for low-strength Bordeaux wine. Not to be despised: there is no more satisfactory daily drink.

Bordeaux Supérieur ★→★★ As above, with slightly more alcohol.

Borie-Manoux Admirable BORDEAUX shippers and château-owners, owned by the Castéja family. Ch'x incl BATAILLEY, BEAU-SITE, DOMAINE DE L'EGLISE, HAUT-BAGES-MONPELOU, TROTTEVIEILLE.

Bouchard Aîné Long-est (1750) burgundy shipper/grower with 62 acres in BEAUNE, MERCUREY, etc. Good, not top quality. Bought in '93 by BOISSET.

Bouchard Père et Fils Important burgundy shipper (est 1731) and grower with 209 acres of excellent v'yds, mainly in the COTE DE BEAUNE, and cellars at the Château de Beaune. Vg, if not quite top quality.

Bouches-du-Rhône Prov r p w ★ VINS DE PAYS from Marseille environs. Robust reds from southern varieties, Cab S, Syrah and Merlot.

Bourg Bx r (w) ★★ 82 83 85 86 88' 89 90 91 Un-fancy claret from E of the Gironde. For châteaux see Côtes de Bourg.

Bourgogne Burg r w (p) ★★ 88' 89 90' 91 92 Catch-all AC for Burgundy, but with theoretically higher standards than basic BORDEAUX. Light but often good flavour, best at 2–3 yrs. Top growers make some bargain beauties; do not despise. BEAUJOLAIS CRUS can also be labelled Bourgogne.

Bourgogne Grand Ordinaire Burg r (w) ★ DYA The lowest Burgundy AC, also allowing Gamay wines. Rare. Whites may incl ALIGOTE, Pinot Bl and Melon de Bourgogne.

Bourgogne Passe-Tout-Grains Burg r (p) ★ Age 1–2 yrs Junior burgundy: 33% Pinot N, 67% Gamay, mixed in the vat. Often enjoyable. Not as 'heady' as BEAUJOLAIS.

Bourgueil Lo r ★★★ 76' 83' 85 86 88 89' 90' 91 92 Normally delicate fruity Cab red from TOURAINE. Deep-flavoured and long-lasting in the best years, ageing like Bordeaux. ST-NICOLAS-DE-BOURGUEIL is often lighter. Growers incl Audebert, Billet, Caslot, Cognard, Druet, Jamet, Lamé-Delille-Boucard, Thouet-Bosseau.

Bouvet-Ladubay The major producer of sparkling SAUMUR, controlled by TAITTINGER. Excellent CREMANT DE LOIRE. 'Saphir' is vintage wine. De luxe 'Trésor' is oak-fermented.

Bouzeron Village of the COTE CHALONNAISE distinguished for the only single-village AC ALIGOTE. Top grower: de Vilaine.

Bouzy Rouge Champ r ★★★ 85 86 88 89 90 91 Still red wine from famous red-grape CHAMPAGNE village. Like light burgundy, ageing early but sometimes lasting well.

Brédif, Marc One of the most important growers and traders of VOUVRAY, owned by LADOUCETTE.

Bricout Brut 82 85 Small CHAMPAGNE house at AVIZE making light wines.

Brouilly Beauj r ★★★ 90 91 92 Biggest of the 10 best CRUS of BEAUJOLAIS: fruity, round, refreshing wine, can age 3–4 yrs. CH DE LA CHAIZE is largest estate. Top growers: Michaud, Dom de Combillaty.

Brut Term for the driest wines of CHAMPAGNE.

Bugey Savoie r p w sp ★→★★ DYA VDQS district for light sparkling, still or half-sparkling wines. Grapes incl Roussette (or Roussanne) and good CHARD. Best from Cerdon and Montagnieu.

Buxy Burg w ★★ Village in AC MONTAGNY with good coop for CHARD.

Buzet SW France r w ★★ 85 86 88 89 90 91 92 Good BORDEAUX-style wines from just SE of Bordeaux. Good value area with well-run cooperative. Best wines are barrel-aged: Ch de Gueyze, Cuvée Napoléon (now Cuvée Baron d'Ardeuil). Also Ch'x de Padère and Sauvagnères.

Cabardès Midi r (p w) ★→★★ 85 86 88 89 90 91 92 Newcomer VDQS region north of Carcassonne, CORBIERES, etc. MIDI and BORDEAUX grapes show promise at Ch Rivals, Ch Ventenac, Coops de Conques sur Orbiel and Pézenas.

Cabernet See Grapes for red wine (pages 8–9).

Cabernet d'Anjou Lo p ★→★★ DYA Delicate, grapey, often rather sweet rosé.

Cabrières Midi p (r) ★★ DYA COTEAUX DU LANGUEDOC vintage best for fragrant rosé from eg Domaine du Temple.

Cahors SW France r ★→★★ 82 83 85 86 88 89 90 91 92 Historically 'black' and tannic from Malbec grapes, now made like BORDEAUX; can be full-bodied and distinct or lighter. Top growers: Baldès (esp 'Prince Probus'), Ch de Caix, Ch de Chambert, Clos la Coutale, Ch St-Didier, Dom Eugénie, Clos de Gamot, Jouffreau, Ch Lagrezette, Ch Latuc, Dom de Paillas, Vigouroux (esp Ch de Haute-Serre). Lighter wines from coop, Caves d'Olt.

Cairanne Rh r p w ★★ 85 86 88 89 90 91 92 Good solid COTES DU RHONE-VILLAGES, esp from Dom Brusset, Dom l'Oratoire St-Martin, Dom Rabasse-Charavin.

Calvet Famous old shippers of BORDEAUX and burgundy, now owned by Allied-Hiram Walker. Some reliable standard wines, esp from Bordeaux.

Canard-Duchêne Brut NV; 'Patrimoine' NV; Rosé; Charles VII NV; Vintage 83 85 Quality CHAMPAGNE house owned by VEUVE-CLICQUOT, hence the Moët-Hennessy group.

Canon-Fronsac Bx r ★★→★★★ 78 82 83' 85 86 88 89' 90 91 92 Full-flavoured tannic reds of increasing quality from small area W of POMEROL. Need less age than formerly (89s vg now). Ch'x: CANON, CANON DE BREM, CANON-MOUEIX, Coustolle, Junayme, Mazeris-Bellevue, Moulin-Pey-Labrie (esp since '88), Toumalin, La Truffière, Vraye-Canon-Boyer. See also Fronsac.

Cantenac Bx r ★★★ Village of the HAUT-MEDOC entitled to the AC MARGAUX. Top châteaux include BRANE-CANTENAC, PALMER, etc.

Cap Corse Corsica w br ★★→★★★ CORSICA's wild N cape. Splendid Muscat; rare soft dry Vermentino white. Vaut le détour, if not le voyage.

Caramany Pyr r (w) ★ 88 89 90 91 92 Notionally superior new AC for part of COTES DU ROUSSILLON-VILLAGES.

Cassis Prov w (r p) ★★ DYA Seaside village E of Marseille known for its lively dry white wine, exceptional for Provence (eg Domaine du Paternel). Not to be confused with cassis, a blackcurrant liqueur made in Dijon.

Castellane, de NV; Croix Rouge 85; Bl de Blancs 82; new Prestige Florens de Castellane 82; Cuvée Commodore Brut 85 Long-established Epernay CHAMPAGNE house. Good rather light wines incl Maxim's house champagne.

Cave Cellar, or any wine establishment.

Cave coopérative Wine-growers' cooperative winery. Coops now account for 55% of all French production. Of all French growers 4 out of 10 are coop members. Almost all coops are now well-run, well-equipped and often make some of the best value wine of their areas.

Cellier des Samsons BEAUJOLAIS/MACONNAIS coop at Quincié with 2,000 grower-members. Widely distributed.

Cépage Variety of vine, eg CHARDONNAY, Merlot.

Cérons Bx w dr sw ★★ 81 83 85 86 88 89 90 91 92 Neighbour of SAUTERNES with some good sweet-wine châteaux, eg Ch de Cérons et de Calvimont, Grand Enclos, Ch Haura. Ch Archambeau also makes vg dry GRAVES.

Chablis Burg w ★★→★★★ **88 89 90 91 92** Distinctive full-flavoured dry minerally wine. Made in N Burgundy of CHARD only, on 10,000 acres (doubled since '85). Top growers incl J-M Brocard, R Dauvissat, Droin, DURUP, FEVRE, Geoffroy, J-P Grossot, LAROCHE, LONG-DEPAQUIT, Michel, PIC, Raveneau, Vocoret. Simple unqualified 'Chablis' may be thin; best is PREMIER or GRAND CRU (see entry below). The modern growers' coop, La Chablisienne, has v high standards, and many different labels.

Chablis Grand Cru Burg w ★★★→★★★★ **78 83 85 86 88 89 90 91 92** In maturity a match for the greatest white burgundies: forceful but often dumb in youth, at best almost SAUTERNES-like with age. There are 7 v'yds: Blanchots, Bougros, Clos, Grenouilles, Preuses, Valmur, Vaudésir. See also Moutonne.

Chablis Premier Cru Burg w ★★★ **85 86 88 89 90 91 92** Technically second-rank but often excellent, more typical of CHABLIS than its GRANDS CRUS. Often outclasses more expensive MEURSAULT and other CHARDS in finesse. Best v'yds incl Côte de Lechet, Fourchaume, Mont de Milieu, Montée de Tonnerre, Montmains, Vaillons. See Chablis for producers.

Chai Building for storing and maturing wine, esp in BORDEAUX.

Chambertin Burg r ★★★★ **69 71 76 78 79 82 83 85 86 87** 88 89 90 91 92 32-acre GRAND CRU producing some of the meatiest, most enduring and best red burgundy, 15 growers, incl BOUCHARD PERE, Camus, Damoy, DROUHIN, MORTET, PONSOT, Rebourseau, ROUSSEAU, Tortochot, Trapet.

Chambertin-Clos de Bèze Burg r ★★★★ **69 71 76 78 79 82 83 85 86 87** 88 89 90 91 92 37-acre neighbour of CHAMBERTIN. Similarly splendid wines. May legally be sold as Chambertin. 10 growers incl B CLAIR, CLAIR-DAU, Damoy, DROUHIN, Drouhin-Larose, FAIVELEY, JADOT, ROUSSEAU, Trapet.

Chambolle-Musigny Burg r (w) ★★★→★★★★ **76 78 82 83 85 86 87 88' 89** 90 91 92 420-acre COTE DE NUITS village with fabulously fragrant, complex, never heavy wine. Best v'yds: Les Amoureuses, part of BONNES-MARES, Les Charmes, MUSIGNY. Growers to note: Barthod, DROUHIN, FAIVELEY, Hudelot-Noëllat, JADOT, Moine-Hudelot, Mugneret, MUGNIER, RION, ROUMIER, Serveau, DE VOGUE.

Champagne Sparkling wine of Pinots N and Meunier and/or CHARD and its region (70,000+ acres 90 miles E of Paris); made by METHODE CHAMPENOISE. Wines from elsewhere, however good, cannot be champagne.

Champigny See Saumur.

Chandon de Briailles, Domaine Small burgundy estate at SAVIGNY. Makes wonderful CORTON (and Corton Blanc) and vg PERNAND-VERGELESSES.

Chanson Père et Fils Growers (with 110 acres) and négociants at BEAUNE.

Chantovent Major brand of VIN DE TABLE, largely from MINERVOIS.

Chapelle-Chambertin Burg r ★★★ **76 78 82 83' 85 86 87** 88 89 90 91 92 13-acre neighbour of CHAMBERTIN. Wine more 'nervous', not so meaty. Top producers: Drouhin-Larose, JADOT, LEROY, Trapet.

Chapoutier Long-established growers and traders of fine Rhône wines.

Charbaut, A et Fils NV; Bl de Blancs; Rosé NV; **79 82 85 87**; Certificate **82 85**; Certificate Rosé **79 82 85** Epernay CHAMPAGNE house. Clean light wines. Good rosé.

Chardonnay See Grapes for white wine (pages 6–8). Also the name of a MACON-VILLAGES commune. Hence Mâcon-Chardonnay.

Charmes-Chambertin Burg r ★★★ **71 76 78 79 82 83 85 86 87** 88 89 90 91 92 76-acre neighbour of CHAMBERTIN. Wine more 'supple', rounder. Growers incl BACHELET, Castagnier, DROUHIN, DUJAC, LEROY, ROTY, ROUSSEAU.

Chartron & Trebuchet Young co (founded '84): some delicate harmonious white burgundies, esp Dom Chartron's PULIGNY-MONTRACHET, Clos de la Pucelle, and BATARD- and CHEVALIER-MONTRACHET. Also good ALIGOTE.

For key to grape variety abbreviations, see pages 6–9.

Chassagne-Montrachet Burg r w ★★★→★★★★ r (★★★) 78 82 83 85 87 88 89 90 91 92; w 76 83 85 86 87 88 89 90 91 92 750-acre COTE DE BEAUNE village with excellent rich dry whites and sterling hefty reds. The whites rarely have the exceptional finesse of PULIGNY-MONTRACHET next door but can be better value. Best v'yds incl part of MONTRACHET, BATARD-MONTRACHET, Boudriottes (r w), Caillerets, CRIOTS-BATARD-MONTRACHET, Morgeot (r w), Ruchottes, CLOS ST-JEAN (r). Growers incl Bachelet-Ramonet, M Colin-Deleger, Delagrange-Bachelet, DROUHIN, J-N Gagnard, GAGNARD-DELAGRANGE, Lamy-Pillot, MAGENTA, MOREY, Niellon, RAMONET-PRUDHON.

Chasseloir, Dom du HQ of the firm of Chéreau-Carré: makers of several excellent AC-leading domaine MUSCADETS (esp Ch du Chasseloir).

Château An estate, big or small, good or indifferent, particularly in BORDEAUX (see pages 55–75). In Burgundy the term 'domaine' is used.

Château d'Arlay Major JURA estate; 160 acres in skilful hands with wines incl vg VIN JAUNE, VIN DE PAILLE, Pinot N and MACVIN.

Château de Beaucastel Rh r w ★★★ 78 79 81 83 85 86' 87 88 89 90 91 92 One of the biggest (173 acres), best-run CHATEAUNEUF-DU-PAPE estates. Deep-hued wines for at least 10 yrs ageing. Small amount of wonderful white to keep 5–10 yrs. Second label: Coudoulet de Beaucastel (vg white). New interest: Beaucastel Estate in California's Central Coast.

Château de la Chaize Beauj r ★★★ 89 90 91 92 The best-known estate of BROUILLY, with 200 acres.

Château Corton-Grancey Burg r ★★★ 71 78 82 83 85 86 88 89 90 91 92 Famous ALOXE-CORTON estate; property of LOUIS LATOUR: benchmark wines.

Château Fortia Rh r (w) ★★★ 78 81 83 84 85 86 88 89 90 91 92 Traditional method CHATEAUNEUF-DU-PAPE property. First class. Owner's father, Baron Le Roy, also fathered the APPELLATION CONTROLEE system in the '20s.

Château de Meursault Burg r w ★★★ 100-acre estate owned by PATRIARCHE with good v'yds and vg wines in BEAUNE, MEURSAULT, POMMARD, VOLNAY. Splendid cellars open to the public for tasting.

Château de Mille Prov r p w ★★ Leading property of the advancing COTES DU LUBERON. A local star.

Château du Nozet Lo w ★★★ 86 88 89 90 91 92 Biggest and best-known estate of POUILLY (FUME) -SUR-LOIRE. Top wine, Baron de L, can be wonderful (at a price).

Château Rayas Rh r (w) ★★★ 78' 79 81 85 86 87 88 89 90 91 92 Famous old-style property of only 38 acres in CHATEAUNEUF-DU-PAPE. Concentrated wines are entirely Grenache, yet can age superbly. Pignan is second label. Also vg Ch Fonsalette, COTES DU RHONE.

Château de Selle Prov r p w ★★ 100-acre estate of OTT family nr Cotignac, Var. Well-known and typical wines. Cuvée Spéciale is largely Cab S.

Château Simone Prov r p w ★★ Age 2–6 yrs Famous old property in Palette; the only one with a name in this AC nr Aix-en-Provence. The red is best: smooth but herby and spicy. White is catching up.

Château Vignelaure Prov r ★★→★★★ 82' 83' 85 86 87 88 89 90 91 92 135-acre Provençal estate nr Aix, making exceptional more-or-less BORDEAUX-style wine with Cab, Syrah and Grenache grapes.

Château-Chalon Jura w ★★★ Unique strong dry yellow wine, like sharpish fino sherry. Usually ready when bottled (at about 6 yrs). A curiosity.

Château-Grillet Rh w ★★★★ 88 89 90 91 92 7.5-acre v'yd: one of France's smallest ACs. Intense fragrant wildly over-expensive wine. Drink young.

Châteaumeillant Lo r p w ★ DYA Tiny VDQS area nr SANCERRE. Light Gamay and Pinot N. Good pale rosé.

Châteauneuf-du-Pape Rh r (w) ★★★ 78' 79 81 83 84 85 86 88 89 90 91 92 7,400 acres nr Avignon with v mixed standards but many fine wines. Best estate wines are dark strong exceptionally long-lived. Others may be light and/or disappointing. White can be heavy: mostly now 'DYA'. Top growers incl ch'x DE BEAUCASTEL, FORTIA, La Nerthe, MONTREDON, RAYAS; Dom les Cailloux, Clos des Papes, VIEUX TELEGRAPHE, etc.

Châtillon-en-Diois Rh r p w ★ DYA Small AC east of the middle Rhône nr Die. Adequate largely Gamay reds; white (some ALIGOTE) mostly made into CLAIRETTE DE DIE.

Chauvenet, F Substantial modern firm in NUITS; buys grapes on contract from good estates to make a wide range of much-appreciated COTE D'OR wines, incl CORTON-CHARLEMAGNE, CHARMES-CHAMBERTIN, etc.

Chave, Gérard To many the superstar grower of HERMITAGE, red and white.

Chavignol Village of SANCERRE with famous v'yd, Les Monts Damnés. Chalky soil gives vivid wines that age 4–5 yrs. Also fromage de chèvre.

Chenonceau, Ch de Lo ★★ Architectural jewel of the Loire producing fair AC Touraine Sauv Bl, Cab and Cot (Malbec).

Chénas Beauj r ★★★ 85 88 89 90 91 92 Smallest BEAUJOLAIS CRU and one of weightiest; neighbour to MOULIN-A-VENT and JULIENAS. Growers incl Benon, Champagnon, Charvet, Ch Chèvres, Robin, the coop.

Chenin Blanc See Grapes for white wine (pages 6–8).

Chevalier-Montrachet Burg w ★★★★ 78 83 85 86 87 88 89 90 91 92 17-acre neighbour of MONTRACHET: similar luxurious wine, perhaps a little less powerful. Incl 2.5-acre Les Demoiselles. Growers incl LATOUR, JADOT, BOUCHARD PERE, CHARTRON & TREBUCHET, Deleger, LEFLAIVE, Niellon, PRIEUR.

Cheverny Lo r p w (sp) ★→★★ DYA Loire VDQS from nr Chambord. Dry crisp whites from Romorantin or Sauv Bl; Gamay, Pinot N or Cab reds; generally light but tasty.

Chevigny, Pascal Producer of fine VOSNE-ROMANEE: next to LA TACHE.

Chevillon, R 21-acre estate at NUITS-ST-GEORGES; outstanding winemaking.

Chignin Savoie w ★ DYA Light soft white from Jacquère grapes for Alpine summers. Chignin-Bergeron is best and liveliest.

Chinon Lo r ★★★ 82 83' 85 86 88 89' 90' 91' 92 Juicy, variably rich Cab F from TOURAINE. Drink cool, young; treat exceptional vintages like BORDEAUX. Top growers: Baudry, Couly-Dutheil (esp Clos de l'Echo), Druet, Joguet, Mabileau, Raffault, Dom de Roncée.

Chiroubles Beauj r ★★★ 88 89 90 91 92 Good but tiny BEAUJOLAIS CRU next to FLEURIE; freshly fruity silky wine for early drinking (1–3 yrs). Growers incl Cheysson, DUBOEUF, Fourneau, Passot, Raousset, and the coop.

Chorey-lès-Beaune Burg r (w) ★★ 83 85 86 87 88 89 90 91 92 Minor AC on flat land N of BEAUNE, notable for 2 fine growers: Jacques Germain (Ch de Chorey) and TOLLOT-BEAUT.

Chusclan Rh r p w ★→★★ 88 89 90 91 Village of COTE DU RHONE-VILLAGES. Middle-weight wines (rosé best) from the coop. Labels incl Cuvée des Monticaud, Seigneurie de Gicon.

Cissac HAUT-MEDOC village just west of PAUILLAC.

Clair, Bruno Recent little domaine at MARSANNAY. Vg wines from GEVREY-CHAMBERTIN (esp CLOS DE BEZE), FIXIN, MOREY-ST-DENIS, SAVIGNY.

Clairet Very light red wine, almost rosé.

Clairette Traditional white grape of the MIDI. Can give soft pretty wine.

Clairette de Bellegarde Midi w ★ DYA AC nr Nîmes: plain neutral white.

Clairette de Die Rh w dr s/sw sp ★★ NV Popular dry or (better) semi-sweet MUSCAT-flavoured sparkling wine from E Rhône; or straight dry CLAIRETTE white, surprisingly ageing well 3–4 yrs. Worth trying.

Clairette du Languedoc Midi w ★ DYA Plain neutral white from nr Montpellier, but watch for improvements.

Clape, La Midi r p w ★→★★ AC of the COTEAUX DU LANGUEDOC. A name to note. Full-bodied wines from limestone hills between Narbonne and the sea. The red gains character after 2–3 yrs, the Malvasia white after even longer. Vg rosé. Some experiments with CHARD.

Claret Traditional English term for red BORDEAUX.

Climat Burgundian word for individual named v'yd, eg BEAUNE Grèves.

Clos A term carrying some prestige, reserved for distinct, usually walled, v'yds, often in one ownership. Frequent in Burgundy and ALSACE. Les Clos is CHABLIS' Grandest Cru.

Clos de Bèze See Chambertin-Clos de Bèze.

Clos des Lambrays Burg r *** 78 83 85 86 87 88' 89 90 91 92 15-acre GRAND CRU v'yd at MOREY-ST-DENIS. Changed hands in '79 after a shaky period. Now, after replanting, looking good (for a v long life).

Clos des Mouches Burg r w *** Splendid PREMIER CRU BEAUNE v'yd, largely owned by DROUHIN. White and red both spicy and memorable.

Clos de la Roche Burg r *** 71 72 76 78 82 83 85' 86 87 88' 89 90 91 92 38-acre GRAND CRU at MOREY-ST-DENIS. Powerful complex wine like CHAMBERTIN for v long ageing. Producers incl BOUCHARD PERE, BOUREE, CASTAGNIER, DUJAC, Lignier, PONSOT, REMY, ROUSSEAU.

Clos du Roi Burg r *** Part of GRAND CRU CORTON. Also a BEAUNE PREMIER CRU.

Clos St-Denis Burg r *** 76 78 79 82 83' 85 86 87 88 89 90 91 92 16-acre GRAND CRU at MOREY-ST-DENIS. Splendid sturdy wine growing silky with age. Growers incl DUJAC, Lignier, PONSOT.

Clos Ste Hune Al w V fine austere Riesling from TRIMBACH.

Clos St-Jacques Burg r *** 71 76 78 79 80 82 83 84 85' 86 87 88' 89 90 91 92 17-acre PREMIER CRU of GEVREY-CHAMBERTIN. Excellent powerful velvety wine, often better (and dearer) than some of the CHAMBERTIN GRANDS CRUS. Main grower: ROUSSEAU.

Clos St-Jean Burg r *** 78 79 82 83' 85 86 87 88 89 90 91 92 36-acre PREMIER CRU of CHASSAGNE-MONTRACHET. Vg red, more solid than subtle, from eg Ch de la Maltroye. NB Domaine RAMONET.

Clos de Tart Burg r *** 76 78 79 82 83' 85' 86 87 88' 89 90 91 92 18-acre GRAND CRU at MOREY-ST-DENIS, owned by MOMMESSIN. At best wonderfully fragrant, whether young or old.

Clos de Vougeot Burg r *** 76 78 82 83 85 86 87 88 89 90 91 92 124-acre COTE DE NUITS GRAND CRU with many owners. Variable, occasionally sublime. Maturity depends on the grower's philosophy, technique and position on hill. Top growers incl CLAIR-DAU, DROUHIN, Drouhin-Laroze, ENGEL, FAIVELEY, GRIVOT, Gros, Hudelot-Noëllat, JADOT, LEROY, Chantal Lescure, MEO-CAMUZET, Mugneret, Rebourseau, ROUMIER.

Coche-Dury 16-acre MEURSAULT domaine (and 1+ acre CORTON-CHARLEMAGNE) with sky-high reputation for oak-perfumed wines. Also vg ALIGOTE.

Cognac Town and region of W France, and its brandy.

Collines Rhodaniennes Rh r w p Popular Rhône VIN DE PAYS. Mainly reds: Merlot, Syrah, Gamay.

Collioure Pyr r ** 82 83 85 86 88 89 90 91 92 Strong dry red from BANYULS area. Tiny production. Top growers include de Baillaury, Guy de Barlande, Dom du Mas Blanc, Dom de la Rectorie, La Tour Vieille.

Comté Tolosan SW r p w Regional VIN DE PAYS for Midi and Pyrenees v'yds. Predominantly red from traditional SW varieties.

Condrieu Rh w **** DYA Outstanding soft fragrant white of great character (and price) from the VIOGNIER grape, planted on only 35+ acres. Top growers: DELAS, Dumazet, GUIGAL, Pinchon, Ch du Rozay, Vernay. CHATEAU-GRILLET is similar. Don't try ageing it.

Corbières Midi r (p w) *→*** 88 89 90 91 92 Good vigorous bargain reds, rarely disappointing at their price. Best growers incl Ch'x Aiguilloux, de Cabriac, des Ollieux, de Quéribus, Dom de Villemajou; Coops de Embrès et Castelmaur, Paziols, St-Laurent-Cabrerisse, etc.

Cordier, Ets D Important BORDEAUX shipper and château-owner, including Ch'x CANTEMERLE, GRUAUD-LAROSE, LAFAURIE-PEYRAGUEY, MEYNEY, TALBOT, and also SANCERRE, Clos de la Poussie.

Cornas Rh r **→**** 78' 79 80 81 83' 84 85' 86 88 89 90 91 92 Expanding 400-acre district south of HERMITAGE. Sturdy dark Syrah wine of vg quality. Needs 5–15 yrs' ageing. Top growers incl de Barjac, Clape, DELAS, JABOULET, Verset.

Corsica (Corse) Strong wines of all colours. Better ACs incl AJACCIO, CAP CORSE, PATRIMONIO, Sartène. VIN DE PAYS: ILE DE BEAUTE!

Corton Burg r **** 76' 78' 82 83 85' 86' 87 88 89 90 91 92 The only GRAND CRU red of the COTE DE BEAUNE. 200 acres in ALOXE-CORTON incl CLOS DU ROI, Les Bressandes. Rich powerful, should age well. Many good growers.

Corton-Charlemagne Burg w ★★★★ 78' 79 82 83 85 86 87 88 89 90 91 92 The white section (one-third) of CORTON. Rich spicy lingering wine, behaves like a red and ages magnificently. Top growers: BONNEAU DU MARTRAY, Dubreuil-Fontaine, JADOT, LATOUR, Rapet.

Costières de Nîmes Midi r p w ★→★★ DYA Large new AC of improving quality from the Rhône delta. Formerly Costières du Gard. NB Ch de Nages, Ch de la Tuilerie ('Dinettes et Croustilles').

Coteaux d'Aix-en-Provence Prov r p w ★→★★★ AC on the move. Established CH VIGNELAURE challenged by Ch'x de Beaupré, Commanderie de la Bargemone, Fonscolombe. See also COTEAUX DES BAUX-EN-PROVENCE.

Coteaux d'Ancenis Lo r p w ★ DYA Light Cab and Gamay reds and rosés, sharpish whites from MUSCADET country.

Coteaux de l'Ardèche See l'Ardèche.

Coteaux de l'Aubance Lo p w dr sw ★★ DYA Light typical minor ANJOU wines. Best: MOELLEUX from Dom Richou, Dom des Rochettes (to age, not DYA).

Coteaux des Baronnies Rh r p w Rhône VIN DE PAYS. Syrah, Merlot, Cab S and CHARD, plus traditional grapes. Promising.

Coteaux des Baux-en-Provence Prov r p w ★→★★★ Neighbour of COTEAUX D'AIX, also gathering speed. NB The excellent Domaine de Trévallon (Cab and Syrah) and Mas de Gourgonnier.

Coteaux Champenois Champ r w (p) ★★★ DYA (whites) The AC for non-sparkling CHAMPAGNE. Vintages (if mentioned) follow those for Champagne. Do not pay inflated prices.

Coteaux du Giennois Lo r p w ★ DYA Up-and-coming Loire VDQS area north of SANCERRE. Light Gamay and Pinot N, Sauvignon à la SANCERRE. Top grower: Balland-Chapuis.

Coteaux du Languedoc Midi r p w ★→★★ Scattered well-above-ordinary Midi AC areas. Best reds (eg CABRIERES, LA CLAPE, FAUGERES, St-Georges-d'Orques, Quatourze, ST-CHINIAN, St-Saturnin) age for 2–3 yrs. Now also some good whites from CHARD, etc. Follow with increasing interest.

Coteaux du Layon Lo w s/sw sw ★★ 79 82 85 86 88' 89 90 91 92 The heart of ANJOU, centred on Rochefort, S of Angers: sweet Chenin Bl with admirable acidity, ageing almost forever, excellent aperitif or dessert. Top ACs: BONNEZEAUX, C du L-Chaume. Top producer: TOUCHAIS.

Coteaux du Loir Lo r p w dr sw ★★ 78 82 83 85 86 88 89' 90 91 92 Small region N of Tours. Occasionally excellent wines of Chenin Bl, Gamay, Cab, etc. Best v'yd: JASNIERES. The Loir is a tributary of the Loire.

Coteaux de la Loire See Anjou-Coteaux de la Loire.

Coteaux du Lyonnais Rh r p (w) ★ DYA Junior BEAUJOLAIS, and whites in keeping. Best EN PRIMEUR.

Coteaux de Peyriac Midi r p ★ DYA The most-used VIN DE PAYS name of the Aude département. Huge quantities.

Coteaux de Pierrevert Rh r p w sp ★ DYA Minor southern VDQS nr Manosque. Well-made coop wine, mostly rosé, with fresh whites.

Coteaux de Saumur Lo w dr sw ★★ DYA Potentially fine semi-sweet Chenin.

Coteaux du Tricastin Rh r p w ★ 85 86 88 89 90 91 92 Fringe COTES DU RHONE of increasing quality from south of Valence. Attractive PRIMEUR red. Domaine de Grangeneuve is best.

Coteaux Varois Prov r p w ★→★★ Substantial new AC zone: California-style Dom de St-Jean de Villecroze makes vg red.

Coteaux du Vendômois Lo r p w ★ DYA Fringe Loire from N of Blois with VDQS rank. Mainly Gamay and Pineau d'Aunis (for rosé).

Côte(s) Means hillside; generally a superior v'yd to those on the plain. Many ACs are prefixed by either 'Côtes' or 'Coteaux', meaning the same. In ST-EMILION distinguishes valley slopes from higher plateau.

Côte Chalonnaise Burg r w sp ★★→★★★ Lesser-known v'yd area between BEAUNE and MACON. See Givry, Mercurey, Montagny, Rully. Alias 'Région de Mercurey'.

Côte de Beaune Burg r w ★★→★★★★ Used geographically: the southern half of the COTE D'OR. Applies as an AC only to parts of BEAUNE itself.

Côte de Beaune-Villages Burg r w ★★ 85 86 87 88 89 90 91 92 Regional APPELLATION CONTROLEE for secondary wines of the classic area. Cannot be labelled 'Côte de Beaune' without either '-Villages' or the village name appended.

Côte de Brouilly Beauj r ★★★ 88 89 90 91 92 Fruity rich vigorous BEAUJOLAIS CRU. One of best. Leaders: Dom de Chavanne, Ch Delachanel, Ch Thivin.

Côte de la Malpère Midi r ★ Recent VDQS for reds half-way in style between BORDEAUX and Midi.

Côte de Nuits Burg r (w) ★★→★★★★ N half of COTE D'OR. Mostly red wine.

Côte de Nuits-Villages Burg r (w) ★★ 85 86 87 88 89 90 91 92 A junior AC for extreme N and S ends of Côte; well worth investigating for bargains.

Côte d'Or Département name applied to the central and principal Burgundy v'yd slopes, consisting of the COTE DE BEAUNE and COTE DE NUITS. The name is not used on labels.

Côte Rôtie Rh r ★★★→★★★★ 78 79 80 82 83' 84 85' 86 88 89 90 91 92 Potentially the finest Rhône red, from just S of Vienne; can achieve complex, almost BORDEAUX-like delicacy with age. Top growers include Champet, CHAPOUTIER, DELAS, Dervieux, Gentaz-Barge, GUIGAL, JABOULET, Jamet, Jasmin, Rostaing, VIDAL-FLEURY.

Côtes d'Auvergne Central France r p (w) ★ DYA Flourishing small VDQS area nr Clermont-Ferrand. Red (at best) like light BEAUJOLAIS. Chanturgues is the best known. Corent is a rosé.

Côtes de Blaye Bx w ★ DYA Run-of-the-mill BORDEAUX white from BLAYE. (Better reds are called PREMIERES COTES DE BLAYE.)

Côtes de Bordeaux Saint-Macaire Bx w dr sw ★ DYA Run-of-the-mill BORDEAUX white from E of SAUTERNES.

Côtes de Bourg Bx r ★→★★ 82 83 85 86 88 89 90 91 92 Appellation used for many of the better reds of BOURG. Ch'x incl DE BARBE, La Barde, DU BOUSQUET, Brûlesécaille, La Croix de Millorit, Falfas, Font Guilhem, Grand-Jour, de la Grave, La Grolet, Guerry, Lalibarde, Lamothe, Mendoce, Peychaud, Rousset, Tayac, de Thau.

Côtes de Castillon Bx r ★→★★ 82 85 86 88 89 90 91 92 Flourishing region just E of ST-EMILION. Similar wines, though a touch lighter. Ch'x incl Beauséjour, La Clarière-Laithwaite, Fonds-Rondes, Haut-Tuquet, Lartigue, Moulin-Rouge, PITRAY, Rocher-Bellevue, Ste-Colombe, Thibaud-Bellevue.

Côtes de Duras Dordogne r w ★ 88 89 90 91 92 Neighbour to BERGERAC, dominated by its v competent coop. Similar light wines.

Côtes du Forez Central France r p ★ DYA Fashionable light Beaujolais-style Gamay red, can be good in warm yrs. VDQS status.

Côtes-de-Francs Bx r w ★★ 82 83 85 86 88' 89 90 91 92 Fringe BORDEAUX from E of ST-EMILION, next door to CASTILLON. Increasingly attractive and tasty wines, esp from Ch'x de Belcier, La Claverie, de Francs, Lauriol, PUYGUERAUD, La Prade.

Côtes de Fronsac See Fronsac.

Côtes du Frontonnais SW France r p →★★ DYA Local wine of Toulouse, gaining admirers everywhere. Ch Bellevue-la-Forêt (250 acres) makes outstanding silky red and rosé 'l'Allégresse'.

Côtes de Gascogne SW w (r) ★→★★ DYA VIN DE PAYS gaining a name for deliciously floral Sauv Bl whites and Ugni Bl, Colombard and Gros Manseng blends, all in bountiful supply. Top growers: Domaine de Biau, Grassa, the Coop de Plaimont.

Côtes du Haut-Roussillon SW France br sw ★→★★ NV Area for VINS DOUX NATURELS N of Perpignan.

Côtes du Jura Jura r p w (sp) ★ DYA Various light tints and tastes. ARBOIS is theoretically better.

Côtes du Luberon Rh r p w sp ★→★★ Improving country wines from N Provence. The stars are Ch de Mille and Ch Val-Joanis, with good largely Syrah red, and whites as well. Others incl a good coop and Ch de la Canorgue.

Côtes du Marmandais Dordogne r p w ★ DYA Light wines from southeast of BORDEAUX. The coop at Cocumont makes most of the best.

Côtes de Montravel Dordogne w dr sw ★ DYA Part of BERGERAC; traditionally medium-sweet wine, now often dry.

Côtes de Provence Prov r p w ★→★★★ Wine of Provence; often with more alcohol than character, though standards are rising with new investment. Commanderie de Peyrassol, Dom Gavoty, DOM OTT, Dom Richeaume are leaders. 60% is rosé, 30% red. See Coteaux d'Aix, Bandol, etc.

Côtes du Rhône Rh r p w ★→★★ **88 89 90 91 92** The basic AC of the Rhône Valley. Best drunk young – even as PRIMEUR. Wide variations of quality due to grape ripeness: tending to rise with alcohol %. See Côtes du Rhone-Villages.

Côtes du Rhône-Villages Rh r p w ★→★★ **88 89 90 91 92** The wine of the 17 best villages of the southern Rhône. Substantial and on the whole reliable. Sometimes delicious. See Beaumes-de-Venise, Cairanne, Chusclan, Laudun, Rasteau, etc.

Côtes Roannaises Central France r ★ DYA Minor Gamay region between Lyon and the Loire.

Côtes du Roussillon Pyr r p w ★→★★ **88 89 90 91 92** Country wine of E Pyrenees. The hefty CARIGNAN reds are best and can be very tasty. Some whites are sharp VINS VERTS.

Côtes du Roussillon-Villages Pyr r ★★ **85 86 88 89 90 91 92** The region's best reds, from 28 communes incl CARAMANY, LATOUR DE FRANCE. Best labels: Cuvée Blanes, Cazes Frères, Ch de Corneilla, Gauby, Ch de Jau, Coop Les Vignerons Catalans. Some producers now choose to renounce AC status and make single variety VINS DE PAYS.

Côtes de St-Mont SW France r w p ★ Promising VDQS from the Gers, not unlike MADIRAN. The same coop as COTES DE GASCOGNE.

Côtes de Thongue Midi r w ★ DYA Above average VIN DE PAYS from the HERAULT. Some good wines coming.

Côtes de Toul E France p r w ★ DYA Very light VDQS wines from Lorraine; mainly VIN GRIS (rosé).

Côtes du Ventoux Prov r (w) ★★ 88 89 90 91 92 Booming AC for tasty reds between the Rhône and Provence. La Vieille Ferme, owned by J-P Perrin of CH DE BEAUCASTEL, is top producer.

Côtes du Vivarais Prov r p w ★ DYA Pleasant country wines from south Massif Central VDQS. Like light COTES DU RHONE: eg Dom de Belvezet.

Coulée de Serrant Lo w dr sw ★★★ **73 76 78 79 81 82 83 85 86** 88 89' 90' 91 92 10-acre Chenin Bl v'yd on Loire's N bank at SAVENNIERES, ANJOU. Intense strong fruity/sharp wine, good aperitif. Ages almost for ever.

Coussergues, Domaine de Midi r w p ★ DYA Large estate in notorious territory nr Beziers. Experiments with CHARD etc producing bargains.

Crémant In CHAMPAGNE means 'creaming' – ie half-sparkling. Since '75 an AC for high quality METHODE TRADITIONELLE sparkling wines from ALSACE, the Loire, BOURGOGNE and most recently LIMOUX – often a notable bargain. The term will be phased out in Champagne.

Crémant de Loire w sp ★★→★★★ NV High quality sparkling wine from ANJOU, TOURAINE and Pays Nantais.

Crépy Savoie w ★★ DYA Light soft Swiss-style white from S shore of Lake Geneva. 'Crépitant' has been coined for its faint fizz.

Criots-Bâtard-Montrachet Burg w ★★★ **78 79 83 85 86 88 89 90** 91 92 4-acre neighbour to BATARD-M. Similar wine without extreme pungency.

Crozes-Hermitage Rh r (w) ★★ **83 86 88 89 90** 91 92 Larger, less distinguished neighbour to HERMITAGE. Often robust excellent reds, but choose carefully: eg Fayolle et Fils, Alain Graillot, Dom de Thalabert of JABOULET, GAEC de la Syrah. Jaboulet's Mule Blanche is good white.

Cru Growth, as in first growth/classed growth – meaning v'yd. Also, in BEAUJOLAIS, one of the top 10 villages.

Cru Bourgeois General term for MEDOC châteaux below CRU CLASSE. There are 250 in the Syndicat, covering 7,000 acres and competing in an annual competition.

Cru Bourgeois Supérieur (Cru Grand Bourgeois) Rank one better than the last – must be barrel-aged. Being phased out by Brussels from '93.

Cru Classé Classed growth. One of the first five official quality classes of the MEDOC, classified in 1855. Also any classed growth of another district (eg GRAVES, ST-EMILION, SAUTERNES).

Cru Exceptionnel Rank above CRU BOURGEOIS SUPERIEUR, immediately below CRU CLASSE. Cru Bourgeois divisions are being phased out as of '93. Now officially suppressed by Brussels – but memories are long.

Cruse et Fils Frères Senior BORDEAUX shipper. Owned by Société des Vins de France. The Cruse family (not the company) owns CH D'ISSAN.

Cussac Village just S of ST-JULIEN. Appellation HAUT-MEDOC. Top ch'x: BEAUMONT, LANESSAN.

Cuve Close Short-cut method of making sparkling wine in a tank. The sparkle dies away in the glass much quicker than with METHODE CHAMPENOISE wine.

Cuvée The wine contained in a cuve or vat. A word of many uses: 'blend' (as in CHAMPAGNE); in Burgundy interchangeable with 'CRU'. Often just refers to a 'lot' of wine.

Cuvée de la Commanderie Pleasant blends of MEDOC, GRAVES and (best) SAUTERNES made for the Commanderie du Bontemps, the ceremonial/promotional body of the Médoc and Graves.

Degré alcoolique Degrees of alcohol, ie percent by volume.

Deiss, Marcel Fine ALSACE grower at Bergheim with 50 acres, incl splendid Ries from GRAND CRU Schoenenberg and GEWURZ from Altenburg at Bergheim.

Delas Frères Old and worthy firm of Rhône wine specialists with v'yds at CONDRIEU, CORNAS, COTE ROTIE, HERMITAGE. Top wines: Condrieu, Marquise de Tourette HERMITAGE (red and white). Owned by DEUTZ.

Delorme, André Leading COTE CHALONNAISE merchants and growers. Specialists in CREMANT DE BOURGOGNE and excellent RULLY.

De Luze, A & Fils BORDEAUX shipper owned by Rémy-Martin of COGNAC.

Demi-Sec Half-dry: in practice more than half sweet. (Eg of CHAMPAGNE.)

Depagneux, Jacques de Cie Well-regarded merchants of BEAUJOLAIS.

Deutz Brut NV; **79 81 82 85** 88; Rosé **82 85** 88; Bl de Blancs **81 82 85** 88 One of the best of the smaller CHAMPAGNE houses. Pioneer of EN PRIMEUR champagne from '75 (finest yrs only). Full-flavoured wines. Luxury brands: Cuvée William Deutz (**79 82 85 88**) and Rosé.

Dirler, Jean-Pierre ALSACE producer of Kessler GRAND CRU: best for Ries.

Domaine Property, particularly in Burgundy.

Dom Pérignon 71 73 75 76 78 82 83 85 **87**; Rosé **78 80 83** 85 Luxury brand of MOET & CHANDON (launched 1936), named after the legendary Abbey cellarmaster who 'invented' CHAMPAGNE. Astonishing consistent quality.

Dopff au Moulin Ancient and top-class family wine house at Riquewihr, ALSACE. Best wines: GEWURZ Eichberg, Ries Schoenenbourg. Pioneers of sparkling wine in Alsace.

Dopff & Irion Another excellent Riquewihr (ALSACE) business. Best wines incl MUSCAT les Amandiers, Ries de Riquewihr.

Doudet-Naudin Burgundy merchant and grower at SAVIGNY-LES-BEAUNE. Vineyards incl BEAUNE-CLOS DU ROI and Redrescul. Unfashionably dark long-lived wines, supplied to Berry Bros & Rudd of London, eventually good.

Dourthe Frères BORDEAUX merchant offering a wide range of ch'x, mainly good CRUS BOURGEOIS, incl BELGRAVE, MAUCAILLOU, TRONQUOY-LALANDE. Beau-Mayne is their well-made brand.

Doux Sweet.

DRC See Romanée-Conti, Domaine de la.

Drouhin, J & Cie Deservedly prestigious Burgundy grower (130 acres) and merchant with highest standards. Cellars in BEAUNE; v'yds in Beaune, CHABLIS, CLOS DE VOUGEOT, MUSIGNY, etc, and Oregon. Top wines incl BEAUNE-CLOS DES MOUCHES, CHABLIS LES CLOS, CORTON-CHARLEMAGNE, GRIOTTE-CHAMBERTIN, PULIGNY-MONTRACHET Les Folatières.

Duboeuf, Georges Top-class BEAUJOLAIS merchant at Romanèche-Thorin. Leader of the region in every sense, with a huge range of admirable wines. Also MOULIN-A-VENT untypically aged in new oak, and white MACONNAIS.

Dubos High-level BORDEAUX négociant.

Duclot BORDEAUX négociant; specialist in top growths. Linked with J-P MOUEIX.

Dujac, Domaine Burgundy grower (Jacques Seysses) at MOREY-ST-DENIS with v'yds in that village, BONNES-MARES, ECHEZEAUX, GEVREY-CHAMBERTIN, etc. Splendidly vivid and long-lived wines. Now planting Cab and CHARD in COTEAUX VAROIS and in MEURSAULT.

Dulong Highly competent BORDEAUX merchant. Breaks all the rules with unorthodox Rebelle blends.

Durup, Jean One of the biggest CHABLIS growers with 140 acres, including DOMAINE DE L'EGLANTIERE and admirable Ch de Maligny.

Duval-Leroy Coteaux Champenois r p w; NV; Brut; Vintage Fleur de Champagne Large progressive Vertus producer with high standards.

Echézeaux Burg r ★★★ 76 78' 79 82 83' 85 86 87 88 89 90 91 92 74-acre GRAND CRU between VOSNE-ROMANEE and CLOS DE VOUGEOT. Can be superlative, fragrant, without great weight, eg ENGEL, Gouroux, Jacqueline Jayer, MONGEARD-MUGNERET, Mugneret, DOM DE LA ROMANEE-CONTI.

The Confrèrie des Chevaliers du Tastevin is the wine fraternity of Burgundy: the world's most famous of its kind. It was founded in 1933 by a group of Burgundian patriots, led by Camille Rodier and Georges Faiveley, to rescue their beloved region from a period of slump by promoting its inimitable wines. Today it regularly holds banquets, with elaborate and sprightly ceremonies, for 600 guests, at its headquarters, the Cistercian château in the Clos de Vougeot. The Confrèrie has branches in many countries and members among lovers of wine all over the world. See also Tastevin, page 52.

Edelzwicker Alsace w ★ DYA Modest light white from mixture of grapes, often fruity and good.

Eguisheim, Cave Vinicole d' ALSACE coop with fine GRAND CRUS Hatchbourg, Hengst, Ollwiller and Spiegel. Owns WILLM.

En Primeur See Primeur.

Engel, R Well-known grower of VOSNE-ROMANEE, CLOS DE VOUGEOT, ECHEZEAUX.

Entre-Deux-Mers Bx w ★ DYA Standard dry white BORDEAUX from between the Garonne and Dordogne rivers. Often a good buy, as techniques improve. Esp ch'x Gournin, Latour-Laguens, Moulin de Launay, ST-BONNET, Séguin, Thieuley etc.

L'Estandon The everyday wine of Nice (AC COTES DE PROVENCE).

l'Etoile Jura w dr sp (sw) ★★ Subregion of the Jura known for stylish whites, incl VIN JAUNE, similar to CHATEAU-CHALON; good sparkling.

Faiveley, J Family-owned growers (with 182 acres) and merchants at NUITS-ST-GEORGES, with v'yds in CHAMBERTIN-CLOS DE BEZE, CHAMBOLLE-MUSIGNY, CORTON, MERCUREY, NUITS (150 acres). Consistent high quality recently. 88s are models. Wines for serious ageing.

Faller, Théo Top ALSACE grower at Dom Weinbach, Kaysersberg. Concentrated firm dry wines needing unusually long ageing, up to 10 yrs.

Faugères Midi r (p w) ★→★★ 88 89 90 91 92 Isolated COTEAUX DU LANGUEDOC village with above-average wine. Gained AC status in '82.

Fessy, Sylvain Dynamic BEAUJOLAIS merchant with wide range.

Fèvre, William Excellent CHABLIS grower with the biggest GRAND CRU holding (40 acres). Spices his top wines with new oak. One whimsy wine he calls Napa Vallée de France. His label is Domaine de la Maladière.

Fiefs Vendéens Lo r p w ★ DYA Up-and-coming VDQS for light wines from the Vendée, S of the W Loire.

Fitou Midi r ★★ 85 86 88 89 90 91 92 Superior CORBIERES red; powerful, ages well. Best from coops at Cascastel, Mont Tuch and Tuchan.

Fixin Burg r ★★ 78 83 85 86 87 88 89 90 91 92 Worthy and under-valued northern neighbour of GEVREY-CHAMBERTIN. Often splendid reds. Best v'yds: Clos du Chapitre, Les Hervelets, Clos Napoléon. Top growers: Bertheau, CLAIR, FAIVELEY, Gelin, Gelin-Moulin.

Fleurie Beauj r ★★★ 88 89 90 91 92 The epitome of a BEAUJOLAIS CRU: fruity scented silky racy. Top wines from Chapelle des Bois, Chignard, DUBOEUF, Ch de Fleurie, the coop.

Fortant de France Midi r p w ★→★★ Brand (dressed to kill) of fair quality single-grape wines from the neighbourhood of Sète. See Skalli.

Frais Fresh or cool.

Frappé Ice-cold.

Froid Cold.

Fronsac Bx r ★→★★★ 82 83 85 86 88 89' 90 91 92 Picturesque area of increasingly fine tannic reds just W of ST-EMILION. Ch'x incl de Carles, DALEM, LA DAUPHINE, Fontenil, Mayne-Vieil, Moulin-Haut-Laroque, LA RIVIERE, La Rousselle, La Valade, La Vieille Cure, Villars. Give them time. See also smaller Canon-Fronsac.

Frontignan Midi br sw ★ NV Strong, sweet and liquorous MUSCAT wine of ancient repute.

Gagnard-Delagrange, Jacques Estimable small (13-acre) grower of CHASSAGNE-MONTRACHET, including some MONTRACHET.

Gaillac SW France r p w dr sw sp ★→★★ mostly DYA Ancient area coming to life. Ch Larroze is the quality leader, others incl Jean Cros, Dom d'Escausses, Dom des Hourtets, Dom de Labarthe and Robert Plageoles. Important coops: Labastide de Lévis (with fruity wines from local Mauzac grapes), La Cave Tecou (esp wood-aged 'Passion'). Slightly fizzy Perlé is value. Reds can age well.

Gamay See Grapes for red wine (pages 8–9).

Gard, Vin de Pays du The Gard département at the mouth of the Rhône is a centre of good VINS DE PAYS; incl Coteaux Flaviens, Pont du Gard, SABLES DU GOLFE DU LION, Salaves, Uzège and Vaunage. Watch this area.

Geisweiler et Fils Big Burgundy merchant and grower. Now owned by the Rehs of the Mosel. Cellars and 50 acres at NUITS-ST-GEORGES, also 150 acres at Bevy in HAUTES-COTES DE NUITS and 30 in the COTE CHALONNAISE.

Gevrey-Chambertin Burg r ★★★ 82 83 85 86 87 88 89 90 91 92 The village containing the great CHAMBERTIN and many other noble v'yds (eg PREMIERS CRUS Cazetiers, Combe aux Moines, CLOS ST-JACQUES, Clos des Varoilles), as well as many more commonplace. Growers incl BACHELET, Boillot, Damoy, DROUHIN, FAIVELEY, JADOT, Leclerc, LEROY, MORTET, ROUSSEAU, ROTY, Roumier, TRAPET, DOM DES VAROILLES.

Gewürztraminer Speciality grape of ALSACE: one of 4 allowed for specified GRAND CRU wines. Perfumed like old roses, often tasting like grapefruit.

Gigondas Rh r p ★★ 78 83 84 85 86 88 89 90 91 92 Worthy neighbour to CHATEAUNEUF-DU-PAPE. Strong full-bodied sometimes peppery wine, eg Dom du Cayron, Dom les Pallières, Dom du Pesquier, Dom Raspail-Ay, Dom St-Gayan, Ch du Trignon.

Giroud, Camille Top small BEAUNE négociant. Wines from old vines keep their growers' individuality.

Gisselbrecht, Louis High quality ALSACE shippers at Dambach-la-Ville.

Givry Burg r w ★★ 83 85 86 87 88 89 90 91 92 Underrated COTE CHALONNAISE village: light but tasty and typical burgundy from eg Dom Joblot, Clos Salomon, BARON THENARD.

Gosset NV Brut; Rosé NV; Grande Réserve **81 82 83 85 86**; Grand Millésime **82 83** 85 88; Grand Rosé **85** 88 Small, v old CHAMPAGNE house at AY. Excellent full wine (esp Grand Millésime). Now linked with PHILIPPONNAT.

Goulaine, Château de The ceremonial showplace of MUSCADET; a noble family estate and its appropriate wine.

Goulet, Georges NV; Rosé **85**; Crémant Bl de Blancs **83 85** High quality Reims CHAMPAGNE house linked with ABEL LEPITRE. Luxury brand: Cuvée du Centenaire (**79 82 83 85**).

Goût Taste, eg goût anglais – as the English like it (ie dry).

Grand Cru One of the top Burgundy v'yds with its own appellation contrôlée. Similar meaning in new ALSACE law (for Ries, GEWURZ, MUSCAT and Pinot Gr only), but more vague elsewhere. In ST-EMILION the third rank of ch'x, incl about 200 properties.

Grand Roussillon Midi br sw ★★ NV Broad AC for MUSCAT and other sweet fortified wines (VINS DOUX NATURELS) of E Pyrenees.

Grande Champagne The AC of the best area of COGNAC.

Grande Rue, La Burg r ★★★ Recently-promoted GRAND CRU in VOSNE-ROMANEE, neighbour to ROMANEE-CONTI. Owners, the Lamarche family, could try harder.

Grands-Echézeaux Burg r ★★★★ **69 71 76 78 79 82 83 85 86 87 88 89 90 91 92** Superlative 22-acre GRAND CRU next to CLOS DE VOUGEOT. Viz: DROUHIN, ENGEL, MONGEARD-MUGNERET, DOM DE LA ROMANEE-CONTI.

Gratien, Alfred and Gratien & Meyer Excellent smaller CHAMPAGNE house (fine v dry long-lasting wine: **79 82 83 85**) and its counterpart at SAUMUR on the Loire. (Vg Cuvée Flamme.)

Graves Bx r w ★→★★★★ Large region S of Bordeaux city with excellent soft earthy reds, and recently much improved dry whites (Sauv Bl-Sém).

Graves de Vayres Bx r w ★ DYA Part of ENTRE-DEUX-MERS; no special character.

Griotte-Chambertin Burg r ★★★★ **76 78' 79 83 85' 86 87 88 89 90 91 92** 14-acre GRAND CRU adjoining CHAMBERTIN. Similar wine, but less masculine, more 'tender'. Growers incl DROUHIN, PONSOT. Griotte means wild cherry.

Grivot, Jean 25-acre COTE DE NUITS domaine, in 5 ACs incl RICHEBOURG, NUITS PREMIERS CRUS, VOSNE-ROMANEE, CLOS DE VOUGEOT, etc. Top quality.

Gros Plant du Pays Nantais Lo w ★ DYA Junior VDQS cousin of MUSCADET, sharper and lighter; made of the COGNAC grape also known as Folle Blanche, Ugni Blanc, etc.

Guigal, E and M Celebrated growers and merchants of CONDRIEU, COTE ROTIE and HERMITAGE. Since '85 owners of VIDAL-FLEURY. By ageing single-v'yd Côte Rôtie (La Landonne, La Mouline, La Turque) in new oak Guigal breaks local tradition (and has lost at least one customer).

Guyon, Antonin Considerable domaine at ALOXE-CORTON with fine wines from CHAMBOLLE-MUSIGNY, CORTON, etc, and HAUTES-COTES DE NUITS.

Haut-Benauge Bx w ★ DYA AC for a limited area in ENTRE-DEUX-MERS.

Hautes-Côtes de Beaune Burg r w ★★ **85 86 87 88 89 90 91 92** Appellation for a dozen villages in the hills behind the COTE DE BEAUNE. Light wines, worth investigating. Top growers: Cornu, Mazilly.

Hautes-Côtes de Nuits Burg r w ★★ **85 86 87 88 89 90 91 92** As above, for COTE DE NUITS. An area on the way up. Top growers: C Cornu, Jayer-Gilles, M Gros. Also has large BEAUNE coop; good esp from GEISWEILER.

Haut-Médoc Bx r ★★→★★★ **70 75 76 78 79 81 82 83 85 86 87 88 89 90 91 92** Big AC including all the best parts of the MEDOC. Most of the zone has communal ACs (eg MARGAUX, PAUILLAC). Some excellent châteaux (eg LA LAGUNE) are simply AC HAUT-MEDOC.

Haut-Montravel Dordogne w dr sw ★ **88 89 90** Medium-sweet BERGERAC.

Haut Poitou Lo w (r) ★→★★ DYA Up-and-coming young VDQS S of ANJOU. Vg whites (CHARD, Sauv) from coop. Has rejected restrictions of AC status.

To decipher codes, please refer to symbols key at front of book, and to 'How to Read an Entry' on page 5.

Heidsieck, Charles NV; **79 81 83 85**; Rosé **81 83 85** Major CHAMPAGNE house of Reims, now controlled by Rémy Martin; also incl Trouillard and de Venoge. Luxury brands: Cuvée Champagne Charlie (**81 82 83**), Blanc des Millénaires (**83**). Fine quality recently; the NV a bargain.

Heidsieck, Monopole NV; Rosé; **79 82 83 85 87** Important CHAMPAGNE merchant and Reims grower now owned by MUMM. Vg luxury brands: Diamant Bleu (**76 79 82 85**), Diamant Rose (**82 85 88**).

Henriot NV; Brut Souverain; Bl de Blancs Crémant NV; **79 82 85 88**; Brut Rosé **81 83 85 88**; Cuvée Baccarat **79 82 83 85 88** Old family CHAMPAGNE house linked with VEUVE CLICQUOT in the Möet Hennessy group. Very big dry style. Luxury private brand: Réserve Baron Philippe de Rothschild.

Hérault Midi The biggest v'yd département in France with 980,000 acres of vines. Production is chiefly of VIN DE TABLE but some good AC COTEAUX DU LANGUEDOC, and, more interestingly, pioneering Vins de Pays de l'Hérault.

Hermitage Rh r w ★★★→★★★★ **71 72 78' 79 80 82 83' 84 85 86 88 89 90 91 92** The 'manliest' wine of France. Dark powerful and profound. Needs long ageing. The white is heady and golden; now usually made for early drinking, though the best wines mature for up to 25 yrs. Top makers: CHAPOUTIER, CHAVE, DELAS, Grippat, GUIGAL, JABOULET, Sorrel.

Hospices de Beaune Historic hospital in BEAUNE, with excellent v'yds (known by 'Cuvée' names) in BEAUNE, CORTON, MEURSAULT, POMMARD, VOLNAY. Wines are auctioned on the third Sunday of each November.

Hugel et Fils The best-known ALSACE growers and merchants. Founded at Riquewihr in 1639 and still in the family. Top wines are: 'Jubilee' and SELECTIONS DES GRAINS NOBLES. Many are sweet, but not all.

Ile de Beauté Name given to VINS DU PAYS from CORSICA. Mostly red.

Impériale BORDEAUX bottle holding 8.5 normal bottles (6.4 litres).

Irancy ('Bourgogne Irancy') Burg r (p) ★★ **85 86 88 89 90 91 92** Good light red made nr CHABLIS from Pinot N and César. The best vintages are long-lived and mature well. To watch.

Irouléguy SW France r p (w) ★★ DYA Agreeable local wines, mainly Tannat reds, of the Basque country.

Jaboulet, Paul Old family firm at Tain, leading growers of HERMITAGE (esp La Chapelle ★★★★) and merchants of other Rhône wines.

Jaboulet-Vercherre & Cie Burgundy merchant house with v'yds (34 acres) in POMMARD, etc, and cellars in BEAUNE. Middling wines.

Jacquart Brut NV, Brut Rosé, Brut **85 87 88** Relatively new ('62) CHAMPAGNE marque; in quantity the sixth largest. Coop based. Luxury brands: Cuvée Nominée Blanc **85**, Cuvée Nominée Rosé **85**. Vg Bl de Blancs Cuvée Spéciale.

Jadot, Louis Much-respected top quality Burgundy merchant house with v'yds (150 acres) in BEAUNE, CORTON etc. Incl former estate of CLAIR-DAU.

Jaffelin Independently run high quality négociant, bought in '92 from DROUHIN by BOISSET.

Jardin de la France Lo r w p One of the four regional VINS DE PAYS. Covers Loire Valley: Gamay and Sauv Bl wines (slightly more red than white), mostly single grape. Top vin de pays de zone: Marches de Bretagne.

Jasnières Lo w (r p) ★★★ **76 78 79 82 83 85 86 88 89 90 91 92** V rare dry rather VOUVRAY-like wine of N TOURAINE.

Jaubertie, Domaine de la English-owned top BERGERAC estate (114 acres). Sumptuous luxury Sauv Bl, Cuvée Mirabelle. Equally fine Réserve red.

Jayer, Henri Tiny VOSNE-ROMANEE domaine acknowledged even by rivals as superlative. (Monsieur J retired in '88 but still watches this and MEO-CAMUZET closely.)

Jeroboam In BORDEAUX a 6-bottle bottle (holding 4.5 litres), or triple magnum; in CHAMPAGNE a double magnum.

Josmeyer Family house at Wintzenheim, ALSACE. Vg long-ageing wines, esp GEWURZ and Pinot Bl. Fine Ries from Hengst GRAND CRU.

Juliénas Burg r ★★★ **89 90 91 92** Leading CRU of BEAUJOLAIS: vigorous fruity wine to keep 2–3 yrs. Growers incl Ch du Bois de la Salle, Dom Bottière, Ch des Capitans, Ch de Juliénas, Dom R Monnet and the coop.

Jura See Côtes de Jura.

Jurançon SW France w sw dr ★★→★★★ **82 83 85 86 88 89 90 91 92** Unusual high-flavoured long-lived speciality of Pau in the Pyrenean foothills, at best like wild-flower SAUTERNES. Not to be missed. Both sweet and dry should age well. Top growers: Barrère, Chigné, Gaillot, Guirouilh, Lamouroux, Larredya, Ramonteu (Dom Cauhapé). Also the coop's Grain Sauvage.

Kaefferkopf Alsace w dr sw ★★★ Ammerschwihr v'yd famous for blends rather than single-grape wines; growers not happy with restrictions of GRAND CRU status.

Kientzheim-Kayserberg Important ALSACE coop for quality as well as style. Esp for GEWURZ.

Kientzler, André Fine ALSACE Ries specialist in Geisburg GRAND CRU: esp VENDANGE TARDIVE and SELECTION DES GRAINS NOBLES. Equally good from Osterberg, occasional 'vins de glaces' (Eisweins).

Kreydenweiss Fine ALSACE grower with 24 acres at Andlau, esp for Pinot Gr (vg from Moenchberg GRAND CRU), Pinot Bl and Ries. Top wine: Kastelberg (Ries ages 20 yrs plus).

Kriter Popular sparkler processed in Burgundy by PATRIARCHE.

Krug Grande Cuvée; Rosé; **64 66 69 71 73 75 76 79 81 82** 85; Clos du Mesnil Bl de Blancs **79 80 82 83** Small but supremely prestigious CHAMPAGNE house. Dense full-bodied v dry wines of superlative quality. Owned by Rémy Martin (but no-one would know).

Kuentz-Bas Top-quality ALSACE grower and merchant at Husseren-les-Châteaux, esp for Pinot Gr (Tokay d'Alsace) and GEWURZ.

Labouré-Gontard Makes high-quality CREMANT DE BOURGOGNE at NUITS.

Labouré-Roi Outstandingly reliable merchant at NUITS-ST-GEORGES. Mostly whites. Many fine domaine wines, esp René Manuel's MEURSAULT, Chantal Lescure's Nuits and CLOS DE VOUGEOT. Vg CHABLIS. Also VOLNAY-SANTENOTS.

Ladoucette, de Leading producer of POUILLY-FUME, based at CH DE NOZET. Luxury brand: Baron de L. Also SANCERRE Comte Lafond.

Lafarge, Michel 23-acre COTE DE BEAUNE estate, with outstanding VOLNAYS.

Lafon, Domaine des Comtes 32-acre top quality Burgundy estate in MEURSAULT, LE MONTRACHET and VOLNAY. Glorious intense wines.

Laguiche, Marquis de Largest owner of LE MONTRACHET. Magnificent wines made by DROUHIN.

Lalande de Pomerol Bx r ★★ **82 83 85 86 88 89 90** Neighbour to POMEROL. Wines similar but less mellow. Top ch'x: Les Annereaux, DE BELAIR, Belles-Graves, La Croix Bellevue, La Croix-St-André, Les Hauts-Conseillants, Les Hauts-Tuileries, Moncets, SIAURAC, TOURNEFEUILLE.

Langlois-Château Producer of sparkling SAUMUR, controlled by BOLLINGER.

Lanson Père & Fils Black Label NV; Rosé NV; Red Label **76 79 81 82 83 85** Important CHAMPAGNE house with cellars at Reims. Luxury brands: Noble Cuvée (**81 85**). Black Label is a reliable fresh NV.

Laroche Important grower (238 acres) and dynamic CHABLIS merchant, incl Domaines La Jouchère and Laroche. Also makes Ch de Puligny-Montrachet and blends good non-regional CHARD.

Latour, Louis Famous Burgundy merchant and grower with v'yds (120 acres) in BEAUNE, CORTON, etc. Among the best for white: CHEVALIER-MONTRACHET, CORTON-CHARLEMAGNE, Les Demoiselles, MONTRACHET, gd value MONTAGNY and ARDECHE CHARD, etc. Developing Pinot N in the Var.

Latour de France r (w) ★→★★ **88 89 90 91 92** New AC in COTES DE ROUSSILLON-VILLAGES.

Latricières-Chambertin Burg r ★★★ **76 78 82 83 85' 86 87 88 89 90 91 92** 17-acre GRAND CRU neighbour of CHAMBERTIN. Similar wine but lighter and 'prettier' eg from FAIVELEY, LEROY, PONSOT, TRAPET.

Laudun Rh r p w ★ Village of COTES DU RHONE-VILLAGES. Attractive wines from the coop incl fresh whites. But Dom Palaquié is better.

Laugel, Michel One of the biggest ALSACE merchant houses at Marlenheim.

Laurent-Perrier NV; Rosé Brut; **78 79 81 82 85 88** Excellent highly successful family-owned CHAMPAGNE house at Tours-sur-Marne. Luxury brands: Cuvée Grand Siècle (a blend of vintages, recently released 81-82-85), Cuvée Alexandre Rosé (82 only). Ultra Brut is best buy. See also Rodet.

Leflaive, Domaine Formerly considered the best of all white burgundy growers, at PULIGNY-MONTRACHET. Best v'yds: Bienvenue- and Chevalier-Montrachet, Clavoillons, Pucelles. Now some wines lack staying power.

Leflaive, Olivier Négociant at PULIGNY-MONTRACHET since '84, now with 22 acres of his own, nephew of the above. Reliable whites and reds, incl less famous ACs. Mostly young-drinking.

Léognan Bx r w ★★★ Top village of GRAVES with its own AC: PESSAC-LEOGNAN. Best ch'x: DOM DE CHEVALIER, HAUT-BAILLY, MALARTIC-LAGRAVIERE.

Leroy Important NEGOCIANT-ELEVEUR at AUXEY-DURESSES with a growing domaine and the finest stocks of old wines in Burgundy. Part-owners of DOM DE LA ROMANEE-CONTI. In '88 bought the 35-acre Noëllat estate in CLOS VOUGEOT, NUITS, ROMANEE-ST-VIVANT, SAVIGNY, etc. Leroy's range, esp of CHAMBERTIN and neighbours, is magnificent.

Lichine, Alexis & Cie BORDEAUX merchants (formerly owned by the late Alexis Lichine), proprietors of CH LASCOMBES. No connection with CH PRIEURE LICHINE.

Lie, sur On the lees. MUSCADET is often bottled straight from the vat, without racking or filtering, for maximum freshness and character.

Limoux Pyr r w ★★ NV Austerely dry non-sparkling version of BLANQUETTE DE LIMOUX (sometimes labelled Limoux Nature) and a good claret-like red from the coop: Anne des Joyeuses. Vinavius (**88 89 90**) is oak-aged and even better. Recently also 'Grand Chardonnay'.

Lirac Rh r p (w) ★★ **85 86 88 89 90 91 92** Next village to TAVEL. Similar wine; the red overtaking the rosé, esp Dom Maby, Dom de la Mordorée, Dom St-Roch, Ch de Segriés.

Listel Midi r p w ★→★★ DYA Vast (4,000-acre+) historic estate on the sandy beaches of the Golfe du Lion. Owned by the giant Salins du Midi salt co. Pleasant light 'vins des sables' incl sparkling. Dom du Bosquet-Canet is a fruity Cab, and Dom de Villeroy makes a fresh BLANC DE BLANCS SUR LIE and CHARD since '89. Also fruity almost non-alcoholic PETILLANT, Ch de Malijay, COTES DU RHONE, and Abbaye de Ste-Hilaire COTEAUX VAROIS.

Listrac-Médoc Bx r ★★→★★★ Village of HAUT-MEDOC next to MOULIS. Best ch'x: CLARKE, FONREAUD, FOURCAS-DUPRE, FOURCAS-HOSTEN.

Long-Depaquit Vg CHABLIS domaine (esp MOUTONNE), owned by BICHOT.

Lorentz Two small quality ALSACE houses at Bergheim: Gustave L and Jerome L, have same management. Esp GEWURZ and Ries from Altenberg de Bergheim and Kanzlerberg.

Loron & Fils Big-scale Burgundy grower and merchant at Pontanevaux; specialist in BEAUJOLAIS and sound VINS DE TABLE.

Loupiac Bx w sw ★★ **76 79 80 83 85 86 88 89 90 91 92** Across the R Garonne from SAUTERNES. Top châteaux: Clos-Jean, Haut-Loupiac, LOUPIAC-GAUDIET, RICAUD, Rondillon.

Lugny ('Mâcon-Lugny') Burg r w sp ★★ **88 89 90 91 92** Village next to VIRE with good active coop. Les Genevrières is sold by LOUIS LATOUR.

Lupé-Cholet & Cie Merchants and growers at NUITS-ST-GEORGES controlled by BICHOT. Best estate wines: Clos de Lupé and Château Gris.

Lussac-St-Emilion Bx r ★★ **82 85 86 88 89 90 91 92** NE neighbour to ST-EMILION. Top ch'x incl Barbe Blanche, Bel Air, DU LYONNAT, Tour de Grenat, Villadière. Coop (at PUISSEGUIN) makes pleasant Roc de Lussac.

France entries also cross-refer to Châteaux of Bordeaux section, pages 55–75.

Macération carbonique Traditional technique of fermentation with whole bunches of unbroken grapes in a closed vat. Fermentation inside each grape eventually bursts it, giving vivid fruity mild wine, not for ageing. Esp in BEAUJOLAIS; now much used in the MIDI and elsewhere.

Machard de Gramont BURGUNDY family estate: cellars in NUITS and v'yds in BEAUNE, Nuits, POMMARD, SAVIGNY. Extremely well-made reds.

Mâcon Burg r w (p) ** 88 89 90 91 92 Sound, usually unremarkable reds, tasty dry (CHARD) whites. Wine with village name (eg Mâcon-Prissé) is better; POUILLY-FUISSE best AC, ST-VERAN also gd. See also Mâcon-Villages.

Mâcon-Lugny See Lugny.

Mâcon Supérieur The same but slightly better, from riper grapes.

Mâcon-Villages Burg w **→*** 88 89 90 91 92 Increasingly well-made typical white burgundies (when not over-produced). Eg Mâcon-Clessé, MACON-LUGNY, Mâcon-Prissé, MACON-VIRE. Best coop is probably Chaintré.

Mâcon-Viré See Mâcon-Villages and Viré.

Macvin Jura w sw ** AC for 'traditional' MARC and grape juice aperitif.

Madiran SW France r *** 82 83 85 86 88 89 90 91 92 Dark vigorous red from ARMAGNAC, like hard but fruity MEDOC with a fluid elegance of its own. Ages 5–10 yrs, but 'barriques' are changing it, not necessarily for the better. Top growers: Ch'x d'Arricau-Bordes, d'Aydié, Barréjat, Dom de Bouscassé, Dom Capmartin, Laplace, Montus, Peyros.

Magenta, Duc de Recently revamped Burgundy estate (30 acres) based at CHASSAGNE-MONTRACHET, managed by JADOT.

Magnum A double bottle (1.5 litres).

Mähler-Besse First-class Dutch wine merchants in BORDEAUX, with a share in CH PALMER. Brands incl Cheval Noir.

Maire, Henri The biggest grower/merchant of JURA wines. Not the best.

Maranges Burg r ** New ('89) AC for 600-odd acres of S COTE DE BEAUNE, beyond SANTENAY, one-third PREMIER CRU. Top/first négociant: JAFFELIN.

Marc Grape skins after pressing; also the strong-smelling brandy made from them (See Italian 'Grappa').

Marcillac SW France r p * DYA Promoted to AC (too hastily?) in '90. Good wines from coop Cave de Valady (rustic reds) and Dom du Cros.

Margaux Bx r **→**** 66 70 75 76 78 79 81 82 83' 85 86 87 88 89 90 91 92 Village of the HAUT-MEDOC making the most 'elegant' red BORDEAUX. AC incl CANTENAC and several other villages. Top ch'x incl MARGAUX, LASCOMBES, RAUSAN-SEGLA, etc.

Margnat Major producer of everyday VIN DE TABLE.

Marne et Champagne, Ste Recent but huge-scale CHAMPAGNE house, owner (since '91) of LANSON and many smaller brands.

Marque déposée Trademark.

Marsannay Burg p w (r) *** 85 86 87 88 89 90 91 92 (rosé DYA) Village nr Dijon with fine light red and delicate Pinot N rosé. Growers incl CLAIR, Dijon University, JADOT, Quillardet, TRAPET.

Mas de Daumas Gassac Midi r w p *** 80 81 82 83 85 86 87 88 89 90 91 92 The one 'first-growth' estate of the LANGUEDOC, producing potent largely Cab wines on apparently unique soil. Also Rosé Frisant and a sumptuous white of blended CHARD, Viognier, Petit Manseng, etc. Now also a vg quick-drinking red, Les Terrasses de Guilhem, from a nearby coop. Sensational quality. VIN DE PAYS status.

Maufoux, Prosper Family firm of burgundy merchants at SANTENAY. Reliable wines, esp whites, keep well. Alias Marcel Amance.

Maury Pyr r sw *→** NV Red VIN DOUX NATUREL from ROUSSILLON.

Mazis (or Mazy) Chambertin Burg r *** 76 78 82 83 85 86 87 88 89 90 91 92 30-acre GRAND CRU neighbour of CHAMBERTIN, sometimes equally potent. Best from FAIVELEY, HOSPICES DE BEAUNE, LEROY, ROTY.

Médoc Bx r ** 78 82 83 85 86 87 88 89 90 91 92 AC for reds of the less good (northern) part of BORDEAUX's biggest and best district. Flavours tend to slight earthiness. HAUT-MEDOC is better. Top châteaux incl LA CARDONNE, GREYSAC, LOUDENNE, LES ORMES-SORBET, POTENSAC, LA TOUR-DE-BY.

Meffre, Gabriel The biggest S Rhône estate, based at GIGONDAS. Includes Ch de Vaudieu, CHATEAUNEUF-DU-PAPE. Variable quality.

Ménétou-Salon Lo r p w ** DYA Attractive light wines from W of SANCERRE: Sauv Bl white, Pinot N red.

Méo-Camuzet V fine domaine in CLOS DE VOUGEOT, NUITS, RICHEBOURG, VOSNE-ROMANEE. HENRI JAYER oversees winemaking.

Mercier & Cie NV; 81 82 83 85 86; Rosé 81 82 83 85 86; 'Extra Rich' One of the biggest CHAMPAGNE houses at Epernay. Controlled by MOET & CHANDON. Good commercial quality. Belle d'Or is premium NV Cuvée.

Mercurey Burg r w ** 83 85 86 87 88 89 90 91 92 Leading red wine village of COTE CHALONNAISE. Good middle-rank burgundy incl more and improving whites. Growers incl Ch de Chamirey, Chanzy, FAIVELEY, Pidault.

Mercurey, Région de The up-to-date name for the COTE CHALONNAISE.

Métaireau, Louis The ringleader of a group of top MUSCADET growers. Expensive well-finished wines.

Méthode champenoise The traditional laborious method of putting bubbles into CHAMPAGNE by refermenting the wine in its bottle. Must be referred to as 'méthode traditionelle' when used outside the region.

Méthode traditionelle See entry above.

Meursault Burg w (r) ***→**** 78 82 83 85 86 88 89 90 91 92 COTE DE BEAUNE village with some of the world's greatest whites: savoury, dry but nutty and mellow. Best v'yds: Charmes, Genevrières, Perrières; also: Goutte d'Or, Meursault-Blagny, Poruzots, Tillets. Top growers incl AMPEAU, COCHE-DURY, Delagrange, Jobard, LAFON, LATOUR, MAGENTA, Manuel, Matrot, CH DE MEURSAULT, Michelot-Buisson, P Morey, G ROULOT. See also Blagny.

Meursault-Blagny See Blagny.

Midi General term for the S of France W of the Rhône delta. Improving reputation, brilliant promise.

Minervois Midi r (p w) br sw *→*** 85 86 88 89 90 91 92 Hilly AC region incl some of the better wines of the MIDI: lively and full of flavour, esp from Dom de Ste-Eulalie, Ch de Gourgazaud and La Livinère. Also sweet MUSCAT de St-Jean de Minervois.

Mis en bouteille au château/domaine Bottled at the château, property or estate. NB dans nos caves (in our cellars) or dans la région de production (in the area of production) are often used but mean little.

Moelleux Mellow. Used of the sweet wines of VOUVRAY, etc.

Moët & Chandon NV; Rosé 81 82 85 86 88; Dry Imperial 76 78 81 82 83 85 86 88 Much the biggest CHAMPAGNE merchant and grower, with cellars in Epernay, and sparkling wine branches in Argentina, Australia, Brazil, California and Spain. Consistent quality. Luxury brand: DOM PERIGNON.

Moillard Big family firm (Domaine Thomas-Moillard) of growers and merchants in NUITS-ST-GEORGES, making full range incl dark and v tasty wines, eg CLOS DU ROI, CLOS DE VOUGEOT, CORTON, etc.

Mommessin, J Major BEAUJOLAIS merchant. Owner of CLOS DE TART. White wines less successful.

Monbazillac Dordogne w sw ** 71 75 76 78 79 80 83 85 86 88 89 90 91 92 Golden SAUTERNES-style wine from BERGERAC. Can age well. Ch Monbazillac and Ch Septy are best known.

Mondeuse Savoie r ** DYA Red grape of SAVOIE. Good vigorous deep-coloured wine. Perhaps Italy's Refosco.

Mongeard-Mugneret 50+-acre VOSNE-ROMANEE estate. Fine ECHEZEAUX, RICHEBOURG, SAVIGNY, VOSNE PREMIER CRU, VOUGEOT, etc.

Monopole V'yd under single ownership.

Montagne-St-Emilion Bx r ** 82 83 85 86 88 89 90 91 92 NE neighbour and largest 'satellite' of ST-EMILION: similar wines and AC regulations; becoming more important each year. Top ch'x: St-André-Corbin, Calon, Faizeau, Haut-Gillet, ROUDIER, Teyssier, DES TOURS, VIEUX-CH-ST-ANDRE.

Montagny Burg w (r) ** 88 89 90 91 92 COTE CHALONNAISE village. Between MACON and MEURSAULT, both geographically and gastronomically. Top producers: LOUIS LATOUR, Michel, Ch de la Saule, Cave Coop de Buxy.

Montée de Tonnerre Burg w *** 86 88 89 90 91 92 Famous and excellent PREMIER CRU of CHABLIS.

Monthélie Burg r (w) **→*** 78 82 83 85 86 87 88 89 90 91 92 Little-known neighbour and sometimes almost equal of VOLNAY. Excellent fragrant reds. Growers incl BOUCHARD PERE, DROUHIN, Garaudet, Ch de Monthélie (de Suremain), Monthélie-Douhairet.

Montlouis Lo w dr sw (sp) ** 75 76 78 82 83' 84 85 86 88' 89 90 91 92 Neighbour of VOUVRAY. Similar sweet or dry long-lived wine.

Montrachet Burg w **** 69 71 78 79 81 82 83 84 85 86 87 88 89 90 91 92 (Both 't's are silent.) 19-acre GRAND CRU v'yd in both PULIGNY- and CHASSAGNE-MONTRACHET. Potentially the greatest white burgundy: strong, perfumed, intense, dry yet luscious. Top wines from LAFON, LAGUICHE (DROUHIN), RAMONET, DOM DE LA ROMANEE-CONTI, THENARD.

Montravel See Côtes de Montravel.

Mont-Redon, Dom de Rh r (w) *** 83 85 86 88 89 90 91 92 Outstanding 235-acre estate in CHATEAUNEUF-DU-PAPE. Reliable fairly early-maturing wines.

Moreau & Fils CHABLIS merchant and grower with 187 acres. Also major table wine producer. Best wine: Clos des Hospices (GRAND CRU).

Morey, Domaines 50 acres in CHASSAGNE-MONTRACHET. Vg wines made by family members, incl BATARD-MONTRACHET.

Morey-St-Denis Burg r *** 76 78 82 83 85 86 87 88 89 90 91 92 Small village with four GRANDS CRUS between GEVREY-CHAMBERTIN and CHAMBOLLE-MUSIGNY. Glorious wine often overlooked. Growers incl Amiot, Castagnier, DUJAC, Groffier, Lignier, Moillard-Grivot, PONSOT, ROUSSEAU, Serveau.

Morgon Burg r *** 85 88 89 90 91 92 The 'firmest' CRU of BEAUJOLAIS, needing time to develop its rich and savoury flavour. Growers incl Aucoeur, Ch de Bellevue, Desvignes, Janodet, Lapierre, Ch de Pizay.

Mortet et Fils, Charles Rich complex red burgundies: GRAND CRU CHAMBERTIN and PREMIER CRU GEVREY CHAMBERTIN (Les Champeaux the best).

Moueix, J-P et Cie The leading proprietor and merchant of ST-EMILION, POMEROL and FRONSAC. Châteaux incl LA FLEUR-PETRUS, MAGDELAINE and part of PETRUS. Now also has a venture in California: see Dominus.

Moulin-à-Vent Burg r *** 85 88 89 90 91 92 The 'biggest' and best wine of BEAUJOLAIS; powerful, meaty and long-lived, eventually can even taste like fine Rhône or burgundy. Many good growers, esp Ch du M-à-V, Ch La Tour du Bief.

Moulis Bx r **→*** Village of the HAUT-MEDOC with its own AC and several CRUS EXCEPTIONNELS: CHASSE-SPLEEN, MAUCAILLOU, POUJEAUX (THEIL), etc. Wines are growing steadily finer.

Mousseux Sparkling.

Mouton Cadet Best-selling brand of blended red and white BORDEAUX.

Moutonne CHABLIS GRAND CRU honoris causa, owned by BICHOT.

Mugnier, J-F 10-acre Ch de Chambolle estate with first-class CHAMBOLLE-MUSIGNY Les Amoureuses and MUSIGNY. Also Bonnes Mares.

Mumm, G H & Cie NV Cordon Rouge; Crémant de Cramant (NV); 79 82 85 88; Rosé 82 85 88 Major CHAMPAGNE grower and merchant owned by Seagram. Luxury brands: René Lalou (79 82 85), Grand Cordon (85; launched '91). The Cramant is superb. Cordon Rouge can be pretty tasteless.

Muré, Clos St-Landelin ALSACE merchant at Rouffach with v'yds in GRAND CRU Vorbourg. Full-bodied wines.

Muscadet Lo w ** DYA Popular, good value, often delicious dry wine from around Nantes. Should never be sharp but should have an iodine tang. Perfect with fish. The best are bottled SUR LIE – on their lees.

Muscadet de Sèvre-et-Maine Wine from the central (best) part of the area.

Muscat Distinctively perfumed grape and its (usually sweet) wine, often fortified as VIN DOUX NATUREL. Made dry in ALSACE.

Muscat de Beaumes-de-Venise See Beaumes-de-Venise.

Muscat de Frontignan Midi br sw ★★ DYA Sweet MIDI MUSCAT. Quality improving.

Muscat de Lunel Midi br sw ★★ NV Ditto. A small area but good.

Muscat de Mireval Midi br sw ★★ NV Ditto, from nr Montpellier.

Muscat de Rivesaltes Midi br sw ★ NV Sweet MUSCAT from large zone near Perpignan.

Musigny Burg r (w) ★★★★ **69 71 76 78 79 82 83 85 86 87 88' 89 90 91 92** 25-acre GRAND CRU in CHAMBOLLE-MUSIGNY. Can be the most beautiful, if not the most powerful, of all red burgundies (and a little white). Best growers: DROUHIN, JADOT, LEROY, MUGNIER, ROUMIER, DE VOGUE.

Nature Natural or unprocessed – esp of still CHAMPAGNE.

Néac Village N of POMEROL. Wines sold as LALANDE DE POMEROL.

Négociant-éleveur Merchant who 'brings up' (ie matures) the wine.

Nicolas, Ets Paris-based wholesale and retail wine merchants controlled by Castel Frères. One of the biggest in France and one of the best.

Nuits-St-Georges r ★★→★★★ **69 71 76 78' 82 83 85' 86 87 88' 89 90 91 92** Important wine town: wines of all qualities, typically sturdy and full-flavoured. Name often shortened to 'Nuits'. Best v'yds incl Les Cailles, Clos de Corvées, Les Pruliers, Les St-Georges, Vaucrains, etc. Many growers and merchants esp Clos de l'Arlot, Chevillon, FAIVELEY, Gouges, GRIVOT, LEROY, MACHARD DE GRAMONT, Michelot, RION.

d'Oc Midi r p w Regional VIN DE PAYS for Languedoc and ROUSSILLON. Esp single-grape wines and VINS DE PAYS PRIMEURS.

Oisly & Thesée, Vignerons de Go-ahead coop in E TOURAINE (Loire), with superior grapes, esp Sauv Bl, Cab, and CHARD. Blended wines labelled Baronnie d'Aignan. Good value.

Orléanais, Vin de l' Lo r p w ★ DYA Small VDQS for light but fruity wines.

Ostertag Little ALSACE domaine at Epfig. Uses new oak for good Pinot N and makes the best Ries and Pinot Gr of GRAND CRU Muenchberg.

Ott, Domaines Top high-quality producer of PROVENCE, incl CH DE SELLE (rosé, red), Clos Mireille (white), Ch de Romassan (NB Réserve Rouge 85).

Pacherenc du Vic-Bilh SW France w sw ★ NV Rare minor speciality of the ARMAGNAC region. Domaine Capmartin's are some of the best.

Paillard, Bruno NV; Crémant Bl de Bls; Rosé; **79 81 83 85** Small but prestigious young CHAMPAGNE house: excellent silky vintage and NV; fair prices.

Palette Prov r p w ★★ Near Aix-en-Provence. Aromatic reds and good rosés from CH SIMONE.

Parigot-Richard Producer of vg CREMANT DE BOURGOGNE at SAVIGNY.

Pasquier-Desvignes V old firm of BEAUJOLAIS merchants nr BROUILLY.

Patriarche One of the bigger firms of burgundy merchants. Cellars in BEAUNE; also owns CH DE MEURSAULT (100 acres), sparkling KRITER, etc.

Patrimonio Corsica r w p ★★→★★★ **90 91 92** Wide range from dramatic chalk hills in N CORSICA. Fragrant reds, crisp whites, fine VINS DOUX NATURELS. Top grower: Gentile.

Pauillac Bx r ★★→★★★★ **66' 70' 75 76 78' 79 81 82' 83 85' 86' 87 88' 89' 90' 91 92** The only BORDEAUX (HAUT-MEDOC) village with 3 first-growths (Châteaux LAFITE, LATOUR, MOUTON) and many other fine ones, famous for high flavour; v varied in style.

Pécharmant Dordogne r ★★ **89 90 91 92** Usually better-than-typical light BERGERAC: more 'meat'. Best: Dom du Haut-Pécharmant, Ch de Tiregand.

Pelure d'oignon 'Onion skin' – tawny tint of certain rosés.

Perlant or Perlé Very slightly sparkling.

Pernand-Vergelesses Burg r (w) ★★★ **78 83 85 86 87 88 89 90 91 92** Village next to ALOXE-CORTON containing part of the great CORTON and CORTON-CHARLEMAGNE v'yds and one other top v'yd: Ile des Vergelesses. Growers incl BONNEAU DU MARTRAY, CHANDON DE BRIAILLES, Delarche, Dubreuil-Fontaine, JADOT, LATOUR, Rapet.

Perrier, Joseph NV; Bl de Blancs NV; Rosé; **76 79 82 83 85** Family-run CHAMPAGNE house with considerable v'yds at Châlons-sur-Marne. Consistent light and fruity style.

Perrier-Jouët NV; Blason de France NV; **76 79 82 85 86** 88 Excellent CHAMPAGNE-growers and makers at Epernay, now linked with MUMM. Luxury brands: Belle Epoque (**79 82 83 85 86** 88) in a painted bottle, Blason de France Rosé (NV). Also Belle Epoque Rosé (**79 82 85 86** 88).

Pessac-Léognan New AC for part of N GRAVES, incl the area of most of the GRANDS CRUS. Since '87 the use of Pessac-Léognan alone has been allowed without adding the name Graves.

Pétillant Slightly sparkling.

Petit Chablis Burg w ** DYA Wine from fourth-rank CHABLIS v'yds. Not much character. Best from coop La Chablisienne.

Pfaffenheim Top ALSACE coop with 500 acres. Strongly individual wines of all varieties incl good Sylvaner. GRANDS CRUS: Goldert, Steinert.

Philipponnat NV; Rosé NV; Reserve Special **82 85 88**; Grand Blanc Vintage **76 81 82 85 86** 88; Clos des Goisses **76 78 79 82 85** 88 Small family-run CHAMPAGNE house: well-structured, long-ageing wines, esp remarkable single v'yd Clos des Goisses, charming rosé. Owners: Marie Brizard.

Piat Père & Fils Important merchants of BEAUJOLAIS and MACON wines at Mâcon, now controlled by Grand Metropolitan. V'yds in MOULIN-A-VENT, also CLOS DE VOUGEOT. BEAUJOLAIS, MACON-VIRE in special Piat bottles maintain a fair standard. Piat d'Or is commercial table wine.

Pic, Albert Fine CHABLIS producer, controlled by DE LADOUCETTE.

Pineau de Charente Strong sweet aperitif of white grape juice and COGNAC.

Pinot See Grapes for white and red wine (pages 6–9).

Piper-Heidsieck NV; Rosé **79 85**; Vintage **76 79 82 85** CHAMPAGNE-makers of old repute at Reims. Rare (**76 79**) and Brut Sauvage (**79 82** 85) are far ahead of their other, rather light wines.

Pol Roger NV; **73 75 76 79 82 85 86** 88; Rosé **75 79 82 85 86** 88; Blanc de Chardonnay **79 82 85 86** 88 Top-ranking family-owned CHAMPAGNE house at Epernay. Esp good NV White Foil, Rosé, Réserve PR and CHARD. Sumptuous luxury cuvée: 'Sir Winston Churchill' (**75 79 82 85**).

Pomerol Bx r **→**** **70 71 75 76 78 79 81 82 83 85 86 88 89 90 92** Next village to ST-EMILION: similar but more plummy and creamy wines, maturing sooner, reliable and delicious. Top châteaux: LA FLEUR-PETRUS, LATOUR-A-POMEROL, PETRUS, TROTANOY, VIEUX CH CERTAN, etc.

Pommard Burg r *** **69 71 76 78 82 83 85 86 87 88 89 90 91 92** The biggest COTE D'OR village. Few superlative wines, but many potent and distinguished ones. Best v'yds: Epenots, HOSPICES DE BEAUNE cuvées, Rugiens. Growers incl Comte Armand, G Billard, Billard-Gonnet, J-M Boillot, de Courcel, Gaunoux, LEROY, MACHARD DE GRAMONT, de Montille, Mussy, Ch de Pommard, Pothier-Rieusset.

Pommery NV; Rosé NV; **82 83 85 87 88** Very big CHAMPAGNE growers and merchants at Reims, bought by Möet-Hennessy in '91. Wines are much improved. The luxury brand, Louise Pommery (**81 82 83 85 87 88**), is outstanding. Louise Pommery Rosé (**82 83 85**).

Ponsot, J M 25-acre estate in MOREY-ST-DENIS. Very high quality.

Pouilly-Fuissé Burg w **→*** **88 89 90 91 92** The best white of the MACON area. At its best (eg Ch Fuissé VIEILLES VIGNES) outstanding, but almost always over-priced compared with (eg) CHABLIS.

Pouilly-Fumé Lo w **→*** **89 90 91 92** 'Gun-flinty', fruity, often sharp white from the upper Loire, next to SANCERRE. Grapes must be Sauv Bl. Good vintages improve for 2–3 yrs. Top producers incl Bailly, Dagueneau, LADOUCETTE, Redde, Renaud, Saget, Ch de Tracy.

Pouilly-Loché Burg w ** POUILLY-FUISSE's neighbour. Similar but scarce.

Pouilly-sur-Loire Lo w * DYA Inferior wine from the same v'yds as POUILLY-FUME but different grapes (Chasselas). Rarely seen today.

Pouilly-Vinzelles Burg w ** **88 89 90 91 92** Neighbour of POUILLY-FUISSE. Similar wine, worth looking for. Value.

Pousse d'Or, Domaine de la 32-acre estate in POMMARD, SANTENAY and esp VOLNAY, where its MONOPOLES Bousse d'Or and Clos des 60 Ouvrées are tannic, powerful and justly famous.

Premier Cru First-growth in BORDEAUX, but the second rank of v'yds (after GRAND CRU) in Burgundy.

Premières Côtes de Blaye Bx r w ★→★★ 82 85 86 88 89 90 91 Restricted AC for better wines of BLAYE, greater emphasis on reds. Ch'x include Barbé, LE BOURDIEU, Charron, l'Escadre, Haut-Sociondo, Le Menaudat, Segonzac, La Tonnelle.

Premières Côtes de Bordeaux Bx r w (p) dr sw ★→★★ Large hilly area E of GRAVES across the R Garonne: a good bet for quality and value, though never brilliant. Largely Merlot. Châteaux incl Carsin, Fayau, Gardera, HAUT-BRIGNON, du Juge, Laffitte (sic), Lamothe, REYNON, Tanesse. An area to watch.

Prieur, Domaine Jacques 35-acre estate all in top Burgundy sites, incl PREMIER CRU MEURSAULT, VOLNAY, PULIGNY- and even LE MONTRACHET. Disappointing in '80s. Now 50% owned by RODET. To watch.

Primeur 'Early' wine for refreshment and uplift; esp BEAUJOLAIS; VINS DE PAYS too. Wine sold 'En Primeur' is offered still in barrel for future delivery.

Prissé See Mâcon-Villages.

Propriétaire-récoltant Owner-manager.

Provence See Côtes de Provence.

Puisseguin St-Emilion Bx r ★★ 82 83 85 86 88 89 90 Eastern neighbour of ST-EMILION, its smallest 'satellite'; wines similar – not so fine but often good value. Ch'x incl La Croix de Berny, LAURETS, Puisseguin, Soleil, Teyssier, Vieux-Ch-Guibeau. Also Roc de Puisseguin from coop.

Puligny-Montrachet Burg w (r) ★★★★ 78 82 83 85 86 87 88 89 90 91 92 Bigger neighbour of CHASSAGNE-MONTRACHET with potentially even more vital and complex rich dry whites. But apparent finesse can be the result of over-production. Best v'yds: BATARD-MONTRACHET, Bienvenue-Bâtard-Montrachet, Champ-Canet, CHEVALIER-MONTRACHET, Clavoillon, Les Combettes, MONTRACHET, Pucelles, etc. Top growers incl AMPEAU, Boillot, BOUCHARD PERE, L Carillon, CHARTRON, DROUHIN, JADOT, LATOUR, LEFLAIVE, Pernot, SAUZET.

Quarts de Chaume Lo w sw ★★★ 75 76 78 79 82 85 86 88 89' 90' 91 92 Famous 120-acre plot in COTEAUX DU LAYON. Chenin Bl grapes. Immensely long-lived intense rich golden wine, esp Dom des Beaumard, Ch de Bellerive, Ch La Suronde.

Quatourze Midi r w (p) ★ 88 89 90 91 92 Minor VDQS area nr Narbonne.

Quincy Lo w ★★ 89 90 91 92 Small area making v dry SANCERRE-style wine of Sauv Bl. Worth trying. Growers: Domaine Mardon, Meunier-Lapha.

Ramonet, Domaine Leading estate in CHASSAGNE-MONTRACHET with 34 acres, incl some MONTRACHET. Vg whites, and red CLOS ST-JEAN.

Rancio Term for the tang of brown wood-aged fortified wine, esp BANYULS and other VDN. A fault in table wines.

Rasteau Rh r br sw (p w dr) ★★ 85' 86 88 89 90 91 92 Village of S Rhône Valley. V sound reds from the Cave des Vignerons. Good strong sweet dessert wine is the (declining) local speciality.

Ratafia de Champagne Sweet aperitif made in CHAMPAGNE of 67% grape juice and 33% brandy. Not unlike PINEAU DE CHARENTE.

Rebourgeon-Mure, Daniel Young-drinking VOLNAY from old family firm based in POMMARD.

Récolte Crop or vintage.

Regnié Beauj r ★★ 89 90 91 92 BEAUJOLAIS village between MORGON and BROUILLY, promoted to CRU in '88. About 1,800 acres. Try DUBOEUF's.

Reine Pédauque, La Burgundy growers and merchants at ALOXE-CORTON. See also André, Pierre.

Remoissenet Père & Fils Fine burgundy merchant (esp for white wines) with a tiny BEAUNE estate. Give his reds time. Also broker for NICOLAS wine shops. Some of best are from DOM THENARD.

Rémy Pannier Important Loire wine merchant at SAUMUR.

Reuilly Lo w (r p) ** **89 90 91 92** Neighbour of QUINCY with similar wine; also good Pinot Gr.

Riceys, Rosé des Champ p *** DYA Minute AC in S CHAMPAGNE for a notable Pinot N rosé. Principal producer: A Bonnet.

Richebourg Burg r **** **69 71 76 78 79 82 83 85 86 87** 88 89 90 91 19-acre GRAND CRU in VOSNE-ROMANEE. Powerful perfumed fabulously expensive wine, among Burgundy's very best. Top growers: BICHOT, GRIVOT, Gros, LEROY, MEO-CAMUZET, DOM DE LA ROMANEE-CONTI.

Riesling See Grapes for white wine (pages 6–8).

Rion, Daniel et Fils 36-acre domaine in Prémeaux (NUITS). Excellent VOSNE-ROMANEE (Les Vignes Rondes, Les Beaumonts), Nuits PREMIERS CRUS and CHAMBOLLE-MUSIGNY-Les Charmes. NB Also Patrice Rion.

Rivesaltes Midi r w br dr sw ** NV Fortified wine of E Pyrenees, some MUSCAT-flavoured. A tradition v much alive, if struggling these days. Top producers: Doms Boudau, Cazes, Château de Calce.

Roche-aux-Moines, La Lo w sw *** **75 76 78 79 82 83 85 86** 88 89' 90' 91 92 60-acre v'yd in SAVENNIERES, ANJOU. Intense strong fruity/sharp wine, needs long ageing.

Rodet, Antonin Substantial burgundy merchant with large (375-acre) estate, esp in MERCUREY (Ch de Chamirey). See also Prieur. Now owned by LAURENT-PERRIER.

Roederer, Louis Brut Premier NV; Rich NV; Brut **71 73 75 76 78 79 81 83 85 86**; Brut Rosé **75 83 85 86** One of best CHAMPAGNE-growers and merchants at Reims. Reliable NV, plenty of flavour. Luxury brand: Cristal Brut (**79 82 83 85 86**), in white glass bottles, needs time.

Romanée, La Burg r **** **76 78 82 83 84 85 86 87** 88 89 90 91 92 2-acre GRAND CRU in VOSNE-ROMANEE, just uphill from ROMANEE-CONTI.

Romanée-Conti Burg r **** **66 71 73 76 78 79 80 81 82** 83 **84** 85 86 87 88 89 90 4.3-acre MONOPOLE GRAND CRU in VOSNE-ROMANEE making 450 cases per year. The most celebrated and expensive red wine in the world, with reserves of flavour beyond imagination. 85, 88 and 90 are astonishing. See next entry.

Romanée-Conti, Domaine de la (DRC) The grandest estate in Burgundy. Includes the whole of ROMANEE-CONTI and LA TACHE and major parts of ECHEZEAUX, GRANDS ECHEZEAUX, RICHEBOURG and ROMANEE-ST-VIVANT. Also a v small part of MONTRACHET and VOSNE-ROMANEE. Crown-jewel prices. Keep DRC wines for decades.

Romanée-St-Vivant Burg r **** **71 76 78 79 80 82 83 84 85 86** 87 88 89 90 91 92 23-acre GRAND CRU in VOSNE-ROMANEE. Similar to ROMANEE-CONTI but lighter and less sumptuous. Top growers: DRC and LEROY.

Ropiteau Burgundy wine-growers and merchants at MEURSAULT. Specialists in Meursault and COTE DE BEAUNE wines.

Rosé d'Anjou Lo p * DYA Pale slightly sw rosé. CAB D'ANJOU should be better.

Rosé de Loire Lo p *→*** DYA AC for dry Loire rosé (ANJOU is sweet).

Roty, Joseph Small grower of classic GEVREY-CHAMBERTIN, esp CHARMES- and MAZIS-CHAMBERTIN. Long-lived wines.

Roumier, Georges 35-acre domaine with exceptional BONNES-MARES, CLOS DE VOUGEOT, MUSIGNY, etc. High standards. Long-lasting reds.

Rousseau, Domaine A Major burgundy grower famous for CHAMBERTIN, etc, of highest quality. Wines are intense, long-lived and mostly GRAND CRU.

Roussette de Savoie Savoie w ** DYA The tastiest of the fresh whites from S of Lake Geneva.

Roussillon Largest producer of VDNS (often 'Grands Roussillons'), lighter MUSCATS now taking over from darker heavier wines. See Côtes du Roussillon.

Ruchottes-Chambertin Burg r *** **71 76 78 79 82 83 85 86 87** 88 89 90 91 92 7.5-acre GRAND CRU neighbour of CHAMBERTIN. Similar splendid long-lasting wine of great finesse. Top growers: LEROY, Mugneret, ROUMIER, ROUSSEAU.

Ruinart Père & Fils NV; Rosé **81 82**; Bl de Blancs 'R' de Ruinart **79 81 85 88** The oldest CHAMPAGNE house, now owned by Moët-Hennessy, with notably fine crisp wines. Luxury brand: Dom Ruinart, Blanc de Blancs (81 82 83). NB the vg mature Rosé. Good value.

Rully Burg r w (sp) ** **88 89 90 91 92** COTE CHALONNAISE village famous for burgundy CREMANT. Still white and red are light but tasty, good value, esp whites. Growers incl DELORME, FAIVELEY, Dom de la Folie, Jacquesson.

Sables du Golfe du Lion Midi p r w * DYA VIN DE PAYS from Mediterranean sand-dunes: esp GRIS DE GRIS from Carignan, Grenache and Cinsaut. Dominated by LISTEL.

Sablet Rh r w (p) ** **89 90 91 92** Admirable COTES DU RHONE village, esp Dom de Boissan, Ch du Trignon, Dom de Verquière.

St-Amour Beauj r ** **89 90 91 92** Northernmost CRU of BEAUJOLAIS: light fruity irresistible. Grower to try: Patissier.

St-André-de-Cubzac Bx r w *→** **85 86 88 89 90 91 92** Town 15 miles NE of BORDEAUX, centre of the minor Cubzaguais region. Sound reds have AC BORDEAUX SUPERIEUR. Incl: Domaine de Beychevelle, Ch du Bouilh, CH DE TERREFORT-QUANCARD, CH TIMBERLAY.

St-Aubin Burg w (r) ** **85 86 88 89 90 91 92** Little-known neighbour of CHASSAGNE-MONTRACHET, up a side-valley. Several PREMIERS CRUS: light firm quite stylish wines. Also sold as COTE DE BEAUNE-VILLAGES. Top growers: Clerget, JADOT, J Lamy, LAMY-PILLOT, H Prudhon, Roux, Thomas.

St-Bris Burg w (r) * DYA Village west of CHABLIS known for fruity ALIGOTE, but chiefly for SAUVIGNON DE ST-BRIS. Also good CREMANT.

St-Chinian Midi r *→** **88 89 90 91 92** Hilly area of growing reputation in COTEAUX DU LANGUEDOC. AC since '82. Tasty southern reds, esp at Berlou.

St-Emilion Bx r **→**** **70 71 75 79 81 82 83 85 86 88 89 90 91 92** The biggest top-quality BORDEAUX district (13,000 acres); solid rich tasty wines from hundreds of châteaux, incl AUSONE, CANON, CHEVAL BLANC, FIGEAC, MAGDELAINE, etc. Also a good coop.

St-Estèphe Bx r **→**** **75 78 79 81 82 83 85 86 87 88 89 90 91 92** Northern village of HAUT-MEDOC. Solid, structured, occasionally superlative wines. Top châteaux: CALON-SEGUR, COS D'ESTOURNEL, MONTROSE, etc, and more notable CRUS BOURGEOIS than any other HAUT-MEDOC commune.

St-Gall Brand name used by Union-Champagne, the vg CHAMPAGNE-growers' coop at AVIZE. The style is usually softer than true BRUT.

St-Georges-St-Emilion Bx r ** **82 83 85 86 88 89 90 91 92** Part of MONTAGNE-ST-EMILION with high standards. Best châteaux: Belair-Montaiguillon, Marquis-St-G, ST-GEORGES, Tour du Pas-St-G.

St-Joseph Rh r (p w) ** **83 85 86 88 89 90 91 92** N Rhône AC of second rank but reasonable price. Vigorous wine often better than CROZES-HERMITAGE, esp from CHAPOUTIER, CHAVE, Grippat, JABOULET.

St-Julien Bx r ***→**** **70 75 76 78 79 81 82' 83' 85' 86 87 88' 89' 90' 91 92** Mid-MEDOC village with a dozen of BORDEAUX's best châteaux, incl three LEOVILLES, BEYCHEVELLE, DUCRU-BEAUCAILLOU, GRUAUD-LAROSE, etc. The epitome of well-balanced red wine.

St-Nicolas-de-Bourgueil Lo r ** **82 83 85 86 88 89' 90' 91 92** The next village to BOURGUEIL: the same lively and fruity Cab F red. Top growers: Ammeaux, Cognard, Jamet, Mabilleau, Taluau.

St-Péray Rh w sp ** NV Rather heavy white from the northern Rhône, much of it made sparkling. A curiosity worth trying once.

St-Pourçain-sur-Sioule Central France r p w *→** DYA Light but venerable local wine of Vichy. Red and rosé made from Gamay and/or Pinot N, white from Tressalier and/or CHARD or Sauv Bl. Recent vintages vastly improved. AC on the way? Top growers: Dom de Bellevue, Ray and good coop.

St-Romain Burg r w ** **85 86 88 89 90 91 92** Overlooked village just behind the COTE DE BEAUNE. Value, esp for firm fresh whites. Reds have a clean 'cut'. Top growers: FEVRE, Jean Germain, Gras, LATOUR, LEROY, Thévenin-Monthélie.

St-Véran Burg w ★★ 89 90 91 92 Next-door AC to POUILLY-FUISSE. Similar but better value: real character from the best slopes of MACON-VILLAGES. Try DUBOEUF's, Dom des Deux Roches' and Dom des Valanges'.

Ste-Croix-du-Mont Bx w sw ★★ 75 76 82 83 86 88 89 90 91 92 Neighbour to SAUTERNES with similar golden wine. No superlatives but well worth trying, esp Clos des Coulinats, Ch Loubens, Ch Lousteau Vieil, Ch du Mont. Often a bargain, esp with age.

Botrytis cinerea (French pourriture noble, German Edelfäule, English noble rot) is a form of mould that attacks the skins of ripe grapes in certain vineyards in warm and misty autumn weather.

Its effect, instead of rotting the grapes, is to wither them. The skin grows soft and flaccid, the juice evaporates through it, and what is left is a super-sweet concentration of everything in the grape except its water content.

The world's best sweet table wines are all made of 'nobly rotten' grapes. They occur in good vintages in Sauternes, the Rhine and the Mosel (where wine made from them is called Trockenbeerenauslese), in Tokaji in Hungary, in Burgenland in Austria, and elsewhere – California and Australia included. The danger is rain on pulpy grapes already far gone in botrytis. All too often, particularly in Sauternes, the grower's hopes are dashed by a break in the weather.

Salon Le Mesnil 71 73 76 79 81 82 85 The original Blanc de Blancs CHAMPAGNE, from Le Mesnil. Fine v dry wine with long keeping qualities. Bought in '88 by LAURENT-PERRIER.

Sancerre Lo w (r p) ★★★ 86 88 89 90 91 92 Very fragrant and fresh Sauv Bl, almost indistinguishable from POUILLY-FUME, its neighbour over the Loire. Top wines can age 5 yrs. Also light Pinot N red (best drunk at 2–3 yrs) and rosé. Top growers incl Bailly, Bonnard, Bourgeois, CORDIER, Cotat, Crochet, Gitton, Jolivet, Pinard and Reverdy.

Santenay Burg r (w) ★★★ 78 79 82 83 85 86 87 88 89 90 91 92 Very worthy, rarely rapturous, sturdy reds from southern COTE DE BEAUNE. Best v'yds: La Comme, Les Gravières, Clos de Tavannes. Top growers: Lequin-Roussot, MOREY, POUSSE D'OR.

Saumur Lo r p w sp ★→★★ Versatile district in ANJOU. Fresh fruity whites, vg CREMANT (producers incl BOUVET-LADUBAY), pale rosés and increasingly good Cab F (see next entry).

Saumur-Champigny Lo r 82 85 86 88 89 90 91 92 Flourishing 10-village AC for fresh Cab F reds ageing remarkably in sunny vintages. Look for Ch'x de Chaintres, du Hureau, Doms Filliatreau, Ruault, coop St-Cyr.

Sauternes Bx w sw ★★→★★★★ 67' 71 75 76' 78 79 80 81 82 83' 85 86' 88' 89' 90 91 District of 5 villages (incl BARSAC) which make France's best sweet wine, strong (14%+ alcohol), luscious and golden, demanding to be aged. Top châteaux are D'YQUEM, CLIMENS, COUTET, GUIRAUD, SUDUIRAUT, etc. Dry wines cannot be sold as Sauternes.

Sauvignon Blanc See Grapes for white wine (pages 6–8).

Sauvignon de St-Bris Burg w ★★ DYA A baby VDQS cousin of SANCERRE, from nr CHABLIS. To try. 'Dom Saint Prix' from Dom Bersan is good.

Sauvion & Fils Ambitious and well-run MUSCADET house, based at the Ch de Cléray. Top wine: Cardinal Richard.

Sauzet, Etienne White burgundy estate at PULIGNY-MONTRACHET. Clearly-defined, well-bred wines, at best superb.

Savennières Lo w dr sw ★★★ 75 76 78 82 83 84 85 86 88 89' 90' Small ANJOU district of pungent long-lived whites, incl Clos du Papillon, COULEE DE SERRANT, Ch d'Epiré, ROCHE-AUX-MOINES.

Savigny-lès-Beaune Burg r (w) ★★★ 78 83 85 86 87 88 89 90 91 92 Important village next to BEAUNE, similar balanced mid-weight wines, often deliciously bright, lively, fruity. Top v'yds: Dominode, Les Guettes, Marconnets, Serpentières, Vergelesses; growers: BIZE, Camus, CHANDON DE BRIAILLES, CLAIR, Ecard, Girard-Vollot, LEROY, Pavelot, TOLLOT-BEAUT.

Savoie E France r w sp ★★ DYA Alpine area with light dry wines like some Swiss or minor Loires. APREMONT, CREPY and SEYSSEL are best-known whites, ROUSSETTE is more interesting. Also good MONDEUSE red.

Schaller, Edgard ALSACE grower in Mandelburg GRAND CRU, Mittelwihr; esp for Ries 'Mambourg Vieilles Vignes'.

Schlumberger ALSACE grower-merchants at Guebwiller. Rich wines incl luscious Kessler GRAND CRU GEWURZ. Fine Kitterlé and Saering Ries.

Schröder & Schÿler Old BORDEAUX merchants, owners of CH KIRWAN.

Sciacarello Red grape of CORSICA's best red and rosé, eg AJACCIO, Sartène.

Sec Literally means dry, though CHAMPAGNE so-called is medium-sweet (and better at breakfast and tea-time than Brut).

Sélection des Grains Nobles (SGN) Description coined by HUGEL for ALSACE equivalent to German Beerenauslese. Grains nobles are individual grapes with 'noble rot' (see page 51).

Sèvre-et-Maine The département containing the best v'yds of MUSCADET.

Seyssel Savoie w sp ★★ NV Delicate pale dry Alpine white, making very pleasant sparkling wine.

Sichel & Co Two famous merchant houses. In BORDEAUX Peter A Sichel runs Maison Sichel and owns CH D'ANGLUDET and part of CH PALMER. In Germany, Peter M F Sichel (of New York) runs Sichel Söhne, makers of BLUE NUN and respected merchants.

Silvaner See Grapes for white wine (pages 6–8).

Sipp, Jean and Louis Ribeauvillé GRAND CRU ALSACE producers competing to make finest Ries (in Kirchberg): Jean's with youthful elegance, Louis' finer when mature.

Sirius Serious oak-aged blended BORDEAUX from Maison SICHEL.

Skalli Dynamic producer of good wines from Cab, Merlot, CHARD, etc, at Sète in the Languedoc. FORTANT DE FRANCE is standard brand. Experimental wines extraordinary.

Sur Lie See Lie and Muscadet.

Syrah See Grapes for red wine (pages 8–9).

Tâche, La Burg r ★★★★ **69 70 71 76 78 79 80 81 82** 83 **84** 85 86 87 88 89 90 91 92 15-acre (1,500 case) GRAND CRU of VOSNE-ROMANEE and one of the best v'yds on earth: dark perfumed luxurious wine. See DOM DE LA ROMANEE-CONTI.

Taittinger NV; Rosé NV; **73 75 76 78 79 80 82 83 85** 86; Collection Brut **78 81 82 83 85** 86 Fashionable Reims CHAMPAGNE growers and merchants with a light touch. Luxury brand: Comtes de Champagne Blanc de Blancs (**79 81 82 83** 85 86). Also vg Rosé (**79 83** 85 86). Also own Champagne Irroy.

Tastevin, Confrèrie des Chevaliers du Burgundy's colourful successful promotion society. Wine with their Tastevinage label has been approved by them and is usually of a fair standard. A tastevin is the traditional shallow silver wine-tasting cup of Burgundy. See also page 37.

Tavel Rh p ★★★ DYA France's most famous, though not her best, rosé: strong and dry. Best growers: Ch d'Aquéria, Bernard, Maby, Dom de la Mordorée, Ch de Trinquevedel. Drink v young.

Tempier, Domaine Top grower of BANDOL, with noble reds and rosé.

Thénard, Domaine The major grower of GIVRY, but best known for his substantial portion (4+ acres) of LE MONTRACHET. Could try harder.

Thorin, J Grower and major merchant of BEAUJOLAIS, owner of the Château des Jacques, MOULIN-A-VENT. Recently bought by Racke of Germany.

Thouarsais, Vin de Lo r w ★ DYA Light Gamay and Sauv VDQS S of SAUMUR.

Tokay d'Alsace See under Pinot Gris (Grapes for white wine – pages 6–8).

Tollot-Beaut Stylish burgundy grower with 50+ acres in the COTE DE BEAUNE, incl Beaune Grèves, CORTON, SAVIGNY- (Les Champs Chevrey) and at CHOREY-LES-BEAUNE where he is based.

Touchais, Moulin Extraordinary luscious COTEAUX DU LAYON from spectacular old stocks of the Touchais family. Vintages back to the '20s are like creamy honey and not over-priced.

Touraine Lo r p w dr sw sp ★→★★★ Big mid-Loire province with immense range of wines, incl dry white Sauv, dry and sweet Chenin Bl (eg VOUVRAY), red CHINON and BOURGUEIL, light red Cabs, Gamays and rosés: often bargains. Amboise, Azay-le-Rideau and Mesland are sub-sections of the AC.

Trapet Two domaines in GEVREY-CHAMBERTIN, both good; esp R Trapet.

Trimbach, F E Distinguished ALSACE grower and merchant at Ribeauvillé. Best wines include the austere Ries CLOS STE-HUNE and GRAND CRU Geisberg.

Turckheim, Cave Vinicole de Perhaps the best coop in ALSACE. Many fine wines incl GRANDS CRUS from 900+ acres.

Tursan SW France r p w ★ Emerging VDQS in the Landes. Sound reds. Ch de Bachen (★★★), owned by the ★★★ chef Michel Gérard, guarantees notoriety and suggests an AC on the way.

Vacqueyras Rh r ★★ 83 85 86 88 89 90 91 92 Neighbour to GIGONDAS and often better value. Try JABOULET's version or Ch de Montmirail.

Val d'Orbieu, Vignerons du Association of some 200 top growers and coops in CORBIERES, COTEAUX DU LANGUEDOC, ROUSSILLON etc with Maison SICHEL, marketing a first-class range of selected MIDI AC wines.

Valençay Lo w ★ DYA VDQS neighbour of CHEVERNY: similar pleasant sharpish wine.

Val-Joanis, Ch de Prov r p w ★★ Impressive new estate making vg COTES DU LUBERON wines. To try.

Vallée du Paradis Midi r w p ★ Popular VINS DE PAYS from Cab and Merlot plus SW local red varieties.

Valréas Rh r (p w) ★★ 85 86 88 89 90 91 92 COTES DU RHONE village with big coop and good mid-weight reds.

Varichon & Clerc Principal makers and shippers of SAVOIE sparkling wines.

Varoilles, Domaine des Burgundy estate of 30 acres, principally in GEVREY-CHAMBERTIN. Tannic wines with great keeping qualities.

Vaudésir Burg w ★★★★ 78 83 85 86 87 88 89 90 91 92 Arguably the best of 7 CHABLIS GRANDS CRUS (but then so are the others).

VDQS Vin Délimité de Qualité Supérieure (see page 21).

Vendange Harvest.

Vendange Tardive Late harvest. In ALSACE equivalent to German Auslese, but stronger and usually less fine.

Veuve Clicquot NV (Yellow label); NV Demi-Sec (White Label); **76 78 79 82 83 85** (Gold Label); and Rosé Reserve **83 85** Historic CHAMPAGNE house of highest standing, now owned by Moët Hennessy. Full-bodied, almost rich wines. Cellars at Reims. Luxury brand: La Grande Dame (**79 83 85**).

Vidal-Fleury, J Long-established shippers and growers of top Rhône wines, esp HERMITAGE and COTE ROTIE. Bought in '85 by GUIGAL.

Vieilles Vignes Old vines – therefore the best wine. Used especially by BOLLINGER and DE VOGUE.

Viénot, Charles Grower-merchant of good burgundy, owned by BOISSET at NUITS. 70 acres in CORTON, Nuits, RICHEBOURG, etc.

Vieux Télégraphe, Domaine du Rh r (w) ★★★ 78' 79 81 83 84 85 86 88 89 90 91 92 A leader in fine vigorous modern CHATEAUNEUF-DU-PAPE.

Vignoble Area of vineyards.

Vin de l'année This year's wine. See Beaujolais, Beaujolais-Villages.

Vin Doux Naturel (VDN) Sweet wine, fortified with wine alcohol, so the sweetness is 'natural', not the strength. The speciality of ROUSSILLON. A vin doux liquoreux is several degrees stronger.

Vin de garde Wine that will improve with keeping. The serious stuff.

Vin Gris 'Grey' wine is v pale pink, made of red grapes pressed before fermentation begins, unlike rosé which ferments briefly before pressing. Oeil de Perdrix means much the same; so does 'blush'.

Vin Jaune Jura w ★★★ Speciality of ARBOIS: odd yellow wine like fino sherry. Normally ready when bottled (at at least 7 yrs old). The best is CHATEAU-CHALON.

Vin nouveau See Beaujolais Nouveau.

Vin de paille Wine from grapes dried on straw mats, consequently v sweet, like Italian passito. Esp in the JURA.

Vin de Pays The junior rank of country wines. No one should overlook this category, the most dynamic in France today. More than 140 vins de pays names have come into active use recently, mainly in the Midi. They fall into three categories: regional (eg Vin de Pays d'Oc for the whole Midi); departmental (eg Vin de Pays du Gard for the Gard département near the mouth of the Rhône), and vins de pays de zone, the most precise, usually with the highest standards. Single-grape vins de pays and vins de pays primeurs (reds and whites, all released on the third Thursday in November) are especially popular. Well-known zonal vins de pays include Coteaux de l'Uzège, Côtes de Gascogne, Val d'Orbieu. Don't hesitate. There are some gems among them, and many charming trinkets.

Vin de Table Standard everyday table wine, not subject to particular regulations about grapes and origin. Choose VINS DE PAYS.

Vin Vert Very light acidic refreshing white wine, a speciality of ROUSSILLON (and v necessary in summer in those torrid parts).

Vinsobres Rh r (p w) ★★ **85 86 88 89 90 91 92** Contradictory name of good southern Rhône village. Potentially substantial reds, but many ordinary.

Viré Burg w ★★ **89 90 91 92** One of the best white wine villages of MACON. Good wines from Clos du Chapitre, JADOT, Ch de Viré, coop.

Visan Rh r p w ★★ **88 89 90 91 92** One of the better southern Rhône villages. Reds much better than whites.

Viticulteur Wine-grower.

Vogüé, Comte Georges de (Now called Dom les Musigny) First-class 30-acre domaine at CHAMBOLLE-MUSIGNY. At best the ultimate BONNES-MARES and MUSIGNY.

Volnay Burg r ★★★ **78 79 82 83 85' 86 87 88 89 90 91 92** Village between POMMARD and MEURSAULT: often the best reds of the COTE DE BEAUNE, not strong or heavy but structured and silky. Best v'yds: Caillerets, Champans, Clos des Chênes, Clos des Ducs, etc. Best growers: D'ANGERVILLE, HOSPICES DE BEAUNE, LAFARGE, LAFON, de Montille, POUSSE D'OR, REBOURGEON-MURE, ROSSIGNOL-FEVRIER.

Volnay-Santenots Burg r ★★★ Excellent red wine from MEURSAULT is sold under this name. Indistinguishable from Premier Cru VOLNAY.

Vosne-Romanée Burg r ★★★→★★★★ **76 78 79 82 83 85 86 87 88 89 90 91 92** Village with Burgundy's grandest CRUS (ROMANEE-CONTI, LA TACHE, etc). There are (or should be) no common wines in Vosne. Many good growers incl Arnoux, Castagnier, CHEVIGNY, ENGEL, GRIVOT, Gros, JAYER, LATOUR, LEROY, MEO-CAMUZET, MONGEARD-MUGNERET, Mugneret, DRC.

Vougeot See Clos de Vougeot.

Vouvray Lo w dr sw sp ★★→★★★★ **76' 78 79 82 83 85 86 88 89' 90' 91 92** Small district of TOURAINE with v variable wines, at their best intensely sweet and almost immortal. Good dry sparkling. Best producers: Allias, BREDIF, Brisebarre, Foreau, Fouguet, Ch Gaudrelle, Huet, Ch Moncontour, Poniatowski.

Willm, A N ALSACE grower at Barr, with vg GEWURZ Clos Gaensbronnel.

'Y' (pronounced 'ygrec') **78 79 80 84 85 86 87 88** Dry wine produced occasionally at CH D'YQUEM.

Ziltener, André Swiss burgundy grower/merchant based at Ch Ziltener, CHAMBOLLE MUSIGNY. Wide range; sound wines.

Zind-Humbrecht 64-acre ALSACE estate in Thann, Turckheim and Wintzenheim. First-rate single-v'yd wines (esp Clos St-Urbain Ries), and v fine from GRANDS CRUS Goldert (GEWURZ and MUSCAT), Hengst and Rangen.

Châteaux of Bordeaux

The three famous vintages of '88, '89 and '90 brought Bordeaux's Amazing Eighties to an end with an unprecedented supply of superb wines. Drinkers in recession could not have handled another great vintage. Frost in April 1991 spared them that, decimating the crop. St-Emilion and Pomerol were the worst hit; the small production in the Médoc and Graves is at least of fair quality. Then, the recession continuing, the 1992 crop was just what the market did not need: a far too copious, swollen by untimely rain. It rained on the flowering in June, it rained in a stormy August and rained again at harvest time in late September. Merlot was washed away, leaving ripe Cabernet to be picked in a fine mid-October.

There is no hurry to stock up with '91 and '92 Bordeaux while cellars are full of better vintages. On the other hand there are many charming 'easy' wines to drink at easy prices while the three great years and the noble 86 mature. The 85s, beautifully mellow and in balance, are tempting now. Never forget though that in Bordeaux the making of a vintage is only the prologue to its long biography.

Over 400 of the best and most widely-distributed châteaux are listed here. Information on the current state of each vintage of most châteaux, and whether its maker regards it as a particular success, is as complete as possible up to the 1992 vintage.

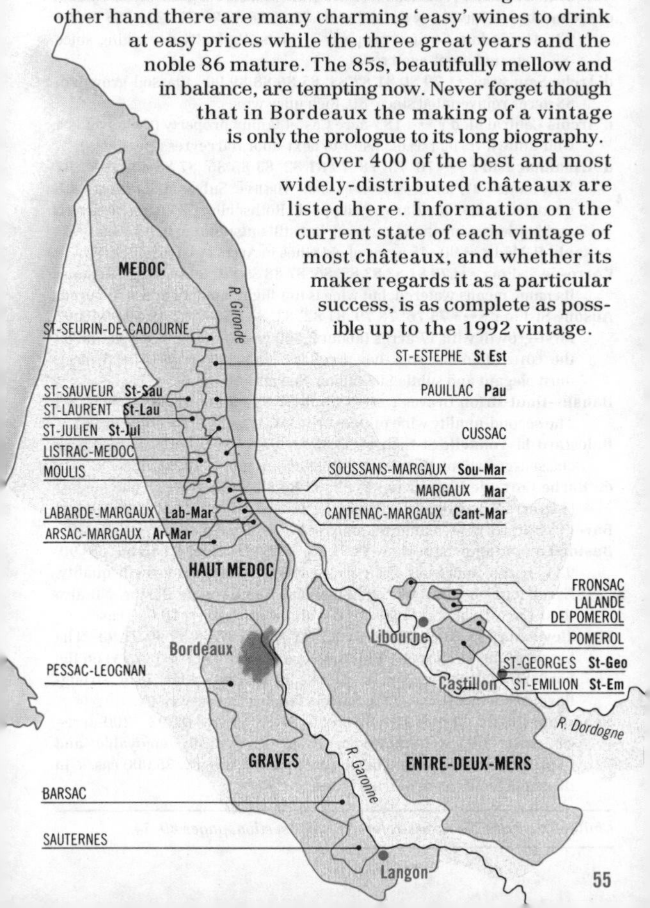

Vintages shown in light type should only be opened now out of curiosity to gauge their future. Vintages shown in bold type are deemed (usually by their makers) to be ready for drinking. Remember though that the French tend to enjoy the vigour of young wines, and that many 82s, 83s, 85s and most good 86s have at least another decade of development in front of them. Vintages marked thus ' are regarded as particularly successful for the property in question.

d'Agassac H-Méd r ★★ **82' 83 85 86 88** 89 90 91 92 Sleeping Beauty 14th-C moated fort. 86 acres v nr Bordeaux suburbs. Same owners as Ch'x CALON-SEGUR and DU TERTRE. Lively wine much drunk in Holland.

d'Alesme Mar r ★★ **78 79 81 82 83 85 86 87** 88' 89 90 Tiny (17-acre) third-growth, formerly 'Marquis-d'Alesme'. Better than its reputation.

Andron-Blanquet St-Est r ★★ **82 83 85' 86** 88 89 90 Sister château to COS-LABORY. 40 acres. Medals since '86.

L'Angélus St-Em r ★★★ **79' 81 82 83' 85 86 87** 88 89' 90' 91 92 Well-sited 57-acre classed-growth on ST-EMILION COTES. A star of recent vintages.

d'Angludet Cant-Mar r ★★→★★★ **61 66 70' 76' 78' 79 80 81' 82 83 85 86 87** 88' 89' 90 91 92 75-acre CRU EXCEPTIONNEL of classed-growth quality owned by Peter A Sichel. Lively fragrant MARGAUX of great style. Value.

d'Archambeau Graves r w dr (sw) ★★ (r) **85 86 88** 89 90 91 92 (w) **88 90'** 91 92 Up-to-date 54-acre property at Illats. Vg fruity dry white; since '85 fragrant barrel-aged reds.

d'Arche Saut w sw ★★ **79 80 81 82 83' 85 86** 88 89 90 Classed-growth of 88 acres rejuvenated since '80. Rich juicy wines.

d'Arcins Central Méd r ★★ 185-acre Castel family property (Castelvin is a well-known VIN DE TABLE). Sister to next-door Barreyres (160 acres).

d'Armailhac Pau r ★★★ **70' 75' 78' 79 81 82' 83** 85 86' 87 88 89 90' 91 92 New name ('91) for CH MOUTON-BARONNE-PHILIPPE. Substantial fifth growth nurtured by the late Baron Philippe de Rothschild. 125 acres: less rich and luscious wine than MOUTON-R, but still outstanding in its class.

Arnauld H-Méd r ★★ 90 45 acres of old vines in Arcins to note since '85.

l'Arrosée St-Em r ★★★ **79 81 82 83 85' 86'** 87 88 89 90 24-acre COTES estate. Its name means watered, but wine is top-flight: opulent and structured.

Ausone St-Em r ★★★★ **75 76' 78 79' 81 82' 83'** 84 85 86' 87 88 89 90 91 92 First-growth with 17 acres (about 2,500 cases) in the best position on the COTES. Famous rock-hewn cellars under the v'yd. The firmest, most elegant and subtle St-Emilion. See also Ch Belair.

Bahans-Haut-Brion Graves r ★★★ NV and **82 83 85 86' 87 88** 89 **90** 91 92 The second-quality wine of CH HAUT-BRION. Worthy of its noble origin.

Balestard-la-Tonnelle St-Em r ★★ **83 85 86'** 87 88 89 90 Historic 30-acre classed-growth on the plateau. Big flavour; more finesse since '85.

de Barbe COTES de Bourg r (w) ★★ **82' 83 85 86 87** 88 89 90 The biggest (148 acres), best-known château of BOURG. Tasty light but fruity Merlot.

Baret Pessac-L r w ★★ Famous name recovered from a lull.

Bastor-Lamontagne Saut w sw ★★ **71 75 76 79 81 82 83 85 86** 88' 89' 90' 92 Large Bourgeois Preignac property of classed-growth quality. Excellent rich wines. Second label: Les Remparts de Bastor. NB also their Ch St-Robert at Pujols for red and white GRAVES. 10,000 cases.

Batailley Pau r ★★★ **70 75 78 79' 81 82' 83' 85 86** 87 88 89 90 91 92 The bigger of the famous pair of fifth-growths (with HAUT-BATAILLEY) on the borders of PAUILLAC and ST-JULIEN. 110 acres. Fine firm strong-flavoured wine. Home of the Castéja family of BORIE-MANOUX.

Beaumont Cussac, H-Méd r ★★ **82 85 86' 87** 88 89' **90'** 91 92 200-acre+ CRU BOURGEOIS, well-known in France for easily enjoyable and improving wines. Second label: Ch Moulin d'Arvigny. 35,000 cases. In the same hands as CH BEYCHEVELLE since '87.

Châteaux entries also cross-refer to France section, pages 20–54.

Beauregard Pom r ★★★ **79' 81 82' 83 85 86 87** 88 **89' 90' 92** 32-acre v'yd with pretty 17th-C château nr LA CONSEILLANTE owned by a bank. Well-made but rather delicate wines to drink quite young. Second label: Benjamin de Beauregard.

Beauséjour-Duffau-Lagarosse St-Em r ★★★ **82 83 85 86 88 89 90'** The other half of the above, 17 acres in old family hands; firm-structured, concentrated and fine.

Beau-Séjour-Bécot St-Em r ★★ **75 78 81 82' 83 85 86' 87 88 89 90' 91 92** Half of the old Beau-Séjour Premier Grand Cru estate on the W slope of the COTES. 45 acres. Controversially demoted in class in '85 but much revved-up since. The Bécots also own CH GRAND-PONTET.

Beau-Site St-Est r ★★ **75' 78' 79 81 82 83 85 86' 87 88 89 90** 55-acre CRU BOURGEOIS EXCEPTIONNEL in same hands as CH BATAILLEY etc. Quality and substance typical of ST-ESTEPHE.

Belair St-Em r ★★★ **71 75' 76' 79' 82' 83' 85' 86' 88' 89' 90' 91 92** Sister château and neighbour of AUSONE with 34.5 acres on the COTES. Wine a shade softer and less complex. V high standard in recent vintages. Makes a NV, Roc-Blanquant, in magnums only.

de Bel-Air Lalande de Pom r ★★ **82' 83 85 86 87** 88' **89' 90 91 92** The best-known estate of L de P, just N of POMEROL. Pomerol-style wine. 37 acres.

Bel-Air-Marquis-d'Aligre Soussans-Mar r ★★ **79' 81 82' 85 86 88 89 90** CRU EXCEPTIONNEL with 42 acres of old vines giving only 3,500 cases. The owner likes gutsy wine.

Belgrave St-Laurent r ★★ **81 82 83 85 86' 87 88 89 90'** Obscure fifth growth in ST-JULIEN's back-country. 107 acres. Managed by DOURTHE since '79. Second label: Diane de Belgrave – since '87.

Bellegrave Listrac r ★★ **82 83 85 86 88 89 90** 38-acre CRU BOURGEOIS making full-flavoured wine with advice from PICHON-LALANDE.

Bel-Orme-Tronquoy-de-Lalande St-Seurin-de-Cadourne (H-Méd) r ★★ **75' 79' 81 82 83 85 86 87 88 89 90 91 92** 60-acre CRU BOURGEOIS N of ST-ESTEPHE. Old v'yd producing tannic wines. More effort now.

Berliquet St-Em r ★★ **79 81 82 83 85 86 88 89 90 91 92** 23-acre Grand Cru Classé recently v well-run (sold by the ST-EMILION coop).

Bertineau St-Vincent Lalande de Pom r ★★ 10 acres owned by top oenologist Michel Rolland (see also Le Bon Pasteur).

Beychevelle St-Jul r ★★★→★★★★ **61 70' 75' 78 81 82' 83 85' 86' 87 88 89 90 91 92** 170-acre fourth growth with the MEDOC's finest mansion. New owners (an insurance company) since '85. Wine of elegance and power, just below the top flight of ST-JULIENS.

Biston-Brillette Moulis r ★★ Another attractive MOULIS. 7,000 cases.

Bonalgue Pom r ★★ Ambitious 2,500-case estate to watch. Les Hautes-Tuileries is sister château. Wines built to age.

Bonnet E-Deux-Mers r w ★★ (w) DYA Big-scale producer (600 acres!) of some of the best ENTRE-DEUX-MERS.

Le Bon Pasteur Pom r ★★★ **70 75 76 79 81 82 83 85 86' 87 88 89 90' 92** Excellent small property (3,500 cases) on the ST-EMILION boundary, owned by consultant oenologist Michel Rolland. Concentrated, sometimes even creamy wines.

Le Boscq St-Est r ★★ **82 83 85 86 87 88 89' 90** Leading CRU BOURGEOIS giving excellent value in tasty ST-ESTEPHE.

Le Bourdieu H-Méd r ★★ **79 81 82 83 85 86 88 89 90'** CRU BOURGEOIS at Vertheuil with sister château Victoria (134 acres in all) known for well-made ST-ESTEPHE-style wines. New owners in '90.

Bourgneuf Pom r ★★→★★★ **81 82 83 85' 86 88 89' 90 92** 22-acre v'yd on chalky clay soil, making fairly rich wines with typically plummy POMEROL perfume. 5,000 cases.

Bouscaut Graves r w ★★ **81 82' 83 85 86' 88 89 90** Classed-growth at Cadaujac bought in '80 by Lucien Lurton of CH BRANE-CANTENAC etc. 75 acres red (largely Merlot); 15 acres white. Never yet brilliant, but slowly getting there.

du Bousquet Côtes de Bourg r ★★ 82 83 85 86 88 89 90' 91 Reliable estate with 148 acres making attractive solid wine.

Boyd-Cantenac Mar r ★★★ 78' 79 81 82' 83' 85 86' 87 88 89 90 91 92 44-acre third growth often producing attractive wine, full of flavour, if not of third growth class. See also Ch Pouget.

Branaire-Ducru St-Jul r ★★★ 75' 78 79' 81 82' 83 85 86 87 88 89' 90' 91 92 Fourth growth of 125 acres, producing notably spicy and flavoury wine in the '70s. The late '80s saw a full-scale revival. New owners in '88. Second label: Duluc (since '88).

Brane-Cantenac Cant-Mar r ★★★ 75' 78' 79 81 82' 83 85 86' 87 88 89 90 Big (211-acre), well-run second growth. Rich, even gamey wines of strong character. Same owners as CH'X BOUSCAUT, CLIMENS, DURFORT-VIVENS, VILLEGEORGE, etc. Second labels: Ch'x Baron de Brane, Notton.

du Breuil Cissac r ★★ 87 88 89 90 Abandoned château bought by owners of CISSAC and restored. To follow.

Brillette Moulis r ★★ 81' 82 83 85' 86 88 89' 90 91 92 70-acre CRU BOURGEOIS. Reliable and attractive. Second label: Berthault Brillette.

La Cabanne Pom r ★★ 79 81 82' 83 86 87 88' 89' 90' 91 92 Highly regarded 25-acre property nr the great TROTANOY. Recently modernized; to follow. Second wine: Dom de Compostelle. See also CH HAUT-MAILLET.

Cadet-Piola St-Em r ★★ 75' 76 78 79 81 82 83' 85' 86 87 88 89' 90 91 92 Distinguished little property just N of the town of ST-EMILION. 3,000 cases. CH FAURIE-DE-SOUCHARD has same owner; less robust wine.

Caillou Saut w sw ★★ 76 81 82 83 85 86 87 88' 89' 90' 91 Well-run second-rank 37-acre BARSAC v'yd for firm fruity wine. Private Cuvée (81 83 85 86 88 89') is a top selection.

Calon-Ségur St-Est r ★★★ 78' 79' 81 82' 83 85' 86' 87 88' 89 90 91 Big (123-acre) third growth of great reputation for fruity hearty wines; less stylish than top ST-ESTEPHES.

Cambon-la-Pelouse H-Méd r ★★ 82 85 86 87 88 89 90 Big (145-acre) accessible CRU BOURGEOIS. A sure bet for fresh typical MEDOC without wood-ageing.

Camensac St-Laurent r ★★ 78 79 81 82' 85 86' 87 88 89 90 91 92 149-acre fifth growth with the same expert direction as LAROSE-TRINTAUDON. Good lively if not exactly classic wines. Second label: La Closerie de Camensac.

Canon Canon-Fronsac r ★★→★★★ 82 83 85 86' 88 89' 90 92 Tiny property of Christian MOUEIX. Long-ageing wine.

Canon St-Em r ★★★ 79' 81 82' 83 85' 86 87 88' 89' 90 92 Famous first-classed-growth with 44+ acres on the plateau W of the town. Conservative methods; v impressive wine, among ST-EMILION's best. Second label (in '91): Clos J Kanon.

Canon-de-Brem Canon-Fronsac r ★★ 81 82' 83 85 86 88 89' 90 92 One of the top FRONSAC v'yds for vigorous wine. MOUEIX property.

Canon-la-Gaffelière St-Em r ★★★ 82 83 85 86' 87 88' 89 90' 92 47-acre classed-growth on the lower slopes of the COTES, under Austrian ownership. Total renovation in '85. Now stylish meaty and impressive.

Canon-Moueix Canon-Fronsac r ★★ 83 85 86 88 89' 90 92 The latest MOUEIX investment in this rising AC. V stylish wine.

Cantegril Graves r ★★ 88 89 90 Good earthy red from CH DOISY-DAENE.

Cantemerle Macau r ★★★ 61 75' 78 81 82 83' 85 86 87 88 89 90 91 92 Superb S MEDOC estate, a romantic château in a wood with 150 acres of vines. Officially fifth growth; potentially much higher for its harmony of flavours. Problems in late '70s, but a new broom (CORDIER) since '81 has restored to potential. New cellars and oak vats in '90.

Cantenac-Brown Cant-Mar r ★★★ 70 78 79 81 82 83 85 86' 87 88 89 90' 91 92 Formerly old-fashioned 77-acre third growth. New owners (same as PICHON-LONGUEVILLE) investing heavily, with J-M Cazes' direction and v promising recent vintages. Big wines. Second label: Canuet.

Capbern-Gasqueton St-Est r ★★ **81 82 83 85 86 88 89 90** Good 85-acre CRU BOURGEOIS; same owner as CALON-SEGUR.

Cap-de-Mourlin St-Em r ★★ **79' 81 82' 83 85 86 87 88 89 90** Well-known 37-acre property of the Cap-de-Mourlin family, owners of CH BALESTARD and CH ROUDIER, MONTAGNE-ST-EM. Rich tasty ST-EMILION.

Carbonnieux Graves r w ★★★ **82 83 85 86' 87 88 89' 90' 91 92** Historic estate at LEOGNAN making rather light reds (since '85 much better). The whites, 50% Sémillon (eg **87 88 89 90 91 92'**), have the structure to age 10 yrs. Ch'x Le Pape and Le Sartre are also in the family.

Cardaillan Graves r ★★ The trusty red wine of the distinguished (SAUTERNES) CH DE MALLE.

La Cardonne Blaignan (Méd) r ★★ **85 86 87 88 89 90 91 92** Large (300-acre+) CRU BOURGEOIS of the northern MEDOC, bought in '73 by the Rothschilds of LAFITE and sold in '90. Fairly simple fruity Médoc, best when young.

Les Carmes-Haut-Brion Graves r ★★ **78 81' 82' 83 85 86 87 88' 89 90 91 92** Small (9-acre) neighbour of HAUT-BRION with higher than Bourgeois standards. Old vintages show its potential. Only 1,500 cases.

Caronne-Ste-Gemme St-Laurent r ★★→★★★ **75 78 79 81 82' 83 84 85 86 87 88 89' 90 91 92** CRU BOURGEOIS EXCEPTIONNEL of 100 acres. Steady stylish quality repays patience. At minor CRU CLASSE level.

CHATEAU
DUCRU-BEAUCAILLOU

Grand Cru Classé

APPELLATION ST-JULIEN
CONTROLEE

Mis en Bouteille au
Château

A Bordeaux Label

A château is an estate – not necessarily with a mansion or a big expanse of vineyard.

Reference to the local classification. It varies from one part of Bordeaux to another.

The appellation contrôlée: look up St-Julien in the France A–Z.

'Bottled at the château' – now the normal practice with classed-growth wines.

Carteau-Côtes-Daugay St-Em ★★ Emerging 5,000-case GRAND CRU; to follow for full-flavoured wines maturing fairly early.

du Castéra Méd r ★★ **82 83 85 86 87 88 89 90'** Historic property at St-Germain (N MEDOC). Recent investment; tasty but not tannic wine.

Certan-Giraud Pom r ★★ **75 79 81 82 83' 85 86 88 89** Small (17-acre) property next to PETRUS. Good, but one expects more.

Certan-de-May Pom r ★★★ **70 75 78 79 81 82' 83' 84 85' 86 87 88 89' 90 91 92** Neighbour of VIEUX CHATEAU CERTAN. Tiny property (1,800 cases) with full-bodied, rich and tannic wine, consistently flying v high.

Chambert-Marbuzet St-Est r ★★ **76 78 79 81 82 83 85 86 87 88 89' 90' 91 92** Tiny (20-acre) sister château of HAUT-MARBUZET. Vg predominantly Cab wine, aged in new oak relatively fast but v tastily.

Chantegrive Graves r w ★★ (w) **82 85 87 88 89 90 91 92'** 215-acre estate, half white, half red; modern GRAVES of high quality. Cuvée Caroline is top white selection, Cuvée Edouard top red. Other labels incl Mayne-Lévêque, Bon-Dieu-des-Vignes.

Chasse-Spleen Moulis r ★★★ **75' 76 78' 79 81' 82' 83' 84 85 86 87 88 89 90 91 92** 180-acre CRU EXCEPTIONNEL of classed-growth quality. Consistently good, usually outstanding, long-maturing wine. Second label: Ermitage de C-S. One of the surest things in Bordeaux.

Chéret-Pitres Graves r w ★→★★ Substantial estate in the up-and-coming village of Portets. Drink young or keep.

Cheval Blanc St-Em r ★★★★ **64 66 70 71 75' 76 78 79 80 81' 82' 83' 84 85' 86 87 88 89 90** This and AUSONE are the 'first growths' of ST-EMILION. Cheval Blanc is richer, more full-blooded, intensely vigorous and perfumed, from 100 acres. Delicious young, and lasts a generation. Second wine: Le Petit Cheval.

Chevalier, Domaine de Graves r w ★★★★ 66 70' 75' 76 78 79' 80 81' 82' 83 84 85 86' 88' 89 90' 91 92 Superb small estate of 36 acres at LEOGNAN. The red is stern at first, richly subtle with age. The white is delicate but matures to rich flavours (79' 81 82 83' 84 85' 87' 88 89 90 91 92).

Chicane Graves r ★★ 85 86 88 89 90' 91 92 Satisfying and reliable product of the Langon merchant Pierre Coste. (Domaine de Gaillat is another.) Drink at 2–6 yrs (the Gaillat a little later).

Cissac Cissac r ★★ 70' 71 75' 76 78' 79 81 82' 83' 84 85 86' 87 88 89 90 91 92 Pillar of the bourgeoisie. 80-acre CRU GRAND BOURGEOIS EXCEPTIONNEL: steady record for tasty, v long-lived wine. Also, since '87, CH DU BREUIL.

Citran Avensan (H-Méd) r ★★ 78' 82 83 85 86 87 88 89' 90 91 92 CRU GRAND BOURGEOIS EXCEPTIONNEL of 178 acres, bought by Japanese in '87. Major works. 89 is turbo-charged. Second label: Moulins de Citran.

Clarke Listrac r (p w) ★★ 82 83 85' 86' 87 88 89' 90 91 92 Huge (350-acre) CRU BOURGEOIS Rothschild development, incl visitor facilities and neighbouring Ch'x Malmaison and Peyrelebade. Also a unique sweet white 'Le Merle Blanc du Ch Clarke'.

Clerc-Milon Pau r ★★★ 75' 76 78' 79 80 81 82' 83 85 86' 87 88 89 90 91 92 Once-forgotten little fifth growth bought by the late Baron Philippe de Rothschild in '70. Now 73 acres with MOUTON input. Not thrilling in the '70s (except 70), but vg 85, 86 (esp), and now 88, 89 and 90.

Climens Saut w sw ★★★★ 71' 75' 76' 78' 79 80' 81 82 83' 85' 86' 88 89 90' 74-acre classed-growth at BARSAC making some of the most stylish (though not the v sweetest) wine in the world for a good 10 yrs' maturing. (Occasional) second label: Les Cyprès. Same owner as CH BRANE-CANTENAC etc.

Clinet Pom r ★★★ 81 82 83 85 86 87 88 89 90 91 92 17-acre property in central POMEROL making intense wines from old vines. Since '86 one of the models for POMEROL.

Clos l'Eglise Pom r ★★★ 75 78 79' 81 83 85 86 88 89' 90 14-acre v'yd on one of the best sites in POMEROL. V fine wine without great muscle or flesh. The same family owns CH PLINCE.

Clos Floridène Graves w ★★ 90' 91 92 Tour de force by one of the best white-wine makers of Bordeaux, Denis Dubourdieu. Oak-aged Sauv to drink young or keep 5 yrs.

Clos Fourtet St-Em r ★★★ 78 79 81 82' 83 85 86 88 89 90 Well-placed 42-acre first growth on the plateau, with cellars almost in the town. Back on form after a middling patch. Same owners as BRANE-CANTENAC, CLIMENS etc.

Clos Haut-Peyraguey Saut w sw ★★ 78 79 81 83 84 85 86' 87 88' 89 90' Tiny production of good medium-rich wine. The vg CRU BOURGEOIS Ch Haut-Bommes is in the same hands.

Clos des Jacobins St-Em r ★★ 75' 78 79 81 82' 83' 85 86 87 88 89' 90 Well-known and well-run little (18-acre) classed-growth owned by the shipper CORDIER. Wines of notable depth and style. NB the 89.

Clos du Marquis St-Jul r ★★ 81 82 83 85 86' 87 88 89' 90 91 92 The second wine of LEOVILLE-LAS-CASES, cut from the same cloth.

Clos René Pom r ★★★ 75 81 82' 83 85 86 87 88 89 90 Leading château W of POMEROL. 38 acres making increasingly concentrated wine. Also sold as Ch Moulinet-Lasserre.

Clos St-Martin St-Em r ★★★ 88 89 90 9 acres in prime spot co-owned with Grandes-Murailles and Côte Baleau; the other two were demoted in the '85 reclassification. A muddle, but taste the wines.

La Closerie-Grand-Poujeaux Moulis r ★★ 85 86 88 89 90 91 92 Small but respected middle-MEDOC property. Also owns neighbouring Ch Bel-Air-Lagrave.

La Clotte St-Em r ★★ 82 83' 85 86 87 88 89 90 92 Tiny COTES GRAND CRU with fragrant supple wine. Drink at the owners' restaurant, La Cadène, in ST-EMILION. Change of winemaker in '90. Second label: Clos Berger Bosson (91).

Colombier-Monpelou Pau r ★★ **81 82 83 85 86' 87 88 89 90' 91 92** Reliable small CRU BOURGEOIS made to a fair standard.

La Conseillante Pom r ★★★★ **70' 75 76 79 81' 82' 83 84 85 86 87 88 89 90' 91 92** 29-acre historic property on the plateau between PETRUS and CHEVAL BLANC. Some of the noblest and most fragrant POMEROL, worthy of its superb position.

Corbin (Giraud) St-Em r ★★ **75 79 81 82' 83 85 86 88 89 90 92** 28-acre classed-growth in N ST-EMILION where a cluster of Corbins occupy the plateau edge. Top vintages are v rich. Same owner as CERTAN-GIRAUD.

Corbin-Michotte St-Em r ★★ **75 81 82 83 85 86 88 89 90** Well-run 19-acre property; 'generous' POMEROL-like wine.

Cordeillan-Bages Pau r ★★ A mere 1,000 cases of full-blooded PAUILLAC from the château-hotel of J-M Cazes (see Lynch-Bages).

Cos-d'Estournel St-Est r ★★★★ **61 66 70 75' 76' 78' 79 81' 82' 83' 84 85' 86' 87 88' 89' 90' 91 92** 140-acre second growth with eccentric chinoiserie tower overlooking CH LAFITE. Always full-flavoured, often magnificent. Now regularly one of best in the MEDOC. Second label: CH DE MARBUZET.

Cos-Labory St-Est r ★★ **81 82 83 85 86 87 88 89 90' 91 92** Little-known fifth growth neighbour of COS-D'ESTOURNEL with 37 acres. Efforts since '85 have raised it steadily to classed-growth form (esp 90). ANDRON-BLANQUET is in effect its second wine.

Coufran St-Seurin-de-Cadourne (H-Méd) r ★★ **81 82' 83 85 86' 87 88 89 90 91 92** Coufran and CH VERDIGNAN, on the northernmost hillock of the HAUT-MEDOC are co-owned. Coufran has mainly Merlot vines; soft supple wine. 148 acres. Ch Soudars is another, smaller sister.

Couhins-Lurton Graves w ★★ **85 86' 88 89 90 91 92** Tiny quantity of v fine oaky Sauv wine for maturing.

Coutet Saut w sw ★★★ **67' 70' 71' 73 75' 76 79 81 82 83' 85 86' 87 88 89 90'** Traditional rival to CH CLIMENS; 91 acres in BARSAC. Usually slightly less rich; at its best equally fine. Cuvée Madame is a v rich selection of the best. A dry GRAVES is sold under the same name.

Couvent des Jacobins St-Em r ★★ **75 78 79' 81 82' 83 85 86 87 88 89 90 92** Well-known 22-acre v'yd on E edge of town. Among the best of its kind. Splendid cellars. Second label: Ch Beau-Mayne.

Le Crock St-Est r ★★ **79 81 82 83 84 85 86 87 88 89 90** Outstanding CRU BOURGEOIS of 74 acres in the same family as CH LEOVILLE-POYFERRE. Among the best CRUS BOURGEOIS of the commune.

La Croix Pom r ★★ **75' 76 79' 81 82 83 85 86 87 88 89 90 91 92** Well-reputed property of 32 acres. Appealing plummy POMEROL with a spine; matures well. Also La C-St-Georges, La C-Toulifaut, Castelot, Clos des Litanies and HAUT-SARPE (St-Em).

La Croix du Casse Pom r ★★ Sister château of CLINET. 22 acres making easy-drinking POMEROL.

La Croix-de-Gay Pom r ★★★ **81 82' 83' 85 86 88' 89 90 91 92** 30 acres in best part of the commune. Recently on fine form. Has underground cellars (rare in POMEROL). La Fleur-de-Gay is the best selection.

Croizet-Bages Pau r ★★ **82' 83 85 86 87 88 89 90 91 92** 52-acre fifth growth (lacking a château or a reputation) with the same owners as CH RAUZAN-GASSIES. Wines with growing vigour (at last) since '86. Fine 89.

Croque-Michotte St-Em r ★★ **75 81 82' 83 85 86 87 88 89 90** 35-acre POMEROL-style classed-growth on the Pomerol border.

de Cruzeau Graves r w ★★ **86 88 89 90 91 92** 100-acre GRAVES-LEOGNAN v'yd recently developed by André Lurton of LA LOUVIERE etc. V high standards; to try. Drink white at 1–3 yrs.

Curé-Bon-la-Madeleine St-Em r ★★★ **75 78 81 82' 83 85 86 88 89 90** Small (12-acre) property among COTES' best; between AUSONE and CANON.

To decipher codes, please refer to symbols key at front of book, and to 'How to Read an Entry' on page 5.

Dalem Fronsac r ★★ 82 83 85 86 88 89 90 91 92 Leading full-blooded FRONSAC.

Dassault St-Em r ★★ 82 83 85 86 88 89 90 Consistent early-maturing middle-weight GRAND CRU. 58 acres.

La Dauphine Fronsac ★★ 85 86 87 88 89 90 92 Old star rejuvenated by J-P MOUEIX.

Dauzac Labarde-Mar r ★★→★★★ 79' 81 82' 83' 84 85 86 87 88 89 90' Substantial fifth growth nr the river S of MARGAUX. Doing better since '79; new owner (an insurance company) in '89. 120 acres. 22,000 cases. Second wine: La Bastide Dauzac.

Desmirail Mar r ★★→★★★ 82 83' 85 86 87 88 89 90 Third growth, now 45 acres. A long-defunct name revived in '81 by Lucien Lurton of BRANE-CANTENAC. So far wines for drinking young.

Doisy-Daëne Barsac w (r) sw dr ★★★ 76' 78 79 80 81 82 83 85 86 88 89' 90' 91 Forward-looking 34-acre estate making crisp oaky dry white and red CH CANTEGRIL as well as notably fine (and long-lived) sweet BARSAC.

Doisy-Dubroca Barsac w sw ★★ 75' 76 78 79 81 83 85 86 87 88 89 90' Tiny (8.5-acre) BARSAC classed-growth allied to CH CLIMENS.

Doisy-Védrines Saut w sw ★★★ 71 75' 76' 78 79 80 81 82' 83' 85 86 88' 89' 90 50-acre classed-growth at BARSAC, nr CLIMENS and COUTET, recently re-equipped. Delicious sturdy rich: for keeping. NB the 89.

La Dominique St-Em r ★★★ 75 78 79 81 82' 83 85 86' 87 88 89 90 45-acre classed-growth next door to CH CHEVAL BLANC; at best almost as arresting. Second label: St Paul de Dominique (91).

Ducluzeau Listrac r ★★ Tiny sister property of DUCRU-BEAUCAILLOU. 10 acres, unusually 90% Merlot.

Ducru-Beaucaillou St-Jul r ★★★★ 61 66 70' 75' 76 78' 79 80 81 82' 83' 84 85' 86' 87 88 89 90 91 92 Outstanding second growth; 120 acres overlooking the river. Second label: La Croix-Beaucaillou. The owner, M Borie, makes classic cedar-scented claret for v long ageing. See also Grand-Puy-Lacoste, Haut-Batailley, Lalande-Borie.

Duhart-Milon-Rothschild Pau r ★★★ 78 79 81 82' 83 85 86 87 88 89 90 Fourth growth neighbour of LAFITE, under the same management. Maturing vines; increasingly fine quality. 110 acres.

Duplessis-Fabre Moulis r ★★ 82 83 85 86 87 88' 89 90 Former sister château of FOURCAS-DUPRE; since '89 owned by DOURTHE (MAUCAILLOU). To watch.

Durfort-Vivens Mar r ★★★ 78' 79' 81 82' 83 84 85' 86 87 88' 89 90 Relatively small (49-acre) second growth owned by M Lurton of BRANE-CANTENAC. Recent wines have structure (lots of Cab S) and class.

Dûtruch-Grand-Poujeaux Moulis r ★★ 81 82' 83 85 86 87 88 89 90 91 92 One of the leaders of MOULIS; full-bodied and tannic wines.

de l'Eglise, Domaine Pom r ★★ 79' 81 82' 83 85 86 88 89 90 Small property: stylish resonant wine distributed by BORIE-MANOUX.

L'Eglise-Clinet Pom r ★★★ 70 71 75 76 78 79 81 82' 83' 84 85' 86 87 88' 89 90 91 92 11 acres. Ranked v nr the top; full fleshy wine. Changed hands in '82; 86 is noble. 1,700 cases. Second label: La Petite Eglise.

L'Enclos Pom r ★★ 70 75 79 82' 83 85 86 87 88 89 90' 91 92 Respected 26-acre property on west side of POMEROL, nr CLOS RENE. Big well-made long-flavoured wine.

L'Evangile Pom r ★★★ 75' 78 79 82' 83' 85' 86 87 88 89 90 33 acres between PETRUS and CHEVAL BLANC. Deep-veined but elegant style. In the same area and class as LA CONSEILLANTE. Bought in '90 by Domaines (Lafite) Rothschild.

de Fargues Saut w sw ★★★ 70' 71' 75' 76' 78 79 80 81 83 85' 86 87 88 89 90 25-acre v'yd by ruined château in same ownership as CH D'YQUEM. Fruity and extremely elegant wines, maturing earlier than Yquem.

Faurie-de-Souchard St-Em r ★★ 85 86 88 89 90 91 92 Small Grand Cru Classé on the COTES. See also Ch Cadet-Piola.

Ferrande Graves r (w) ★★ 79 81 82 83 85 86 87 88 89 90 91 Major estate of Castres: 100+ acres. Easy enjoyable red and good white at 1–4 yrs.

Ferrière Mar r ★★ **75 78 79 81 82 83 85 86 87 88 89 90** Phantom third growth; only 10+ acres. Now in same capable hands as CHASSE-SPLEEN.

Feytit-Clinet Pom r ★★→★★★ **75' 79 81 82' 83 85' 86 87 88' 89' 90 92** Little property nr LATOUR-A-POMEROL. Fine ripe wines. Managed by J-P MOUEIX.

Why do the Châteaux of Bordeaux have such a large section of this book devoted to them? The reason is simple: collectively they form by far the largest supply of high-quality wine on earth. A single typical Médoc château with 150 acres (some have far more) makes approximately 26,000 dozen bottles of identifiable wine each year – the production of two or three California 'boutique' wineries.

The tendency over the last two decades has been to buy more land. Many classed-growths have expanded very considerably since their classification in 1855. The majority has also raised its sights and invested the good profits of the past decade in better technology.

Fieuzal Graves r (w) ★★★ **78' 79 81 82' 83 84 85' 86' 87 88 89 90' 91 92 (w) 91' 92** 75-acre classed-growth at LEOGNAN. Finely made, memorable wines of both colours esp since '84. Whites since '85 are 4–8-yr keepers. Second label: Ch le Bonnat.

Figeac St-Em r ★★★★ **70' 75' 76' 78 79 81 82' 83 84 85' 86 87 88 89 90** Famous first growth neighbour of CHEVAL BLANC. 98-acre gravelly v'yd gives one of Bordeaux's most stylish, rich but elegant wines, maturing relatively quickly but lasting almost indefinitely.

Filhot Saut w sw dr ★★ **75 76' 79' 82' 83' 85 86' 87 88 89 90' 91** Second-rank classed-growth with splendid château, 148-acre v'yd. Lightish (Sauv) sweet wines for fairly early drinking, a little dry, and red. 'Crème de Tête' in '90 extremely rich.

La Fleur St-Em r ★★ **75 78 79 81 82' 83 85 86 88 89' 90 92** 16-acre COTES estate; consistently fruity wines. Now managed by J-P MOUEIX.

La Fleur-de-Gay See La Croix-de-Gay.

La Fleur-Pétrus Pom r ★★★★ **70 75' 78 79 81' 82 83' 85 86 87 88' 89' 90 92** 18-acre v'yd flanking PETRUS and under same management. Exceedingly fine plummy wines; POMEROL at its most stylish.

Fombrauge St-Em r ★★ **79 81 82' 83 85 86 87 88' 89 90** 120-acres at St-Christophe-des-Bardes, E of ST-EMILION, with Danish connections. Reliable mainstream St-Emilion making great efforts. Second label: Ch Maurens.

Fonbadet Pau r ★★ **70 76 78 79 81' 82' 83 84 85 86 87 88 89 90' 91 92** CRU BOURGEOIS of solid reputation. 38 acres next to PONTET-CANET. Old vines; wine needs long bottle-age. Value.

Fonplégade St-Em r ★★ **75 78 79 81 82' 83 85 86 87 88 89 90** 48-acre Grand Cru Classé on the COTES W of ST-EMILION in the Armand Moueix group. Firm and long-lasting.

Fonréaud Listrac r ★★ **78' 79 81 82 83 85' 86' 87 88 89 90 91 92** One of the bigger (96 acres) and better CRUS BOURGEOIS of its area. New broom (and barrels) since '83. See also Ch Lestage.

Fonroque St-Em r ★★★ **70 75' 78 79 81 82 83' 85' 86 87 88 89' 90' 92** 48 acres on the plateau N of ST-EMILION. J-P MOUEIX property. Big deep dark wine that nonetheless opens up quite young.

Les Forts de Latour Pau r ★★★ **70' 75 78' 79 80 81 82' 83 84 85 86** 90 The second wine of CH LATOUR; well worthy of its big brother. For long unique in being bottle-aged at least 3 yrs before release; since '90 offered EN PRIMEUR as well. V fine 82 and 90.

Fourcas-Dupré Listrac r ★★ **70' 75 78' 79 81 82' 83' 85' 86' 87 88 89' 90 91 92** Top-class 100-acre CRU BOURGEOIS EXCEPTIONNEL making consistent and elegant wine. To follow. Second label: Ch Bellevue-Laffont.

Fourcas-Hosten Listrac r ★★→★★★ **70 75 78' 79 81 82' 83' 85 86' 87 88 89 90 91 92** 96-acre CRU BOURGEOIS currently considered the best of its (underestimated) commune. Firm wine with a long life.

Franc-Mayne St-Em r ★★ 85 86 87 88 89' 90' '89 acquisition of AXA Insurance. 18 acres run by J-M Cazes (see Lynch-Bages). Expect high standards. Ch'x La Fleur-Pourret and Petit-Figeac (total 19 acres) are in the same stable.

de France Pessac-L r w ★★ Well-known GRAVES, 65 acres red, 10 white recently replanted. Recent reds notable.

La Gaffelière St-Em r ★★→★★★ 70 78 79 81 82' 83' 85 86' 87 88' 89' 90 92 61-acre first growth at the foot of the COTES below CH BEL-AIR. Elegant, not rich wines; worth its rank since '82, after a bad patch.

La Garde Graves r (w) ★★ 81 82' 83' 84 85 86 88 89 90 91 92 Substantial property making reliably sound red.

Le Gay Pom r ★★★★ 70 75' 76' 78 79 82' 83' 85 86 88 89' 90' 92 Outstanding 14-acre v'yd on N edge of POMEROL. Same owner as CH LAFLEUR; under J-P MOUEIX management since '85. Now producing regularly noble wine.

Gazin Pom r ★★★ 81 82 83 85 86 87' 88 89' 90' 91 92 Large property (for POMEROL) with 58 acres next to PETRUS. Inconsistent up to '85; now back on top form. Distributed (except tiny '91 crop) by J-P MOUEIX. Second label: Ch l'Hospitalet.

Gilette Saut w sw ★★★ 37 49 53 55 59 61 62 Extraordinary small Preignac château which stores its sumptuous wines in cask to a great age. Only about 5,000 bottles of each. Ch Les Justices is the sister château.

Giscours Labarde-Mar r ★★★ 70 71' 75' 76 78' 79' 81' 82' 83 84 85 86 87 88 89' 90 91 92 Splendid 182-acre third growth S of CANTENAC. Dynamically run with excellent vigorous wine in '70s; '80s less sure-footed. Ch La Houringue is baby sister.

du Glana St-Jul r ★★ 81 82' 83 85 86 88 89 90 91 92 Big CRU BOURGEOIS in centre of ST-JULIEN. Undemanding; undramatic.

Gloria St-Jul r ★★★ 70' 75' 76 78' 79 80 81 82' 83 85 86 87 88 89 90 91 92 Outstanding CRU BOURGEOIS making wine of vigour and finesse, up to classed-growths in quality. 110 acres. In '82 the owner, the late Henri Martin, bought CH ST-PIERRE. Recent return to long-maturing style.

Grand-Barrail-Lamarzelle-Figeac St-Em r ★★ 78 79 82' 83 85 86 87 88 89 90 91 92 48-acre property S of FIGEAC, incl Ch La Marzelle. Well-reputed and popular, if scarcely exciting.

Grand-Corbin-Despagne St-Em r ★★→★★★ 70 75 76 78 79 81 82' 83 85 86 88 89 90' 91 92 One of biggest and best GRANDS CRUS on CORBIN plateau.

Grand-Mayne St Em ★★ 82 83 84 85 86 87 88 89 90 40-acre Grand Cru Classé on W COTES. To watch.

Grand-Pontet St-Em r ★★ 82' 83 85 86' 87 88 89 90 91 92 35 acres beside CH BEAU-SEJOUR BECOT; both revitalized since '85.

Grand-Puy-Ducasse Pau r ★★★ 78 79 81 82' 83 85 86 87 88 89 90 91 92 Well-known little fifth growth bought in '71, renovated and enlarged to 90 acres under expert management. A best buy. Second label: Ch Artiges-Arnaud.

Grand-Puy-Lacoste Pau r ★★★ 70 75 76 78' 79' 81' 82' 83 85' 86' 87 88 89 90 91 92 Leading fifth growth famous for excellent full-bodied vigorous PAUILLAC. 110 acres among the 'Bages' châteaux, owned by the Borie family of DUCRU-BEAUCAILLOU. Second label: Lacoste-Borie.

Gravas Saut w sw ★★ 83' 85 86 88 89' 90' Small BARSAC property; impressive firm wine. NB Cuvée Spéciale.

La Grave, Domaine Graves r w ★★ 82 83 85 86 87 88 89 90' 91 92 Innovative little estate with lively reds; delicious oak-aged whites. Made at CH DE LANDIRAS by Peter Vinding-Diers.

La Grave-Trigant-de-Boisset Pom r ★★★ 75' 76' 78 79 81' 82' 83 85 86' 87 88 89' 90 92 Verdant château with small but first-class v'yd owned by CHRISTIAN MOUEIX. Elegant beautifully structured POMEROL.

Gressier-Grand-Poujeaux Moulis r ★★→★★★ 70 75' 78 79' 81 82 83' 85 86 87 88 89 90 Good CRU BOURGEOIS, neighbour of CHASSE-SPLEEN. Fine firm wine with a good track record for repaying patient cellaring.

Greysac Méd r ** **81' 82 83 85 86 88 89 90 91 92** Elegant 140-acre property. Easy early-maturing wines popular in US.

Gruaud-Larose St-Jul r *** **70' 75' 76 78' 79 81 82' 83 85 86 87 88 89 90 91 92** One of the biggest and best-loved second growths. 189 acres. Smooth rich stylish claret. Owned by CORDIER. Excellent second wine: Sarget de Gruaud-Larose.

Guadet-St-Julien St-Em ** **79 81 82 83 85 86 87 88 89 90' 92** Extremely well-made wines from v small Grand Cru Classé.

Guiraud Saut w (r) sw (dr) *** **76 78' 79' 81 82 83' 85 86' 87 88 89' 90'** Restored classed-growth of top quality. 250+ acres. At best excellent sweet wine of great finesse, and a small amount of red and dry white. The 86, 88, 89 and 90 will be superb in time.

Guiteronde du Hayot Saut ** 75-acres in BARSAC; known for finesse and value.

La Gurgue Mar r ** **79 81 82 83' 85' 86 87 88 89 90** Small, well-placed 30-acre property, for MARGAUX of the fruitiest sort. From owners of CHASSE-SPLEEN. To watch.

Hanteillan Cissac r ** **81 82' 83 85' 86 87 88' 89 90 91 92** Large (200-acre+) v'yd renovated since '73. V fair Bourgeois wine. Ch Laborde is second quality. 50,000 cases.

Haut-Bages-Averous Pau r **→*** **82' 83 85 86 87 88 89 90 91 92** The second wine of CH LYNCH BAGES. Delicious easy drinking.

Haut-Bages-Libéral Pau r ** **78 82' 83 84 85 86' 87 88 89' 90 91 92** Lesser-known fifth growth of 64 acres (next to Latour) in same stable as CHASSE-SPLEEN. Results are excellent, full of PAUILLAC vitality.

Haut-Bages-Monpelou Pau r ** **81 82' 83 85 86 87 88 89' 90 91 92** 25-acre CRU BOURGEOIS stable-mate of CH BATAILLEY on former DUHART-MILON land. Good minor PAUILLAC.

Haut-Bailly Graves r *** **70' 78 79' 81' 82 83 85 86' 87 88 89 90 92** 70-acre+ estate at LEOGNAN, famous for ripe round intelligently-made sometimes 'feminine' wine since '79. Second label: La Parde de H-B.

Haut-Batailley Pau r *** **70' 75' 78' 79 81 82' 83 85 86 87 88 89' 90 91 92** Smaller part of fifth growth BATAILLEY estate: 49 acres. Often in a gentler vein than sister ch, GRAND-PUY-LACOSTE. Second wine: La Tour-d'Aspic.

Haut-Bergey Pessac-L r ** 40 acres, largely Cab; fragrant delicate GRAVES.

Haut-Bommes See Clos Haut-Peyraguey.

Haut-Brignon Premières Côtes r w * Big producer of standard wines at Cénac, owned by major CHAMPAGNE coop. Do not confuse with the next!

Haut-Brion Pessac (Graves) r (w) **** **61 64 66 70' 71' 75' 76 78' 79' 80 81 82 83 84 85' 86' 87 88 89' 90' 91 92** The oldest great château of Bordeaux and the only non-MEDOC first growth of 1855. 108 acres. Beautifully harmonious, never aggressive wine. Particularly good since '75. A little full dry white in **78 79 81 83 85 86 87 88 89 90 91 92**. See Bahans-Haut-Brion, La Mission-Haut-Brion.

Haut-Maillet Pom ** **84 85 86 88 89 90 91 92** 12-acre sister château of LA CABANNE. Well-made gentle wines.

Haut-Marbuzet St-Est r **→*** **70 75' 76 78' 79 80 81 82' 83 85 86 87 88 89 90 91 92** The best of many good ST-ESTEPHE CRUS BOURGEOIS. 100 acres, 60% Merlot. Second-label châteaux CHAMBERT-MARBUZET, MACCARTHY, MacCarthy-Moula, Tour de Marbuzet are in same hands. New oak gives them all classic style.

Haut-Pontet St-Em r ** **70 75 78 79 81 82' 83 85 86 88 89 90** 12-acre v'yd of the COTES well deserving its GRAND CRU status. 2,500 cases.

Haut-Quercus St-Em r ** **83 85 86 88 89' 90** Oak-aged coop wine to a v high standard.

Haut-Sarpe St-Em r ** **79 81 82 83' 85 86 87 88 89 90 91 92** Grand Cru Classé (6,000 cases) with elegant château and park. Same owner as CH LA CROIX, POMEROL.

Hortevie St-Jul r ** **81 82 83 85' 86 87 88 89 90 91 92** One of the few ST-JULIEN CRUS BOURGEOIS. This tiny v'yd and its bigger sister TERREY-GROS-CAILLOU are shining examples.

Houissant St-Est r ★★ 78 79 81 82 83 85 86 87 88 89 90 91 92 Typical robust well-balanced ST-ESTEPHE CRU BOURGEOIS also called Ch Leyssac; well-known in Denmark.

d'Issan Cant-Mar r ★★★ 70 75' 78 79 81 82' 83' 85 86 87 88 89 90' 91 92 Beautifully restored moated château with 75-acre third growth v'yd well-known for fragrant, virile but delicate wine. Second label: Ch de Candale.

Kirwan Cant-Mar r ★★★ 78 79' 81 82' 83' 85 86 87 88' 89 90' 91 92 Well-run 86-acre third growth owned by SCHRODER & SCHYLER. Mature v'yds giving ever tastier wines.

Labégorce Mar r ★★ 75' 78 79 81' 82' 83' 85 86 87 88 89 90 91 92 Substantial 69-acre property N of MARGAUX producing long-lived wines of true Margaux quality.

Labégorce-Zédé Mar r ★★→★★★ 75' 78 79 81' 82' 83' 85 86' 87 88 89' 90 91 92 Outstanding CRU BOURGEOIS on the road N from MARGAUX. 62 acres. Typically delicate and fragrant, truly classic since '81. The same family as VIEUX CHATEAU CERTAN. Second label: Domaine Zédé. Also 23 acres of AC Bordeaux: 'Z'.

Lacoste-Borie The second wine of CH GRAND-PUY-LACOSTE.

Lafaurie-Peyraguey Saut w sw ★★★ 75' 76' 78' 80 81' 82 83' 85 86 87 88 89 90 Fine classed-growth of only 49 acres at Bommes, belonging to CORDIER. After a lean patch, good, rich and racy wines.

Lafite-Rothschild Pau r ★★★★ 70' 75' 76' 78 79 81' 82' 83 84 85 86' 87 88' 89' 90' 91 92 First growth of fabulous style and perfume in its great vintages, which keep for decades. Resplendent since '76. Amazing circular cellars opened '87; joint ventures in Chile ('88), California ('89), Portugal ('92). Second wine: MOULIN-DES-CARRUADES. 225 acres. Also owns CH'X LA CARDONNE, DUHART-MILON, L'EVANGILE, RIEUSSEC.

Lafleur Pom r ★★★★ 70' 75' 78 81 82' 83 85 86 88 89' 90 12-acre property just N of PETRUS. Resounding wine of the tannic, less 'fleshy' kind. Same owner as LE GAY. Second wine: Pensées de Lafleur.

Lafleur-Gazin Pom r ★★ 70 75' 78 79 81 82' 83 85' 86 87 88' 89 90 92 Distinguished small J-P MOUEIX estate on the NE border of POMEROL.

Lafon-Rochet St-Est r ★★ 70' 79 81 82 83' 85 86 87 88 89 90 Fourth growth neighbour of CH COS D'ESTOURNEL, restored in the '60s and again recently. 110 acres. Rather hard dark full-bodied ST-ESTEPHE reluctant to 'give'. Same owner as CH PONTET-CANET. Second label: Numéro 2.

Lagrange Pom r ★★★ 70' 75' 78 81 82' 83 85' 86 87 88 89' 90' 92 20-acre v'yd in the centre of POMEROL run by the ubiquitous house of J-P MOUEIX. Rising profile for flavour/value.

Lagrange St-Jul r ★★★ 70 75 79 81 82 83 84 85' 86' 87 88 89' 90 91 92 Formerly run-down third growth inland from ST-JULIEN, bought by Suntory at the end of '83. 280 acres now in tiptop condition. A property to follow. Second wine: Les Fiefs de Lagrange (83' 85 86 87 88 89 90 91 92).

La Lagune Ludon r ★★★ 70' 75' 76' 78' 79 81 82' 83' 85 86' 87 88' 89' 90' 91 92 Well-run ultra-modern 160-acre third growth in the extreme S of the MEDOC. Attractively rich wines with marked oak; steadily v high quality. Owned by CHAMPAGNE AYALA.

Lalande-Borie St-Jul r ★★ 79 81 82 83 85 86 87 88 89 90' 91 92 A baby brother of the great DUCRU-BEAUCAILLOU created from part of the former v'yd of CH LAGRANGE.

Lamarque Lamarque (H-Méd) r ★★ 81' 82 83' 85 86' 87 88 89 90 91 92 Splendid medieval fortress of the central MEDOC with 113 acres giving admirable and improving wine of high Bourgeois standard.

Lamothe Bergeron H-Méd r ★★ 150 acres at CUSSAC makes 25,000 cases of reliable claret. Run by GRAND-PUY-DUCASSE.

Châteaux entries also cross-refer to France section, pages 20–54.

Landiras Graves w r ** (w) 88' 89 90 91 92' Medieval ruin in S GRAVES replanted in '80s by Peter Vinding Diers. 50 acres Sém, 10 red. See also Domaine La Grave.

Lanessan Cussac (H-Méd) r **→*** 78' 79 81 82 83 85 86' 87 88 89 90 91 92 Distinguished 108-acre CRU BOURGEOIS EXCEPTIONNEL just S of ST-JULIEN. Can be classed-growth quality. Fine rather than burly but ages v well. The same family owns Ch'x de Ste-Gemme, Lachesnaye, La Providence.

Langoa-Barton St-Jul r *** 70' 75' 76 78' 79 81 82' 83 85 86' 87 88 89' 90' 91 92 49-acre third growth sister château to LEOVILLE-BARTON. V old family property with impeccable standards, and value. Second wine: Lady Langoa.

Médoc: The Class System

The Médoc has 60 crus classés, ranked in 1855 in five classes. In a separate classification it has 18 Crus Grands Bourgeois Exceptionnels and 41 Crus Grands Bourgeois (which must age their wine in barrels), and 68 Crus Bourgeois. (The terms Grand Bourgeois and Exceptionnel are not acceptable to the EC, and are therefore no longer used on labels.)

Apart from the first growths, the five classes of 1855 are now considerably jumbled in quality, with some second growths at fifth growth level and vice versa. They also overlap in quality with the Crus Exceptionnels. (Besides the official 18, another 13 châteaux are unofficially acknowledged as belonging to this category.) The French are famous for logic.

Larcis-Ducasse St-Em r ** 66 78 81 82' 83 85 86 87 88 89 90 91 92 The top property of St-Laurent, E neighbour of ST-EMILION, on COTES next to CH PAVIE. 30 acres in fine situation. Long-lived wines in keeping.

Larmande St-Em r ** 75' 78 79 81 82 83 85 86 87 88 89 90' Substantial 54-acre property related to CAP-DE-MOURLIN. Replanted, re-equipped and now making rich strikingly scented wine.

Laroque St-Em r ** 75' 78 79 81 82' 83 85 86 88 89 90 91 92 Important 108-acre v'yd on the ST-EMILION COTES in St-Christophe.

Larose-Trintaudon St-Laurent r ** 79 82 83 85 86 87 88 89 90 91 92 The biggest v'yd in the MEDOC: 425 acres. Modern methods make reliable fruity and charming CRU BOURGEOIS wine. New management in '89 and second label Larose St-Laurent.

Laroze St-Em r ** 79 81 82 83 85 86 87 88' 89 90' 91 92 Big v'yd (74 acres) on W COTES. Fine lightish wines from sandy soil; soon enjoyable.

Larrivet-Haut-Brion Graves r (w) ** 75' 76 79' 81 82' 83 85 86 87 88 89 90 91 92 Little property at LEOGNAN with perfectionist standards. Also 500 cases of barrel-fermented white to age up to 10 yrs.

Lascombes Mar r (p) *** 70' 75' 78 79 81 82 83 85 86 87 88' 89 90' 91 92 240-acre second growth owned by British brewers Bass-Charrington, lavishly restored. After a poor patch, new vigour since '82. A second growth needs the severest standards. Second wine: Ch Segonnes.

Latour Pau r **** 61 62 64 66 67 70' 71 73 75' 76 78' 79 80 81 82' 83 84 85 86' 87 88' 89' 90' 91' 92 First growth considered the grandest statement of the MEDOC. Rich, intense and almost immortal wines in great years, nearly always classical and pleasing even in weak ones, from 150 acres sloping to the R Gironde. Some controversy over style in early '80s but Latour always needs time to show its hand. British-owned (though different co since '89). Second wine: LES FORTS DE LATOUR.

Latour-Martillac Graves r w ** (r) 81 82' 83 85' 86 87 88' 89 90 91 92 Small but serious property at Martillac. 10 acres of white grapes; 37 of black. The white can age admirably (85 86 88 89 90 91 92). The owner is resurrecting the neighbouring Ch Lespault.

Latour-à-Pomerol Pom r **** 70' 76' 79' 81' 82 83 85' 86 87 88 89 92 Top growth of 19 acres under MOUEIX management. POMEROL of great power and perfume, yet also ravishing finesse.

des Laurets St-Em r ** 78 79 81 82 83 85 86 88 89' 90' 92 Major property in PUISSEGUIN-ST-EMILION and MONTAGNE-ST-EMILION (to the E) with 160 acres of vineyard on the COTES (producing 40,000 cases). Sterling wines sold by J-P MOUEIX.

Laville-Haut-Brion Graves w **** 79 81 82 83 85' 86 87' 88 89' 90 91 92 A tiny production of one of the v best white GRAVES for long succulent maturing, made at CH LA MISSION-HAUT-BRION.

Léoville-Barton St-Jul r *** 61 66 70' 75' 76 78' 79 80 81 82' 83 84 85 86 87 88 89 90 91 92 90-acre portion of the great second growth Léoville v'yd in Anglo-Irish hands of the Barton family for over 150 years. Powerful classic claret; traditional methods, v fair prices. Major investment is raising already v high standards. See also Langoa-Barton.

Léoville-Las-Cases St-Jul r **** 61 66 70' 75' 76 78' 79 81 82 83 84 85 86 87 88 89' 90' 91 92 The largest portion of the old Léoville estate, adjacent to LATOUR; 210 acres, with one of the highest reputations in Bordeaux. Elegant complex powerful rather austere wines, built for immortality. Second label, CLOS DU MARQUIS, is also outstanding.

Léoville-Poyferré St-Jul r *** 75' 79 81 82 83 84 85 86' 87 88 89 90 91 92 For years the least outstanding of the Léovilles; since '80 again living up to the great name. 156 acres. Second label: Ch Moulin-Riche.

Lestage Listrac r ** 81 82' 83 85 86' 87 88 89 90 91 92 130-acre CRU BOURGEOIS in same hands as CH FONREAUD. Light, quite stylish wine aged in oak since '85. Second wine: Ch Caroline.

Lilian-Ladouys St-Est ** 89 90 Recent creation: a 50-acre CRU BOURGEOIS with high ambitions and real early promise. To watch.

Liot Barsac w sw ** 75' 76 82 83 85 86 88 89' 90' 92 Consistent fairly light golden wines from 50 acres.

Liversan St-Sauveur r ** 81 82' 83 85 86' 87 88 89 90 91 92 116-acre Grand Cru Bourgeois inland from PAUILLAC. Change of regime in '84 greatly improved standards. Second wine: Ch Fonpiqueyre.

Livran Méd r ** 81 82' 83 85 86 88 89 90 91 92 Big CRU BOURGEOIS at St-Germain in the N MEDOC. Consistent round wines (half Merlot).

Loudenne St-Yzans (Méd) r ** 82' 83 85 86' 87' 88 89' 90 91 92 Beautiful riverside château owned by Gilbeys since 1875. Well-made CRU BOURGEOIS red and an increasingly delicious dry white from 120 acres. The white is best at 2–3 yrs (90 91 92').

Loupiac-Gaudiet Loupiac w sw ** 85 86 87 88 89 90 91 92 Reliable source of good value almost-SAUTERNES, just across the R Garonne. 7,500 cases.

La Louvière Graves r w **→*** (r) 81 82' 83 85 86 87 88 89 90 91 92 (w) 86 88 89 90 91 92 Noble 135-acre estate at LEOGNAN restored by the ubiquitous Lurton family (BRANE-CANTENAC etc). Excellent white for drinking or maturing, and red recently of classed-growth standard.

de Lussac St-Em r ** 82 83 85 86 88 89' 90 91 92 One of the best estates in LUSSAC-ST-EMILION (to the NE).

Lynch-Bages Pau r (w) ***→**** 61' 66 70 75' 78' 79 81 82' 83' 84 85' 86' 87 88 89' 90' 91 92 Always popular, but now one of PAUILLAC's regular stars. 200 acres making rich robust wine: deliciously brambly; aspiring to greatness. Esp notable recently. Second wine: HAUT-BAGES-AVEROUS. From '90, a little intense oaky white. The owner, J-M Cazes, also directs PICHON-LONGUEVILLE etc for AXA Insurance.

Lynch-Moussas Pau r ** 81 82 83 85 86 87 88 89 90 91 92 Fifth growth restored by the director of CH BATAILLEY since '69. Now 60+ acres are making serious wine, gaining depth as the young vines age.

du Lyonnat Lussac-St-Em r ** 82 83 85 86' 88 89 90 91 92 120-acre estate with well-distributed reliable wine.

MacCarthy St-Est r ** The second label of CHAMBERT-MARBUZET.

Macquin-St-Georges St-Em r ** 85 86 88 89 90 91 92 Steady producer of delicious 'satellite' ST-EMILION at ST-GEORGES.

Magdelaine St-Em r ★★★ 70' 71' 73 75 76 78 79 81 82 83' 85' 86 88 89 90 92 Leading COTES first growth: 28 acres next to AUSONE owned by J-P MOUEIX. Beautifully balanced full-flavoured wine. Substantial new investment ('92) promises even better things.

Magence Graves r w ★★ Go-ahead 45-acre property in S GRAVES. Sauv-flavoured dry white and fruity red. Both age well 2–6 yrs.

Malartic-Lagravière Graves r (w) ★★★ (r) 70' 75' 78 82' 83 85 86' 87 88 89 90 91 92 (w) 82 83 85 86 87' 88 89 90 91 92 Well-known LEOGNAN classed-growth of 53 acres. Well-structured rather hard red and a v little excellent fruity Sauv white, hard to resist young, but worth cellaring. Bought in '90 by LAURENT-PERRIER.

Malescasse Lamarque (H-Méd) r ★★ 79' 81 82 83 85 86 87 88 89 90 91 92 Renovated CRU BOURGEOIS with 100 acres in good situation. Second label: Le Tana de Malescasse.

Malescot-St-Exupéry Mar r ★★★ 75' 78' 79 81 82' 83' 85 86 87 88 89 90 91 92 Third growth of 84 acres. Often tough when young, eventually fragrant and stylish MARGAUX. New consultant from '90 augurs well.

de Malle Saut w r sw dr ★★★ (w sw) 75 76 78 79 80 81' 82' 83 85 86' 88 89' 90' 91 Beautiful château with Italian gardens at Preignac. 124 acres. Good sweet and dry white and red (GRAVES) DU CARDAILLAN (★★).

de Malleret H-Méd r ★★ 82 83 85 86 88 89' 90 An aristocrat's domaine. The Marquis du Vivier makes 25,000 cases of fine gentlemanly claret at Le Pian, among forests just N of Bordeaux.

de Marbuzet St-Est r ★★ Second label of COS-D'ESTOURNEL: correspondingly good.

Margaux Mar r (w) ★★★★ 61 70 78' 79 80 81' 82' 83' 84 85' 86' 87 88 89' 90' 91 92 First growth (with 209 acres of vines), the most penetrating and fabulously perfumed of all in its (v frequent) best vintages. Pavillon Rouge (81 82' 83 84 85 86 87 88 89 90' 91 92) is the second wine. Pavillon Blanc is the best white (Sauv) wine of the MEDOC (79 80 81 82 83 84 85 86 87 88 89 90 91 92).

Marquis-d'Alesme See d'Alesme.

Marquis-de-Terme Mar r ★★→★★★ 75' 81' 82 83 85 86' 87 88 89 90 91 92 Renovated fourth growth of 84 acres. Fragrant, fairly lean style has developed since '85, with more Cab S.

Martinens Mar r ★★ 81 82 83 85 86 87 88 89 90 91 92 Worthy 75-acre CRU BOURGEOIS at CANTENAC; new barrels since '89.

Maucaillou Moulis r ★★ 75' 78 79 81 82 83' 85' 86' 87 88 89 90 91 92 130-acre CRU BOURGEOIS with CRU CLASSE standards, property of DOURTHE family. Richly fruity Cap de Haut-Maucaillou is second wine.

Mazeyres Pom r ★★ Consistent, useful lesser POMEROL. 5,000 cases.

Méaume Bx Supérieur r ★★ An Englishman's domaine, out of the mainstream, N of POMEROL. Since '80 has built a solid reputation for vg daily claret to age 4–5 yrs. 7,500 cases.

Meyney St-Est r ★★→★★★ 75' 78' 79 81 82' 83 85 86 87 88 89 90 91 92 Big (125-acre) riverside property next door to CH MONTROSE, one of the best of many steady CRUS BOURGEOIS in ST-ESTEPHE. Owned by CORDIER. Second label: Prieur de Meyney.

Millet Graves r w (p) ★★ (r) 82 83 85 86 88 89 90 (w) 91 92 Useful GRAVES. Second label, Ch Renon: mainly white; drink young.

La Mission-Haut-Brion Graves r ★★★★ 61 64 66 71' 74 75' 76 78' 79 80 81 82' 83 84 85' 86 87 88 89' 90' 91 92 Neighbour and long-time rival to CH HAUT-BRION; since '84 in the same hands. New equipment in '87. Serious grand old-style claret for long maturing; 'bigger' wine than Haut-Brion. 30 acres.

Monbousquet St-Em r ★★ 78' 79' 81 82 83 85' 86 88' 89 90 91 92 Attractive early-maturing wine from deep gravel soil: lasts well.

Monbrison Arsac-Mar r ★★ 81 82 83 84 85 86 87 88' 89' 90 91 92 A new name to watch in MARGAUX. Top Bourgeois standards. 4,000 cases plus 2,000 of second label, Ch Cordet.

Montrose St-Est r ★★★ 61 66 70' 75' 76 78' 79 81 82' 83 84 85 86' 87 88 89' 90' 91 92 158-acre family-run second growth well-known for deeply coloured forceful old-style claret. Vintages 79–86 (except 82) were lighter, but recent Montrose is almost ST-ESTEPHE's answer to CH LATOUR. Second wine: La Dame de Montrose.

Moulin du Cadet St-Em ★★ 75' 81 82' 83 85 86 88 89' 90 92 First-class little v'yd on the COTES, owned by MOUEIX.

Moulin-des-Carruades The second-quality wine of CH LAFITE.

Moulin-à-Vent Moulis r ★★ 81 82' 83 85 86 87 88 89 90' 91 92 60-acre property in the forefront of this booming AC. Lively forceful wine. LA TOUR-BLANCHE (MEDOC) has same owners.

Moulinet Pom r ★★★ 75 78 79 81 82 83 85 86 87 88' 89 90 92 One of POMEROL's bigger châteaux, 45 acres on lightish soil; wine lightish also.

Mouton-Baronne-Philippe See d'Armailhac.

Mouton-Rothschild Pau r ★★★★ 61 66 70' 71 75' 76 78' 79 81 82' 83 84 85 86' 87 88 89' 90' 91 92 Officially a first growth since '73, though for 40 yrs worthy of the title. 175 acres (87% Cab S) make majestic rich wine (also, from '91, white Aile d'Argent). Also the world's greatest museum of art relating to wine. Baron Philippe, the greatest champion of the MEDOC, died in '88, to be succeeded by his daughter Philippine. See also Opus One, California.

Nairac Saut w sw ★★ 73 75 76' 78 79 80 81 82 83' 85 86' 88 89 90' Perfectionist BARSAC classed-growth. Wines to lay down for a decade.

Nenin Pom r ★★★ 70' 75' 78 85' 86 87 88' 89 90 Well-known 66-acre estate; on a (v necessary) upswing since '85.

d'Olivier Graves r w ★★ (r) 82 83 85 86 87 88 89' 90' 91 92 (w) 91 92 90-acre classed-growth, surrounding a moated castle at LEOGNAN. 9,000 cases red, 12,000 white. New broom in '89 has upgraded quality drastically.

Les Ormes-de-Pez St-Est r ★★→★★★ 75' 78' 79 81' 82' 83' 84 85 86' 87 88 89' 90' 91 92 Outstanding 72-acre CRU BOURGEOIS owned by CH LYNCH-BAGES. Increasingly notable full-flavoured ST-ESTEPHE.

Les Ormes-Sorbet Méd r ★★ 78 82 83 85 86 87 88 89 90 91 92 Emerging 10,000-case producer of good solid red aged in new oak at Couquèques. A leader of the N MEDOC. Second label: Ch de Conques.

Palmer Cant-Mar r ★★★★ 61' 66' 70 71' 75' 76 78' 79' 81 82 83' 84 85 86' 87 88' 89 90 91 92 The star of CANTENAC: a third growth often of nearly first growth quality. Wine of power flesh delicacy and much Merlot. 110 acres with Dutch, British, French owners. Second wine: Réserve du Général.

Pape-Clément Graves r (w) ★★★ 75' 78' 82 83 85' 86' 87 88' 89' 90' Ancient v'yd at Pessac with record of seductive scented not ponderous reds. Early '80s poor: new resolve (and more white) since '85.

de Parenchère r (w) ★ Steady supply of useful AC Ste-Foy Bordeaux from handsome château with 125 acres.

Patache d'Aux Bégadan (Méd) r ★★ 81 82' 83' 85 86 88 89' 90' 91 92 90-acre CRU BOURGEOIS of the N MEDOC. Fragrant largely Cab wine with the earthy quality of its area.

Paveil (de Luze) Mar r ★★ 81 82' 83' 85 86' 87 88 89' 90' 91 92 Old family estate at SOUSSANS. Small but highly regarded.

Pavie St-Em r ★★★ 75' 78 79' 81 82' 83' 84 85 86' 87 88 89' 90' Splendidly-sited first growth; 92 acres mid-slope on the COTES. Rich and tasty and on top form since '82. PAVIE-DECESSE and La Clusière in same family.

Pavie-Decesse St-Em r ★★ 24 acres challenging their big brother (above).

Pavie-Macquin St-Em r ★★ 82 83 85' 86 87 88 89 90 91 92 Reliable 25-acre COTES v'yd E of ST-EMILION. Organic winemaking. Second label: Les Chênes.

Pavillon Rouge (Blanc) du Château Margaux See Ch Margaux.

Pedesclaux Pau r ★★ 75 78 79 81 82' 83 85 86 87 88 89 90' 91 92 50-acre fifth growth on the level of a good CRU BOURGEOIS. Solid strong wines that Belgians love. Second labels: Bellerose, Grand-Duroc-Milon.

Petit-Village Pom r ★★★ 75' 78 79 81 82' 83 85 86 88 89' 90' 91 92 Top property revived. 26 acres next to VIEUX CHATEAU CERTAN, same owner (AXA) as CH PICHON-LONGUEVILLE since '89. Powerful plummy wine.

Pétrus Pom r ★★★★ 61 64 66 67 70' 71' 73 75' 76' 78 79' 80 81 82' 83 84 85' 86 88' 89' 90 92 The great name of POMEROL. 28 acres of gravelly clay giving massively rich and concentrated wine. 95% Merlot vines. Each vintage adds lustre (NB no 91). The price too is legendary.

Peyrabon St-Sauveur r ★★ 81 82 83 85 86 87 88 89 90 91 92 Serious 132-acre CRU BOURGEOIS popular in the Low Countries. Also La Fleur-Peyrabon (only 12 acres).

Peyreau St-Em r ★★ Sister château of Clos l'Oratoire.

Peyre-Labade Listrac ★★ Second label of CH CLARKE.

de Pez St-Est r ★★★ 70' 75' 76 78' 79 81 82' 83 85 86' 87 88 89 90 91 92 Outstanding CRU BOURGEOIS of 60 acres. As reliable as any of the classed-growths of the village and nearly as fine.

Phélan-Ségur St-Est r ★★ 75' 81 82' 85 86 87 88 89 90 91 92 Big and important CRU BOURGEOIS (125 acres): some fine old vintages. 83, 84 were faulty and had to be withdrawn, but from '86 things have gone well.

Pibran Pau r ★★ 89 90 91 92 Small CRU BOURGEOIS allied to PICHON-LONGUEVILLE. V classy wine with real PAUILLAC drive.

Pichon-Lalande (formerly Pichon-Longueville, Comtesse de Lalande) Pau r ★★★★ 61 66 70' 75' 76 78' 79' 81 82' 83' 84 85' 86' 87 88 89' 90' 91 92 Second growth neighbour to CH LATOUR. 148 acres. Consistently among the v top performers; long-lived wine of fabulous breed for those who like it luscious, even in lesser yrs. Second wine: Réserve de la Comtesse. Rivalry across the road (next entry) is worth watching.

Pichon-Longueville (formerly Baron de Pichon-Longueville) Pau r ★★★ 78 79' 81 82' 83 85 86' 87 88' 89' 90' 91 92 77-acre second growth whose wines have varied widely. Since '87 owned by AXA Insurance, run by J-M Cazes (LYNCH-BAGES). Revitalized winemaking matches spectacular building programme. Second label: Les Tourelles de Longueville.

Le Pin Pom r ★★★ 90' A mere 500 cases of Merlot, with same owners as VIEUX CHATEAU CERTAN. A perfectionist miniature.

Pindefleurs St-Em r ★★ 79 81 82' 83 85 86 88 89 90 92 Steady 23-acre v'yd on light soil. Second label: Clos Lescure.

St-Emilion: the class system
St-Emilion has its own class system, revised in 1985. At the top are 2 Premiers Grands Crus Classés 'A': Châteaux Ausone and Cheval Blanc. Then come 9 Premiers Grands Crus Classés 'B'. 63 châteaux were elected as Grands Crus Classés (seeking re-election in 1994). Another 170-odd are classed simply as Grands Crus, a rank renewable each year after official tastings. St-Emilion Grand Cru is therefore the very approximate equivalent of Médoc Crus Bourgeois and Grand Bourgeois.

Pique-Caillou Graves r ★★ 85 86 87 88 89 90 91 92 Nr Bordeaux airport. Refurbished; delicate charming wine. Also next-door Ch Chênevert.

Piron Graves w (r) ★★ Seductively fruity white.

de Pitray Castillon r ★★ 82 83 85 86 87 88 89 90 91 92 Large (62-acre) v'yd on COTES DE CASTILLON E of ST-EMILION. Good flavoursome chewy wines.

Plagnac Méd r ★★ 81 82 83 85 86 88 89 90 91 92 CRU BOURGEOIS at BEGADAN restored by CORDIER. To follow.

Plince Pom r ★★ 75 79 81 82 83 85 86 88 89 90 92 Reputable 20-acre property nr Libourne. Attractive lightish wine from sandy soil.

La Pointe Pom r ★★→★★★ 81 82 83' 85 86 87 88 89' 90' 92 Prominent 63-acre estate, well-made, but relatively spare of flesh until new consultant in '86. 89 is terrific. LA SERRE is in the same hands.

Pontac-Monplaisir Graves r (w) ★★ 87 89 90 91 92 Another GRAVES property offering delicious white and fragrant red.

Pontet-Canet Pau r ★★★ **70 75' 78' 79' 81' 82' 83 85 86 87 88 89 90 91 92** 182-acre neighbour to MOUTON-R. Dragged its feet for many yrs. Owners (same as LAFON-ROCHET) have shown new resolve since '85. Should make potent long-lived wines. Second label: Les Hauts de Pontet.

Pontoise-Cabarrus H-Méd r ★★ Useful and improving 60-acre CRU BOURGEOIS at ST-SEURIN. Wines need 5–6 yrs.

Potensac Méd r ★★ **78' 79 81' 82' 83 85' 86 87 88 89' 90' 91 92** The best-known CRU BOURGEOIS of the N MEDOC. The neighbouring châteaux Lassalle and Gallais-Bellevue belong to the same family, the Delons, owners of LEOVILLE-LAS-CASES. Class shows.

Pouget Mar ★★ **78 79 81 82' 83 85 86 87 88 89 90** 19-acre v'yd attached to BOYD-CANTENAC. Same owners since 1906. Similar, rather lighter wines.

Poujeaux (Theil) Moulis r ★★ **70' 75' 76 78 79' 81 82' 83' 85' 86 87 88 89' 90' 91 92** Family-run CRU EXCEPTIONNEL of 120 acres. 20,000-odd cases of characterful tannic and concentrated wine for a long life. Second label: La Salle de Poujeaux. Also Ch Arnauld.

Prieuré-Lichine Cant-Mar r ★★★ **70 75 78' 81 82' 83' 85 86' 87 88 89' 90 91 92** 143-acre fourth growth brought to the fore by the late Alexis Lichine. Excellent full-bodied and fragrant MARGAUX.

Puy-Blanquet St-Em r ★★ **75' 81 82' 83 85 86 88 89' 90** The major property of St-Etienne-de-Lisse, E of ST-EMILION, with over 50 acres. Early-maturing St-Em in early '80s; now firming up well.

Puygueraud Côte de Francs r ★★ **85 86 88 89' 90 92** Leading château of this rising district. Wood-aged wines of surprising class. Ch Laclaverie and Les Charmes-Godard follow the same lines.

Rabaud-Promis Saut w sw ★★ **75 76 79 81 83' 85 86 88' 89 90** 74-acre classed-growth at Bommes. To follow since '85.

Rahoul Graves r w ★★ **(r) 78' 81 82 83 85 86 87 88 89 90' 91 92 (w) 86' 88 89' 90' 91 92** 37-acre v'yd at Portets making particularly good wine in the '80s from maturing vines; 80% red. White also oak-aged.

Ramage-la-Bâtisse H-Méd r ★★ **82 83' 85 86 88 89' 90 91 92** Potentially outstanding CRU BOURGEOIS of 130 acres at ST-SAUVEUR, N of PAUILLAC. Increasingly good since '85. Ch Tourteran is second wine.

Rausan-Ségla Mar r ★★★ **70' 81 82 83' 84 85 86' 88' 89' 90' 91 92** 106-acre second growth famous for its fragrance; a great MEDOC name trying hard to regain its rank since '82. New British owners (and splendid wine) in '89. Second wine: Ségla.

Rauzan-Gassies Mar r ★★ **61 75' 78' 79' 82 83 85 86 88 89 90 91 92** 75-acre second-growth neighbour of the last with little excitement to report for two decades, now perking up – but still far to go.

Raymond-Lafon Saut w sw ★★★ **75 76 78' 79 80' 81' 82 83' 85 86 87 88 89 90 91 92** Serious SAUTERNES estate of 44 acres run by the ex-manager of YQUEM. Splendid wines for long ageing. Among the top Sauternes.

de Rayne-Vigneau Saut w sw ★★★ **76' 83 85 86' 88 89 90' 91 92** 164-acre classed-growth at Bommes. Standard sweet wine and dry Rayne Sec.

Respide-Médeville Graves w (r) ★★ **(w) 86 87 88 89 90 91 92'** One of the better unclassified white wine châteaux. Full-flavoured wines for ageing. (NB 85 Cuvée Kauffman.) Drink the reds at 2–4 yrs.

Reynon Premières Côtes r w ★★ 100 acres producing fragrant white from old Sauv vines (VIEILLES VIGNES). Also CLOS FLORIDENE barrel-fermented white and red since '85. DYA white and serious red (**85 86 88' 89 90 91 92**). Second wine (red): Ch Reynon-Peyrat.

Reysson Vertheuil (H-Méd) r ★★ **82' 83 85 86 87 88 89 90** Recently replanted 120-acre CRU BOURGEOIS in Japanese hands.

Ricaud Loupiac w sw (r dr) ★★ **(w) 81 82 83' 85 86' 88 89 90 91 92** Substantial grower of almost SAUTERNES-like wine just across the river. New owners are working hard. It ages well.

For key to grape variety abbreviations, see pages 6–9.

Rieussec Saut w sw ★★★ 71' 75' 80 81 82 83' 85 86' 87 88' 89' 90' 91 92 Worthy neighbour of CH D'YQUEM with 136 acres in Fargues, bought in '84 by the (Lafite) Rothschilds. Not the sweetest; can be exquisitely fine. Also dry 'R' and super-wine Crème de Tête.

Ripeau St-Em r ★★ 81 82 83 85 86 87 88 89 90 Steady GRAND CRU in the centre of the plateau. 40 acres.

La Rivière Fronsac r ★★ 85' 86 87 88' 89 90 The biggest and most impressive FRONSAC property. Tannic but juicy wines win prizes in youth and stay young for a decade.

de Rochemorin Graves r (w) ★★ 82 83 85 86 87 88 89 90 91 92 An important restoration at Martillac by CH LA LOUVIERE's owner: 165 acres of maturing vines promise great things. Oaky whites to keep 4–5 yrs.

Romer-du-Hayot Saut w sw ★★ 81 82 83 85 86' 88 89 90 Classed-growth with a growing reputation. La Guiteronde (BARSAC) is sister château.

de Roquetaillade-la-Grange Graves r w ★★ 89 90 91 92 Substantial estate establishing a name for fine red (S) GRAVES.

Roudier Montagne-St-Em r ★★ 75-acre 'satellite': classic ST-EMILION flavour.

Rouget Pom r ★★ 75' 76' 78 79 81 82' 83 85' 86 88 89 90 Attractive old estate on the N edge of POMEROL. Good without polish; needs age.

Royal St-Emilion Brand name of the important and dynamic growers' coop. See also Berliquet, Haut-Quercus.

Ruat-Petit-Poujeaux Moulis r ★★ 82 85 86 88 89 90 91 92 45-acre v'yd gaining in reputation for vigorous wine, to drink in 5–6 yrs.

St-André-Corbin St-Em r ★★ 79' 81 82' 83 85' 86 88 89 90 92 54-acre estate in MONTAGNE- and ST-GEORGES-ST-EM: long record of above average wines.

St-Bonnet Méd r ★★ 81 82 83 85 86 89 90 91 92 Big N MEDOC estate at St-Christoly. V flavoury wine.

St-Estèphe, Marquis de St-Est r ★ 82 86 88 89 90 The growers' coop; bigger but not as interesting as formerly.

St-Georges St-Georges-St-Em r ★★ 82 85' 86 87 88 89' 90 92 Noble 18th-C château overlooking the ST-EMILION plateau from the hill to the N. 125 acres; vg wine sold direct to the public.

St-Georges-Côte-Pavie St-Em r ★★ 81 82 83' 85' 86 88 89' 90' 92 Perfectly placed little v'yd on the COTES. Run with dedication (and served by Air France First Class).

St-Pierre St-Jul r ★★★ 70' 78' 81' 82' 83' 85 86' 87 88 89 90 Small (42-acre) fourth growth bought in '82 by the late Henri Martin of CH GLORIA. V stylish and consistent classic ST-JULIEN.

de St-Pierre Graves w (r) ★★ Main-line white of notable character and flavour to drink young or keep. Also red.

de Sales Pom r ★★★ 75' 81 82' 83 85 86 88 89 90 92 Biggest v'yd of POMEROL (116 acres), attached to grandest château. Not often poetry, but at least lucid prose. Second labels: Ch'x Chantalouette, du Delias.

Saransot-Dupré Listrac r (w) ★★ 86 88 89 90 Small property performing well since '86. Also LISTRAC's only (?) white.

Sénéjac H-Méd r (w) ★★ 78 79 81 82' 83' 85 86' 87 88 89 90' 91 92 60-acre CRU BOURGEOIS in S MEDOC run with zeal by a New Zealander. All-Sém white to age (89 90 91 92). Second label: Domaine de l'Artigue.

La Serre St-Em r ★★ 81 82 83 85 86 88' 89 90 Small GRAND CRU, same owner as LA POINTE. Reliably tasty.

Siaurac Lalande de Pom r ★★ Substantial, consistent; nr POMEROL. 57 acres.

Sigalas-Rabaud Saut w sw ★★★ 75 76' 78 79 80 82 83' 85 86 87 88' 89' 90' 91 92 The smaller part of the former Rabaud estate: 34 acres in Bommes making first-class sweet wine in a fresh grapey style.

Siran Labarde-Mar r ★★ 61 66 70 75' 78' 79 81 82' 83 85 86 88 89 90 74-acre property approaching CRU CLASSE quality.

Smith-Haut-Lafitte Graves r (w) ★★ (r) 82' 85 86 88 89 90 91 92 (w, age 2–3 yrs) Classed-growth at Martillac: 122 acres (14 of white). New British owners (same as RAUSAN-SEGLA) in '89. Formerly light wines now more concentrated. Second label: Les Hauts de Smith.

Sociando-Mallet H-Méd r ★★ 70 75 78 79 81 82 83 85 86 88 89 90 91 92 Splendid CRU GRAND BOURGEOIS at ST-SEURIN in the north. 65 acres. Conservative big-boned wines to lay down for years.

Soudars H-Méd r ★★ Sister to COUFRAN; new CRU BOURGEOIS doing v well.

Soutard St-Em r ★★→★★★ 70' 71 75' 76 78' 79 81 82' 83 85' 86 87 88' 89 90 91 92 Excellent reliable 48-acre classed-growth. Potent; long-lived.

Suduiraut Saut w sw ★★★ 67 70 76' 78 79' 81 82' 83' 84 85 86 88' 89 90' One of the best SAUTERNES – though now rarely super-rich. Over 173 acres potentially of the top class. Selection: Cuvée Madame (82 83 86).

du Tailhas Pom r ★★ 5,000 cases. POMEROL of the lighter kind, near FIGEAC.

Taillefer Pom r ★★ 81 82 83 85 86 88' 89 90 92 45-acre property on the edge of POMEROL owned by the Armand Moueix family (see also Fonplégade). 10 yrs is plenty.

Talbot St-Jul r (w) ★★★ 70' 75' 78' 79 81 82' 83 85 86' 87 88' 89 90 91 92 Important 240-acre fourth growth, sister to GRUAUD-LAROSE. Wine similarly attractive: rich, satisfying, reliable and gd value. Vg second label: Connétable Talbot. White is 'Caillou Blanc'.

Tayac Soussans-Mar r ★★ 81 82 83 85 86 87 88 89 90 MARGAUX's biggest CRU BOURGEOIS. Reliable if not noteworthy.

de Terrefort-Quancard Bx r w ★★ Huge producer of good value wines at ST-ANDRE-DE-CUBZAC on the road to Paris. Rocky subsoil contributes to surprising quality. 33,000 cases. Drink at 2–5 yrs.

Terrey-Gros-Caillou St-Jul ★★ 79 82 83 85 86' 87 88 89' 90 91 92 Sister-château to HORTEVIE; equally noteworthy and stylish.

du Tertre Arsac-Mar r ★★★ 70' 75 79' 81 82' 83' 85 86 87 88' 89' 90 91 92 Fifth growth isolated S of MARGAUX; restored to excellence by the owner of CALON-SEGUR. Fragrant and long-lived.

Tertre-Daugay St-Em r ★★★ 78 79 81 82' 83' 85 86 87 88 89 90 92 Small, spectacularly sited GRAND CRU. Restored to its proper rank and quality since '78 by the owner of LA GAFFELIERE.

Le Tertre-Rôteboeuf St-Em ★★→★★★ 85 86 87 88 89 90 A new star making concentrated, even dramatic, largely Merlot wine since '83. The 'roast beef' of the name gives the idea.

Thieuley E-Deux-Mers r p w ★★ 85 86 88 89 90 Substantial supplier esp of clairet (rosé) and grapey Sauv. But reds are aged in oak.

Timberlay Bx r (w) ★ 185 acres at ST-ANDRE-DE-CUBZAC. Pleasant light wines to age 2–5 yrs.

Toumilon Graves r w ★★ Little château in St-Pierre-de-Mons to note. Fresh and charming red and white.

La Tour-Blanche Saut w (r) sw ★★★ 76 81' 82 83' 85 86 87 88 89' 90 91 Historic leader of SAUTERNES, now a government wine college. Coasted in '70s; now closer to its (very) high rank.

La Tour-de-By Bégadan (Méd) r ★★ 79' 81 82' 83 85' 86 87 88' 89' 90' 91 92 V well-run 144-acre CRU BOURGEOIS in N MEDOC steadily increasing its reputation for sturdy, impressive yet instantly appealing wine.

La Tour-Carnet St-Laurent r ★★ 79 81 82' 83 85 86 87 88 89' 90 91 92 Fourth growth with medieval fortress, reborn after total neglect. Lightish wine (much bolder since '86). Second wine: Sire de Comin.

La Tour-Figeac St-Em r ★★ 79 81 82' 83 85 86 88 89 90 34-acre GRAND CRU between CH FIGEAC and POMEROL. Wines worthy of the site.

La Tour-Haut-Brion Graves r ★★★ 70 78 79 81 82' 83 85 86 87 88 89 90 91 92 Formerly second label of CH LA MISSION-HAUT-BRION. Up to '83 a plainer, v tannic wine for long life. Now a separate v'yd: easier wines.

La Tour-Haut-Caussan Méd r ★★ Ambitious small (23-acre) estate at Blaignan attracting admiration.

La Tour-du-Haut-Moulin Cussac (H-Méd) r ★★ 81 82 83 85 86 87 88 89 90 91 Conservative producer of intense wines among v top CRUS BOURGEOIS.

La Tour-de-Mons Soussans-Mar r ★★ 70' 75' 78 81 82' 83 85 86' 87 88' 89' 90' 91 92 Distinguished CRU BOURGEOIS of 87 acres, 3 centuries in the same family. After a dull patch, back to CRU CLASSE form.

Tour du Pas St-Georges St-Em r ** Wine from 40 acres of ST-GEORGES-ST-EMILION made by AUSONE winemaker. V stylish; to follow.

La Tour-du-Pin-Figeac St-Em r ** 26-acre GRAND CRU worthy of restoration.

La Tour-du-Pin-Figeac-Moueix St-Em r ** 81 82 83 85 86 88' 89 90 92 Another 26-acre section of the same old property, owned by the Armand Moueix family. Splendid site; powerful wines.

La Tour-St-Bonnet Méd r ** 81 82' 83 85 86 87 88 89 90 91 92 Consistently well-made N MEDOC from St-Christoly. 100 acres.

Tournefeuille Lalande de Pom r ** 81' 82' 83' 85 86 88 89 90' 91 92 Best-known château of NEAC. 43 acres making v sound wine.

des Tours Montagne-St-Em r ** 82 83 85 86 88 89 90 Spectacular château with modern 170-acre v'yd. Sound easy wine.

Toutigeac, Domaine de E-Deux-Mers r (w) * 89 90 (w) 91 92 Enormous producer of useful Bordeaux at Targon.

Tronquoy-Lalande St-Est r ** 70 75 78 79 81 82' 83 85 86 88 89 90 40-acre CRU BOURGEOIS making typical high-coloured ST-ESTEPHE needing long ageing. Distributed by DOURTHE.

Troplong-Mondot St-Em r **→*** 82' 83 85' 86 87 88' 89' 90 70 acres well-sited on the COTES above CH PAVIE (and with the same owners). To follow, esp since '86. Second wine: Mondot.

Trotanoy Pom r **** 61' 70' 71' 73 75' 76' 78 79 81 82 83 84 85' 86 87 88 89 90 92 Usually the second POMEROL, after PETRUS, from the same stable. Only 27 acres; but a glorious fleshy perfumed wine.

Trottevieille St-Em r *** 79' 81 82' 83 85' 86 87 88 89 90 GRAND CRU of 27 acres on the COTES. Dragged its feet for yrs. Same owners as BATAILLEY have raised their sights since '85. To watch.

Le Tuquet Graves r w ** Big estate at Beautiran. Light fruity wines; the white better.

Verdignan Méd r ** 81 82 83 85 86 87 88 89' 90 91 92 Substantial Bourgeois sister to CH COUFRAN. More Cab than Coufran.

Vieux Château Certan Pom r *** 71 75 78 79 81 82' 83 85 86' 87 88' 89 90 92 Traditionally rated close to PETRUS in quality, but totally different in style; almost HAUT-BRION build. 34 acres. Same (Belgian) family owns LABEGORCE-ZEDE and tiny POMEROL, Le Pin. See also Puygueraud.

Vieux-Château-St-André St-Em r ** 79' 81 82' 83 85' 86 87 88' 89 90 91 92 Small v'yd in MONTAGNE-ST-EMILION owned by the leading wine-maker of Libourne. To follow. 2,500 cases.

Villegeorge Avensan r ** 81 82 83' 85 86 87' 88 89 90 24-acre CRU BOURGEOIS to the N of MARGAUX; same owner as BRANE-CANTENAC. Enjoyable rather tannic wine. Sister château: Duplessis (Hauchecorne).

Villemaurine St-Em r ** 82' 83 85' 86 88 89 90 91 92 Small GRAND CRU with splendid cellars well-sited on the COTES by the town. Firm wine with a high proportion of Cab.

Vray-Croix-de-Gay Pom *** 75' 81 82' 83 85 86 87 88 89 90 92 V small ideally situated v'yd in the best part of POMEROL. Rich slow wines.

Yon-Figeac St-Em r ** 81 82 83 85 86 88 89 90 59-acre GRAND CRU to follow for savoury and scented wine.

d'Yquem Saut w sw (dr) **** 67' 71' 73 75' 76' 77 78 79 80 81 82 83' 84 85 86' 87 88' 89' (90' 91 to come) The world's most famous sweet-wine estate. 250 acres making only 500 bottles per acre of v strong intense luscious wine, kept 4 yrs in barrel. Most vintages improve for at least 15 yrs. Also dry Ygrec ('Y') in 78 79 80 84 85 (86 v little) 87 88.

More Bordeaux châteaux are listed under Canon-Fronsac, Côtes de Bourg, Côtes-de-Castillon, Côtes de France, Fronsac, Lalande de Pomerol, Loupiac, Premières Côtes de Blaye, Premières Côtes de Bordeaux, St-André-de-Cubzac, Ste-Croix-du-Mont in the A–Z of France, pages 20–54.

Italy

1992 may prove to have been the turning point in the reputation and fortunes of the Italian wine industry, whose genial chaos has always tended to mask its real values and qualities. January 23 that year saw the enactment of a completely revised version of the seriously discredited DOC legislation, which for 30 years has caused confusion among consumers and militated against both quality and innovation.

'Law 164' is intended to end all the old anomalies, but especially that by which a vino da tavola, officially the lowest grade of wine classification, was frequently a much better (and more expensive) wine than one made within the statutory requirements of a DOC – or even a DOCG, formerly the most elevated appellation available (see page 83).

Eventually (though this may take many years) the new laws will bring Italian appellations very close in spirit to those of France, where all the stress is on geography. They are also intended (like the French laws) to discourage the marketing of high quality wines simply by grape variety name.

Law 164 is most graphically represented by a pyramid, whose base is the humble vino da tavola. No geographical (or varietal) claims can be made at this level: only a brand name. The next level is a new institution, intended to mirror the French vin de pays and known as IGT (Indicazione Geografica Tipica). IGTs can use the geographical name and the grape name (strictly in that order). The principal is that 'varietal' identification must remain secondary to geographical. Above the IGT come the DOC and DOCG. In these bands the label can carry information as specific as a single vineyard (vigna) name – but only by sacrificing quantity for quality.

Thus the highest rank in the pyramid will be a vigna wine from within a DOCG zone. But whereas the rank of DOCG was formerly limited to a dozen famous areas, it will now become the right of any DOC which has performed well enough for five years. Conversely a DOC which functions poorly will lose its rank (some 50 are already threatened). Even more radically, an outstanding proprietorial wine 'which does honour to Italy' may be eligible for its own DOCG.

A distinct advantage of the pyramid system is that producers in a DOC zone can decide at vintage time how high they are going to pitch their wine. Self-discipline can give them the right to the top appellation; high yields and lower concentration will automatically demote them down the pyramid.

There is very much more detail to the new Law, and much that only experience will finally determine, but it is a convincingly bold attempt to sort out the minestrone of the old system. No doubt the German government will pay due heed.

Meanwhile, as always, the best advice is to be bold. Do not cling limply to familiar names: look for distinctive labels on distinctive bottles. But be prepared to pay more for quality.

The following abbreviations are used in the text:

Ab	Abruzzi	**F-VG**	Friuli-Venezia Giulia	**Sar**	Sardinia
Ap	Apulia	**Lat**	Latium	**Si**	Sicily
Bas	Basilicata	**Lig**	Liguria	**T-AA**	Trentino-Alto Adige
Cal	Calabria	**Lom**	Lombardy	**Tus**	Tuscany
Cam	Campania	**Mar**	Marches	**Umb**	Umbria
E-R	Emilia-Romagna	**Pie**	Piedmont	**VdA**	Valle d'Aosta
				Ven	Veneto
				fz	frizzante
				pa	passito

Abbazia di Rosazzo A leading estate of COLLI ORIENTALI. White Ronco delle Acacie and di Corte and red dei Roseti are vg single-v'yd wines.

Abboccato Semi-sweet.

Adanti Umbrian maker of good red SAGRANTINO DI MONTEFALCO, VDT BIANCO D'ARQUATA and Rosso d'Arquata (a vg BARBERA-Canaiolo-MERLOT blend). Also good CAB S. Value.

Aglianico del Vulture Bas DOC r dr (s/sw sp) *** **82 85 86 87** 88 90 91 92 Among the best wines of S Italy. Ages well to rich aromas. Called vecchio after 3 yrs, RISERVA after 5. Top growers: Fratelli D'Angelo (also makes vg pure Aglianico VDT Canneto), Paternoster.

Alba Major wine centre of PIEDMONT, on R Tanaro, S of Turin.

Albana di Romagna E-R DOCG w dr s/sw (sp) **(*) DYA Italy's first DOCG for white wine, though it is hard to see why. Albana is the grape. Cold fermentation now robs it of what little character it had. FATTORIA PARADISO makes some of the best. AMABILE is often better than dry. FATTORIA ZERBINA's botrytis-sweet PASSITO is outstanding.

Alcamo Si DOC w * Soft neutral whites. Rapitalà is the best brand.

Aleatico Excellent red Muscat-flavoured grape, chiefly of the south.

Aleatico di Gradoli Lat DOC r sw fz ** Aromatic fruity; alcohol 17.5%. Made nr Viterbo N of Rome.

Aleatico di Puglia Ap DOC r sw fz ** ALEATICO grapes make a little good dessert wine. 2 distinct types: 15% or 18.5% alcohol.

Alezio Ap DOC p (r) ** 89 90 91 92 Recent DOC at Salento, esp for delicate rosé. Top grower: Caló.

Allegrini Top quality producer of Veronese wines, incl fine VALPOLICELLA from prime new v'yds and vg AMARONE. NB **90**.

Altare Reputed small producer of BAROLO and BARBERA VDT Vigna Larigi.

Altesino Highly regarded estate producing BRUNELLO DI MONTALCINO and VDT Palazzo Altesi.

Alto Adige T-AA DOC r p w dr sw sp *→*** DOC covering 20 different wines, usually named after their grape varieties, in 33 villages around Bolzano. The best are white. This largely German-speaking region is often called Südtirol.

Ama, Castello di Modern CHIANTI CLASSICO estate nr Gaiole. San Lorenzo, Bertinga, La Casuccia and Bellavista are excellent top wines. Vg CHARD, SAUV, MERLOT (Vigna L'Apparita).

Amabile Semi-sweet, but usually sweeter than ABBOCCATO.

Amaro Bitter. When prominent on a label the content is not wine but 'bitters'.

Amarone High-octane version of VALPOLICELLA; potent dry impressive and long-lived. See also Recioto.

Anghelu Ruju Port-like version of Sardinian CANNONAU from SELLA & MOSCA.

Anselmi, Roberto A leader in SOAVE with his single-v'yd Capitel Foscarino and exceptional sweet dessert RECIOTO dei Capitelli.

Antinori, Marchesi L & P Immensely influential long-established Tuscan house of the highest repute producing first-rate CHIANTI (esp PEPPOLI, Tenute Marchese Antinori and Badia a Passignano) and ORVIETO. Distinguished for pioneering new VDT styles, eg TIGNANELLO, SOLAIA, CERVARO DELLA SALA. The Marchese Piero A could be called the Voice of Italy in world wine circles. See also Prunotto.

Aquileia F-VG DOC r w ** 88 89 **90** 91 92 12 single-grape wines from around town of Aquileia on border of Slovenia. Good REFOSCO.

Argusto Oak-aged DOLCETTO from BANFI.

Arneis Pie w **→*** DYA At last a white worthy of BAROLO country. A revival of an ancient grape to make fragrant light wine. Now DOC under Roero, a zone N of Alba. Good producers incl Ceretto (Blangé), BRUNO GIACOSA, Angelo Negri, VIETTI.

Artimino Ancient hill-town W of Florence, known for its DOCG CARMIGNANO.

Assisi Umb r (w) ** DYA Rosso and Bianco di Assisi are v attractive VDT. Drink cool.

Asti Major wine centre of PIEDMONT.

Asti Spumante Pie DOC w sp ** NV Immensely popular sweet and v fruity Muscat sparkling wine. V low in alcohol.

Attems, Conti Famous old COLLIO estate with range of good typical wines (esp PINOT GRIGIO) now run by COLLAVINI.

Avignonesi MONTEPULCIANO house with range of good wines incl VINO NOBILE, blended red Grifi, first-rate CHARD, SAUV, MERLOT and superlative VIN SANTO.

Azienda agricola/agraria A farm producing crops, often incl wine.

Azienda/casa vinicola Wine firm using bought-in grapes and/or wines.

Azienda vitivinicola A (specialized) wine estate.

Badia a Coltibuono *** Fine CHIANTI-maker in an old abbey at Gaiole with a restaurant and collection of old vintages. Also produces VDT SANGIOVETO (82 83 85 86 88 90).

Banfi (Castello or Villa) The production department of the biggest US importer of Italian wine. Huge plantings at MONTALCINO, incl Syrah, PINOT N, CAB, CHARD, etc, are part of a drive for quality plus quantity. BRUNELLO is proving excellent. Centine is ROSSO DI MONTALCINO. In PIEDMONT Banfi produces vg sparkling Banfi Brut, Principessa GAVI, BRACCHETO D'ACQUI, PINOT GR.

Barbacarlo Lom r dr sw sp ** 88 89 90 91 92 Delicate wines with typical bitter-almond taste, from OLTREPO PAVESE.

Barbaresco Pie DOCG r ***→**** 85 86 87 88 89 90 Neighbour of BAROLO from the same grapes. Perhaps marginally less sturdy. At best palate-cleansing, deep, subtle and fine. At 4 yrs becomes RISERVA. Producers incl CERETTO, GAJA, BRUNO GIACOSA, Marchesi di Gresy, Nada, Pelissero, Produttori del B, PRUNOTTO, Alfredo Roagna, Bruno Rocca.

Barbera Dark acidic red grape, the second most planted in Italy after SANGIOVESE; a speciality of PIEDMONT also used in Lombardy, Emilia-Romagna and other northern provinces. Its best wines follow

Barbera d'Alba Pie DOC r **→*** 85 86 87 88 89 90 91 92 Tasty tannic fragrant red. SUPERIORE can age 7 yrs or more. Round ALBA, NEBBIOLO is sometimes added to make a VDT (some barrique-aged 100% BARBERA is also vdt). Top producers incl A CONTERNO, GAJA, Grasso, PRUNOTTO, G MASCARELLO, Scavino, VIETTI, VOERZIO.

Barbera d'Asti Pie DOC r **→*** 85 86 87 88 89 90 91 92 For real BARBERA-lovers: solely Barbera grapes, tangy and appetizing, drunk young or aged up to 7 yrs. Top growers incl La Barbatella, Bertelli, Boffa, Braida, Brema, Cascina Castle't, Chiarlo, Coppo, Scarpa, Trinchero, Viarengo.

Barbera del Monferrato Pie DOC r *→** 88 89 90 91 92 Easy-drinking Barbera from a large area in the province of Alessandria and ASTI. Pleasant, slightly fizzy, sometimes sweetish.

Barberani Leading ORVIETO producer; Calcaia is sweet, botrytis-affected.

Barco Reale Tus DOC r ** DOC for junior wine of CARMIGNANO; same grapes.

Bardolino Ven DOC r (p) ** DYA Pale light slightly bitter red from E shore of Lake Garda. Bardolino CHIARETTO is even paler and lighter. Top makers: GUERRIERI-RIZZARDI, Fratelli Zeni.

Barolo Pie DOCG r ***→**** 79 82 85' 86 88 89 90 Small area S of ALBA with one of the highest-rated Italian red wines; rich tannic alcoholic (min 13°) dry but deep in flavour. From NEBBIOLO grapes. Ages for up to 15 yrs (RISERVA after 5). Best producers incl ALTARE, CERETTO, Clerico, CONTERNO, CORDERO, GIACOSA, Elio Grasso, Giovanni Manzone, Marcarini, MASCARELLO, PIO CESARE, PRUNOTTO, RATTI, Rinaldi, ROCCHE DEI MANZONI, Sandrone, Scavino, VIETTI, VOERZIO.

Bava ASTI firm with well-presented range of sound PIEDMONT wines.

Bellavista FRANCIACORTA estate rivalling CA'DEL BOSCO for brisk subtle sparkling. Also notable Crémant. Good VDT reds from CAB and PINOT N.

Berlucchi, Guido Italy's biggest producer of sparkling METODO CLASSICO, at FRANCIACORTA. Steady quality.

Bertani Well-known producers of quality Veronese wines (SOAVE, VALPANTENA, VALPOLICELLA, etc) incl aged AMARONE and white VDT Catullo.

Bianco White.

Bianco d'Arquata Umb w ★★ 89 90 91 92 See Adanti.

Bianco di Custoza Ven DOC w (sp) ★★ DYA Twin of SOAVE from W of Verona; often beats it in quality.

Bianco di Pitigliano Tus DOC w ★ DYA Soft fruity lively wine from nr Grosseto.

Bianco Vergine della Valdichiana Tus DOC w ★ DYA Pale dry light wine from Arezzo. But what music in the name.

Biancolella Ischia's best white. A VDT from D'AMBRA.

Bigi, Luigi & Figlio Famous producers of ORVIETO and other wines of Umbria and Tuscany. Their TORRICELLA v'yd produces vg dry Orvieto.

Biondi-Santi The original producer of BRUNELLO in MONTALCINO. His Il Greppo v'yd is 45 acres. Prices are v high but old vintages unique.

Boca Pie DOC r ★★ 85 88 89 90 91 92 From same grape as BAROLO (NEBBIOLO) in N of PIEDMONT. Look for Poderi ai Valloni.

Bolla Famous Veronese firm producing VALPOLICELLA, SOAVE, etc. Top wines: Castellaro (one of the v best SOAVES), Creso (red and white), Jago.

Bonarda Minor red grape (alias Croatina) widely grown in PIEDMONT, Lombardy, Emilia-Romagna and blended with BARBERA.

Bonarda (Oltrepò Pavese) Lom DOC r ★★ 89 90 91 92 Soft fresh often FRIZZANTE red from S of Pavia.

Bosca, Luigi PIEDMONT producers of ASTI SPUMANTE and vermouths.

Boscarelli, Poderi Small estate with vg VINO NOBILE DI MONTEPULCIANO.

Brachetto d'Acqui Pie DOC r sw (sp) ★★ DYA Sweet sparkling red with enticing Muscat aroma.

Bramaterra Pie DOC r ★★ 85 88 89 90 91 92 Neighbour to GATTINARA. NEBBIOLO grapes predominate in a blend.

Breganze Ven DOC ★→★★★ 85 86 87 88 90 91 92 A catch-all for many varieties around Vicenza. CAB and PINOT BL are best. Top producers: B Bartolomeo, MACULAN.

Bricco Term for a high (and by implication vg) hillside v'yd in PIEDMONT.

Bricco del Drago Pie vdt 85 86 88 89 90 Original long-lived blend of DOLCETTO and NEBBIOLO from Cascina Drago.

Bricco Manzoni Pie r ★★★ 82 85 88 89 90 91 92 V successful blend of NEBBIOLO and BARBERA from Monforte d'Alba.

Bricco dell'Uccellone Pie r ★★★ 85 86 87 88 89 90 91 92 Barrique-aged BARBERA from the Braida firm of the late Giacomo Bologna. Bricco della Bigotta and Ai Suma are others.

Brindisi Ap DOC r ★★ Strong NEGROAMARO. Best is Patriglione from Taurino.

Brunello di Montalcino Tus DOCG r ★★★→★★★★ 82 83 85 86 88 90 91 92 With BAROLO, Italy's most celebrated red: strong full-bodied high-flavoured long-lived. RISERVA after 5 yrs. Montalcino is 25 miles S of Siena. Producers incl ALTESINO, Argiano, BANFI, Fattoria dei Barbi, BIONDI-SANTI, CAPARZO, Case Basse, Cerbaiona, Col d'Orcia, COSTANTI, LISINI, Poggio Antico, POGGIONE, Salvioni, Talenti. See also Rosso di Montalcino (value).

Brusco dei Barbi Tus r ★★ 88 89 90 91 92 Lively variant on BRUNELLO using old CHIANTI GOVERNO method.

Bukkuram Celebrated MOSCATO DI PANTELLERIA from De Bartoli.

Ca'del Bosco FRANCIACORTA estate making some of Italy's v best sparkling wine, CHARD, and excellent reds (see ZANELLA).

Ca'Ronesca Big new COLLIO winery with good range incl red blend 'Sariz'.

Cabernet Sauvignon Much used in NE Italy and increasingly (esp in VDT) in Tuscany, PIEDMONT and the south.

Cafaggio, Villa Solid CHIANTI CLASSICO estate. Good red VDT: Solatio Basilica.

Caldaro or Lago di Caldaro T-AA DOC r ★→★★ DYA Alias KALTERERSEE. Light soft slightly bitter-almond red from SCHIAVA grapes. CLASSICO from a smaller area is better. From a huge area.

Caluso Passito Pie DOC w sw (fz) ★★ Made from Erbaluce grapes left to dry; delicate scent, velvety taste. Tiny production from a large area. Best from Bianco, Ferrando.

Cannonau di Sardegna Sar DOC r (p) dr s/sw ** 88 89 90 91 92 Cannonau (Grenache) is Sardinia's basic red grape; its wine often formidably strong (min 13.5% alc for DOC), but mild in flavour.

Cantina Cellar or winery.

Cantina Sociale Growers' coop.

Capannelle Good producer of Tuscan VDT (formerly CHIANTI CLASSICO), though overrated and (like a number of its class) overpriced.

Caparzo, Tenuta MONTALCINO estate with excellent BRUNELLO La Casa; also CHARD and red blend Ca'del Pazzo.

Capezzana, Tenuta di (or Villa) The Tuscan estate (W of Florence) of the ancient Contini Bonacossi family. Excellent CHIANTI Montalbano and CARMIGNANO. Also vg Bordeaux-style red, GHIAIE DELLA FURBA.

Capri Cam DOC r p w * Famous island with widely abused name. Better to drink ISCHIA.

Carema Pie DOC r ** 85 88 89 90 91 92 Old speciality of N PIEDMONT. Best from Luigi Ferrando (or the CANTINA SOCIALE).

Carignano del Sulcis Sar DOC r p **→*** Well-structured red with capacity for ageing. Best: Terre Brune from CANTINA SOCIALE di Santadi.

Carmignano Tus DOCG r *** 85 86 88 90 91 92 Section of CHIANTI using 10% CAB to make reliably good, and some v fine, wine. See Capezzana.

Carpenè Malvolti Leading producer of classic PROSECCO and other sparkling wines at Conegliano, Veneto.

Carso F-VG DOC r w 88 89 90 91 92 DOC nr Trieste incl good MALVASIA. Terrano del C is a REFOSCO red. Top grower: Edi Kante.

Casa fondata nel... Firm founded in...

Castel del Monte Ap DOC r p w ** 85 86 88 90 91 92 Dry fresh well-balanced southern wines. The red is RISERVA after 3 yrs. Rosé most widely known. RIVERA's Il Falcone stands out.

Castel San Michele T-AA r ** 85 86 87 88 90 A good red of CAB and MERLOT from the Trentino Agricultural College nr Trento. Also the name of a good white from Incrocio Manzoni.

Castell'in Villa Vg CHIANTI CLASSICO estate.

Castellare Small but admired CHIANTI CLASSICO producer with first-rate SANGIOVESE VDT I Sodi di San Niccoló and sprightly GOVERNO del Castellare, a modern version of old-style CHIANTI.

Castello d'Albola Famous CHIANTI CLASSICO estate owned by ZONIN.

Castello di Cacchiano First-rate CHIANTI CLASSICO estate at Gaiole.

Castello della Sala ANTINORI's estate at ORVIETO. Borro is the regular white. Top wine is Cervaro della Sala: CHARD and GRECHETTO aged in oak.

Castello di San Polo in Rosso CHIANTI CLASSICO estate with first-rate red VDT Cetinaia (aged in standard casks, not barriques).

Castello di Uzzano Famous old CHIANTI CLASSICO estate at Greve.

Castello di Verrazzano Important CHIANTI CLASSICO estate near Greve.

Castello di Volpaia First-class CHIANTI CLASSICO estate at Radda, making VDT red Balifico, which contains CAB, and COLTASSALA.

Càvit (Cantina Viticoltori) Group of good quality coops near Trento. Wines incl MARZEMINO, CAB, PINOTS N, BL and GR, Nosiola. Top wines: Brume di Monte (red and white) and sparkling Graal.

Cellatica Lom DOC r ** DYA Blended light slightly bitter red.

Cerasuolo Ab DOC p ** The ROSATO version of MONTEPULCIANO D'ABRUZZO.

Cerasuolo di Vittoria Si r *→*** 88 89 90 91 92 Cherry-red from southernmost Sicily, best made by COS. Giuseppe Coria makes a fine matured non-DOC version.

Ceretto High-quality grower of BARBARESCO (called Bricco Asili), BAROLO (Bricco Rocche), top BARBERA D'ALBA (Piana), CHARD (La Bernardina), DOLCETTO and ARNEIS.

To decipher codes, please refer to symbols key at front of book, and to 'How to Read an Entry' on page 5.

Cervaro See Castello della Sala.

Cerveteri Lat DOC w dr s/sw ★ DYA Sound wines produced NW of Rome between Bracciano and the sea.

Chardonnay Has recently joined permitted varieties for several N Italian DOCs (eg T-AA, FRANCIACORTA, F-VG). Most of the best (eg from ANTINORI, FELSINA, GAJA, LUNGAROTTI) are still only VDT.

Chianti Tus DOCG r ★→★★ 88 90 91 92 The lively local wine of Florence and Siena. Fresh fruity and tangy, still sometimes sold in straw-covered flasks. Mostly made to drink young. Of the subdistricts, RUFINA and Colli Fiorentini can make CLASSICO-style RISERVAS. Montalbano, Colli Senesi, Aretini and Pisani make lighter wines.

Chianti Classico Tus DOCG r ★★→★★★ 85 86 87 88 89 90 91 92 (Riserva) 83 85 86 88 90 Senior Chianti from the central area. Its old pale astringent style is becoming rarer as top estates opt for either darker tannic wines or softer and fruitier ones. Outstanding producers incl AMA, CASTELLARE, CASTELL'IN VILLA, FELSINA, FONTERUTOLI, FONTODI, ISOLE E OLENA, QUERCIABELLA, San Giusto. Members of the Consorzio use the badge of a black rooster, but several top firms do not belong.

Chianti Putto Tus DOCG r ★→★★ DYA From a league of producers outside the CLASSICO zone. The neck-label, a pink cherub, is now rarely seen.

Chiaretto Rosé (the word means 'claret') produced esp around L Garda. See Bardolino, Riviera del Garda.

Cinqueterre Lig DOC w dr sw pa ★★ Fragrant fruity white from the steep coast nr La Spezia. The PASSITO is known as SCIACCHETRA (★★→★★★).

Cinzano Major Vermouth company also known for its ASTI SPUMANTE from PIEDMONT, and Florio MARSALA. Owns MONTALCINO estate of Col d'Orcia.

Cirò Cal DOC r (p w) ★★ 85 86 87 88 89 90 91 92 V strong red from Gaglioppo grapes; fruity white (to drink young). Top wines: Caparra & Siciliani, Librandi, Ronco dei Quattroventi and single-v'yd Donna Madda from San Francesco.

Classico Term for wines from a restricted area within the limits of a DOC. By implication, and often in practice, the best of the district. Applied to sparkling wines it denotes the méthode traditionelle.

Collavini, Cantina Quality producer of COLLIO, COLLI ORIENTALI and GRAVE DEL FRIULI wines: PINOT GR, RIES, MERLOT, PINOT N and sparkling. See Attems.

Colle Picchioni Estate S of Rome making the best MARINO white; also red (CAB-MERLOT) VDT, Vigna del Vassallo, perhaps Latium's best.

Colli Hills. Occurs in many wine-names.

Colli Albani Lat DOC w dr s/sw (sp) ★→★★ DYA Soft fruity white of the Roman hills.

Colli Berici Ven DOC r p w ★★ 86 88 90 91 92 Hills S of Vicenza. CAB is the best wine.

Colli Bolognesi E-R DOC r p w ★★ DYA (w) 85 86 87 88 90 91 92 SW of Bologna. 8 wine types, 5 grape varieties. TERRE ROSSE is top estate.

Colli Euganei Ven DOC r w dr s/sw (sp) ★→★★ DYA A DOC SW of Padua for 7 wines. Red is adequate; white and sparkling soft and pleasant.

Colli Orientali del Friuli F-VG DOC r w dr sw 88 89 90 91 92 20 different wines (18 named after their grapes) are made under this DOC on hills E of Udine. Whites esp are vg. Top producers: ABBAZIA DI ROSAZZO, Borgo del Tiglio, Livon, RONCO DEL GNEMIZ, Torre Rosazza, Volpe Pasini.

Colli Piacentini E-R DOC r p w ★→★★ DYA DOC incl traditional GUTTURNIO and MONTEROSSO VAL D'ARDA among 11 types grown S of Piacenza. Good fizzy MALVASIA. Most wines FRIZZANTE.

Colli del Trasimeno Um DOC r w ★→★★ 88 90 91 92 Often lively wines from the province of Perugia.

Collio F-VG DOC r w ★★ 88 89 90 91 92 19 different wines, 17 named after their grapes, from a small area between Udine and Gorizia on the Slovenian border. Vg whites, esp SAUV, PINOT BIANCO and PINOT GRIGIO. Best from: La Castellada, Dorigo, L FELLUGA, GRAVNER, JERMANN, Primosic, Radikon, SCHIOPETTO, Villa Russiz.

Coltassala Tus r ★★★ 85 86 87 88 90 Notable VDT red of SANGIOVESE from the ancient CHIANTI CLASSICO estate of CASTELLO DI VOLPAIA at Radda.

Coltiva-Gruppo Italiano Vini Complex of coops and wineries, apparently the world's third largest producer. Sells 10% of all Italian wine, incl eg BIGI, FOLONARI, FONTANA CANDIDA, LAMBERTI, MELINI, Negri...

Conterno, Aldo Highly regarded grower of BAROLO, etc, at Monforte d'Alba. Good GRIGNOLINO, FREISA, vg CHARD 'Printanier' and 'Bussia d'Oro'. Best BAROLO is La Cicalla.

Contratto PIEDMONT firm known for ASTI SPUMANTE, BAROLO, etc.

Copertino Ap DOC r (p) ★★ 87 88 89 90 91 92 Savoury age-worthy dark red wine of NEGROAMARO from the heel of Italy. Look for the RISERVA from the coop.

Cordero di Montezemolo-Monfalletto Tiny producer of good BAROLO.

Cori Lat DOC w r dr sw ★ DYA Soft pleasant wines made 30 miles south of Rome.

Cortese di Gavi See Gavi. (Cortese is the grape.)

Cortese (Oltrepò Pavese) Lom DOC w ★→★★ DYA Delicate fresh white from W Lombardy.

Corvo-Duca di Salaparuta Si r w ★★→★★★ Popular Sicilian wines. Sound dry reds, pleasant soft whites. Excellent new barrique red called Duca Enrico (85 86 87 88 89 90 91 92).

Costanti, Conti Tiny estate producing top quality BRUNELLO DI MONTALCINO.

D'Ambra Top producer of ISCHIA wines.

Darmagi Pie r ★★★★ 82 83 85 86 87 88 89 90 91 92 CAB S from GAJA in BARBARESCO has become PIEDMONT'S most discussed VDT red.

Decugnano dei Barbi Top ORVIETO estate with an ABBOCCATO version known as 'Pourriture Noble', and a good red VDT.

Under the laws in place up to 1992 (see Introduction, page 76) the top category of Italian wine was DOCG, denominazione di origine controllata e garantita. It was awarded only to certain wines from top quality zones, which were bottled and sealed with a government seal by the producer. The first five areas to be 'guaranteed' were Barolo, Barbaresco, Brunello di Montalcino, Chianti and Vino Nobile di Montepulciano. The sixth (and first white) was Albana di Romagna, for no discernible reason. Then came Carmignano, Torgiano, Gattinara and Sagrantino. But it should be remembered that many of Italy's best wines are not yet covered by the DOC system and are officially only vino da tavola (referred to here as VDT). Examples are Bricco Manzoni, Sassicaia, Tignanello, Venegazzù, etc, etc.

Di Majo Norante Lone star of Molise on the Adriatic with vg Biferno DOC MONTEPULCIANO and white Falanghina under the Ramitello label. Also lighter, more aromatic Molí. Fine value. To watch for new ideas.

Dolce Sweet.

Dolceacqua See Rossese di Dolceacqua.

Dolcetto Popular low-acid red grape of PIEDMONT. Its smooth dark wine can age well. Makes the everyday wine of BAROLO- and BARBARESCO-producing areas and gives its name to the

Dolcetto d'Acqui Pie DOC r ★ DYA Pale quick-maturing table wine from south of ASTI.

Dolcetto d'Alba Pie DOC r ★★ DYA Among the best DOLCETTI, with a trace of bitter almond.

Dolcetto di Diano d'Alba Pie DOC ★★ DYA A rival to DOLCETTO D'ALBA; often more potent.

Dolcetto di Dogliani Pie DOC r ★★ DYA Often regarded as the top DOLCETTO subregion.

Dolcetto di Ovada Pie DOC r ★★ DYA Reputedly the sturdiest and longest-lived of DOLCETTI.

Donnafugata Si r w ★★ Zesty Sicilian whites (best are Vigna di Gabri, Damaskino). Also sound red.

Donnaz VdA DOC ★★ **85 88 89 90 91 92** A mountain NEBBIOLO, fragrant pale and faintly bitter. Aged for a statutory 3 yrs. Now part of the VALLE D'AOSTA regional DOC.

Duca Enrico See Corvo-Duca di Salaparuta.

Elba Tus r w (sp) ★ DYA Decent dry red. The island's white is drinkable with fish.

Enfer d'Arvier VdA DOC r ★★ **88 89 90 91** Alpine speciality (see Donnaz); pale pleasantly bitter light red.

Enoteca Wine library. There are many, the impressive original being the Enoteca Italiana of Siena. Also used for wine shops or restaurants.

Erbaluce di Caluso See Caluso Passito.

Est! Est!! Est!!! Lat DOC w dr s/sw ★ DYA Unextraordinary white from Montefiascone, north of Rome. Has traded for centuries on its odd-ball name.

Etna Si DOC r p w ★→★★ **88 89 90 91 92** Wine from the volcanic slopes. The red is warm, full, balanced and can age well; the white is distinctly grapey. See Villagrande.

Falerio dei Colli Ascolani Mar DOC w ★ DYA Made nr Ascoli Piceno. A pleasant fresh fruity summer wine.

Falerno del Massico Cam DOC r w ★★ **88 89 90 91 92** As Falernum, the best-known wine of ancient times. Strong red from AGLIANICO, fruity white from Falanghina. Good producer: Villa Matilde.

Fara Pie DOC r ★★ **85 88 89 90 91 92** Good NEBBIOLO wine from Novara, N PIEDMONT. Fragrant; worth ageing. Small production. Best is Dessilani's Caramino.

Faro Si DOC r ★★ **88 89 90 91 92** Strong Sicilian red from the Straits of Messina. Made only (and rather well) by Bagni.

Favorita Pie w ★→★★ Dry fruity white making friends in BAROLO country. From eg Negro, Sant'Orsola, VOERZIO.

Fazi-Battaglia Well-known producer of VERDICCHIO, etc. White Le Moie VDT is pleasant. Also owns Fassati, impressive for VINO NOBILE DI MONTEPULCIANO.

Felluga Brothers Livio and Marco (Russiz SUPERIORE) have separate companies in the COLLIO and COLLI ORIENTALI. Both are highly esteemed.

Felsina-Berardenga CHIANTI CLASSICO estate with famous RISERVA Vigna Rancia and VDT Fontalloro.

Ferrari Firm making some of Italy's best dry sparkling wines nr Trento, TRENTINO-ALTO ADIGE. Giulio Ferrari RISERVA is best.

Fiano di Avellino Cam w ★★→★★★ **90 91 92** Considered the best white of Campania. Smooth and dry but not remarkable. MASTROBERARDINO'S Vignadora is best.

Fiorano Lat r w dr s/sw ★★ **88 89 90 91 92** Interesting Roman reds of CAB and MERLOT, whites of Sémillon.

Flaccianello della Pieve See Fontodi.

Florio The major producer of MARSALA, controlled by CINZANO.

Foianeghe T-AA vdt r (w) ★★ **86 88 89 90** Trentino CAB-MERLOT red to age 7–10 yrs. White is PINOT BL-CHARD-TRAMINER. Top grower: Conti Bossi Fedrigotti.

Folonari Large run-of-the-mill merchant of Lombardy.

Fontana Candida One of the biggest producers of FRASCATI. Single-v'yd Santa Teresa stands out.

Fontanafredda Big historic producer of PIEDMONT wines, incl BAROLO from single v'yds and a range of ALBA DOCs. Also vg sparkling.

Fonterutoli High quality CHIANTI CLASSICO estate at Castellina with noted VDT Concerto and RISERVA Ser Lapo.

Le Fonti, Fattoria CHIANTI estate of 30 acres. Panzano still uses ancient 'promisco' mixed cultivation. Good eco-wine.

Fontodi Top CHIANTI CLASSICO estate at Panzano producing highly regarded RISERVA, VDT Flaccianello and white vdt 'Meriggio' (a PINOT BIANCO-SAUV-TRAMINER blend).

Franciacorta Pinot Lom DOC w (p sp) ★★→★★★ Pleasant soft white and some vg sparkling wines made of PINOTS BL, N or GR and CHARD. CA'DEL BOSCO is outstanding. BELLAVISTA, Cavalleri and Monte Rossa also vg.

Franciacorta Rosso Lom DOC r ★★ 88 89 90 91 92 Lightish red of mixed CAB and BARBERA from Brescia.

Frascati Lat DOC w dr s/sw sw (sp) ★→★★ DYA Best-known wine of the Roman hills: should be soft ripe golden, tasting of whole grapes. Most is disappointingly neutral today: look for dated wines from small producers (eg Conte Zandotti, Villa Simone, or Santa Teresa from FONTANA CANDIDA). A sweet version is known as Cannellino.

Freisa Pie r dr s/sw sw (sp) ★★ DYA Usually v dry (except nr Turin), often FRIZZANTE red, said to taste of raspberries and roses. With enough acidity it can be highly appetizing, esp with salami.

Frescobaldi Ancient noble family, leading pioneers of CHIANTI at NIPOZZANO, E of Florence. Also white POMINO and PREDICATO SAUV BL (Vergena) and CAB (Mormoreto). See also Montesodi.

Friuli-Venezia Giulia The NE province on the Slovenian border. Many wines; the DOCs COLLIO and COLLI ORIENTALI include most of the best.

Frizzante (fz) Semi-sparkling. Used to describe wines such as LAMBRUSCO.

Gaja Old family firm at BARBARESCO with inspired direction of Angelo G. Top quality (and price) PIEDMONT wines, esp BARBARESCO (single v'yds Sorì Tildin, Sorì San Lorenzo, Costa Russi) and BAROLO Sperss (since '88). Now setting trends with excellent CHARD (Gaja & Rey and less expensive Rossj-Bass), CAB (DARMAGI). Also less successful SAUV BL. Vignarey is excellent BARBERA, Vignabajla delicious DOLCETTO.

Galestro Tus w ★ V light grapey white from eponymous shaley soil in CHIANTI country.

Gambellara Ven DOC w dr s/sw (sp) ★ DYA Neighbour of SOAVE. Dry wine similar. Sweet (known as RECIOTO DI GAMBELLARA) agreeably fruity. Also VIN SANTO.

Gancia Famous ASTI SPUMANTE house also producing vermouth and dry sparkling. New Torrebianco estate in Apulia is making good VDT whites: CHARD, SAUV, PINOT BL.

Garganega Principal white grape of SOAVE.

Garofoli, Gioacchino Quality leader of the Marches (nr Ancona). Notable style in VERDICCHIO Macrina and Serra Fiorese; also sparkling. ROSSO CONERO Piancarda and Grosso Agontano are outstanding.

Gattinara Pie DOCG r ★★→★★★ 82 85 86 88 89 90 V tasty big-scale BAROLO-type red from N PIEDMONT (made from NEBBIOLO, locally known as Spanna). Best are Monsecco and single-v'yd wines from Antoniola. Other good producers: Nervi, Travaglini.

Gavi (or Cortese di Gavi) Pie w ★★★ DYA At best substantial subtle dry white of CORTESE grapes. La Scolca is best known, Castello di Tassarolo top quality, La Giustiniana and Tenuta San Pietro admirable. But high prices are rarely justified.

Ghemme Pie DOC r ★★→★★★ 82 85 86 88 89 90 Neighbour of GATTINARA, rival in quality but rare. Best is Antichi Vigneti di Cantalupo.

Ghiaie della Furba Tus r ★★★ 85 86 88 89 90 Bordeaux-style VDT CAB blend from the admirable TENUTA DI CAPEZZANA, CARMIGNANO.

Giacobazzi Well-known producers of LAMBRUSCO nr Modena.

Giacosa, Bruno Inspired loner: outstanding BARBARESCO, BAROLO and other PIEDMONT wines at Neive. Remarkable ARNEIS white, PINOT N sparkling.

Girò di Cagliari Sar DOC r dr sw ★ A formidably alcoholic red, most sympathetic when some of its sugar content is left unfermented.

Goldenmuskateller Aromatic ALTO ADIGE grape made into irresistible dry white, esp by TIEFENBRUNNER.

Governo Old Tuscan custom, enjoying mild revival with some producers, in which dried grapes/musts are added to young wine to induce secondary fermentation and give a slight prickle – sometimes instead of chaptalising.

Gradi Degrees (of alcohol), ie percent by volume.

Grai, Giorgio Merchant/consultant to top ALTO ADIGE and other estates.

Grappa Spirit made from grape pomace (the skins etc after pressing).

Grattamacco Top Tuscan producer on coast outside classic centres (nr SASSICAIA S of Bolgheri). Vg Grattamacco SANGIOVESE-CAB blend.

Grave del Friuli F-VG DOC r w ★★ 88 89 90 91 92 DOC covering 15 different wines, 14 named after their grapes, from nr the Slovenian border. Good MERLOT and CAB.

Gravner COLLIO estate encompassing a range of excellent whites, led by CHARD and SAUV.

Grechetto White grape with more flavour than the ubiquitous TREBBIANO, increasingly used in Umbria.

Greco di Bianco (or Greco di Gerace) Cal DOC w sw ★★ 86 87 88 89 90 91 92 An original smooth and fragrant dessert wine from Italy's toe. See also Mantonico.

Greco di Tufo Cam DOC w (sp) ★★→★★★ 90 91 92 One of the best white wines of the south, fruity and slightly 'wild' in flavour. A character. MASTROBERARDINO makes single-v'yd Vignadangelo.

Grignolino d'Asti Pie DOC r ★ DYA Pleasant lively standard light red of PIEDMONT.

Grumello Lom DOC r ★★ 85 86 88 89 90 91 92 NEBBIOLO wine from VALTELLINA. Can be delicate (or meagre).

Guerrieri-Gonzaga Top producer in TRENTINO; esp VDT San Leonardo, ★★★ CAB-MERLOT blend.

Guerrieri-Rizzardi Top producer of BARDOLINO and other Veronese wines from various family estates.

Gutturnio dei Colli Piacentini E-R DOC r dr (s/sw) ★★ 88 89 90 91 92 BARBERA-BONARDA blend from the hills of Piacenza, often FRIZZANTE.

Inferno Lom DOC r ★★ 85 86 88 89 90 Similar to GRUMELLO and, like it, classified as VALTELLINA SUPERIORE.

Ischia Cam DOC w (r) ★→★★ DYA The wine of the island off Naples. Slightly sharp white SUPERIORE is best of the DOC. But top producer D'Ambra makes better VDT whites BIANCOLELLA and Forestera and red PER'E PALUMMO.

Isole e Olena Top CHIANTI CLASSICO estate with fine red VDT Cepparello. Vg VIN SANTO, and l'Eremo SYRAH.

Isonzo F-VG DOC r w ★★ 88 89 90 91 92 DOC covering 19 wines (17 varietals) in the northeast. Best whites and CAB (esp from Stelio Gallo) compare with neighbouring COLLIO wines.

Jermann Estate in COLLIO producing top-ranked VDT, incl singular VINTAGE TUNINA oak-aged white blend and lighter vinnae. Also fresh Capo Martino (91).

Kalterersee German name for LAGO DI CALDARO.

Lacryma (or Lacrima) Christi del Vesuvio Cam r p w dr (sw fz) ★→★★ DYA Famous but ordinary range of wines in great variety from Vesuvius. (DOC name is Vesuvio.) MASTROBERARDINO produces the only good example.

Lageder, Alois The lion of the Bolzano (ALTO ADIGE) DOCs: SANTA MADDALENA, etc. Exciting wines, incl barrel-aged CHARD and CAB Löwengang. Single-v'yd SAUV BL is called Lehenhof, PINOT BL Haberlehof, PINOT GR Benefizium Porer.

Lago di Caldaro See Caldaro.

Lagrein T-AA DOC r p ★★→★★★ 85 86 88 89 90 91 A Tyrolean grape with a bitter twist. Good fruity wine – at best v appetizing. The rosé is called Kretzer, the dark Dunkel.

Lamberti Substantial producers of SOAVE, VALPOLICELLA, BARDOLINO, etc at Lazise on the E shore of Lake Garda. NB LUGANA and VDT Turà.

Lambrusco DOC (or not) r p (w) s/sw ★ DYA Bizarre highly popular fizzy red (or artificially white), generally drunk SECCO in Italy but best known in its sweet version in the US.

Lambrusco Grasparossa di Castelvetro E-R DOC r dr s/sw sp ** DYA Often rivals the foregoing. Acidic: good with rich food.

Lambrusco Salamino di Santa Croce E-R DOC r dr s/sw sp * DYA Similar to above. Fruity smell, high acidity and a thick 'head'.

Lambrusco di Sorbara E-R DOC r (w) dr s/sw sp ** DYA The best of the LAMBRUSCOS. From nr Modena.

Langhe The hills of central PIEDMONT, home of BAROLO, BARBARESCO, etc. DOC for certain varieties. The name is seen on many VDT.

Latisana F-VG DOC r w ** 88 89 90 91 92 DOC for 13 varietal wines from some 50 miles NE of Venice. Particularly good TOCAI FRIULANO.

Leone de Castris Large but variable producer of Apulian wines with an estate at SALICE SALENTINO, near Lecce.

Lessona Pie DOC r ** 85 86 88 89 90 Soft dry claret-like wine from the province of Vercelli. NEBBIOLO, Vespolina and BONARDA grapes.

Liquoroso Means strong and usually sweet (whether fortified with alcohol or not), eg Tuscan VINSANTO.

Lisini Small estate producing some of the finest recent vintages of BRUNELLO.

Loazzolo Pie DOC w sw *** 89 90 91 92 New DOC for Moscato dessert wine from botrytised air-dried grapes: expensive and sweet. Best producer is Luja.

Locorotondo Ap DOC w (sp) * DYA Pleasantly fresh southern white.

Lugana Lom DOC w (sp) *** DYA One of the best whites of S Lake Garda: fragrant smooth full of body and flavour. Visconti is best producer.

Lungarotti The leading producer of TORGIANO wine, with cellars, hotel and wine museum nr Perugia. Also some of Italy's best CHARD (Miralduolo and Vigna I Palazzi) and PINOT GR. See Torgiano.

Maculan The top producer of DOC BREGANZE. Also Torcolato, dessert VDT (***) and Prato di Canzio (CHARD, PINOT BL and PINOT GR).

Malvasia Important white or red grape of chameleon character but low acidity. Used all over Italy for dry and sweet, still, FRIZZANTE and sparkling wines. A frequent dry white of the NE, but also an ingredient of CHIANTI. An outstanding mature example is TORRICELLA.

Malvasia di Cagliari Sar DOC w dr s/sw sw ** 89 90 91 92 Interesting strong Sardinian wine, fragrant and slightly bitter.

Malvasia di Casorzo d'Asti Pie DOC r sw sp ** DYA Fragrant grapey sweet red, sometimes sparkling.

Malvasia di Castelnuovo Don Bosco Pie DOC r sw (sp) ** DYA Interrupted fermentation gives very sweet aromatic red.

Malvasia delle Lipari Si DOC w sw (pa fz) *** 86 87 88 89 90 91 92 Among the very best Malvasias, aromatic and rich, from the volcanic Lipari or Aeolian Islands N of Sicily. Top producer: Carlo Hauner.

Malvoisie de Nus VdA DOC w dr s/sw *** Rare Alpine white, with a deep bouquet of honey. Small production and high reputation. Can age remarkably well.

Manduria (Primitivo di) Ap DOC r s/sw (dr sw fz) ** 88 89 90 91 92 Heady red, naturally strong but often fortified. From nr Taranto. Primitivo is a southern grape related to California's Zinfandel.

Mantonico Cal w dr sw fz ** 85 86 87 88 89 90 91 92 Fruity deep amber dessert wine from Reggio Calabria. Can age remarkably well. See also Greco di Bianco.

Marino Lat DOC w dr s/sw (sp) ** DYA A neighbour of FRASCATI with similar wine, often a better buy. Look for COLLE PICCHIONI brand.

Marrano Umb w ** Pungent GRECHETTO white grown by BIGI nr ORVIETO.

Marsala Si DOC br dr s/sw sw fz **→*** NV Sherry-type wine invented by the Woodhouse Brothers from Liverpool in 1773; excellent aperitif or for dessert, but mostly used in the kitchen. The dry ('virgin'), sometimes made by the solera system, must be 5 yrs old. Top producers: FLORIO, Pellegrino, Rallo, VECCHIO SAMPERI.

Martina Franca Ap DOC w (sp) * DYA Bland southern white, cousin to LOCOROTONDO.

Martini & Rossi Well-known vermouth and sparkling wine house, also famous for its splendid wine museum in Pessione, nr Turin.

Marzemino (del Trentino) T-AA DOC r ★→★★ 89 90 91 92 Pleasant local red of Trento. Fruity; slightly bitter. See Cávit.

Mascarello The name of 2 top producers of BAROLO, etc: Bartolo M and Giuseppe M & Figli. Look for the latter's BAROLO Monprivato.

Masi, Agricola Well-known conscientious and reliable specialist producers of VALPOLICELLA, RECIOTO, SOAVE, etc, incl fine red Campo Fiorin and vg single-v'yd AMARONE. Also look for excellent new red Toar.

Mastroberardino The leading wine producer of Campania (by far). Wines incl FIANO DI AVELLINO, GRECO DI TUFO, LACRYMA CHRISTI and TAURASI.

Melini Important long-established producers of CHIANTI CLASSICO at Poggibonsi.

Meranese di Collina T-AA DOC r ★ DYA Light red of Merano, known in German as Meraner Hügel.

Merlot Adaptable red Bordeaux grape widely grown in NE Italy and elsewhere. Top Tuscan producers (AMA, AVIGNONESI, ORNELLAIA) make the best. In the NE it tends to taste more like Cab Franc. Merlot DOCs include the following:

Merlot dell'Alto Adige T-AA ★★→★★★ Good growers: Haas, Schreckbichl.

Merlot di Aprilia Lat DOC r ★ Harsh at first, softer after 2–3 yrs.

Merlot Colli Berici Ven DOC r ★→★★ Pleasantly light and soft. Campo del Lago VDT from Villa dal Ferro is one of Italy's best MERLOTS.

Merlot Colli Orientali del Friuli F-VG DOC r ★★ 88 89 90 91 92 Pleasant herby character, best at 2–3 yrs (RISERVA). Some ages well, notably Vigne dal Leon. L'Altromerlot from Torre Rosazza also good.

Merlot Collio F-VG DOC r ★★ 88 89 90 91 92 Grassy scent, sometimes slightly bitter. Best at 2–3 yrs. Vg VDT from Borgo del Tiglio.

Merlot Grave del Friuli F-VG DOC r ★→★★ 88 89 90 91 92 Pleasant light wine, usually best at 1–2 yrs, but potentially a keeper.

Merlot Isonzo F-VG DOC r ★→★★ 88 90 91 92 Neighbour to COLLIO on flat land. Dry herby agreeable light wine.

Merlot Lison-Pramaggiore Ven DOC r ★★ 86 88 90 91 A cut above most other Merlots. RISERVA after 2 yrs.

Merlot del Piave Ven DOC r ★→★★ 88 90 91 92 Sound tasty light red, usually best at 2–4 yrs.

Merlot del Trentino T-AA DOC r ★→★★ 86 88 89 90 Full flavour, slightly grassy scent; RISERVA after 2 yrs. (ALTO ADIGE has better; esp from Margreid and Siebeneich v'yds.)

Metodo classico or tradizionale Terms increasingly in use to identify méthode traditionelle sparkling wines. (See also Classico.)

Monica di Sardegna Sar DOC r ★ DYA Monica is the grape. An ordinary dry light red.

Monsanto Esteemed CHIANTI CLASSICO estate, esp for Il Poggio v'yd.

Montalcino Small town in the province of Siena, Tuscany, famous for its deep red BRUNELLO and lighter ROSSO DI MONTALCINO.

Monte Vertine Top estate at Radda in CHIANTI. VDT Le Pergole Torte (100% SANGIOVETO) is one of Tuscany's best (★★★★). Also Sodaccio (Sangioveto plus Canaiolo) and fine VINSANTO.

Montecarlo Tus DOC w r ★★ DYA (w) Traditional white wine area in N Tuscany: smooth delicate TREBBIANO blended with a range of better grapes. Now applies to a CHIANTI-style red too (eg Rosso di Cercatoia).

Montecompatri Colonna Lat DOC w s/sw ★ DYA A neighbour of FRASCATI. Similar wine.

Montefalco Umb DOC r dr sw ★★ 88 89 90 91 92 M Rosso is standard red; SAGRANTINO (named for the grape) has sweetness and bite. ADANTI's Rosso d'Arquata VDT stands out.

For key to grape variety abbreviations, see pages 6–9.

Montepulciano An important red grape of central-east Italy as well as the famous Tuscan town (see next entry).

Montepulciano, Vino Nobile di See Vino Nobile di Montepulciano.

Montepulciano d'Abruzzo (or Molise) Ab (or Mol) DOC r p ★★ 85 87 88 89 90 91 92 At its best one of Italy's tastiest reds, full of flavour and warmth, from the Adriatic coast round Pescara. See also Cerasuolo, Valentini.

Monterosso (Val d'Arda) E-R DOC w dr sw (sp) ★ DYA Agreeable minor often FRIZZANTE white from Piacenza (DOC COLLI PIACENTINI).

Montesodi Tus r ★★★ 83 85 86 88 90 Tip-top CHIANTI Rufina RISERVA from FRESCOBALDI.

Morellino di Scansano Tus DOC r ★→★★ Local SANGIOVESE of the Maremma, the S Tuscan coast. Cherry-red, lively and tasty to drink young. Fattorie Le Pupille is good.

Moscadello di Montalcino Tus DOC w sw (sp) ★★ DYA Traditional wine of MONTALCINO, much older than BRUNELLO. Sweet white fizzy MOSCATO. Good producers: BANFI, POGGIONE.

Moscato Fruitily fragrant grape grown all over Italy.

Moscato d'Asti Pie DOC w sw sp ★★ DYA Low-strength sweet fruity sparkler, delicious from Bera, Dogliotti, Gatti, Rivetti, Saracco, Vignaioli di Santo Stefano. ASTI SPUMANTE is the (theoretically) superior version.

Moscato dei Colli Euganei Ven DOC w sw (sp) ★★ DYA Golden wine, fruity and smooth, from nr Padua.

Moscato (Oltrepò Pavese) Lom DOC w sw (sp) ★ DYA The Lombardy equivalent of MOSCATO D'ASTI. Rarely as good.

Moscato di Pantelleria Si DOC w sw (sp fz pa) ★★★ Italy's best Muscat, from the island of Pantelleria off the Tunisian coast; rich fruity and aromatic. Ages well. Top wine: BUKKURAM.

Moscato di Sorso Sennori Sar DOC w sw (fz) ★ DYA Strong golden dessert wine from Sassari, N Sardinia.

Moscato di Trani Ap DOC w sw fz ★★★ Another golden dessert wine, sometimes fortified, with a 'bouquet of faded roses'. NB the unfortified version from Fratelli Nugnes.

Müller-Thurgau Makes wine to be reckoned with in TRENTINO-ALTO ADIGE and FRIULI, esp TIEFENBRUNNER'S Feldmarschall.

Nasco di Cagliari Sar DOC w dr sw (fz) ★★ Sardinian speciality with light bitter taste, high alcohol content.

Nebbiolo The best red grape of PIEDMONT and Lombardy.

Nebbiolo d'Alba Pie DOC r dr s/sw (sp) ★★ 85 86 87 88 89 90 91 Like lightweight BAROLO; sometimes easier to appreciate than the more powerful classic wine. ROERO is a new DOC from N of ALBA.

Negroamaro Literally 'black bitter'; Apulian red grape with potential for quality. See Copertino.

Nipozzano, Castello di The FRESCOBALDI estate E of Florence producing MONTESODI CHIANTI. The most important outside the CLASSICO zone.

Nosiola (Trentino) T-AA DOC w dr sw ★★ DYA Light fruity white from dried Nosiola grapes. Also good VINSANTO. Best from Pravis: Le Frate.

Nozzole Famous estate, owned by RUFFINO, in the heart of CHIANTI CLASSICO N of Greve. Also good CAB.

Nuragus di Cagliari Sar DOC w ★ DYA Lively Sardinian white, not too strong.

Oliena Sar r ★★ Interesting strong fragrant CANNONAU red; a touch bitter.

Oltrepò Pavese Lom DOC r w dr sw sp ★→★★ DOC applicable to 14 wines produced in the province of Pavia, mostly named after their grapes. Top growers incl Cabanon, Doria, Mairano, Tenuta Mazzolino, Monsupello, Montelio.

Ornellaia Tus ★★★ 85 86 87 88 89 90 91 92 New 130-acre estate of LODOVICO ANTINORI nr Bolgheri on Tuscan coast. To watch for CAB-MERLOT and SAUV BL called Poggio delle Gazze. Also Masseto, vg straight Merlot, and blend La Volte (since '91).

Orvieto Umb DOC w dr s/sw ★★→★★★ DYA The classical Umbrian golden white: smooth and substantial; formerly rather dull but recently more interesting, esp in sweet versions. Orvieto CLASSICO is better. Only the finest examples (eg BIGI, BARBERANI, DECUGANO DEI BARBI) age well. But see Castello della Sala.

Pagadebit di Romagna E-R DOC w dr s/sw DYA Pleasant traditional 'payer of debts' from around Bertinoro.

Paradiso, Fattoria Century-old family estate near Bertinoro (E-R). Good ALBANA and PAGADEBIT and unique red BARBAROSSA. Vg SANGIOVESE.

Parrina Tus r w ★★ 89 90 91 92 Light red and fresh appetizing white from S Tuscany.

Pasolini Dall'Onda Noble family with estates in CHIANTI Colli Fiorentini and Romagna, producing fine traditional-style wines.

Passito (pa) Strong sweet wine from grapes dried on the vine or indoors.

Pelaverga Pie r ★★ 89 90 91 92 Pale red with spicy perfume, from Verduno. Good producers: Alessandria, Bel Colle, Castello di Verduno.

Peppoli Estate owned by ANTINORI, producing excellent CHIANTI CLASSICO in a full round youthful style – first vintage 85.

Per'e Palummo Cam r ★★ Appetizing light tannic red from island of ISCHIA.

Petit Rouge VdA ★★ 88 89 90 91 92 Good dark lively REFOSCO-like red. Part of VALLE D'AOSTA DOC.

Piave Ven DOC r w ★→★★ 88 90 (w DYA) Flourishing DOC NW of Venice covering 8 wines, 4 red and 4 white, named after their grapes. CAB, MERLOT and RABOSO reds can all age.

Picolit (Colli Orientali del Friuli) F-VG DOC w s/sw sw ★★★ 88 90 Delicate well-balanced sweet dessert wine with exaggerated reputation. Rather like Jurançon. Ages up to 6 yrs, but wildly overpriced.

Piedmont (Piemonte) The most important Italian region for top quality wine. Turin is the capital, ASTI and ALBA the wine centres. See Barbaresco, Barbera, Barolo, Dolcetto, Grignolino, Moscato, etc.

Pieropan Outstanding producer of SOAVE that for once deserves its fame.

Pigato New DOC under Riviera Ligure di Ponente. Often outclasses VERMENTINO as Liguria's finest white, with rich texture and structure.

Pighin, Fratelli Solid producers of COLLIO and GRAVE DEL FRIULI.

Pinot Bianco (Pinot Bl) Popular grape in NE, esp good for sparkling wine.

Pinot Bianco (Alto Adige) T-AA DOC w ★★ DYA Some of Italy's best and longest-lived wine of this variety.

Pinot Bianco (dei Colli Berici) Ven DOC w ★★ DYA Straight satisfying dry white.

Pinot Bianco (Colli Orientali del Friuli) F-VG DOC w ★★ DYA Good white; smooth rather than showy.

Pinot Bianco (Collio) F-VG DOC w ★★ DYA Similar to above.

Pinot Grigio Tasty low-acid white grape increasingly popular in NE Italy. Best from ALTO ADIGE, COLLIO. Also in eg Tuscany (from AMA, BANFI).

Pinot Grigio (Collio) F-VG DOC w ★★ DYA Fruity soft agreeable dry white. The best age well.

Pinot Grigio (Grave del Friuli) F-VG DOC w ★ DYA Second choice to COLLIO or COLLI ORIENTALI.

Pinot Grigio (Oltrepò Pavese) Lom DOC w (sp) ★ DYA Lombardy's PINOT GR is usually at least adequate.

Pinot Nero T-AA DOC r ★★ 88 89 90 91 92 Pinot Nero (Noir) gives lively light wine in much of NE Italy, incl TRENTINO and esp ALTO ADIGE. Vg results from Cantina Sociale Colterenzio-Schreckbichl, Castelfeder, Haas, Niedrist. RISERVA after 2 yrs. Also fine sparkling. Promising trials elsewhere.

Pio Cesare A producer of top-quality red wines of PIEDMONT, incl BAROLO.

Podere Il Palazzino Small estate with admirable CHIANTI CLASSICO and VDT Grosso Sanese.

Poggione, Tenuta Il Perhaps the most consistent estate for BRUNELLO and ROSSO DI MONTALCINO.

Pojer & Sandri Top producers of TRENTINO VDT MULLER-T and CHARD.

Pomino Tus DOC w (r br) *** 85 86 87 88 90 Fine white, partly CHARD (Il Benefizio is 100%), and a SANGIOVESE-CAB-MERLOT-PINOT N blend. Also VINSANTO. From FRESCOBALDI.

Predicato Name for 4 kinds of VDT from central Tuscany, illustrating the current headlong rush from tradition. P del Muschio is CHARD and PINOT BL; P del Selvante is SAUV BL; P di Biturica is CAB S with SANGIOVESE, P di Cardisco is SANGIOVESE straight. RUFFINO's Cabreo brand wines are examples.

Primitivo di Apulia See Manduria.

Prosecco di Conegliano-Valdobbiadene Ven DOC w dr s/sw (sp) **→*** DYA Popular sparkling wine of the NE. Slight fruity bouquet, the dry pleasantly bitter, the sweet fruity; the best are known as Superiore di Cartizze. Carpené-Malvolti is leading producer, now challenged by Canevel, Cardinal, Nino Franco, Pino Zardetto and others.

Prunotto, Alfredo Very serious ALBA company with vg BARBARESCO, BAROLO, NEBBIOLO, etc. Now controlled by ANTINORI.

Querciabella Up-coming CHIANTI CLASSICO estate with excellent red VDT Camartina and a dream of a white VDT, Bâtard Pinot (PINOTS BL and GR).

Quintarelli, Giuseppe True artisan producer of VALPOLICELLA, RECIOTO and AMARONE, at the top in both quality and price.

Raboso del Piave (now DOC) Ven r ** 86 88 90 91 92 Powerful sharp interesting country red; needs age.

Ramandolo See Verduzzo Colli Orientali del Friuli.

Ramitello See Di Majo Norante.

Rampolla, Castello dei Top CHIANTI CLASSICO estate at Panzano; also excellent CAB-based VDT Sammarco.

Rapitalà See Alcamo.

Ratti, Renato Maker of vg BAROLO and other ALBA wines. The late Signor Ratti (d '88) was a highly respected leader of the PIEDMONT industry.

Ravello Cam r p w ** 88 89 90 91 Among the best wines of Campania: full dry red, fresh white. Caruso is the best-known brand. Episcopio-Vuillemier makes better wines.

Recioto Wine made partly of half-dried grapes. Speciality of Veneto since the great days of the Venetian empire.

Recioto di Gambellara Ven DOC w s/sw sp * DYA Sweetish golden wine, often half-sparkling.

Recioto di Soave Ven DOC w s/sw (sp) ** 87 88 90 91 92 SOAVE made from selected half-dried grapes: sweet fruity fresh slightly almondy; high alcohol. Top makers: ANSELMI, PIEROPAN.

Recioto della Valpolicella Ven DOC r s/sw sp ** 85 86 88 90 Strong late-harvested red, sometimes sparkling. 'Amabile' is sweet.

Recioto della Valpolicella Amarone Ven DOC r **** 81 83 85 86 88 90 Dry version of the above; strong concentrated flavour, rather bitter. Impressive and expensive. Now properly called just Amarone.

Refosco (Colli Orientali del Friuli) F-VG DOC r ** 88 90 91 92 Full-bodied dry red; RISERVA after 2 yrs. Refosco is said to be the same grape as the Mondeuse of Savoie (France). It tastes like it.

Refosco (Grave del Friuli) F-VG DOC r ** 88 90 91 92 Similar to above but slightly lighter.

Regaleali Si w p r ** 86 87 88 89 90 91 92 Perhaps the best Sicilian producer; situated between Palermo and Caltanissetta to the SE.

Ribolla (Colli Orientali del Friuli and Collio) F-VG DOC w *→*** DYA Thin NE white. The best come from COLLIO.

Ricasoli Famous Tuscan family, 'inventors' of CHIANTI, whose Chianti Classico is named after their Brolio estate and castle.

Riecine Tus r (w) *** First-class CHIANTI CLASSICO estate at Gaiole, created by an Englishman, John Dunkley. Also VDT La Gioia di Riecine.

Riesling Used to mean Italian Ries (Ries Italico or Welschriesling). German (Rhine) Riesling, now ascendant, is Riesling Renano.

Riesling (Alto Adige) DOC w ** **90 91 92** Can often be Italy's best RIES.

Riesling (Oltrepò Pavese) Lom DOC w (sp) ** The Lombardy version, quite light and fresh. Occasionally sparkling. Keeps well. Made of both types of RIES.

Riesling (Trentino) T-AA DOC w ** DYA Delicate, slightly acid, v fruity.

Riserva Wine aged for a statutory period, usually in barrels.

Riunite One of the world's largest coop cellars, nr Reggio Emilia, producing huge quantities of LAMBRUSCO and other wines.

Rivera Reliable winemakers at Andria, near Bari, with good red Il Falcone and CASTEL DEL MONTE rosé. Also Vigna al Monte label.

Riviera del Garda Chiaretto Ven, Lom DOC p ** DYA Charming cherry-pink fresh and slightly bitter, from SW Garda.

Riviera del Garda Rosso Ven DOC r ** **88 90 91** Red version of the above; ages surprisingly well.

Rocche dei Manzoni, Podere Go-ahead estate at Monforte d'Alba. Excellent BAROLO (best: Vigna Big), BRICCO MANZONI, ALBA wines, CHARD (L'Angelica) and Valentino Brut sparkling.

Roero DOC r ** DYA New name for a drink-me-quick NEBBIOLO from ALBA. Can be delicious.

Ronco Term for a hillside v'yd in FRIULI-VENEZIA GIULIA.

Ronco del Gnemiz Tiny property with outstanding COLLI ORIENTALI DOCs and VDT CHARD made in barriques.

Rosa del Golfo Ap p dr ** DYA An outstanding VDT rosé of ALEZIO.

Rosato Rosé.

Rosato del Salento Ap p *→** DYA Strong but refreshing southern rosé from round Brindisi.

Rossese di Dolceacqua Lig DOC r ** **90 91 92** Well-known fragrant light red of the Riviera. Can be as clean as claret.

Rosso Red.

Rosso d'Arquata See Adanti.

Rosso delle Colline Lucchesi Tus DOC r *→** **88 89 90 91 92** Produced round Lucca but not greatly different from CHIANTI.

Rosso Cònero Mar DOC r *** **85 86 88 89 90 91 92** Some of the best MONTEPULCIANO (varietal) reds of Italy, eg Garofoli's Grosso Agontano, Moroder's RC Riserva, Umani Ronchi's Cumaro and San Lorenzo.

Rosso di Montalcino Tus DOC r **→*** **88 89 90 91 92** DOC for younger wines from BRUNELLO grapes. Still variable but potentially a winner if the many good producers are not too greedy over prices.

Rosso di Montepulciano Tus DOC r ** **90 91 92** Equivalent of the last for junior VINO NOBILE, recently introduced and yet to establish a style.

Rosso Piceno Mar DOC r *→** **88 89 90 91** Stylish Adriatic red. Can be SUPERIORE from classic zone nr Ascoli. Best incl Cocci Grifoni, Villamagna.

Rubesco The excellent popular red of LUNGAROTTI; see Torgiano.

Rubino di Cantavenna Pie DOC r ** DYA Lively red, principally BARBERA, from a well-known coop SE of Turin.

Ruchè di Castagnole Monferrato DOC r (sw) *** Blend of BARBERA and GRIGNOLINO, barrel-aged and aromatic.

Ruffino Perhaps the biggest and best known of all CHIANTI merchants, at Pontassieve. RISERVA Ducale and Santedame are the top wines. NB new PREDICATO wines (red and white Cabreo) and CAB Il Pareto.

Rufina Important subregion of CHIANTI in the hills E of Florence.

Sagrantino di Montefalco Umb DOCG r sw ** **90 91 92** A little dry and even less sweet red. See also Montefalco.

Salice Salentino Ap DOC r ** **83 85 86 87 88 89 90 91 92** Strong red from NEGROAMARO grapes. RISERVA after 2 yrs; smooth when mature. Top makers: Francesco Candido, De Castris, Taurino, Vallone.

San Felice Rising star in CHIANTI with fine CLASSICO Poggio Rosso. Also red VDT Vigorello and PREDICATO di Biturica.

San Giusto a Rentennano One of the best CHIANTI CLASSICO producers. Delicious but v rare VINSANTO. Excellent VDT red Percarlo.

San Severo Ap DOC r p w ★ Sound neutral southern wine.

Sangiovese or Sangioveto Principal red grape of Italy, esp Tuscany. Many forms incl the noble BRUNELLO (of MONTALCINO) and Prugnolo Gentile (of MONTEPULCIANO). Also the following:

Sangiovese d'Aprilia Lat DOC p ★ DYA Strong dry rosé from S of Rome.

Sangiovese di Romagna E-R DOC r ★★ 87 88 89 90 91 92 Pleasant standard red; gains character with a little age.

Santa Maddalena T-AA DOC r ★ DYA Typical SCHIAVA Tyrolean red with bitter aftertaste.

Santa Margherita The Veneto winery that popularized PINOT GR, now on a broad base with many good wines.

Sassella (Valtellina) Lom DOC r ★★★ 85 86 88 89 90 Considerable NEBBIOLO wine, tough when young. Known since Roman times; mentioned by Leonardo da Vinci. Neighbour to INFERNO, etc.

Sassicaia Tus r ★★★★ 81 82 83 85 86 88 89 90 91 92 Outstanding pioneer CAB, Italy's best, from the Tenuta San Guido of the Incisa family, at Bolgheri nr Livorno.

Sauvignon Sauvignon Blanc is working v well in NE, perhaps best at TERLANO, ALTO ADIGE. Vg in COLLIO and COLLI ORIENTALI.

Sauvignon (Colli Berici) Ven DOC w ★ DYA The Vicenza version.

Sauvignon (Colli Orientali del Friuli) F-VG DOC w ★★→★★★ 89 90 91 92 This and the COLLIO version (next) vary from thin and simple to Sancerre-like and splendid. Top producers: Torre Rosazza, Vigne dal Leon.

Sauvignon (Collio) F-VG DOC w ★★→★★★ 89 90 91 92 See above. Top wines from La Castellada, GRAVNER, Edi Kante, Primosic, SCHIOPETTO, Villa Russiz.

Sauvignon (Isonzo) F-VG DOC w ★★→★★★ 90 91 92 V full fruity white, increasingly good quality. Top producers: Pecorari, Vie di Romans.

Savuto Cal DOC r p ★★ 90 91 92 Fragrant juicy wine from the provinces of Cosenza and Catanzaro.

Schiava High-yielding red grape of TRENTINO-ALTO ADIGE with characteristic bitter aftertaste, used for LAGO DI CALDARO, SANTA MADDALENA, etc.

Schiopetto, Mario Legendary pioneer of COLLIO with brand-new 20,000-case winery for excellent SAUVIGNON, MALVASIA, etc.

Sciacchetrà See Cinqueterre.

Secco Dry.

Sella & Mosca Major Sardinian growers and merchants at Alghero. Their port-like Anghelu Ruju is good. Also pleasant white TORBATO and delicious light fruity VERMENTINO Cala Viola (DYA).

Selvapiana CHIANTI RUFINA estate. Top wine is RISERVA Bucerchiale.

Settesoli Sicilian growers' coop with range of sometimes vg table wines.

Sforzato (Valtellina) Lom DOC r ★★★ 82 83 85 86 88 89 90 92 Valtellina equivalent of RECIOTO AMARONE made with partly dried grapes. Velvety, strong, ages remarkably well. Also called Sfursat.

Sizzano Pie DOC r ★★ 85 86 87 88 89 90 Attractive full-bodied red produced at Sizzano in the province of Novara, mostly from NEBBIOLO. Ages up to 10 yrs.

Soave Ven DOC w ★★→★★★ DYA Famous mass-produced Veronese white. Should be fresh with v attractive texture. Standards are rising (at last). S CLASSICO is more restricted and better. Top growers are ANSELMI, BOSCAINI, PIEROPAN. See also Bolla.

Solaia Tus r ★★★★ 78 79 82 83 85 86 88 90 V fine Bordeaux-style VDT of CAB S and a little SANGIOVESE from ANTINORI; first made in '78. Extraordinarily influential in shaping VDT (and Italian) philosophy.

Solopaca Cam DOC r w ★★ 89 90 91 92 Up-and-coming from nr Benevento; rather sharp when young, the white soft and fruity.

Sorni T-AA r w ★★ DYA From Trento. Light and soft. Drink young.

Spanna See Gattinara.

Spumante Sparkling, as in sweet ASTI or many good dry wines, incl both METODO CLASSICO (best from TRENTINO, ALTO ADIGE, FRANCIACORTA) and tank-made cheapos.

Squinzano Ap DOC r p ★ Strong southern red from Lecce.

Stravecchio Very old.

Südtirol The local name of German-speaking ALTO ADIGE.

Super Tuscans Term coined for high-price novelties from Tuscany, usually involving CAB and barriques.

Superiore Wine that has undergone more ageing than normal DOC and contains 1% more alcohol.

Taurasi Cam DOC r ★★★ 82 83 85 86 87 88 89 90 91 92 The best Campanian red, from MASTROBERARDINO of Avellino. Harsh when young. RISERVA after 4 yrs. Radici (since '86) is Mastroberardino's top estate bottling.

Tedeschi, Fratelli Leading small producer of VALPOLICELLA, RECIOTO and AMARONE. Vg Capitel San Rocco red and white VDT.

Terlano T-AA DOC w ★★→★★★ DYA A DOC for 8 white wines from the province of Bolzano, named by their grapes, esp outstanding SAUV. Terlaner in German.

Teroldego Rotaliano T-AA DOC r p ★★→★★★ 88 89 90 91 92 The attractive local red of Trento. Blackberry-scented; slight bitter aftertaste; can age v well. Top maker: Foradori.

Terre di Ginestra Si w ★★ Good VDT from Cataratto, SW of Palermo.

Terre Rosse Distinguished small estate nr Bologna. Its CAB, CHARD, SAUV BL, PINOT GR, RIES, even Viognier, etc, are the best of the region.

Tiefenbrunner Leading grower of some of the very best ALTO ADIGE white and red wines at Schloss Turmhof, Kurtatsch (Cortaccio).

Tignanello Tus r ★★★★ 82 83 85 86 88 90 Pioneer and still leader of the new style of Bordeaux-inspired Tuscan reds, made by ANTINORI.

Tocai (Colli Berici) Ven DOC w ★ DYA A more modest wine.

Tocai Friulano (Collio) ★★ DYA NE Italian white grape; no relation of Hungarian or Alsace Tokay. The TOCAIS of the COLLI ORIENTALI DEL FRIULI and COLLIO are best.

Tocai (Grave del Friuli) F-VG DOC w ★★ DYA Similar to TOCAI DI LISON; generally rather milder.

Tocai di Lison Ven DOC w ★★ DYA From E Veneto. Pleasant faintly fruity CLASSICO is better.

Tocai di San Martino della Battaglia Lom DOC w ★★ DYA Small production S of Lake Garda. Light, slightly bitter.

Torbato di Alghero Sar w (pa) ★★ DYA Good N Sardinian table wine. Top maker: SELLA & MOSCA.

Torgiano (Rubesco di) Umb DOCG r w ★★★ 85 87 88 90 The creation of the LUNGAROTTI family. Excellent red from nr Perugia, comparable with top CHIANTI CLASSICO. Rubesco is the standard quality. RISERVA Vigna Monticchio is superb; keep 10 yrs. VDT San Giorgio involves CAB to splendid effect. White Torre di Giano, of TREBBIANO and GRECHETTO, also ages well. See also Lungarotti.

Torricella Tus w ★★★ 85 86 87 88 90 Remarkable aged, soft, buttery MALVASIA dry white from Brolio. Produced by BARONE RICASOLI.

Toscana Tuscany.

Traminer Aromatico T-AA DOC w ★★→★★★ DYA Delicate aromatic rather soft Gewürz.

Trebbiano Principal white grape of Tuscany, found all over Italy. Ugni Blanc in French. Sadly a waste of good v'yd space, with v rare exceptions.

Trebbiano d'Abruzzo Ab, Mol DOC w ★→★★ DYA Gentle neutral slightly tannic. From round Pescara. VALENTINI is much the best producer (also of MONTEPULCIANO D'ABRUZZO).

Trebbiano d'Aprilia Lat DOC w ★ DYA Heady, mild, rather yellow. From S of Rome.

Trebbiano di Romagna E-R DOC w dr s/sw (sp) ★ DYA Clean pleasant white from nr Bologna.

Trentino T-AA DOC r w dr sw ★→★★★ DOC for as many as 20 different wines, mostly named after their grapes. Best are CHARD, PINOT BL, MARZEMINO, TEROLDEGO and esp VINSANTO. The region's capital is Trento.

Umani Ronchi A leading producer of quality wines of the Marches; notably VERDICCHIO (Casal di Serra and Villa Bianchi) and ROSSO CONERO (Cumaro and San Lorenzo).

Val d'Arbia Tus DOC w ★→★★ DYA Another DOC for a pleasant white and VIN SANTO from CHIANTI country.

Valcalepio Lom DOC r w ★ From nr Bergamo. Pleasant red; lightly scented fresh white.

Valdadige T-AA DOC r w dr s/sw ★ Name for the simple wines of the Adige Valley – in German 'Etschtaler'.

Valentini, Edoardo Perhaps the best traditionalist maker of TREBBIANO and MONTEPULCIANO D'ABRUZZO.

Valgella (Valtellina) Lom DOC r ★★ 85 86 88 89 90 One of the VALTELLINA NEBBIOLOS: good dry red. RISERVA at 4 yrs.

Valle d'Aosta VdA DOC Regional DOC for 15 Alpine wines incl DONNAZ. A mixed bag. Vg from monastery-run Institut Agricole Regional.

Valle Isarco T-AA DOC w ★→★★ DYA A DOC applicable to 5 varietal wines made NE of Bolzano. Good MULLER-T, SILVANER.

Valpantena Valley in the VALPOLICELLA zone. Rival to CLASSICO. See Bertani.

Valpolicella Ven DOC r ★→★★★ 89 90 91 92 Attractive light red from nr Verona; most attractive when young. Delicate nutty scent, slightly bitter taste. (None of this is true of junk Valpolicella sold in litre and bigger bottles.) CLASSICO more restricted; SUPERIORE has 12% alcohol and 1 yr of age. Best wines from ALLEGRINI, MASI, QUINTARELLI.

Valtellina Lom DOC r ★★→★★★ 88 89 90 91 92 A DOC for tannic wines made mainly from Chiavennasca (NEBBIOLO) grapes in Sondrio province, N Lombardy. V SUPERIORE are GRUMELLO, INFERNO, SASSELLA, VALGELLA.

Vecchio Samperi Si ★★★ The outstanding estate of MARSALA today, although not DOC. A dry aperitif not unlike amontillado sherry. The owner, De Bartoli, also makes DOC Marsalas.

Velletri Lat DOC r w dr s/sw ★ DYA Agreeable Roman dry red and smooth white. Drink young.

Vendemmia Harvest or vintage.

Venegazzù Ven r w sp ★★★ Remarkable rustic Bordeaux-style red produced from CAB grapes nr Treviso. Rich bouquet, soft warm taste. 'Della Casa' and 'Capo di Stato' are best quality. Also sparkling.

Verdicchio dei Castelli di Jesi Mar DOC w (sp) ★→★★★ DYA Ancient famous and pleasant fresh pale white from nr Ancona, dating back to the Etruscans. CLASSICO is more restricted. Traditionally comes in amphora-shaped bottles; today also standard bottles, notably from Brunori, Bucci, GAROFOLI, Monteschiavo, UMANI RONCHI; also FAZI-BATTAGLIA.

Verdicchio di Matelica Mar DOC w (sp) ★★ DYA Similar to the last, though less well-known. Bigger wines than Jesi.

Verdiso Rare native white grape of NE Italy, used with PROSECCO.

Verduzzo (Colli Orientali del Friuli) F-VG DOC w dr s/sw sw ★★→★★★ 88 89 90 91 92 Full-bodied white from a native grape. The best sweet is called Ramandolo. Top makers: Dario Coos, Giovanni Dri.

Verduzzo (del Piave) Ven DOC w ★ DYA A dull little white.

Vermentino Lig w DOC ★★ DYA Best seafood white of Riviera: from Pietra Ligure and San Remo. DOC is Riviera Ligure di Ponente. See Pigato.

Vermentino di Gallura Sar DOC w ★★ DYA Soft dry rather strong white from N Sardinia.

Vernaccia di Oristano Sar DOC w dr (sw fz) ★★★ 75 78 81 83 85 87 88 91 92 Sardinian speciality, like light sherry, a touch bitter, full-bodied and interesting. SUPERIORE with 15.5% alcohol and 3 yrs of age. Top producer Contini also makes ancient solera wine Antico Gregori.

Vernaccia di San Gimignano Tus DOC w (fz) ** **91 92** Should be a distinctive strong highly-flavoured wine from nr Siena. Michelangelo's favourite. Much today is light and bland, but there are signs of improvement. Try Teruzzi & Falchini, Montenidoli, Puthod or (old-style) Pietrafitta. RISERVA after 1 yr.
Vernaccia di Serrapetrona Mar DOC r s/sw sp ** DYA From Macerata; aromatic, with pleasantly bitter aftertaste.
Vernatsch German for SCHIAVA.
Vicchiomaggio Important CHIANTI CLASSICO estate near Greve. Famous if not brilliant.
VIDE An association of better-class Italian producers for marketing their estate wines from many parts of Italy.
Vietti Excellent small producer of some of PIEDMONT'S most characterful wines, incl BAROLO. At Castiglione Falletto in Barolo region.
Vigna A single vineyard – see Introduction, page 76.
Vignamaggio Historic, beautiful and vg CHIANTI CLASSICO estate nr Greve.
Villagrande Imposing old estate on the slopes of Mt Etna, Sicily. DOC ETNA.
Vino da arrosto 'Wine for roast meat', ie good robust dry red.
Vino Nobile di Montepulciano Tus DOCG r *** 83 85 86 87 88 90 91 92 Impressive CHIANTI-like red with bouquet and style, rapidly making its name and fortune. RISERVA after 3 yrs. Best estates incl AVIGNONESI, Bindella, BOSCARELLI, Le Casalte, Fattoria del Cerro, Contucci, Poliziano, Talosa, Tenuta Trerose, Valdipiatta.
Vino novello Italy's equivalent of France's primeurs (as in Beaujolais).
Vino da pasto 'Mealtime wine', ie nothing special.
Vino da tavola (vdt) 'Table wine': intended to be the humblest class of Italian wine, with no specific geographical or other claim to fame, but recently the category to watch (with reasonable circumspection and a wary eye on the price) for top-class wines not conforming to DOC regulations. New laws introduced in '92 will phase out this situation (see Introduction, page 76).
Vin Santo di Gambellara Ven DOC w sw ** Powerful velvety golden; made near Vicenza and Verona.
Vin Santo Toscano Tus w s/sw **→*** Aromatic rich and smooth. Aged in v small barrels called caratelli. Can be astonishing.
Vinsanto or **Vin(o) Santo** Term for certain strong sweet wines esp in Tuscany: usually PASSITO. Can be v fine, esp in Tuscany and TRENTINO.
Vintage Tunina F-VG w *** **88 89 90 91 92** A notable blended white from the JERMANN estate.
Voerzio, Roberto Young pace-setter in BAROLO producing refreshing wines.
Volpe Pasini Ambitious COLLIO ORIENTALI estate, esp for good SAUV and red blend Le Marne.
VQPRD Often found on the labels of DOC wines to signify Vini di Qualità Prodotti in Regioni Delimitate.
Zagarolo Lat DOC w dr s/sw ** DYA Neighbour of FRASCATI; similar wine.
Zanella, Maurizio Owner of CA'DEL BOSCO. His name is on his top CAB-MERLOT blend, one of Italy's best.
Zerbina, Fattoria New leader in Romagna with best ALBANA DOCG to date (a rich PASSITO), good SANGIOVESE and a barrique-aged Sangiovese-CAB VDT called Marzeno di Marzeno.
Zibibbo Si w sw ** Fashionable MOSCATO from the island of Pantelleria.
Zonin One of Italy's biggest privately owned estates and wineries, based at GAMBELLARA, with DOC VALPOLICELLA, etc. Other large estates are at ASTI and in CHIANTI, San Gimignano and FRIULI. Also at Barboursville, Virginia, USA.

Germany

Two decades of drift and demoralization in Germany's cellars have taken a terrible toll. They began with the 1971 Wine Laws, which encouraged low standards, over-production and confusing (not to say misleading) labelling. Demoralization, greed and fraud made matters worse. And so did the weather: 20 years with only four really good vintages.

But quality is reasserting itself. The world is aware once more that Germany's wines reach unassailable levels – when they are made of the right grapes. Above all, of Riesling. Four fine vintages have been matched by new determination among winemakers. Germany's best growers have at last resolved to ignore the laws that encourage inflation of quantity and dilution of quality, and make the best wine they can. They have turned their backs on sugar-watery wines. A large number are now being made dry or close to dry, with sweetness reserved as the exception, for Spätlesen and Auslesen and not always even for these. Growers are experimenting with barrique-ageing (though not of Riesling) to open up new stylistic possibilities and supply top restaurants. On the home market these fine dry wines are all the rage: abroad they have yet to be really appreciated.

Officially, all German wines are classified according to the ripeness of their grapes. Most German wine (like most French) needs sugar added before fermentation to make up for missing sunshine and increase its strength. But unlike in France, German wine from grapes ripe enough not to need extra sugar is made and sold as a separate product: Qualitätswein mit Prädikat, or QmP. Within this top category, natural sugar content is expressed by traditional terms in ascending order of ripeness: Kabinett, Spätlese, Auslese, Beerenauslese, Trockenbeerenauslese.

Qualitätswein bestimmter Anbaugebiete (QbA), the second level, is for wines that needed additional sugar before fermentation. The third level, Tafelwein, has no pretensions to quality.

Though there is much more detail in the laws, this is the gist of the quality grading. It differs completely from the French system in ignoring geographical difference. There are (at least as yet) no Grands Crus, no Premiers Crus. In theory all any German vineyard has to do to make the best wine is to grow the ripest grapes – even of inferior varieties.

The law distinguishes only between degrees of geographical exactness. In labelling quality wine the growers or merchants are given a choice. They can (and generally do) label the relatively small quantities of their best wine with the name of the precise vineyard or Einzellage. Germany has about 2,600 Einzellage names. Obviously only a relative few are famous enough to help sell the wine. Therefore the 1971 law created a second class of vineyard name: the Grosslage. A Grosslage is a group of neighbouring Einzellagen of supposedly similar character. Because there are fewer Grosslage names, and far more wine from each, they have the advantage of familiarity – a poor substitute for hard-earned fame.

Thirdly, growers or merchants may choose to sell their wine under a regional name: the word is Bereich. To cope with the

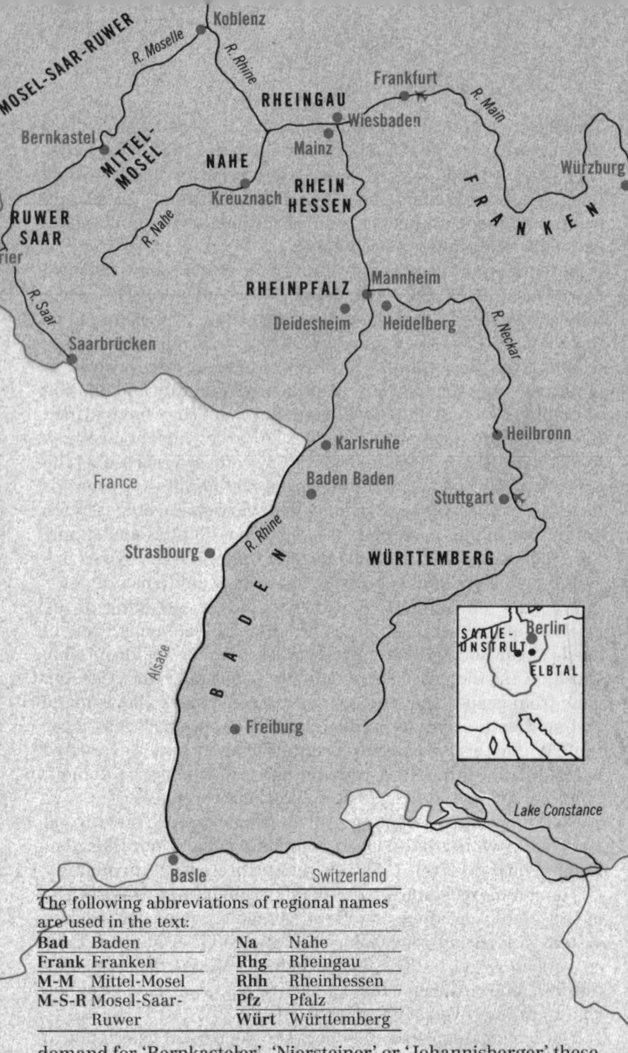

The following abbreviations of regional names are used in the text:

Bad	Baden	**Na**	Nahe
Frank	Franken	**Rhg**	Rheingau
M-M	Mittel-Mosel	**Rhh**	Rheinhessen
M-S-R	Mosel-Saar-Ruwer	**Pfz**	Pfalz
		Würt	Württemberg

demand for 'Bernkasteler', 'Niersteiner' or 'Johannisberger' these world-famous names have been made legal for large districts. 'Bereich Johannisberg' is the whole of Rheingau. By this logic the whole of the Médoc could be Margaux. Beware the Bereich.

More and more growers and estates are now using their own simplified labels to avoid confusion and clutter. Some use the village name only, not mentioning the vineyard, or indeed omit even this and sell top wines under their brand name alone in the Italian fashion. But before Germany can fully recover her rightful place, two things are needed: the banning of inferior grapes such as Müller-Thurgau from the best areas, and a thoroughgoing classification of which those areas are. It is after all, and in Germany above all, the vineyard and the producer that count.

Recent vintages

Mosel-Saar-Ruwer

Mosels (including Saar and Ruwer wines) are so attractive young that their keeping qualities are not often enough explored and wines older than about 7 yrs are unusual. But well-made Riesling wines of Kabinett class gain from 5 or more in bottle, Spätlese by 10 yrs or so, and Auslese and Beerenauslese by anything from 10–30 yrs.

As a rule, in poor yrs the Saar and Ruwer make sharp thin wines, but in the best years they can surpass the whole world for elegance and thrilling steely 'breed'.

1992 A very large crop, threatened by cold and rain in October. Mostly good QbA, but 30% QmP, some exceptional, esp in Mittelmosel.
1991 A diverse vintage. Bad frost damage in Saar and Ruwer, but many fine Spätlesen in Mittelmosel.
1990 Superb vintage, though small. Many QmP wines are the finest for 20 years.
1989 Large and outstandingly good, with noble rot giving many Auslesen etc. Saar best; Mittelmosel overproduced.
1988 Excellent vintage. Much ripe QmP, esp in Mittelmosel. For long keeping.
1987 Rainy summer but warm Sept/Oct. 90% QbA wines, crisp and lively, to drink soon.
1986 Fair Riesling year despite autumn rain: 13% QmP wines, mostly Kabinett. For drinking.
1985 A modest summer but beautiful autumn. 40% of harvest was QmP. Riesling vintage from best v'yds, incl Eiswein. Many need keeping.
1984 A late and rainy year. Two-thirds QbA, one-third Tafel- or Landwein. Almost no QmP. Avoid.
1983 The best between 76 and 88; 31% Spätlese; Auslesen few but fine. No hurry to drink.
1982 A huge ripe vintage marred by rain which considerably diluted the wines. Most is plain QbA but good sites made Kabinett, Spätlese and Auslese. Drink up.
1981 A wet vintage but some good Mittelmosels up to Spätlese. Also Eiswein. Drinking well.
1980 A terrible summer. Some pleasant wines but little more. Avoid.
1979 A patchy vintage after bad winter damage. But several excellent Kabinetts and better. Light but well-balanced wines should be drunk up. Auslesen will still improve.
1978 V late and rather small. Generally to be avoided. Drink up.
1977 Big vintage of serviceable quality, mostly QbA. Drink up.
1976 Vg small vintage, with some superlative sweet wines and almost no dry. Most wines now ready; the best will keep.
1975 Vg; many Spätlesen and Auslesen. Almost all now ready.
1971 Superb, with perfect balance. At its peak.

Older fine vintages: 64, 59, 53, 49, 45.

Rheinhessen, Nahe, Pfalz, Rheingau

Even the best wines can be drunk with pleasure when young, but Kabinett, Spätlese and Auslese Riesling wines gain enormously in character by keeping for longer. Rheingau wines tend to be longest-lived, improving for 15 yrs or more, but wines from the Nahe and Palatinate can last as long. Rheinhessen wines usually mature sooner, and dry Franken wines are best at 3–6 yrs.

1992 Very large vintage, would have been great but for October cold and rain. A third QmP wines of rich stylish quality.
1991 A good middling vintage in most regions, though light soils in Pfalz suffered from drought. Some fine wines will emerge.
1990 Small but exceptionally fine. High percentage of QmP to lay down.
1989 Summer storms reduced crop in Rheingau. Vg quality elsewhere, up to Auslese level.
1988 Not quite so outstanding as the Mosel, but comparable with 83. Drinking well.
1987 Good average quality: lively round and fresh. 80% QbA, 15% QmP. Now drinking well.
1986 Well-balanced Rieslings, mostly QbA but some Kabinett and Spätlese, esp in Rheinhessen and Nahe. Good botrytis wines in Pfalz.
1985 Sadly small crops, but good quality, esp Riesling. Average 65% QmP. Keep the best.
1984 Poor flowering and ripening. Three-quarters QbA. Nothing to wait for.
1983 Vg Rieslings, esp in the Rheingau and central Nahe. Generally about half QbA, but plenty of Spätlesen, now excellent to drink.
1982 A colossal vintage gathered in torrential rain. All 82s should be drunk up.
1981 Rheingau poor, Nahe and Rheinhessen better, Pfalz best. Drink up.
1980 Bad weather from spring to autumn. Only passable wines. Avoid.
1979 Few great wines but many typical and good, esp in Palatinate. Drink up.
1978 Satisfactory vintage saved by late autumn. 25% QmP, but v few Spätlesen. Drink up.
1977 Big and useful; few Kabinett wines or better. Drink up.
1976 The richest vintage since 21 in places. Very few dry wines. Balance less consistent than 75. Generally mature.
1975 A splendid Riesling yr, a high percentage of Kabinett and Spätlesen. Drink soon.
1971 A superlative vintage, now at its peak.

Older fine vintages: 69, 67, 64, 59, 53, 49, 45.

NB On the German vintage notation

Vintage notes after entries in the German section are given in a different form from those elsewhere, to show the style of the vintage as well as its quality. Three styles are indicated:

Bold type (eg **90**) indicates classic, super-ripe vintages with a high proportion of natural (QmP) wines, including Spätlese and Auslese.

Normal type (eg 92) indicates 'normal' successful vintages with plenty of good wine but no great preponderance of sweeter wines.

Italic type (eg *84*) indicates cool vintages with generally poor ripeness but a fair proportion of reasonably successful wines, tending to be over-acid. Few or no QmP wines, but correspondingly more selection in the QbA category. Such wines sometimes mature better than expected.

Where no mention is made the vintage is generally not recommended, or most of its wines have passed maturity.

Achkarren Bad w (r) ★★ Village on the KAISERSTUHL, known esp for SILVANER, RULANDER. Best site: Schlossberg. Good wines: DR HEGER and coop.

Adelmann, Graf Grower with 37 acres at Kleinbottwar, WURTTEMBERG. Uses the name'Brussele'. Reds best.

Ahr Ahr r ★→★★ **76** 83 **85** 87 **88 89 90** 91 92 Germany's best-known red-wine area, south of Bonn. Very light, pale SPATBURGUNDER, esp from Kloster Marienthal, Meyer-Näkel, STATE DOMAIN.

Amtliche Prüfungsnummer See Prüfungsnummer.

Anheuser Name of two growers of the NAHE, August (★) and Paul (★★★).

APNr Abbreviation of AMTLICHE PRUFUNGSNUMMER.

Assmannshausen Rhg r ★→★★★ **71** 75 **76** 83 **85** 87 **88 89 90** 91 92 RHEINGAU village known for its usually pale, sometimes sweet reds. Top v'yd: Höllenberg. Grosslagen: Steil and Burgweg. Growers incl August Kesseler, Robert König, VON MUMM, and the STATE DOMAIN at ELTVILLE.

Auslese Specially selected wine with high natural sugar content; the best affected by 'noble rot' (Edeldfäule) and correspondingly unctuous in flavour.

Avelsbach M-S-R (Ruwer) w ★★★ **71** 75 **76** 83 **85** 87 **88 89 90 91** 92 Village nr TRIER. Supremely delicate wines. Growers: BISCHOFLICHE WEINGUTER, Staatliche Weinbaudomäne (see Staatsweingut). Grosslage: Römerlay.

Ayl M-S-R (Saar) w ★★★ **71** 75 **76** 83 **85** 87 **88** 89 **90 91** 92 One of the best villages of the SAAR. Top v'yd: Kupp. Grosslage: SCHARZBERG. Growers incl BISCHOFLICHE WEINGUTER, LAUERBURG, WAGNER.

Bacchus Modern, perfumed, even kitsch, grape, best for sweet wines.

Bacharach Romantic old town, a tourist centre of the MITTELRHEIN.

Bacharach (Bereich) ★→★★ District name for the southern MITTELRHEIN v'yds downstream from the RHEINGAU. Steely racy RIESLINGS, some v fine. Growers incl TONI JOST, Ratzenberger.

Baden Huge SW area of scattered wine-growing. The style is substantial, generally dry, relatively low in acid, good for mealtimes. Fine Pinots etc and SPATBURGUNDER, less RIES. Best areas: KAISERSTUHL, ORTENAU.

Badische Bergstrasse/Kraichgau (Bereich) Widespread district of N BADEN. RIES and RULANDER are best.

Badischer Winzerkeller New name for the ZBW, Germany's (and Europe's) biggest coop, at BREISACH; 25,000 members with 12,000 acres, producing almost half of BADEN's wine at all quality levels.

Badisches Frankenland (Bereich) Minor district name of N BADEN; FRANKEN-style wines.

Bad Dürkheim Pfz w (r) ★★→★★★ **76** 83 **85** 86 87 **88 89 90** 91 92 Main town of the MITTELHAARDT, with the world's biggest barrel (converted into a tavern). Scene of a vast and ancient September wine festival, the 'Wurstmarkt'. Top v'yds: Michelsberg, Spielberg. Grosslagen: Feuerberg, Hochmess, Schenkenböhl. Top growers: Darting, FITZ-RITTER, Karst, KOEHLER-RUPRECHT, Schäfer.

Bad Kreuznach Nahe w ★★→★★★ **75 76 79 83 85 86 87 88 89 90 91 92** Main town of the NAHE with some of its best wines. Many fine v'yds, incl Brückes, Kahlenberg, Krötenpfuhl. Grosslage: Kronenberg. Growers incl ANHEUSER, Finkenauer, PLETTENBERG.

Balbach Erben, Bürgermeister One of the best-known NIERSTEIN growers. 44 acres, 80% RIES. Best v'yd: Pettenthal.

Barriques Some German growers are experimenting with fashionable new-oak small-barrel ageing. A quick route to notoriety and higher prices, it can be positive for SPATBURGUNDER, WEISSBURGUNDER or GRAUBURGUNDER, but not RIES.

Bassermann-Jordan 117-acre MITTELHAARDT family estate with many of the best v'yds in DEIDESHEIM, FORST, RUPPERTSBERG, etc. 100% RIES and a formidable track-record.

Becker, J B Dedicated family estate and brokerage house at WALLUF. 30 acres in ELTVILLE, MARTINSTHAL, Walluf. Specialist in dry RIESLINGS.

Beerenauslese Extremely sweet and luscious wine from selected exceptionally ripe individual berries, their sugar and flavour usually concentrated by 'noble rot'. Very rare and expensive.

Bercher KAISERSTUHL estate; 40 acres of white and red Pinots at Burkheim. Good dry wines.

Bereich District within an Anbaugebiet (region). The word on a label should be treated as a warning. As a rule do not buy. See Introduction and under Bereich names, eg Bernkastel (Bereich).

Bergweiler-Prüm-Erben, Weingut Zacharias, See Pauly-Bergweiler, Dr.

Bernkastel M-M w ★★→★★★★ **71 75 76 79 83** ***84*** **85 86 87 88 89 90 91 92** Top wine town of the MITTELMOSEL; the epitome of RIES. Best v'yds: Doctor (8 acres), Graben, Lay. Grosslagen: Badstube (★★★) and Kurfürstlay (★★). Top growers incl FRIEDRICH WILHELM GYMNASIUM, KERPEN, LAUERBURG, LOOSEN, PAULY-BERGWEILER, PRUM, Studert-Prüm, THANISCH, WEGELER-DEINHARD.

Bernkastel (Bereich) Wide area of deplorably mixed quality but hopefully flowery character. Mostly MULLER-T. Includes all the MITTELMOSEL.

Biffar, Josef Rising star DEIDESHEIM estate. 40 acres (also WACHENHEIM) of RIES. Intense classic wines.

Bingen Rhh w ★★→★★★ **71 75 76 83 85 87 88 89 90 91 92** Town on Rhine and NAHE with fine v'yds, incl Scharlachberg. Grosslage: Sankt Rochuskapelle. Top grower: VILLA SACHSEN.

Bingen (Bereich) District name for west RHEINHESSEN.

Bischöfliche Weingüter Famous M-S-R estate at TRIER, a union of the cathedral properties with 2 other famous charities, the Bischöfliches Priesterseminar and the Bischöfliches Konvikt. 260 acres of top v'yds, esp in SAAR and RUWER, but wines recently disappointing.

Blue Nun The best-selling brand of LIEBFRAUMILCH, from SICHEL.

Bocksbeutel Flask-shaped bottle used for FRANKEN wines.

Bodenheim Rhh w ★★ Village nr NIERSTEIN with full earthy wines, esp from Silberberg. Top growers: Kühling-Gillot, Liebrecht.

Bodensee (Bereich) Minor district of S BADEN, on Lake Constance.

Brauneberg M-M w ★★★ **71 75 76 83 85 86 87 88 89 90 91 92** Village nr BERNKASTEL with 750 acres. Excellent full-flavoured RIES. Best v'yd: Juffer-SONNENUHR. Grosslage: Kurfürstlay. Growers incl FRITZ HAAG, WILLI HAAG, Paulinshof, PAULY-BERGWEILER, RICHTER.

Breisach Bad Frontier town on RHINE nr KAISERSTUHL. Seat of the largest German coop, the BADISCHER WINZERKELLER.

Breisgau (Bereich) Minor district of BADEN, just north and east of KAISERSTUHL. Best known for very pale pink WEISSHERBST.

Breuer, Weingut G Family estate of 36 acres in RUDESHEIM, with 6 acres of Berg Schlossberg. Fine quality and new ideas, incl sparkling wine (87) blended from RIES plus Pinots Bl and Gr.

Buhl, Reichsrat von Historic PFALZ family estate. 160 acres in DEIDESHEIM, FORST, RUPPERTSBERG, etc. Recently leased by Japanese firm.

Bundesweinprämierung The German State Wine Award, organized by DLG (see below): gives great (Grosse), silver or bronze medallion labels.

Bürgerspital zum Heiligen Geist Ancient charitable estate at WURZBURG. 333 acres in Würzburg, RANDERSACKER, etc, make often magnificent rich dry wines, esp from SILVANER and RIES.

Bürklin-Wolf, Dr Famous PFALZ family estate. 247 acres in WACHENHEIM, FORST, DEIDESHEIM and RUPPERTSBERG. Vg 89s.

Castell'sches, Fürstlich Domänenamt Historic 142-acre princely estate in STEIGERWALD. Noble FRANKEN wines: SILVANER, RIESLANER. Also SEKT.

Chardonnay A small acreage of Chard has been experimentally, and sometimes illegally, planted – it is now legal in the PFALZ and BADEN-WURTTEMBERG.

Charta Organization of top RHEINGAU estates making dry RIES. Wines made to far higher standards than dismally permissive laws require.

Christoffel, J J Tiny domaine in ERDEN, GRAACH, WEHLEN, URZIG. Polished RIES.

Crusius 30-acre family estate at TRAISEN, NAHE. Vivid RIES from Bastei, Rotenfels and SCHLOSSBOCKELHEIM. Felsenberg can age v well. Also good SEKT and freshly fruity SPATBURGUNDER dry rosé.

Deidesheim Pfz w (r) **→**** 71 75 76 83 85 86 87 88 89 90 91 92 Biggest top-quality wine village of PFALZ with 1,000 acres. Rich high-flavoured lively wines. Also Sekt. Top v'yds incl Grainhübel, Hohenmorgen, Kalkofen, etc. Grosslagen: Hofstück (**), Mariengarten (***). Top growers: BASSERMANN-JORDAN, Biffar, BURKLIN-WOLF, DEINHARD, VON BUHL.

Deinhard Famous old Koblenz merchants and growers of top-quality wines in RHEINGAU, MITTELMOSEL, RUWER and PFALZ (see Wegeler-Deinhard), also makers of vg SEKT (eg brand name: Lila). Their Heritage range of single-village (DEIDESHEIM, HOCHHEIM, JOHANNISBERG, etc) TROCKEN wines are well-made but singularly austere. Leaders in both quality and new ideas.

Deinhard, Dr Fine 62-acre family estate: many of DEIDESHEIM's best v'yds.

Deutscher Tafelwein Officially the term for humble German wines. Now confusingly the flag of convenience for some top novelties (eg BARRIQUE wines) as well.

Deutsches Weinsiegel A quality seal (ie neck label) for wines which have passed a statutory tasting test. Seals are: yellow for dry, green for medium-dry, red for medium-sweet.

Deutsche Weinstrasse Tourist road of southern PFALZ, Bockenheim to SCHWEIGEN.

DLG (Deutsche Landwirtschaftgesellschaft) The German Agricultural Society at Frankfurt. Awards national medals for quality.

Dhron See Neumagen-Dhron.

Diabetiker Wein Wine with minimal residual sugar (less than 4 grams per litre); thus suitable for diabetics – or those who like very dry wine.

Diel auf Burg Layen, Schlossgut Fashionable 30-acre NAHE estate; known for ageing RULANDER and WEISSBURGUNDER in French BARRIQUES. Also fine traditional RIES.

Dom German for 'cathedral'. Wines from the famous TRIER cathedral properties have 'Dom' before the v'yd name.

Domäne German for 'domain' or 'estate'. Sometimes used alone to mean the 'State domain' (STAATLICHE WEINBAUDOMANE).

Dönnhoff, Weingut Hermann 23-acre NAHE estate with exceptionally fine RIES from NIEDERHAUSEN, Oberhausen, etc.

Dornfelder New red grape making deep-coloured everyday wines in PFALZ.

Durbach Baden w (r) **→*** 76 83 85 87 88 89 90 91 92 Village with 775 acres of BADEN's best v'yds. Top growers: H Männle, von Neveu, SCHLOSS STAUFENBERG, Wolf-Metternich. Choose their KLINGELBERGERS (RIES) and KLEVNERS (TRAMINER). Grosslage: Fürsteneck.

Edel Means 'noble'. Edelfäule means 'noble rot': the condition which gives the greatest sweet wines (see page 51).

Egon Müller zu Scharzhof Top SAAR estate of 32 acres at WILTINGEN. Its delicate racy SCHARZHOFBERGER RIESLINGS are among the world's greatest wines, esp in AUSLESEN-producing vintages. The best Auslesen are given gold capsules. 89s and 90s are sublime honeyed immortal. Le Gallais is a second estate in WILTINGER Braune Kupp.

Eiswein Wine made from frozen grapes with the ice (ie water content) discarded, thus v concentrated in flavour and sugar, of BEERENAUSLESE ripeness or more. Rare and v expensive. Sometimes produced as late as January or February following the vintage. Alcohol content can be as low as 5.5%. High acidity gives them v long life.

Eitelsbach M-S-R (Ruwer) w ★★→★★★ **71 75 76 83 85 87 88 89 90 91 92** RUWER village now part of TRIER, incl superb KARTHAUSERHOFBERG estate. Grosslage: Römerlay.

Elbling Traditional grape widely grown on upper MOSEL. Can be sharp and tasteless but capable of great freshness and vitality in the best conditions (eg at Nittel in the OBERMOSEL).

Elbtal Sachsen Former E German wine region of 750 acres on the outskirts of Dresden and Meissen. MULLER-T dominant; also WEISSBURGUNDER, TRAMINER, etc. Schloss Wackerbarth makes good SEKT Graf von Wackerbarth.

Eltville Rhg w ★★→★★★ **71 75 76 83 85 86 87 88 89 90 91 92** Major wine town with cellars of RHEINGAU STATE DOMAIN, FISCHER and VON SIMMERN estates. Excellent wines. Top v'yd: Sonnenberg. Grosslage: Steinmächer.

Enkirch M-M w ★★→★★★ **71 76 83 85 87 88 89 90 91** Minor MITTELMOSEL village, often overlooked but with lovely light tasty wine. Grosslage: Schwarzlay. Top v'yds: Batterieberg, Zeppwingert. Top grower: IMMICH-BATTERIEBERG.

Erbach Rhg w ★★★→★★★★ **71 76 83 85 86 87 88 89 90 91 92** Top RHEINGAU area: powerful perfumed wines, incl the great MARCOBRUNN; other top v'yds: Schlossberg, Siegelsberg. Major estates: SCHLOSS REINHARTSHAUSEN, SCHLOSS SCHONBORN. Also BECKER, KNYPHAUSEN, VON SIMMERN, etc.

Erben Word meaning 'heirs', often used on old-established estate labels.

Erden M-M w ★★→★★★ **71 75 76 83** *84* **85 86 87 88 89 90 91 92** Village between Urzig and Kröv: noble full-flavoured vigorous wine. Top v'yds: Prälat, Treppchen. Grosslage: Schwarzlay. Growers incl BISCHOFLICHE WEINGUTER, Stefan Ehlen, LOOSEN, Meulenhoff, MONCHHOF, Nicolay.

Erzeugerabfüllung Bottled by producer. Being replaced by 'GUTSABFULLUNG'.

Escherndorf Frank w ★★→★★★ 76 83 87 88 89 90 91 92 Important wine town near WURZBURG. Similar tasty dry wine. Top v'yds: Berg, Lump. Grosslage: Kirchberg. Growers incl JULIUSSPITAL.

Eser, Weingut August 20-acre RHEINGAU estate at OESTRICH. V'yds also in HALLGARTEN, RAUENTHAL (esp Gehrn, Rothenberg), WINKEL. Model wines.

Eser, Hans Hermann JOHANNISBERG family estate. 45 acres. RIESLINGS that justify the great Johannisberg name.

Filzen M-S-R (Saar) w ★★→★★★ **76 83 85 87 88 89 90 91 92** Small SAAR village nr WILTINGEN. Grower to note: Piedmont.

Fischer, Weingut Dr 60-acre OCKFEN, WAWERN estate: generally high quality.

Fischer Erben, Weingut 18-acre RHEINGAU estate at ELTVILLE with highest traditional standards. Long-lived classic wines.

Fitz-Ritter Reliable BAD DURKHEIM estate. 54 acres, fine RIES.

Forschungsanstalt See Hessische Forschungsanstalt.

Forst Pfz w ★★→★★★★ **71 75 76 83 85 86 87 88 89 90 91 92** MITTELHAARDT village with 500 acres of Germany's best v'yds. Ripe richly fragrant full-bodied but subtle wines. Top v'yds: Jesuitengarten, Kirchenstück, Ungeheuer. Grosslagen: Mariengarten, Schnepfenflug. Top growers: BASSERMANN-JORDAN, DEINHARD, Mosbacher, Spindler, Werlé.

To decipher codes, please refer to symbols key at front of book, and to 'How to Read an Entry' on page 5.

Franken Franconia: region of excellent distinctive dry wines, esp SILVANER, always bottled in round-bellied flasks. The centre is WURZBURG. Bereich names: MAINDREIECK, STEIGERWALD. Top producers: BURGERSPITAL, JULIUSSPITAL, WIRSCHING, etc.

Freiburg Baden w (r) ★→★★ DYA Wine centre in N of MARKGRAFLERLAND. Good GUTEDEL.

Freinsheim Pfz w r ★★ Well-known village of MITTELHAARDT with high proportion of RIES. Aromatic spicy wines. Top grower: LINGENFELDER.

Friedrich Wilhelm Gymnasium Superb 111-acre charitable estate based in TRIER with v'yds in BERNKASTEL, GRAACH, OCKFEN, TRITTENHEIM, ZELTINGEN, etc, all M-S-R. Sound wines and good value.

Fuhrmann See Pfeffingen.

Gallais Le See Egon Müller.

Geheimrat 'J' Brand-name of good very dry RIES SPATLESE from WEGELER-DEINHARD, OESTRICH, since '85. Epitomizes new thinking.

Geisenheim Rhg w ★★→★★★ **71 76 83 85 86 87 88 89 90 91 92** Village famous for Germany's best-known wine school and fine aromatic wines. Best v'yds incl Kläuserweg, Rothenberg. Grosslagen: Burgweg, Erntebringer. Many top growers (eg SCHLOSS SCHONBORN) have v'yds here.

Gemeinde A commune or parish.

Gewürztraminer (or Traminer) Spicy grape, speciality of Alsace, used a little in Germany, esp PFALZ, RHEINHESSEN and BADEN.

Gimmeldingen Pfz w ★→★★ **76** 83 85 87 88 89 **90** 91 92 Village just S of MITTELHAARDT. At their best, similar wines. Grosslage: Meerspinne. Top grower: MULLER-CATOIR.

Goldener Oktober Brand of RHINE and MOSEL blends from ST-URSULA.

Graach M-M w ★★→★★★ **71 75 76 83** *84* 85 86 87 88 89 90 91 92 Small village between BERNKASTEL and WEHLEN. Top v'yds: Domprobst, Josephshöfer. Grosslage: Münzlay. The many top growers include: KESSELSTATT, LOOSEN, PRUM, WILLI SCHAEFER, SELBACH-OSTER, WEINS-PRUM.

Grans-Fassian Fine 25-acre MOSEL estate at Leiwen. V'yds there and in PIESPORT, TRITTENHEIM.

Grauburgunder Synonym of RULANDER or Pinot Gris.

Remember that vintage information for German wines is given in a different form from the ready/not ready distinction applying to other countries. Read the explanation on page 100.

Grosser Ring Group of top (VdP) MOSEL-SAAR-RUWER estates.

Grosslage See Introduction, pages 97–8.

Grosvenor, G & M Wine-brokers of JOHANNISBERG and exporters of many fine estate wines.

Gunderloch Excellent 30-acre NACKENHEIM estate, perhaps the best in RHEINHESSEN today. 70% RIES. Best from N Rothenberg, but all are vg.

Guntersblum Rhh w ★→★★ **76** 83 85 88 89 **90** 91 92 Big wine town S of OPPENHEIM. Grosslagen: Krötenbrunnen, Vogelsgärten. Top grower: RAPPENHOF.

Guntrum, Louis Fine 164-acre family estate in NIERSTEIN, OPPENHEIM, etc, and merchant house with high and reliable standards. Fine SILVANERS and GEWURZ as well as RIES.

Gutedel German word for the Chasselas grape, used in S BADEN.

Gutsabfüllung Estate-bottled. A new term limited to qualified estates.

Gutsverwaltung Estate administration.

Haag, Fritz and Willi Two small high quality estates at BRAUNEBERG. Fritz Haag is in the v top league.

Haart, Reinhold Small estate emerging as the best in PIESPORT.

Halbtrocken Medium-dry (literally 'semi-dry'). Containing less than 18 but more than 9 grams per litre unfermented sugar. An increasingly popular category of wine intended for mealtimes, often better balanced than TROCKEN. All CHARTA wines are halbtrocken.

Hallgarten Rhg w ★★→★★★ 71 76 83 85 86 87 88 89 90 91 92 Small wine town behind HATTENHEIM. Robust full-bodied wines, mysteriously seldom seen.

Hallgarten, House of Well-known London-based wine merchant.

Hattenheim Rhg w ★★→★★★★ 71 75 76 83 85 87 88 89 90 91 92 Superlative 500-acre wine town. V'yds incl Nussbrunnen, Mannberg, Pfaffenberg, STEINBERG (ORTSTEIL), Wisselbrunnen, etc. Grosslage: Deutelsberg. MARCOBRUNN lies on ERBACH boundary. Many fine estates incl KNYPHAUSEN, RESS, SCHLOSS SCHONBORN, VON SIMMERN, STATE DOMAIN, etc.

Heger, Dr Some of BADEN's best SPATBURGUNDER reds come from old vines on this 28-acre IHRINGEN estate. Also fine GRAUBURDUNDER, WEISSBURGUNDER.

Heilbronn Würt w r ★→★★ 76 83 85 87 88 89 90 91 92 Wine town with many small growers and a big coop. Best wines are RIESLINGS. Seat of DLG competition. Top growers: Amalienhof, Drautz-Able, Heinrich.

Hessen, Prinz von Wide-ranging 75-acre estate in JOHANNISBERG, WINKEL, KIEDRICH and ELTVILLE. An under-achiever. Wines incl 'Kurhessen' Sekt (transfer and méthode traditionelle).

Hessische Bergstrasse w ★★→★★★ 76 83 85 87 88 89 90 91 92 Smallest wine region in former West Germany (1,000 acres), N of Heidelberg. Pleasant RIES from STATE DOMAIN v'yds in Bensheim, Bergstrasser Coop, Heppenheim and Stadt Bensheim.

Hessische Forschungsanstalt für Wein-Obst-& Gartenbau Famous wine school and research establishment at GEISENHEIM, RHEINGAU. Good wines incl reds. The name on the label is Forschungsanstalt.

Heyl zu Herrnsheim Leading 72-acre NIERSTEIN estate, 60% RIES, with an excellent record.

Hochgewächs A superior level of QBA RIES, esp in MOSEL-SAAR-RUWER.

Hochheim Rhg w ★★→★★★ 71 75 76 79 83 *84* 85 86 87 88 89 90 91 92 600-acre wine town 15 miles E of main part of RHEINGAU. Similar fine wines with an earthy intensity and fragrance of their own. Top v'yds: Domdechaney, Hölle, Kirchenstück, Königin Viktoria Berg (12-acre monopoly of Hupfeld of OESTRICH, sold only by DEINHARD). Grosslage: Daubhaus. Growers incl Aschrott, Hupfeld, FRANZ KUNSTLER, RESS, SCHLOSS SCHONBORN, STAATSWEINGUT, WERNER.

Hock English term for Rhine wine, derived from HOCHHEIM.

Hoensbroech, Weingut Reichsgraf zu Top KRAICHGAU estate. 37 acres. Excellent dry KABINETT WEISSBURGUNDER and SILVANER eg Michelfelder Himmelberg. Some of BADEN's best wines.

Hövel, Weingut von Very fine SAAR estate at OBERMOSEL (Hütte has 12-acre monopoly) and in SCHARZHOFBERG.

Huesgen, Adolph Important merchant house at TRABEN-TRARBACH.

Huxelrebe Modern, very aromatic grape variety, mainly for dessert wines.

Ihringen Bad r w ★→★★★ 83 85 86 87 88 89 90 91 92 One of the best villages of the KAISERSTUHL, BADEN. Proud of its SPATBURGUNDER red, WEISSHERBST and vg SILVANER. Top growers: Heger, Stigler.

Ilbesheim Pfz w ★→★★ 83 85 87 88 89 90 91 92 Base of important growers' coop of SUDLICHE WEINSTRASSE 'Deutsches Weintor'. See also Schweigen.

Immich-Batterieberg The top estate of ENKIRCH. 15 acres. Sole owner of Batterieberg v'yd.

Ingelheim Rhh r w ★ 85 88 89 90 91 92 Town opposite the RHEINGAU historically known for SPATBURGUNDER.

Iphofen Frank w ★★→★★★ 75 76 79 *83* 85 87 88 89 90 91 92 Village E of WURZBURG. Superb top v'yd: Julius-Echter-Berg. Grosslage: Burgweg. Growers: JULIUSSPITAL, Ruck, STAATLICHER HOFKELLER, WIRSCHING.

Jahrgang Year – as in 'vintage'.

Johannisberg Rhg w ★★→★★★★ 71 75 76 83 85 86 87 88 89 90 91 92 260-acre village with superlative subtle RIES. Top v'yds incl Hölle, SCHLOSS JOHANNISBERG, Klaus, etc. Grosslage: Erntebringer. Many good growers. But beware 'Bereich Johannisberg' wines (see next entry).

Johannisberg (Bereich) District name for the entire RHEINGAU.

Johner, Karl-Heinz Tiny BADEN estate at Bischoffingen in the front line for new-look SPATBURGUNDER and oak-aged WEISSBURGUNDER.

Josephshöfer Fine v'yd at GRAACH, the sole property of VON KESSELSTATT.

Jost, Toni Perhaps the top estate of the MITTELRHEIN. 25 acres, mainly RIES, in BACHARACH and also in the RHEINGAU.

Juliusspital Ancient religious charity at WURZBURG with 374 acres of top FRANKEN v'yds and many of the region's best wines. Look for its SILVANERS.

Kabinett The term for the lightest category of natural, unsugared (QMP) wines. Low in alcohol (RIES averages 7–9%) but capable of sublime finesse. Do not hurry to drink.

Kaiserstuhl (Bereich) One of the top districts of BADEN, with a notably warm climate and volcanic soil. Villages incl ACHKARREN, IHRINGEN. Grosslage: Vulkanfelsen.

Kallstadt Pfz w (r) ★★→★★★ 76 83 85 86 87 88 89 90 91 92 Village of N MITTELHAARDT. Fine rich wines. Top v'yds: Annaberg, Saumagen. Grosslagen: Feuerberg, Kobnert. Growers incl Henninger, KOEHLER-RUPRECHT, Schüster.

Kammerpreismünze See Landespreismünze.

Kanzem M-S-R (Saar) w ★★★ 71 75 76 83 85 87 88 89 90 91 92 Small neighbour of WILTINGEN. Top v'yd: Altenberg. Grosslage: SCHARZBERG. Growers incl Othegraven, Reverchon. Best is J P Reinert.

Karlsmühle Hotelier in MERTESDORF, making top-grade RUWERS in his monopole v'yd: Lorenzhof.

Karthäuserhofberg Top RUWER estate of 46 acres at Eitelsbach. Easily recognized by bottles with only a neck-label. Recently back on top form, esp with Gold Capsule AUSLESEN.

Kasel M-S-R (Ruwer) w ★★→★★★ 71 75 76 83 85 86 87 88 89 90 91 92 Village with stunning flowery light wines. Best v'yd: Nies'chen. Grosslage: Römerlay. Top growers: KARLSMUHLE, VON KESSELSTATT, WEGELER-DEINHARD.

Keller Wine cellar.

Kellerei Winery.

Kerner Modern grape variety, earlier-ripening than RIES, of fair quality but without the inbuilt harmony of Riesling.

Kerpen, Weingut Heribert Tiny top-class estate in BERNKASTEL, GRAACH, WEHLEN.

Kesselstatt, von The biggest private MOSEL estate, 600 yrs old. Some 150 acres in GRAACH, KASEL, PIESPORT, WILTINGEN, etc, plus substantial rented or managed estates, making aromatic, generously fruity MOSELS. Now belongs to Günther Reh (Leiwen). Excellent wines since '88.

Kesten M-M w ★→★★★ 71 75 76 83 85 86 87 88 89 90 91 92 Neighbour of BRAUNEBERG. Best wines (from Paulinshofberg v'yd) similar. Grosslage: Kurfürstlay. Top grower: Paulinshof.

Kiedrich Rhg w ★★→★★★★ 71 76 83 85 86 87 88 89 90 91 92 Neighbour of RAUENTHAL; almost as splendid and high-flavoured. Top v'yds: Gräfenberg, Sandgrub, Wasseros. Grosslage: Heiligenstock. Growers incl: FISCHER, KNYPHAUSEN, STATE DOMAIN, WEIL, etc.

Klevner (or Clevner) Red Klevner (synonym, Blauer Frühburgunder) grown in WURTTEMBERG is supposedly either a mutation of Pinot N or Italian Chiavenna, an early-ripening black Pinot. Also an ORTENAU (BADEN) synonym for TRAMINER.

Klingelberger BADEN term for the RIESLING, esp at DURBACH.

Kloster Eberbach Glorious 12th-C Cistercian Abbey in the forest at HATTENHEIM, RHEINGAU. Its monks planted the STEINBERG. Now STATE DOMAIN property and HQ of the German Wine Academy.

Klüsserath M-M w ★★→★★★ 76 83 85 88 89 90 91 92 Minor MOSEL village, good yrs worth trying. Best v'yd: Bruderschaft. Grosslage: St-Michael. Top growers: FRIEDRICH WILHELM GYMNASIUM, Kirsten.

Knyphausen, Weingut Freiherr zu Noble 50-acre estate on former Cistercian land (see Kloster Eberbach) in ELTVILLE, ERBACH, HATTENHEIM, KIEDRICH and MARCOBRUNN. Top RHEINGAU wines, many dry.

Koehler-Ruprecht Highly-rated little (22-acre) estate; the top grower in KALLSTADT, PFALZ. Ultra-traditional winemaking; v long-lived dry RIESLINGS from K Saumagen are memorable.

Kraichgau Small BADEN region S of Heidelberg. Top grower: HOENSBROECH.

Kreuznach (Bereich) District name for the entire northern NAHE. See also Bad Kreuznach.

Kröv M-M w ★→★★★ 88 89 90 91 92 Popular tourist resort famous for its Grosslage name: Nacktarsch, meaning 'bare bottom'. Wines to avoid.

Künstler, Franz Outstanding 12.5-acre HOCHHEIM estate, esp for H Hölle and H Kirchenstück and model CHARTA wines.

Landespreismünze Prizes for quality at state, rather than national, level. Considered by some more discriminating than DLG medals.

Landwein A category of better quality TAFELWEIN (the grapes must be slightly riper) from 15 designated regions. It must be TROCKEN or HALBTROCKEN. Similar in intention to France's vin de pays.

Lauerburg One of the 4 owners of the famous Doctor v'yd, with 10 acres, all in BERNKASTEL. Often excellent racy wines.

Liebfrauenstift 26-acre v'yd in city of Worms; origin of 'LIEBFRAUMILCH'.

Liebfraumilch A much abused name, accounting for 50% of all German wine exports – much to the detriment of Germany's better products. Legally defined as a QBA 'of pleasant character' from RHEINHESSEN, PFALZ, NAHE or RHEINGAU, of a blend with at least 51% RIESLING, SILVANER, KERNER or MULLER-T. Most is mild, semi-sweet wine from Rheinhessen and Pfalz. The rules now say it must have more than 18 grams per litre unfermented sugar. Sometimes v cheap and of inferior quality, depending on brand or shipper. Its definition makes a mockery of the term 'Quality Wine'.

Lieser M-M w ★→★★ 71 76 83 85 86 87 88 89 90 91 92 Little-known neighbour of BERNKASTEL. Lighter wines. Grosslage: Kurfürstlay.

Leitz, J Fine little RUDESHEIM family estate for elegant dry RIES.

Lingenfelder, Weingut Small, innovative estate at Grosskarlbach, PFALZ, making some of Germany's best burgundy-style SPATBURGUNDER and full-bodied RIES, etc.

Loosen, Weingut Dr 20-acre St-Johannishof estate in BERNKASTEL, ERDEN, GRAACH, URZIG, WEHLEN. Lovely quality in recent vintages.

Lorch Rhg w (r) ★→★★ 71 76 83 85 87 88 89 90 91 92 At extreme W end of RHEINGAU. Some fine light RIES, more like MITTELRHEIN wines. Best grower: von Kanitz.

Löwenstein, Fürst 66-acre FRANKEN estate: classic dry powerful wines. 45-acre HALLGARTEN property is rented by MATUSCHKA-GREIFFENCLAU.

Maindreieck (Bereich) District name for central FRANKEN, incl WURZBURG.

Marcobrunn Historic RHEINGAU v'yd; one of Germany's best. See Erbach.

Markgräflerland (Bereich) District S of Freiburg, BADEN. Typical GUTEDEL wine can be delicious refreshment when drunk v young, but best wines are the -BURGUNDERS: WEISS-, GRAU- and SPAT-. Also Sekt.

Martinsthal Rhg w ★★→★★★ 71 75 76 83 85 86 87 88 89 90 91 92 Little-known neighbour of RAUENTHAL. Top v'yds: Langenberg, Wildsau. Grosslage: Steinmächer. Growers incl BECKER, Diefenhardt.

Matuschka-Greiffenclau, Graf Erwein Owner of the ancient SCHLOSS VOLLRADS estate and tenant of the WEINGUT FURST LOWENSTEIN at HALLGARTEN. A principal spokesman for German high quality wine, dedicated to dry wines and their combination with food.

Maximin Grünhaus M-S-R (Ruwer) w ★★★★ 71 75 76 79 83 85 86 87 88 89 90 91 92 Supreme RUWER estate of 80 acres at MERTESDORF. Wines of firm elegance to mature 20 yrs+.

Mertesdorf See Maximin Grünhaus and Karlsmühle.

Mittelhaardt The north-central and best part of PFALZ, incl DEIDESHEIM, FORST, RUPPERTSBERG, WACHENHEIM, largely planted with RIESLING.

Mittelhaardt-Deutsche Weinstrasse (Bereich) District name for the northern and central parts of PFALZ.

Mittelheim Rhg w ★★→★★★ 71 75 76 83 85 86 87 88 89 90 91 92 Relatively minor village between WINKEL and OESTRICH.

Mittelmosel The central and best part of the MOSEL, incl BERNKASTEL, PIESPORT, WEHLEN, etc. Its best sites are (or should be) entirely RIES.

Mittelrhein Northern Rhine area of domestic importance, incl BACHARACH and Boppard. Some attractive steely RIESLING.

Mönchhof High quality 12-acre estate in ERDEN, URZIG, WEHLEN and ZELTINGEN.

Morio-Muskat Stridently aromatic grape variety now on the decline.

Mosel The TAFELWEIN name of the area. All quality wines from the Mosel must be labelled MOSEL-SAAR-RUWER. (Moselle is the French – and English – spelling for this beautiful river.)

Moselland, Winzergenossenschaft The biggest coop of the M-S-R, based at BERNKASTEL, incl Saar-Winzerverein at WILTINGEN. Its 5,200 members produce 25% of M-S-R wines (incl méthode traditionelle Sekt), but nothing above average.

Mosel-Saar-Ruwer (M-S-R) 31,000-acre QUALITATSWEIN region between TRIER and Koblenz. Incl MITTELMOSEL, RUWER, SAAR and lesser areas. The natural home of RIES.

Müller-Catoir Outstanding estate of NEUSTADT, PFALZ, with 40 acres and many varieties, incl barrel-aged reds. A name to conjour with.

Müller zu Scharzhof, Egon See Egon Müller.

Müller-Thurgau Fruity early-ripening, usually low-acid grape variety; the commonest in PFALZ and RHEINHESSEN, NAHE, BADEN and FRANKEN, and increasingly planted in all areas, incl MOSEL. Should be banned from top v'yds by law.

Mumm, von 173-acre estate in JOHANNISBERG, RUDESHEIM, etc. Under the same control as SCHLOSS JOHANNISBERG, but not up to the same standard.

Münster Nahe w ★→★★★ 71 75 76 83 85 86 87 88 89 90 91 92 Best village of N NAHE, with fine delicate wines. Grosslage: Schlosskapelle. Top growers: Kruger-Rumpf, STATE DOMAIN.

Nackenheim Rhh w ★→★★★ 75 76 83 85 86 87 88 89 90 91 92 Neighbour of NIERSTEIN; best wines (N Rothenberg) similar. Grosslagen: Spiegelberg (★★), Gutes Domtal (★). Top growers: GUNDERLOCH, GUNTRUM.

Nahe Tributary of the Rhine and high quality wine region. Balanced fresh and clean but full-, even earthy-flavoured wines; the best are RIES. TWO BEREICHE: KREUZNACH and SCHLOSS BOCKELHEIM.

Nahesteiner Brand name of new NAHE HALBTROCKEN blend of RIES, SILVANER and MULLER-T. V sound standard; not too dry.

Neckerauer, Weingut Klaus Out-of-the-way but interesting 40-acre estate at Weissenheim-am-Sand, on sandy soil in N PFALZ. Impressive but unpredictable range.

Neef M-S-R w ★→★★ 71 76 83 85 87 88 89 90 91 92 Village of lower MOSEL with one fine v'yd: Frauenberg.

Neipperg, Graf von 71-acre top WURTTEMBERG estate at Schwaigern, esp known for red wines and TRAMINER.

Neumagen-Dhron M-M w ★★ Neighbour of PIESPORT with fine but neglected vineyards.

Neustadt Central town of PFALZ with a famous wine school.

Niederhausen Nahe w ★★→★★★★ 71 75 76 83 85 86 87 88 89 90 91 Neighbour of SCHLOSS BOCKELHEIM and HQ of the NAHE STATE DOMAIN. Wines of grace and power. Top v'yds incl: Hermannsberg, Hermannshöhle. Grosslage: Burgweg. Top growers: CRUSIUS, DONNHOFF, Hehner-Kilz, Schneider, STATE DOMAIN.

Nierstein (Bereich) Large E RHEINHESSEN district of v mixed quality.

Nierstein Rhh w ★→★★★ **71 75 76 83 85** 86 87 **88 89 90** 91 92 Famous but treacherous name. 1,300 acres incl superb v'yds: Bruderberg, Olberg, Pettenthal, etc, and their Grosslagen: Rehbach, Spiegelberg, Auflangen. Ripe aromatic wines with great 'elegance'. But beware Grosslage Gutes Domtal: no guarantee of anything. Growers to choose incl BALBACH, H Braun, GUNDERLOCH, GUNTRUM, HEYL ZU HERRNSHEIM, St-Anthony, G A Schneider, Seebrich, Strub.

Nobling New white grape variety giving light fresh wine in BADEN, esp MARKGRAFLERLAND.

Norheim Nahe w ★→★★★ **71 76 79 83 85** 86 87 **88 89 90** 91 92 Neighbour of NIEDERHAUSEN. Top v'yds: Kafels, Kirschheck, Klosterberg. Grosslage: Burgweg. Growers: P ANHEUSER, CRUSIUS.

Novum Completely new style of wine from SICHEL, softened by malolactic fermentation. Aromatic, gentle and versatile.

Germany's quality levels

The official range of qualities in ascending order are as follows:

(1) Deutscher Tafelwein: sweetish light wine of no special character. (Unofficially, can be very special.)

(2) Landwein: dryish Tafelwein with some regional style.

(3) Qualitätswein: dry or sweetish wine with sugar added before fermentation to increase its strength, but tested for quality and with distinct local and grape character.

(4) Kabinettwein: dry or dryish natural (unsugared) wine of distinct personality and distinguishing lightness. Can be very fine.

(5) Spätlese: stronger, often sweeter than Kabinett. Full-bodied. The trend today is towards drier or even completely dry Spätlese.

(6) Auslese: sweeter, sometimes stronger than Spätlese, often with honey-like flavours, intense and long.

(7) Beerenauslese: very sweet and usually strong, intense; can be superb.

(8) Eiswein: (Beeren- or Trockenbeerenauslese) concentrated, sharpish and very sweet. Extraordinary and everlasting.

(9) Trockenbeerenauslese: intensely sweet and aromatic; alcohol slight.

Oberemmel M-S-R (Saar) w ★★→★★★ **71 75 76 83 85** 86 87 **88 89 90** 91 92 Next village to WILTINGEN. V fine wines from Hütte, Karlsberg, etc. Grosslage: SCHARZBERG. Top growers: VON HOVEL, VON KESSELSTADT.

Obermosel (Bereich) District name for the upper MOSEL above TRIER. Generally uninspiring wines from the ELBLING grape, unless v young.

Ockfen M-S-R (Saar) w ★★→★★★ **71 75 76 83 85** 86 87 **88 89 90** 91 92 200-acre village with superb fragrant austere wines. Top v'yd: Bockstein. Grosslage: SCHARZBERG. Growers incl DR FISCHER, FRIEDRICH WILHELM GYMNASIUM, WAGNER, ZILLIKEN.

Oechsle Scale for sugar content of grape juice (see page 204).

Oestrich Rhg w ★★→★★★ **71 75 76 83 85** 86 87 **88 89 90** 91 92 Big village; variable but capable of splendid RIES AUSLESE. V'yds incl Doosberg, Klosterberg, Lenchen. Grosslage: Gottesthal. Major growers: Auerbach, AUGUST ESSER, WEGELER-DEINHARD.

Offene weine Wine by the glass: the way to order it in wine villages.

Oppenheim Rhh w ★→★★★ **71 75 76 83 85** 86 87 **88 89 90** 91 92 Town S of NIERSTEIN with a spectacular 13th-C church. Best wines (Kreuz, Sackträger) similar. Grosslagen: Guldenmorgen (★★★), Krötenbrunnen (★). Growers incl GUNTRUM, Carl Koch.

Ortenau (Bereich) District just S of Baden-Baden. Good KLINGELBERGER (RIES), SPATBURGUNDER and RULANDER. Top village: DURBACH.

Ortsteil Independent part of a community allowed to use its estate and vineyard name without the village name, eg SCHLOSS JOHANNISBERG, STEINBERG.

Palatinate English for RHEINPFALZ.

Pauly-Bergweiler, Dr Fine 27-acre estate based at BERNKASTEL. V'yds there and in WEHLEN, etc. Also Nicolay wines from URZIG and ERDEN.

Perlwein Semi-sparkling wine.

Pfalz 56,000-acre v'yd region S of RHEINHESSEN (see Mittelhaardt and Südliche Weinstrasse.) Grapes ripen to relatively high degrees. The classics are rich wines, with TROCKEN and HALBTROCKEN increasingly fashionable (and well made). Biggest RIES producer after M-S-R. Until recently, known as 'Rheinpfalz'.

Pfeffingen, Weingut Messrs Fuhrmann and Eymael make outstanding RIES and SCHEUREBE on 26 acres of UNGSTEIN.

Piesport M-M w ★★→★★★★ 71 75 76 83 85 86 87 88 89 90 91 92 Tiny village with famous vine amphitheatre, gives (at best) glorious gentle fruity RIES. Top v'yd: Goldtröpfchen. Treppchen, on flatter land, is far inferior. Grosslage: Michelsberg (mainly MULLER-T; avoid). Top growers: HAART, KESSELSTATT, Reuscher-Haart, Weller-Lehnert.

Plettenberg, von 100-acre estate at BAD KREUZNACH. Wines recently poor.

Portugieser Second-rate red-wine grape now often used for WEISSHERBST.

Prädikat Special attributes or qualities. See QmP.

Prüfungsnummer The official identifying test-number of a quality wine.

Prüm, J J Superlative and legendary 34-acre MOSEL estate in BERNKASTEL, GRAACH, WEHLEN, ZELTINGEN. Delicate but long-lived wines, esp in WEHLENER SONNENUHR: 81 KABINETT still young.

Prüm Erben, S A Small separate part of the Prüm family estate for WEHLENERS etc – but not in the class of the above.

Qualitätswein bestimmter Anbaugebiete (QbA) The middle quality of German wine, with sugar added before fermentation (as in French 'chaptalisation'), but controlled as to areas, grapes, etc.

Qualitätswein mit Prädikat (QmP) Top category, incl all wines ripe enough to be unsugared, from KABINETT to TROCKENBEERENAUSLESE. See Introduction, pages 97–8.

Randersacker Frank w ★★→★★★ 76 *83* 86 87 88 89 **90** 91 92 Leading village for distinctive dry wine. Top v'yd: Pfülben. Grosslage: Ewig Leben. Growers incl BURGERSPITAL, Göbel, STAATLICHER HOFKELLER, JULIUSSPITAL, Schmitt.

Rappenhof, Weingut 90-acre RHEINHESSEN estate at Alsheim with wide range incl BARRIQUE-aged CHARD and deep-coloured SPATBURGUNDER.

Rauenthal Rhg w ★★★→★★★★ 71 75 76 83 85 86 87 88 89 **90** 91 92 Supreme village for spicy complex wine. Top v'yds incl Baiken, Gehrn, Wulfen. Grosslage: Steinmächer. Growers: ESER, SCHLOSS REINHARTSHAUSEN, SCHLOSS SCHONBORN, VON SIMMERN, STATE DOMAIN.

Rebholz Top grower of SUDLICHE WEINSTRASSE. Many varieties on 25 acres at Siebeldingen.

Ress, Balthasar RHEINGAU estate with 50 acres of good land, cellars in HATTENHEIM. Also runs SCHLOSS REICHARTSHAUSEN. Variable wines; highly original artists' labels. Managed by Stephan Ress.

Restsüsse Unfermented grape sugar remaining in (or more often added to) wine to give it sweetness. New TROCKEN wines have v little, if any.

Rheinburgengau (Bereich) District name for MITTELRHEIN v'yds around the Rhine gorge. Wines with 'steely' acidity needing time to mature.

Rheinfront, Winzergenossenschaft The leading NIERSTEIN coop, with way above average standards.

Rheingau The best v'yd region of the Rhine, W of Wiesbaden. 7,000 acres. Classic substantial but subtle RIESLING. BEREICH name for the whole region: JOHANNISBERG.

Rheinhessen Vast region (61,000 acres of v'yds) between Mainz and Worms, bordered by the river NAHE, mostly second-rate, but incl top wines from NACKENHEIM, NIERSTEIN, OPPENHEIM, etc.

Rheinhessen Silvaner (RS) New uniform label for dry wines from SILVANER – designed to give a modern quality image to the region.

Rheinpfalz See Pfalz.

Rhodt Village of SUDLICHE WEINSTRASSE with well-known Rietburg coop. Agreeable fruity wines. Grosslage: Ordensgut.

Richter, Weingut Max Ferd 37-acre MITTELMOSEL family estate, based at Mülheim. Fine barrel-aged RIES from: BRAUNEBERG (Juffer-SONNENUHR), GRAACH, Mülheim (Helenenkloster), WEHLEN (usually models).

Rieslaner Cross between SILVANER and RIES; has made fine AUSLESEN in FRANKEN, where most is grown. Also fine from MULLER-CATOIR.

Riesling The best German grape: fine, fragrant, fruity, long-lived. Only CHARDONNAY can compete as the world's best white grape.

Roseewein Rosé wine made of red grapes fermented without their skins.

Rotwein Red wine.

Rüdesheim Rhg w ★★→★★★★ 71 75 76 79 *81* 82 83 *84* 85 86 87 88 89 90 91 92 Rhine resort with 650 acres of excellent v'yds; the 3 best called Rüdesheimer Berg–. Full-bodied wines, fine-flavoured, often remarkable in 'off' vintages. Grosslage: Burgweg. Most top RHEINGAU estates own some Rüdesheim v'yds.

Rüdesheimer Rosengarten RUDESHEIM is also the name of a NAHE village near BAD KREUZNACH. Do not be misled by the ubiquitous blend going by this name. It has nothing to do with RHEINGAU Rüdesheim. Avoid.

Ruländer PINOT GRIS: grape giving soft full-bodied wine, alias (as dry wine) GRAUBURGUNDER. Best in BADEN and southern PFALZ.

Ruppertsberg Pfz w ★★→★★★ 75 76 83 85 86 87 88 89 90 91 92 Southern village of MITTELHAARDT. Top v'yds incl Hoheburg, Linsenbusch, Reiterpfad. Grosslage: Hofstück. Growers incl BASSERMANN-JORDAN, VON BUHL, BURKLIN-WOLF, DEINHARD.

Ruwer Tributary of MOSEL nr TRIER. V fine delicate but highly aromatic and well-structured wines. Villages incl EITELSBACH, KASEL, MERTESDORF.

Saale-Unstrut Region in former E Germany, 1,000 acres around the confluence of these two rivers at Naumburg, near Leipzig. Terraced v'yds of WEISSBURGUNDER, SILVANER, GUTEDEL, etc and red PORTUGIESER and SPATBURGUNDER have Cistercian origins. Quality leader: Staatsweingut Naumburg.

Saar Tributary of MOSEL S of RUWER. Brilliant austere 'steely' RIES. Villages incl AYL, OCKFEN, Saarburg, SERRIG, WILTINGEN (SCHARZHOFBERG). Grosslage: SCHARZBERG. Many fine estates.

Saar-Ruwer (Bereich) District covering these 2 regions.

St-Ursula Well-known merchants at BINGEN.

Salm, Prinz zu Owner of SCHLOSS WALLHAUSEN and President of VDP.

Salwey, Weingut Leading BADEN estate at Oberottweil, esp for RIESLING, WEISSBURGUNDER and RULANDER.

Schaefer, Willi The finest grower of GRAACH (but only 5 acres).

Scharzberg Grosslage name of WILTINGEN and neighbours.

Scharzhofberg M-S-R (Saar) w ★★★★ 71 75 76 83 85 86 87 88 89 90 91 92 Superlative 67-acre SAAR v'yd: austerely beautiful wines, the perfection of RIESLING. Do not confuse with above. Top estates: EGON MULLER, VON HOVEL, VON KESSELSTATT.

Schaumwein Sparkling wine.

Scheurebe Fruity grape of high quality (and RIESLING parentage) esp used in PFALZ.

Schillerwein Light red or rosé QBA, speciality of WURTTEMBERG (only).

Schlossböckelheim Nahe w ★★→★★★★ 71 75 76 79 83 85 86 87 88 89 90 91 92 Village with the best NAHE v'yds, incl Felsenberg, Kupfergrube. Firm yet delicate wine. Grosslage: Burgweg. Top growers: CRUSIUS, DONNHOF, STATE DOMAIN.

Schlossböckelheim (Bereich) District name for the whole S NAHE.

Schloss Groenesteyn Formerly top-grade RHEINGAU estate (80 acres) in KIEDRICH and RUDESHEIM. Not on top form.

For key to grape variety abbreviations, see pages 6–9.

Schloss Johannisberg Rhg w ★★★★ 76 79 83 85 86 87 88 89 90 91 92 Famous RHEINGAU estate of 86 acres owned by Prince Metternich and the Oetker family. The 'first growth' of the Rhine, back on form since '88 after going through a less brilliant spell. Wines incl fine SPATLESE and KABINETT TROCKEN, yet one feels still more could be achieved with this truly great v'yd.

Schloss Reichartshausen 10-acre HATTENHEIM v'yd run by RESS.

Schloss Reinhartshausen Fine 175-acre estate in ERBACH, HATTENHEIM, KIEDRICH, etc. Changed hands in '87. The mansion is now a hotel.

Schloss Salem 188-acre estate of Margrave of BADEN near L Constance in S Germany. MULLER-T and WEISSHERBST.

Schloss Saarstein SERRIG estate of 25 acres with consistently fine RIESLINGS.

Schloss Schönborn One of the biggest and best RHEINGAU estates, based at HATTENHEIM. Full-flavoured wines, at best excellent. Also vg SEKT.

Schloss Staufenberg 69-acre DURBACH estate of the Margrave, BADEN. Best wines are KLINGELBERGER.

Schloss Vollrads Rhg w ★★★→★★★★ 71 76 83 85 86 87 88 89 90 91 Great estate at WINKEL since 1300. 116 acres producing generally dry and austere RHEINGAU RIES. TROCKEN and HALBTROCKEN wines are the speciality; some would like to see rather less austerity. The owner, Graf MATUSCHKA-GREIFFENCLAU, leads the 'German wine with food' campaign, rents the LOWENSTEIN estate and runs DR WEIL.

Schloss Wallhausen The 25-acre NAHE estate of the PRINZ ZU SALM, one of Germany's oldest. 65% RIES. Vg TROCKEN.

Schmitt, Gustav Adolf Merchant house with fine old 250-acre family estate at NIERSTEIN. Has fallen sadly behind the times.

Schoppenwein Café (or bar) wine: ie wine by the glass.

Schubert, von Owner of MAXIMIN GRUNHAUS.

Schwarzer Adler, Weingut The Keller brothers make some of BADEN's best GRAUBURGUNDER and WEISSBURGUNDER, also SPATBURGUNDER, on 35 acres at Oberbergen.

Schweigen Pfz w ★→★★ 85 86 87 88 89 90 91 92 Southernmost PFALZ village with important coop, DEUTSCHES WEINTOR. Grosslage: Guttenberg. Best grower: BECKER, whose range incl SPATBURGUNDER reds.

Sekt German (QBA) sparkling wine, best when label specifies RIES, WEISSBURGUNDER or SPATBURGUNDER. Sekt bA is the same but from a specified area.

Selbach-Oster 15-acre ZELTINGEN estate now among MITTELMOSEL leaders.

Serrig M-S-R (Saar) w ★★→★★★ 71 75 76 83 85 86 87 88 89 90 91 Village known for 'steely' wine, excellent in sunny yrs. Top grower: VEREINIGTE HOSPITIEN. Grosslage: SCHARZBERG. Growers also incl SCHLOSS SAARSTEIN, BERT SIMON.

Sichel, Söhne H Famous wine merchants of London and Mainz based at Alzey, RHEINHESSEN. Owners of BLUE NUN LIEBFRAUMILCH and creators of revolutionary NOVUM.

Silvaner The third most-planted German white grape, usually underrated, best in FRANKEN. But look for good Silvaners from RHEINHESSEN and KAISERSTUHL, too.

Simmern, Langwerth von Top 120-acre family estate at ELTVILLE. Famous v'yds: Baiken, Mannberg, MARCOBRUNN, etc. Some of the v best, most elegant RHEINGAU RIES.

Simon, Weingut Bert One of largest SAAR estates. 80 acres: KASEL, SERRIG.

Sonnenuhr Sundial. Name of several v'yds, esp one at WEHLEN.

Spätburgunder Pinot Noir: the best red-wine grape in Germany, esp in BADEN and WURTTEMBERG and, increasingly, PFALZ – though its wines are not widely appreciated outside their country.

Spätlese Late Harvest. One better (stronger/sweeter) than KABINETT RIESLING. Wines to age at least 5 yrs. Dry Spätlesen can be v fine.

Staatlicher Hofkeller The Bavarian STATE DOMAIN. 287 acres of finest FRANKEN v'yds with spectacular cellars under the great baroque Residenz at WURZBURG. Wines less spectacular.

Staatsweingut (or Staatliche Weinbaudomäne) The State wine estates or domains, the principal of which are: KLOSTER EBERBACH, SCHLOSS-BOCKELHEIM, TRIER.

State Domain See Staatsweingut.

Steigerwald (Bereich) District name for E part of FRANKEN.

Steinberg Rhg w ★★★→★★★★ **71 75 76 79 83 85 86 87 88 89 90 91 92** Famous 79-acre walled v'yd at HATTENHEIM planted by Cistercians 700 yrs ago. Now property of the STATE DOMAIN, ELTVILLE. Some glorious wines.

Steinwein Wine from WURZBURG'S best v'yd, Stein. In the past the term was loosely used for all FRANCONIAN wine.

Stuttgart Chief city of WURTTEMBERG, producer of some pleasant wines (esp RIES), recently beginning to be exported.

Südliche Weinstrasse (Bereich) District name for the southern PFALZ. Quality has improved tremendously in the last 25 yrs. See Ilbesheim, Schweigen, Siebeldingen.

Tafelwein Table wine. The vin ordinaire of Germany. Frequently blended with other EC wines. But DEUTSCHER TAFELWEIN must come from Germany alone and may be excellent. (See also Landwein.)

Thanisch, Weingut Wwe Dr H 16-acre BERNKASTEL family estate of top quality, incl part of Doctor v'yd.

Traben-Trarbach M-M w ★★ **76 83 85 86 87 88 89 90 91 92** Major wine town of 800 acres, 87% of it RIES. Top v'yds: Ungsberg, Würzgarten. Grosslage: Schwarzlay. Top grower: RICHTER.

Traisen Nahe w ★★★ **71 75 76 79 83 85 86 87 88 89 90 91 92** Small village incl superlative Bastei and Rotenfels v'yds, making RIES of great concentration and class. Top grower: CRUSIUS.

Traminer See Gewürztraminer.

Trier M-S-R w ★★→★★★ Important wine city of Roman origin, on the MOSEL, adjacent to RUWER, now also including AVELSBACH and EITELSBACH. Grosslage: Römerlay. The big Mosel charitable estates have their cellars here.

Trittenheim M-M w ★★ **71 75 76 83 85 87 88 89 90 91 92** Attractive light wines from the S end of the MITTELMOSEL. Top v'yds were Altärchen, Apotheke, but they now incl second-rate flat land. Grosslage: Michelsberg (Avoid). Top growers: GRANS-FASSIAN, Milz.

***Trocken** 'Dry'. By law trocken on a label means with a maximum of 9 grams per litre unfermented sugar. The new wave in German winemaking upsets the old notion of sweetness balancing acidity and embraces an austerity of flavour that can seem positively Lenten. It is much harder to make good dry wines in German conditions, and non-initiates should not expect to fall in love at first sip. To be good, trocken wines need substantial body or alcohol; more than most Riesling Kabinett wines have to offer. Weissburgunder trocken is more satisfying. Halbtrockens are friendlier. Spätlesen (or QbA) often make the best trocken wines. Auslese trocken sounds like a contradiction in terms – and usually tastes like one. Do not be confused by the apparent link with Trockenbeerenauslesen (see below): they are unrelated.*

Trockenbeerenauslese The sweetest and most expensive category of German wine, extremely rare and with concentrated honey flavour, made from selected shrivelled grapes affected by 'noble rot' (botrytis). TBA for short. See also Edel. Edelbeerenauslese would be a less confusing name for these wines.

Trollinger Common (pale) red grape of WURTTEMBERG; locally v popular.

Ungstein Pfz w ★★→★★★ **71 75 76** 83 85 86 87 88 89 90 91 92 MITTELHAARDT village with fine harmonious wines. Top v'yd: Herrenberg. Top growers: Darting FITZ-RITTER, PFEFFINGEN, K Schäfer. Grosslagen: Honigsäckel, Kobnert.

Urzig M-M w ★★★ 71 75 76 83 85 86 87 88 89 90 91 Village famous for lively spicy wine. Top v'yd: Würzgarten. Grosslage: Schwarzlay. Growers incl J J Christoffel, DR LOOSEN, MONCHHOF, WEINS-PRUM.

Valckenberg, P J Major merchants and growers at Worms, with Madonna LIEBFRAUMILCH and a small estate producing good RIES. Also dry Ries.

VdP Verband Deutscher Prädikats und Qualitätsweingüter. An important association of premium growers. President: PRINZ ZU SALM.

Vereinigte Hospitien 'United Hospitals'. Ancient charity at TRIER with large holdings in PIESPORT, SERRIG, TRIER, WILTINGEN, etc; but wines recently disappointing.

Verwaltung Administration (of property/estate etc).

Villa Sachsen Well-known 67-acre BINGEN estate; Japanese shareholding.

Wachenheim Pfz w ★★★→★★★★ 71 75 76 79 83 85 86 87 88 89 90 91 92 840 acres, incl exceptionally fine RIES. V'yds incl Böhlig, Gerümpel, Rechbächel. Top grower: BURKLIN-WOLF. Grosslagen: Mariengarten, Schenkenböhl, Schnepfenflug.

Wagner, Dr Saarburg estate. 20 acres of RIES. Fine wines incl TROCKEN.

Waldrach M-S-R (Ruwer) w ★★ 76 83 85 88 89 90 91 92 Some charming light wines. Grosslage: Römerlay.

Walluf Rhg w ★★ 75 76 79 83 85 87 88 89 90 91 92 Neighbour of ELTVILLE; formerly Nieder- and Ober-Walluf. Underrated wines. Grosslage: Steinmächer. Growers incl BECKER.

Walporzheim Ahrtal (Bereich) District name for the whole AHR valley.

Walthari-Hof Much-discussed estate at Edenkoben, PFALZ, making wine without recourse to the usual sulphur dioxide.

Wawern M-S-R (Saar) w ★★→★★★ 71 75 76 83 85 87 88 89 90 91 92 Small village with fine RIES. Grosslage: SCHARZBERG.

Wegeler-Deinhard 136-acre RHEINGAU estate. V'yds: GEISENHEIM, MITTELHEIM, OESTRICH, RUDESHEIM, WINKEL, etc. Consistent quality; dry SPATLESE, classic AUSLESE, finest EISWEIN. Also 67 acres in MITTELMOSEL, incl major part of BERNKASTELER Doctor, WEHLENER SONNENUHR, etc, 46 acres in MITTELHAARDT (DEIDESHEIM, FORST, RUPPERTSBERG). Only best sites are named on labels. See also GEHEIMRAT 'J'.

Wehlen M-M w ★★★→★★★★ 71 75 76 83 85 86 87 89 90 91 92 Neighbour of BERNKASTEL with equally fine, somewhat richer wine. Top v'yd: SONNENUHR. Top growers: KERPEN, LOOSEN, PRUM, WEGELER-DEINHARD, WEINS-PRUM. Grosslage: Münzlay.

Weil, Dr Fine 84-acre estate at KIEDRICH, now owned by Suntory of Japan.

Weinbaugebiet Viticultural region. For TAFELWEIN (eg MOSEL, RHEIN, SAAR).

Weingut Wine estate.

Weinkellerei Wine cellars or winery. See Keller.

Weins-Prüm, Dr Classic MITTELMOSEL estate; 12 acres at WEHLEN. WEHLENER SONNENUHR is top wine.

Weinstrasse Wine road. Scenic route through v'yds. Germany has several. The most famous is the Deutsche Weinstrasse in PFALZ.

Weintor, Deutsches See Schweigen.

Weissburgunder Pinot Blanc. One of the better grapes for TROCKEN and HALBTROCKEN wines: low acidity, high extract. Also much used for Sekt.

Weissherbst Usually pale pink wine of QBA standard or above, from a single variety, even occasionally BEERENAUSLESE, the speciality of BADEN, PFALZ and WURTTEMBERG. Currently fashionable in Germany.

Werner, Domdechant Fine 25-acre family estate on the best slopes of HOCHHEIM. 95% RIES.

Werner Klein (Mossbacher Hof) 25-acre estate, 90% RIES, in FORST and DEIDESHEIM. Good TROCKEN wines.

Wiltingen M-S-R (Saar) w ★★→★★★★ 71 75 76 83 85 86 87 88 89 90 91 92 The centre of the SAAR. 790 acres. Beautiful subtle austere wine. Top v'yds incl Braune Kupp, SCHARZHOFBERG (ORTSTEIL). Grosslage (for the whole SAAR): SCHARZBERG. Top growers: EGON MULLER, LE GALLAIS, VON KESSELSTATT, etc.

Winkel Rhg w ★★★→★★★★ **71 75 76 83 85 86 87 88 89 90 91 92** Village famous for full fragrant wine, incl SCHLOSS VOLLRADS. V'yds incl Hasensprung, Jesuitengarten. Grosslagen: Erntebringer, Honigberg. Growers incl DEINHARD, PRINZ VON HESSEN, VON MUMM, RESS, SCHLOSS SCHONBORN, etc.

Winningen M-S-R w ★★ Village of lower MOSEL nr Koblenz, producing some fine delicate RIES. Top v'yds: Röttgen, Uhlen. Growers: Dötsch, von Heddesdorf, Heymann-Löwenstein, Richter.

Wintrich M-M w ★★→★★★ **71 75 76 83 85 86 87 88 89 90 91 92** Neighbour of PIESPORT; similar wines. Top v'yds: Ohligsberg, Sonnenseite. Grosslage: Kurfürstlay. Good grower: R HAART.

Remember that vintage information for German wines is given in a different form from the ready/not ready distinction applying to other countries. Read the explanation on page 100.

Winzergenossenschaft Wine-growers' cooperative, often making sound and reasonably priced wine. Referred to in this text as 'coop'.

Winzerverein The same as the above.

Wirsching, Hans Leading estate in IPHOFEN, FRANKEN. Firm elegant dry wines. 100 acres in top v'yds: Julius-Echter-Berg, Kalb, etc.

Wonnegau (Bereich) District name for S RHEINHESSEN.

Wolff Metternich BADEN's best dry (and sweet) RIESLINGS from noble 87-acre estate at DURBACH.

Württemberg Vast S area, little known for wine outside Germany. Some good RIES esp from Neckar Valley. Also TROLLINGER.

Würzburg Frank ★★→★★★★ **71 76 79 81** *83* **85 86 87 88 89 90 91 92** Great baroque city on the Main, centre of Franconian (FRANKEN) wine: fine, full-bodied and dry. Top v'yds: Innere, Leiste, Pfaffenberg, Stein. No Grosslage. See also Maindreieck. Growers incl: BURGERSPITAL, JULIUSSPITAL, STAATLICHER HOFKELLER.

Zell M-S-R w ★→★★ **76 83 88 89 90 91 92** The best-known lower MOSEL village, esp for its awful Grosslage: Schwarze Katz ('Black Cat'). RIES on steep slate gives aromatic light wines. Top grower: Kallfelz.

Zell (Bereich) District name for whole lower MOSEL from Zell to Koblenz.

Zeltingen M-M w ★★→★★★★ **71 75 76 79 83 85 86 87 88 89 90 91 92** Important MOSEL village next to WEHLEN. Typically lively crisp RIES. Top v'yds: Schlossberg, SONNENUHR. Grosslage: Münzlay. Many estates hold v'yds here, the best being PRUM, SELBACH-OSTER.

Zilliken, Forstmeister Geltz Former estate of the Prussian royal forester at Saarburg and OCKFEN, SAAR. Racy minerally RIESLINGS. Great EISWEIN.

Zwierlein, Freiherr von 55-acre family estate in GEISENHEIM. 100% RIES.

Switzerland

Switzerland has no truly great wines, but almost all (especially whites) are enjoyable and satisfying – and very expensive. Switzerland has some of the world's most efficient and productive vineyards; costs are high and nothing less is viable. All the most important are in French-speaking areas, along the south-facing slopes of the upper Rhône Valley and Lake Geneva, respectively the Valais and the Vaud. Wines from German- and Italian-speaking zones (see map) are mostly drunk locally. Wines are known by place names, grape names and legally controlled type names and are usually drunk young. 1993 saw the establishment of a Swiss cantonal and federal appellation system, but controlled indication of orgin is still under discussion.

Aargau Wine-growing canton in E Switzerland. Best for light RIES-SILVANER, rich BLAUBURGUNDER and pleasant country wines.

Aigle Vaud r w ★★→★★★ Well-known for balanced whites and supple reds.

Aligoté White Burgundy variety doing well in the VALAIS and GENEVA.

Amigne Traditional white grape of the VALAIS, esp around VETROZ. Full-bodied tasty wine, often made sweet.

Arvine Old VALAIS white grape (also 'Petite Arvine'): dry and sweet, elegant long-lasting wines with characteristic salty finish. Best in SIERRE, SION.

Beerliwein Original name for wine of destemmed E Swiss BLAUBURGUNDER (now general practice). Today used for wine fermented on skins traditionally rather than in pressure tanks.

Bern Swiss capital and canton of same name. V'yds in W (BIELERSEE) and E (Thunersee, Laufental: BLAUBURGUNDER, RIES-SILVANER); 610 acres.

Béroche, La Neuchâtel r p w ★→★★ Wine-growing region on Lake Neuchâtel incl communes of Gorgier, St-Aubin, Fresens, Vaumarcus.

Bex Vaud r w ★★ CHABLAIS appellation, esp for red wines.

Bielersee r p w ★→★★ Wine region on N shore of the Bielersee (dry light CHASSELAS, PINOT N, SPEZIALITATEN) and at the foot of Jolimont.

Blauburgunder German-Swiss name for PINOT N.

Bonvillars Vaud r p w ★★ Characterful red from N shore of Lake Neuchâtel.

Bündner Herrschaft Grisons r p w ★★→★★★ Best E Swiss wine region incl top villages: Malans, Jenins, Maienfeld, Fläsch. Serious BLAUBURGUNDER ripens unusually well, cask-aged is vg. Also matured CHARD.

Calamin Vaud w ★★→★★★ Village next to DEZALEY: lush fragrant whites.

Chablais Vaud w (r) ★★→★★★ Robust full-bodied reds and whites from VAUD subsection. Best villages: AIGLE, BEX, Ollon, VILLENEUVE, YVORNE.

Chamoson Valais r w ★★→★★★ Largest VALAIS commune, esp for SILVANER.

Chardonnay Long-established in W, now also in more favourable parts.

Chasselas (Gutedel) Top white grape of west, neutral in flavour so takes on local character: svelte (GENEVA), full refined (VAUD), robust fragrant (VALAIS), pleasantly sparkling (BIELERSEE, L Neuchâtel, Murtensee).

Completer Native white grape surviving only in GRISONS. Aromatic generous wines which keep well.

Cornalin Local red grape making VALAIS speciality; dark spicy v strong wine. Best from SALGESCH, SIERRE.

Cortaillod Neuchâtel r (p w) ★★ Small village S of NEUCHATEL making good CHASSELAS and OEIL DE PERDRIX, but esp famous for PINOT N.

Côte, La Vaud r p w ★→★★★ Largest VAUD wine area, on N shore of Lake Geneva. Whites with finesse; harmonious reds.

Cotes de l'Orbe Vaud r p w ★★ Light fruity reds from N VAUD appellation between NEUCHATEL and Lake Geneva.

Dézaley Vaud w (r) ★★★ Famous LAVAUX v'yd on slopes above L Geneva, once tended by Cistercian monks. Unusually powerful CHASSELAS, needs ageing. Red Dézaley is a GAMAY-PINOT N-MERLOT-SYRAH rarity.

Dôle Valais r ★★→★★★ Appellation for blend of (at least 51%) PINOT N with GAMAY: full-bodied, supple. Dôle Blanche is a v lightly pressed rosé. Eg from MARTIGNY, SIERRE, SION, VETROZ.

Epesses Vaud w (r) ★★→★★★ LAVAUX appellation: supple full-bodied whites.

Ermitage The Marsanne grape; a VALAIS SPEZIALITAT. Concentrated full-bodied dry white, often with residual sugar. Esp from FULLY, SION.

Federweisser E Swiss name for white wine from BLAUBURGUNDER pressed immediately after harvest.

Fendant Valais w ★→★★ VALAIS appellation for CHASSELAS. Wide range of wines. Better ones now use village names only (FULLY, SION, etc).

Flétri/Mi-flétri Late-harvested grapes from which sweet and slightly sweet wine (respectively) is made; SPEZIALITAT in VALAIS.

Fribourg Small W Swiss region (260 acres, nr VULLY and Lake Neuchâtel). Esp for CHASSELAS, BLAUBURGUNDER, GAMAY, SPEZIALITATEN.

Fully Village nr MARTIGNY making excellent ERMITAGE and GAMAY.

Gamay The red Beaujolais grape abounds in W. Fairly thin wine.

Geneva Capital of, and west Swiss wine canton; the third largest (3,700 acres). Key areas: Mandement, Entre Arve et Rhône, Entre Arve et Lac. Mostly CHASSELAS, GAMAY. Also RIES-SILVANER, PINOT N, good ALIGOTE.

Gewürztraminer Grown in Switzerland as a SPECIALITAT variety.

Glacier, Vin du (Gletscherwein) Fabled oxidized white (from rare Rèze grape) of Val d'Anniviers; offered by thimbleful to visiting dignitaries.

Goron DOLE that fails to make the grade (83° Oechsle).

Grand Cru Quality designation for top wines. Implication differs by canton: in VALAIS and GENEVA used where set requirements fulfilled, in VAUD, for any top-of-the-range wine.

Grisons (Graubünden) Mountain canton, partly in E (BUNDNER HERRSCHAFT, Churer Rheintal; esp BLAUBURGUNDER) and partly in TICINO (Misox, esp MERLOT); 910 acres. Tiny quantities of Puschlav wine (Italian grapes).

Heida (Païen) Old VALAIS white grape for country wine of upper V (originally from v'yds at 1,000 m+), so successful that now in lower V too.

Humagne Native white grape (a SPEZIALITAT). Humagne Rouge (unrelated, from the VALAIS) also sold. Mostly from CHAMOSON and Leytron.

Lagewein (Origin-describing names.) In Switzerland 'Clos', 'Domaine', 'Château' or 'Abbaye' may only be used when the exclusive origin.

Landwein (Vin de pays) Traditional light easy white and esp red from E.

Lausanne Capital of VAUD. No longer with v'yds in town area, but long-time owner of classics: Abbaye de Mont, Château Rochefort (LA COTE); Clos des Moines, Clos des Abbayes, Dom de Burignon (LAVAUX). Pricey.

Lavaux Vaud r w ★→★★★ Scenic wine region on N shore of Lake Geneva. Delicate refined whites, good reds. Best from CALAMIN, Chardonne, DEZALEY, EPESSES, Lutry, St-Saphorin, Vevey-Montreux, Villette.

Martigny Valais w r ★★ Lower VALAIS commune esp for HUMAGNE rouge.

Merlot Grown in Italian Switzerland (TICINO) since '20s (after phylloxera destroyed local varieties). Quality. Also used with Cab S. See also Viti.

Mont d'Or, Domaine du Valais w s/sw ★★→★★★ Well-sited property nr SION: rich concentrated demi-sec wines, notable SILVANER.

Morges Vaud r p w ★→★★ LA COTE/VAUD appellation: fruity balanced reds.

Muscat Grown in VAUD as a SPEZIALITAT variety.

Neuchâtel City and canton on N shore of lake (W Switz). Owns v'yds from L Neuchâtel to BIELERSEE. Mainly CHASSELAS: fragrant lively. PINOT N also good (esp OEIL DE PERDRIX). PINOT GR and CHARD increasing.

Nostrano Word meaning 'ours', applied to lesser red wine of TICINO, made from native and Italian grapes (Bondola, Freisa, Barbera, etc).

Oeil de Perdrix Pale PINOT N rosé. Esp from NEUCHATEL and the VAUD.

Perlan Name for usually thin CHASSELAS grown in the GENEVA area.

Pinot Gris Widely planted white grape for dry and residually sweet wines. Makes v fine Spätlese in VAUD (called Malvoisie).

Pinot Noir Top Swiss red grape. Best: BUNDNER HERRSCHAFT, NEUCHATEL, VAUD.

Rauschling Old white ZURICH grape; esp for quality fruit and elegant acidity.

Riesling (Petit Rhin) Mainly in the VAUD. Excellent botrytis wines.

Riesling-Silvaner Swiss for Müller-THURGAU (E's top white; SPEZIALITAT in W).

St-Gallen E Swiss wine canton nr L Constance. Esp for BLAUBURGUNDER, RIES-SILVANER, SPEZIALITATEN. Incl Alstätten, Berneck, Rhine Valley, Thal.

Salquenen Valais r w ★→★★ Village nr SIERRE. First to use 'GRAND CRU'.

Salvagnin Vaud r ★→★★ GAMAY and/or PINOT N appellation. (See also Dôle.)

Schaffhausen E Swiss canton and town on R Rhine. Esp BLAUBURGUNDER; also some RIESLING-SILVANER and SPEZIALITATEN (eg Perle von Alzey).

Schafis Bern r p w ★→★★ Top wine commune of BIELERSEE and the name for all wines from its N shore. Twann is similar.

Sierre Valais r w ★★→★★★ Resort and famous wine town. Known for Fendant, PINOT N, ERMITAGE, Malvoisie.

Sion Valais r w ★→★★★ Capital/wine centre of VALAIS. Esp FENDANT de Sion.

Silvaner (Johannisberg, Gros Rhin) Common SPEZIALITAT in VAUD. Heady and spicy: some with residual sweetness, some Spätlese.

Spezialitäten (Spécialités) Wines of unusual grapes: vanishing local Gwass, Elbling, Bondola, etc, or modish Chenin Bl, Sauv, Cab (first grown experimentally). Eg VAUD: 38 of its 42 varieties are considered 'spezialitäten'.

Süssdruck Dry bright red wine retaining residual sweetness.

Thurgau E Swiss canton beside Bodensee (625 acres). Top wines from Warth, Seebachtal, Rhine Valley, south shore of the Untersee (esp BLAUBURGUNDER). Good RIES-SILVANER (ie Müller-T, born in the region).

Ticino Italian-speaking S Switzerland (with Misox), growing mainly MERLOT (good from mountainous Sopraceneri region). Trying out Cab S (cask-matured Bordeaux style), Sauv Bl, Sém, Merlot rosé.

Valais The Rhône Valley from the Grimselpass round to St Gingolph on L Geneva: the largest, most varied (and sunniest) wine canton in W Switzerland. Nr perfect climatic conditions; 42 grape varieties: FENDANT, SILVANER, GAMAY, PINOT N, plus many SPEZIALITES.

Vaud Region of L Geneva and the Rhône. W Switzerland's second largest wine canton incl LA COTE, LAVAUX, CHABLAIS and appellations Côtes de l'Orbe, Bonvillars, VULLY. CHASSELAS stronghold. Also GAMAY, PINOT N etc.

Vétroz Valais w r ★★→★★★ Top village nr SION, esp famous for AMIGNE.

Vevey-Montreux Vaud r w ★★ Up-and-coming appellation of LAVAUX. Famous wine festival held about every 30 years; next in 1999.

Villeneuve Vaud w (r) ★★→★★★ Nr L Geneva: powerful yet refined whites.

Viti Quality designation for the traditional MERLOT wine of TICINO.

Vully Vaud w (r) ★→★★ Good refreshing sparkling from Rhine catchment.

Winzerwy Quality label (E Swiss) for cantons AARGAU, Appenzell, Basel, BERN, GRAUBUNDEN, ST-GALLEN, SCHAFFHAUSEN, THURGAU and ZURICH.

Yvorne Vaud w (r) ★★★ Top CHABLAIS appellation: strong fragrant whites.

Zürich Capital of largest E wine canton (same name). Mostly BLAUBURGUNDER; also PINOT GR and GEWURZ, and esp RIES-SILVANER and RAUSCHLING.

Spain & Portugal

The following abbreviations are used in the text:

Alen	Alto Alentejo	**Cas-León**	Castilla-León	**R Alt**	Rioja Alta
Alg	Algarve	**Cat**	Catalonia	**R Ala**	Rioja Alavesa
And	Andalucia	**Est**	Estremadura	**R B**	Rioja Baja
Ara	Aragón	**Ext**	Extremadura	**Trás-os-M**	Trás-os-Montes
B Al	Beira Alta	**Gal**	Galicia		
B Lit	Beira Littoral	**Lev**	Levante		
Cas-La M	Castilla-La Mancha	**Min**	Minho	**g**	vino generoso
		Nav	Navarra	**res**	reserva

Spain and Portugal have had eight years, since they joined the European Community, to modernize their venerable wine industries. Much has been done and there is much to do. The continuing state of ferment is highly productive, and some splendid new wines have appeared, both in the few traditional quality areas and in former bulk-wine regions.

Currently in Spain (apart from sherry country), Catalonia, Rioja, Navarra, Galicia, Rueda and Ribera del Duero still hold most interest; in Portugal (apart from port and madeira) Bairrada, the Douro, the Ribatejo, Alentejo and Estremadura, and the Minho. In Portugal especially, newly delimited areas are tending to overshadow such old appellations as eg Dão.

The following listing includes the best and most interesting types and regions of each country, whether legally delimited or not. Geographical references (see map above) are to the autonomies and demarcated regions (DOs) of Spain, and the provinces of Portugal.

Sherry, port and madeira, the greatest glories of these nations, have a chapter to themselves on pages 134–140.

Spain

AGE, Bodegas Unidas R Alt r w (p) dr sw res ★→★★ 73 74 75 78 80 81 82 83 84 85 88 Large BODEGA making a wide range of wines. Red MARQUES DE ROMERAL and Siglo GRAN RESERVA are best.

Alavesas, Bodegas R Ala r (w) res ★★→★★★ 73 74 75 76 78 80 81 83 84 85 86 87 91 Pale orange-red Solar de Samaniego was always one of the most delicate of the soft, fast-maturing Alavesa wines. But quality since '83 has been seriously variable; some wines excessively light.

Albariño Aromatic high-quality white grape of GALICIA and its wine. The Zona del Albariño, together with the Condado de Tea and El Rosal, has recently been demarcated under the name Rías Baixas. Its cold-fermented wines are some of Spain's best (at appropriate prices).

Alella Cat r w (p) dr sw ★★ Small demarcated region just N of Barcelona. Pleasantly fruity wines. (See Marfil, Marqués de Alella, Parxet.)

Alicante Lev r (w) ★ DO. Wines still tend to be earthy and overstrong.

Almendralejo Ext r w ★ Wine centre of Extremadura. Much of its wine is distilled to make the spirit for fortifying sherry. See Lar de Barros.

Aloque Cas-La M r ★ DYA A light (though not in alcohol) variety of VALDEPENAS, made by fermenting red and white grapes together.

Alvear And g ★★★ The largest producer of excellent sherry-like aperitif and dessert wines in MONTILLA-MORILES.

Ampurdán, Cavas del Cat w p r sp res ★→★★ Producers of big-selling white Pescador, red Cazador table wines and cuve close sparklers.

Año Year: 4° Año (or Años) means 4 yrs old when bottled. Common on labels in the past, but now being discontinued in favour of vintage years, or terms such as CRIANZA.

Bach, Masia Cat r p w dr sw res ★★→★★★ 70 74 78 80 81 82 83 85 Spectacular villa-winery nr SAN SADURNI DE NOYA, owned by CODORNIU. Formerly known for luscious oaky white Extrísimo Bach; now for dry white Extrísimo and good red RESERVAS.

Banda Azul R Alt r ★★ 75 76 80 81 84 85 86 Big-selling CRIANZA wine from Bodegas PATERNINA.

Baron de Ley RB r (w) res ★★★ 85 86 Newish concern linked with EL COTO: good single-estate wines.

Barril, Masia Cat r br res ★★ 81 83 86 87 88 89 Tiny family estate in DO PRIORATO: powerful fruity reds – the 83 was 18°! – and superb RANCIO.

Berberana, Bodegas R Alt r (w) res ★→★★★ 70 73 74 75 76 78 80 81 82 83 84 85 86 87 88 The fruity, full-bodied reds are best: the young Carta de Plata, the **84 85** Carta de Oro CRIANZA, the velvety RESERVAS.

Berceo, Bodegas R Alt r w p res ★★→★★★ 70 78 85 87 Sister cellar in HARO of BODEGAS GURPEGUI. Vg Gonzalo de Berceo GRAN RESERVA.

Beronia, Bodegas R Alt r w res ★★→★★★ 73 75 77 78 80 81 82 83 84 85 87 88 Small modern BODEGA making reds in traditional oaky style, and fresh 'modern' whites. Owned by Gonzalez Byass (see page 136).

Bilbainas, Bodegas R Alt r w (p) dr sw sp res ★★ 70 72 73 75 76 78 80 81 82 83 84 85 87 Large BODEGA in HARO. Wide and usually reliable range includes dark Viña Pomal, lighter Viña Zaco, Vendimia Especial RESERVAS and Royal Carlton CAVA.

Blanco White.

Bodega Spanish for (i) a wineshop; (ii) a concern occupied in the making, blending and/or shipping of wine; and (iii) a cellar.

Campo Viejo, Bodegas R Alt r (w) res ★→★★★ 70 71 73 75 76 78 80 81 82 83 84 85 88 Branch of Bodegas y Bebidas, one of Spain's largest wine companies. Makes the popular and tasty young San Asensio and some big fruity red RESERVAS, esp Marqués de Villamagna.

Can Rafols dels Caus Cat r w ★★ 84 85 86 87 88 Young small PENEDES BODEGA: own-estate fruity Cab, pleasant white Chard-Xarel-lo-Chenin.

Cañamero Ext w ★ Remote village nr Guadalupe whose wines grow FLOR and behave almost like sherry.

Caralt, Cavas Conde de Cat r w sp res ** **73 78 80 81 82 83 84 85 86 87** CAVA wines from an outpost of FREIXENET; also pleasant still wines.

Cariñena Ara r (p w) * Demarcated region and large-scale supplier of strong everyday wine, dominated by coops. Now being invigorated (and its wines lightened) by modern technology.

Casar de Valdaiga Cas-León r w ** Fruity red made by Pérez Carames in EL BIERZO, north of LEON.

Castellblanch Cat w sp ** PENEDES CAVA firm, owned by FREIXENET. Currently much praised for Brut Zéro and slightly sweeter Cristal Seco.

Castillo Ygay 25 34 42 62 68 See Marqués de Murrieta.

Cava The official term for any Spanish sparkling wine made by the 'méthode traditionelle', and the DO covering the areas up and down Spain where it is made.

Cenalsa Nav r w ** 89 90 Large firm blending and maturing coop-made wines and shipping a range from NAVARRA, incl a flowery new-style white and a fruity red, Agramont.

Cenicero Wine township in the RIOJA ALTA with ancient Roman origins.

Cepa Wine or grape variety.

Cervera, Lagar de Gal w *** DYA Makers of one of best ALBARINOS: flowery and intensely fruity with subdued bubbles and a long finish.

Chacolí w (r) * DYA Alarmingly sharp, often fizzy, wine from the Basque coast, now possessing its own DO, which applies to all 116 acres! It contains only 9–11% alcohol.

Chaves, Bodegas Gal w ** **89 90** (DYA) Small family firm making good, fragrant, slightly acidic ALBARINO.

Chivite, Bodegas Julián Nav r w (p) dr sw res ** **81 82 83 84 86 87 88 89** Biggest BODEGA in NAVARRA. Full-bodied fruity red wines and a flowery well-balanced white. See Gran Feudo.

Clarete Traditional term, now banned by the EC, for light red wine (occasionally dark rosé).

Codorníu Cat w sp **→*** One of the two largest firms in SAN SADURNI DE NOYA making good CAVA: v high tech, 10 million bottles ageing in cellars. Non Plus Ultra is matured. Many prefer the fresher Ana de Codorníu, the Première Cuvée Brut (86 87) and the Chard (88).

Compañía Vinícola del Norte de España (CVNE) R Alt r w (p) dr sw res **→*** **70 73 74 75 76 78 80 81 82 83 84 85 86 87 89** Top RIOJA BODEGA. The CRIANZA is among the best young red RIOJAS, and Monopole one of the best slightly oaky whites. Excellent red Imperial and Viña Real RESERVAS. CVNE is pronounced 'coonay'.

Conca de Barberá Cat w (r p) Demarcated region growing Parellada grapes for making CAVA, shortly to be incorporated in the DO PENEDES. Its best wine is TORRES MILMANDA Chard.

Consejo Regulador Official organization for the defence, control and promotion of a DENOMINACION DE ORIGEN.

Contino R Ala r res *** **74 75 76 78 80 81 82 84 85** Superb single-v'yd red made by a subsidiary of COMPANIA VINICOLA DEL NORTE DE ESPANA.

Corral, Bodegas R Alt r (p w) res ** **73 75 78 80 81 85 87** Long-est RIOJA BODEGA now in new premises at Navarrete. Best known: red Don Jacobo.

Cosecha Crop or vintage.

Cosecheros Alaveses R Ala r ** 87 88 89 91 Up-and-coming RIOJA coop, esp for good young unoaked red Artadi.

Criado y embotellado por... Grown and bottled by...

Crianza Literally 'nursing'; the ageing of wine. New or unaged wine is 'sin crianza' or 'joven' (young). Wines labelled 'crianza' must be at least 2 yrs old, of which 1 yr is spent in barrel, and must not be released before the third year.

Cumbrero See Montecillo, Bodegas.

Spain entries also cross-refer to Sherry, Port & Madeira, pages 134–140.

De Muller Cat br (r w) ★★→★★★ Venerable TARRAGONA firm specializing in altar wines, gd PRIORATO, superb sumptuous v old SOLERA-aged dessert wines. Incl Priorato DULCE, PAXARETE. Also fragrant Moscatel Seco.

Denominación de Origen (DO) Official wine region (see page 119).

Denominación de Origen Calificada (DOCa) Classification for wines of the highest quality; only Rioja benefits so far (since '91).

Diaz e Hijos, Jesús Cas-La M r w p res ★★→★★★ **86 87 90 91** Unoaked reds from this small BODEGA near Madrid win many prizes and have been compared with those of RIOJA and Catalonia.

Domecq R Ala r (w) res ★★→★★★ **73 74 76 78 80 81 82 83 84 85 88** RIOJA outpost of sherry firm. Best wines are fruity red Domecq Domain, exceptional in '76, and Marqués de Arienzo RESERVAS.

Dulce Sweet.

Elaborado y añejado por... Made and aged by...

El Bierzo Cas-León Region N of LEON demarcated in '90. See Casar de Valdaiga, Palacio de Arganza.

El Coto, Bodegas R Ala r (w) res ★★ **70 75 76 78 80 81 82 84 85 86 87 88** BODEGA best known for light soft red El Coto and Coto de Imaz.

Espumoso Sparkling (but see Cava).

Evena Nav Government-funded research station revolutionizing NAVARRA wines. Run by JAVIER OCHOA.

Fariña, Bodegas Cas-León r w res ★★ **82 85 86 89** Rising star of new DO TORO: good spicy reds. Gran Colegiata is cask-aged; Colegiata not.

Faustino Martínez R Ala r w (p) res ★★ **70 72 73 74 75 76 78 80 81 82 83 85 86** Good reds. Light fruity white Faustino V. GRAN RESERVA is Faustino I. Do not be put off by the repellent fake-antique bottles.

Felix Solis Cas-La M r ★★ BODEGA in VALDEPENAS setting a new pace with oak-aged reds, Viña Albali, RESERVAS **(78 81 83 88)** and fresh white.

Ferrer, José L Mallorca r res ★★ **78 80 84 85 86** The best-known BODEGA of Mallorca, at Binissalem. Second best known is Vinos Oliver, at Felanitx.

Fillaboa, Granxa Gal w ★★ DYA Newly established small firm making delicately fruity wine from ALBARINO.

Franco-Españolas, Bodegas R Alt r w dr sw res ★→★★ **64 70 73 74 75 76 78 79 81 82 85 87** Reliable LOGRONO wines. Bordón is fruity red. Semi-sweet white Diamante is a Spanish favourite. Also vg GRAN RESERVA white.

Freixenet Cavas Cat w sp ★★→★★★ Large producer of CAVA, rivalling CODORNIU in size through many acquisitions. Range of good sparkling wines, notably its inexpensive Cordon Negro in black bottles, Brut Nature (87), Reserva Real and Premium Cuvée DS (85). Also owns Gloria Ferrer in California, the champagne house Henri Abelé in Reims and a sparkling wine plant in Mexico. Paul Cheneau is low-price brand.

Galicia Rainy northwest Spain; region to watch for fresh aromatic whites.

Generoso (g) Aperitif or dessert wine rich in alcohol.

Gonzalez y Dubosc, Cavas Cat w sp ★★ A branch of the sherry giant GONZALEZ BYASS. Pleasant sparkling wines exported as 'Jean Perico'.

Gran Feudo Nav w res ★★ Brand name of fragrant white, refreshing rosé, soft plummy red; the best-known wines from CHIVITE.

Gran Reserva See Reserva.

Gran Vas Pressurized tanks (French cuves closes) for making cheap sparkling wines; also used to describe this type of wine.

Gurpegui, Bodegas R B r (p w) res ★ **88 89** Large family firm making inexpensive wines from the RIOJA BAJA, labelled as Viñadrian, incl a fresh rosé. See also Berceo.

Haro The wine centre of the RIOJA ALTA, a small but stylish old town.

Hill, Cavas Cat w r sp res ★★ **83 84 86 87 88** Old PENEDES firm making fresh dry white Blanc Cru, good Gran Civet and Gran Toc reds and a delicate reserva Oro Brut CAVA.

Huelva And r w br ★→★★ Demarcated region W of Cádiz. White table wines and sherry-like GENEROSOS, formerly an important resource of 'Jerez' for blending.

Irache, SL Nav r p (w) res ★★ 78 81 82 85 87 91 Well-known BODEGA for sound everyday reds.

Jean Perico See Gonzalez y Dubosc.

Jerez de la Frontera The capital city of sherry (see page 137).

Joven (vino) Young, unoaked wine.

Jumilla Lev r (w p) ★→★★ Demarcated region in mountains N of Murcia. Its overstrong (up to 18%) wines are being lightened by earlier picking and better winemaking, esp by French-owned Bodegas VITIVINO, eg their Altos de Pío.

Juvé y Camps Cat w sp ★★→★★★ Family firm aiming for and achieving top quality CAVA, from free-run juice only, esp Reserva de la Familia (88).

Laguardia Picturesque walled town at the centre of the RIOJA ALAVESA.

Lagunilla, Bodegas R Alt r ★★ 81 82 83 84 85 86 87 Modern firm owned by the British Grand Met Co. Easy oaky light reds incl Viña Herminia and GRAN RESERVA.

Lan, Bodegas R Alt r (p w) res ★★→★★★ 70 73 75 78 80 81 82 85 86 Huge modern BODEGA, lavishly equipped and making aromatic red RIOJAS, incl the good Lanciano and Lander and fresh white Lan Blanco.

Lar de Barros Ext r res ★★ 83 84 86 87 88 Meaty RESERVAS from Bodegas Inviosa, the first wines from remote Extremadura to make their mark outside Spain. Also Lar de Larres GRAN RESERVAS (80 82 84 86).

La Rioja Alta, Bodegas R Alt r w (p) dr (sw) res ★★→★★★ 64 68 70 73 76 78 80 81 82 83 84 85 86 87 Excellent wines, esp red CRIANZA Viña Alberdi, velvety Ardanza Reserva, lighter Araña Reserva, splendid Reserva 904 and marvellous RESERVA 890. Now making only reservas and GRAN RESERVAS.

León Cas-León r p w ★→★★ 78 81 82 83 84 85 91 Northern region to watch: fruity, dry and refreshing wines, esp from Vinos de León, the former unfortunately named VILE (eg young Coyanza, more mature Palacio de Suzman, full-blooded Don Suero RESERVA). See also El Bierzo.

León, Jean Cat r w res ★★★ 74 75 77 78 79 80 81 82 83 84 85 Small firm owned by a Los Angeles restaurateur. Good oaky Chard, deep full-bodied Cab that repays long bottle-ageing, though less so since '80.

Logroño First town of the RIOJA region. HARO has more charm (and BODEGAS).

López de Heredia R Alt r w (p) dr sw res ★★→★★★ 64 68 70 73 76 78 80 81 82 83 84 85 86 87 Superb startlingly old-established BODEGA in HARO with exceptionally long-lasting, v traditional wines. Viña Tondonia reds and whites are delicate and fine; Viña Bosconia fine and beefy.

López Hermanos Málaga ★★ Large BODEGA for commercial MALAGA wines, incl popular Málaga Virgen and Moscatel Flor de Málaga.

Los Llanos Cas-La M r (p w) res ★★ 75 78 81 82 83 84 86 87 One of the growing number of VALDEPENAS BODEGAS to age wine in oak. Señorío de Los Llanos GRAN RESERVA was remarkably seductive in '79, but recent bottles have been inconsistent. To watch. Also a clean fruity white, Armonioso.

Magaña, Bodegas Nav r res ★★★ 80 81 82 83 85 Tiny young BODEGA making excellent red with Merlot (vines bought from Pétrus), Cab S.

Málaga And br sw ★★→★★★ Demarcated region around city of Málaga. At their best its dessert wines can resemble tawny port. See Scholtz.

Majorca JOSE FERRER, Miguel Oliver and Jaume Mesquida make the only wines of any interest on the island. On the whole, drink Catalan.

Mancha, La Cas-La M r w ★→★★ Large demarcated region N and NE of VALDEPENAS. Mainly white wines, the reds lacking the liveliness of the best Valdepeñas but showing signs of improvement. To watch.

Marfil Cat r w (p) ★★ Means 'ivory'. Brand name of Alella Vinícola (Bodegas Cooperativas), oldest-established and v traditional producer in ALELLA. Now making a lively new-style dry white.

Marqués de Alella Cat w (sp) ★★ 86 87 88 89 (DYA) Light and fragrant white ALELLA wines from PARXET, some from Chard (incl barrel-fermented 'Allier' 91), made by modern methods. Also CAVA.

Marqués de Cáceres, Bodegas R Alt r p w res ★★→★★★ **70 73 75 76 78 80 81 82 83 86 87** Good red RIOJAS made by modern French methods from CENICERO (R Alt) grapes; also a surprisingly light and fragrant white (DYA); and new oak-aged white.

Marqués de Griñon Cas-La M r w ★★★ **82 83 84 85 87** Enterprising nobleman making v fine Cab nr Toledo, S of Madrid, a region not known for wine. Also refreshing white from Verdejo grapes in RUEDA.

Marqués de Monistrol, Bodegas Cat w p r sp dr sw res ★★ **75 77 78 80 82 85 89** Old BODEGA now owned by Martini & Rossi. Refreshing whites, esp the Vin Nature, a good red RESERVA and an odd sweet red wine.

Marqués de Murrieta R Alt r p w res ★★★→★★★★ **34 42 52 60 62 64 68 70 73 74 75 76 78 79 80 81 82 83 84 85 86** Historic, much-respected BODEGA near LOGRONO making some of the best of all RIOJAS. Also soft and fruity red Etiqueta Blanca, superb red CASTILLO YGAY, an 'old-style' oaky white – dry, fruity and worth bottle-ageing (eg currently Blanco Ygay 70) – and a wonderful old-style ROSADO. Quality wavering?

Marqués del Puerto R Alt r (p w) res ★★→★★★ **73 76 78 80 81 83 84 86 87 88** Small concern founded as Bodegas López Agos now owned by Bodegas y Bebidas: red RESERVA Señorío de Agos highly praised in Spain.

Marqués de Riscal R Ala r (p w) res ★★→★★★ **64 65 68 78 80 81 82 83 84 85 86 87** The best-known BODEGA of the RIOJA ALAVESA. Its red wines are relatively light and dry. Old vintages are v fine; some more recent ones have disappointed; current ones are back on form. Baron de Chirel, 50% Cab S, new in '86, is magnificent. Whites from RUEDA, incl a vg Sauv Bl, are some of the best from this region.

Marqués de Romeral R Alt r w ★★ **76 78 80** Everyday Romeral and GRAN RESERVA are both vg value.

Martínez-Bujanda R Ala r p w res ★★★ **70 73 75 78 80 81 84 85 86 87 88 89** Refounded ('85) family-run RIOJA BODEGA, remarkably equipped. Excellent wines, incl fruity SIN CRIANZA and irresistible ROSADO as well as noble Valdemar RESERVAS.

Martínez Lacuesta R Alt r res ★★ **70 73 76 84 85 86 87 88** For long a main supplier to Iberia airlines, Lacuesta has bounced back with first-rate Campeador **80, 81** and **83.**

Mascaró, Cavas Cat r p w sp ★★→★★★ Maker of some of the best Spanish brandy, good sparkling wine, lemony refreshing dry white Viña Franca, and good (85) Anima Cab S.

Mauro, Bodegas Cas-León r ★★ **80 81 83 84** 85 86 87 89 Young BODEGA in Tudela del Duero nr Valladolid with vg round fruity Tinto del País (Tempranillo) red. Not DO as it is made by Bodegas Sainz in RUEDA.

Méntrida Cas-La M r w Demarcated region W of Madrid, source of everyday red wine.

Milmanda ★★★ 86 88 89 See Conca de Barberá, Torres.

Monopole See Compañía Vinícola del Norte de España (CVNE).

Montánchez Ext r g ★ Village near Mérida whose red wines grow FLOR yeast like FINO sherry.

Montecillo, Bodegas R Alt r w (p) res ★★★ **75 76 78 80 81 82 84** 85 88 'State of the art' RIOJA BODEGA owned by OSBORNE (see page 138). Red and fresh dry white Cumbrero are among the best CRIANZA wines. Viña Monty is the worthy RESERVA. GRAN RESERVA Especial is first rate.

Montecristo, Bodegas ★★ Well-known brand of MONTILLA-MORILES wines.

Monterrey Gal r ★ Region near the N border of Portugal; strong wines like those of VERIN.

Montilla-Moriles And g ★★→★★★ Demarcated region nr Córdoba. Its crisp sherry-like FINO and AMONTILLADO contain 14–17.5% natural alcohol and remain unfortified. At best, singularly toothsome aperitifs.

Muga, Bodegas R Alt r (w sp) res ★★★ **70 73 75 76 78 80 81 82 84 85 86 87 88** Small family firm in HARO, making some of RIOJA's best reds by strictly traditional methods. Wines are light but highly aromatic, with long complex finish. Best is Prado Enea. Whites and CAVA less good.

Navajas, Bodegas R Alt r w res ★★ 82 83 85 87 Small firm with bargain reds, CRIANZAS and RESERVAS, fruity and full-bodied.

Navarra Nav r p (w) ★★ Demarcated region; mainly rosés and sturdy reds, now well launched on stylish Tempranillo and Cab reds, some RESERVAS up to RIOJA standards. See Cenalsa, Chivite, Magaña, Ochoa, etc.

Nuestro Padre Jésus del Perdón, Coop de Cas-La M r w ★→★★ 85 86 88 91 DYA Look for bargain fresh white Lazarillo and more-than-drinkable Yuntero; 100% Cencibel (alias Tempranillo) aged in oak.

Ochoa Nav r p w res ★★→★★★ **82 84 85 87 88 89** Small family BODEGA now producing an excellent white, but better known for its well-made red and rosé wines, incl outstanding 100% Tempranillo, 100% Cab S, and a blend of both.

Olarra, Bodegas R Alt r (w p) res ★★→★★★ **70 73 75 76 78 80 81 82 83 84 85** 87 Vast modern BODEGA nr LOGRONO, one of the showpieces of RIOJA, making good red and white wines and excellent Cerro Añon RESERVAS. Since '81, Añares is the top reserva.

Rioja's Characteristic Style

To the Spanish palate the taste of luxury in wine is essentially the taste of (American) oak. Oak contains vanillin: hence the characteristic vanilla flavour of all traditional Spanish table wines of high quality – exemplified by the reservas of Rioja (red and white). Fashion swung (perhaps too far) against the oaky flavour of old Rioja whites but the pendulum is swinging back, although to subtler oak flavours than in the old days. The marriage of ripe fruit and oak in red Rioja is still highly appreciated.

Palacio, Bodegas R Ala r p w res ★★ **70 73 81 82 85** 87 Glorioso was for a long time one of the best of RIOJA RESERVAS. After Seagram bought the BODEGA in '72 it went to pieces, but is now much improved.

Palacio de Arganza Cas-León r p (w) res ★★ **70 74 76 79 80** 83 85 Best-known BODEGA in the new DO of EL BIERZO, between LEON and Galicia. The somewhat variable red Almena del Bierzo is well worth trying.

Palacio de Fefiñanes Gal w res ★★★ Famous for untypical ALBARINO. No bubbles and oak-aged 3–5 yrs.

Parxet Cat w p sp ★★ Makers of excellent fresh fruity CAVA and elegant MARQUES DE ALELLA whites from ALELLA.

Paternina, Bodegas R Alt r w (p) dr sw res ★→★★ **73 75 76 78 82** 83 86 A household name, esp for BANDA AZUL red and Banda Dorada white (oaked and unoaked styles). The Conde de los Andes label was fine; **64, 70, 73** were outstanding, but recent vintages are disappointing. Most consistent red is Viña Vial.

Paxarete Traditional intensely sweet dark brown almost chocolatey speciality of TARRAGONA. Not to be missed. See De Muller.

Pazo Gal r p w ★★ DYA Brand name of the RIBEIRO coop, whose wines are akin to VINHOS VERDES. Rasping red is the local favourite. Pleasant slightly fizzy Pazo and Xeito whites are safer; Viña Costeira has quality.

Peñafiel Cas-León r w res ★★ **76 79 80 82 83 85 86 87 89** Village on R Duero nr Valladolid. Best wines: fruity reds from Bodega Ribero Duero, incl tasty Protos Reserva. Tasty does not always mean agreeable.

Penedès Cat r w sp ★→★★★ Demarcated region including Vilafranca del Penedès, SAN SADURNI DE NOYA and SITGES. See also Torres.

Perelada Cat w (r p) sp ★★ In the demarcated region of Ampurdán on the Costa Brava. Best known for sparkling, both CAVA and GRAN VAS.

Pérez Pascuas Hermanos Cas-León r (p) res ★★★ **81 83** 85 86 87 89 91 Immaculate tiny family BODEGA in RIBERA DEL DUERO. In Spain its fruity and complex red Viña Pedrosa is rated one of the country's best.

Pesquera Cas-León r ★★→★★★ **80 82 84 85 86 87 88** RIBERA DEL DUERO red made in small quantity by Alejandro Fernandez. Robert Parker has rated it on a level with Bordeaux Grands Crus. Janus is a special (even more expensive) bottling.

Piqueras, Bodegas Cas-La M r ★★ 82 83 85 87 Small family BODEGA. Some of LA MANCHA's best reds: Castillo de Almansa CRIANZA, Marius GRAN RES.

Priorato Cat br r ★★★ 85 87 88 89 Demarcated region, an enclave of TARRAGONA, known for alcoholic RANCIO wines and also for splendidly full-bodied, almost black reds, often used for blending, but at its brambly best one of Spain's triumphs. Lighter blended Priorato is a good carafe wine in Barcelona. See De Muller, Scala Dei, Barril.

Protos See Peñafiel.

Raimat Cat r w p sp ★★→★★★ (Cab) 76 81 82 83 84 85 86 87 88 89 Thrillingly clean, structured and highly promising wines from the new DO of Costers del Segre nr Lérida, planted by CODORNIU with Cab, Chard and other foreign vines. Also a good 100% Chard CAVA.

Rancio Maderized (brown) white wine.

Raventos i Blanc Cat w sp ★★→★★★ 85 86 87 Excellent CAVA aimed at top of market, also fresh El Preludi white (91).

Real Divisa, Bodegas R Alt r res ★★ 73 80 81 82 85 86 87 90 Small and picturesque old BODEGA at Abalos, one of the few in RIOJA growing all its own fruit. Noted for its Marqués de Legarda RESERVAS.

Remélluri La Granja R Ala r res ★★★ 74 76 79 80 81 83 84 85 87 Small estate (since '70), making vg traditional red RIOJAS.

René Barbier Cat r w res ★★ 83 85 86 87 89 Owned by FREIXENET, known for fresh white Kraliner and red RB RESERVAS.

Reserva (res) Good quality wine matured for long periods. Red reservas must spend at least 1 yr in cask and 2 in bottle; gran reservas 2 in cask and 3 in bottle. Thereafter many continue to mature for decades.

Ribeiro Gal r w (p) ★→★★ Demarcated region on N border of Portugal making wines similar in style to Portuguese VINHOS VERDES – and others.

Ribera del Duero Historic demarcated region E of Valladolid, now revealed as excellent for Tinto Fino (Tempranillo) reds. Vintages are somewhat variable and prices high. See Peñafiel, Pérez Pascuas, Pesquera, Torremilanos, Vega Sicilia. Also Mauro.

Rioja Cas-León r p w sp **64 66 68 70 73 75 76 78 80 81 82 83 85 86** 87 88 89 90 Upland region along River Ebro in N of Spain producing most of the country's best table wines in some 60 BODEGAS DE EXPORTACION. Its famous reds are mostly from Tempranillo. Other grapes and/or oak added depending on fashion and vintage. Subdivided into 3 areas:

Rioja Alavesa N of the R Ebro, produces fine red wines, mostly light in body and colour but particularly aromatic.

Rioja Alta S of the R Ebro and W of LOGRONO, grows most of the finest, best-balanced red and white wines; also some rosé.

Rioja Baja Stretching E from LOGRONO, makes coarser red wines, high in alcohol and often used for blending.

Riojanas, Bodegas R Alt r (w p) res ★★→★★★ 70 73 74 75 76 78 80 81 82 83 84 85 88 Old BODEGA making good traditional Viña Albina. Its Monte Real RESERVAS are big and mellow.

Rioja Santiago R Alt r (p w dr sw) res ★→★★ 78 81 83 84 85 86 87 88 90 BODEGA at HARO with brands incl the biggest-selling bottled SANGRIA. Its top reds, Condal and Gran Enologica, are respectable.

Rosado Rosé.

Rovellats Cat w p sp ★★→★★★ Small family firm making only good (and expensive) CAVAS, stocked in some of Spain's best restaurants.

Rovira, Pedro Cat r p br w dr sw res ★→★★ Large firm with BODEGAS in the DOs TARRAGONA, Terra Alta and PENEDES. A wide range.

Rueda Cas-León br w ★→★★ Small historic demarcated area W of Valladolid. Traditional producer of FLOR-growing, sherry-like wines with up to 17° alcohol, now making fresh whites, incl those of the MARQUES DE RISCAL (eg oak-aged 'Limousin' 87) and MARQUES DE GRINON. Its secret weapon is the Verdejo grape.

Ruiz, Santiago Gal w ★★★ DYA Small prestigious BODEGA, now owned by Bodegas LAN, in new Galicia DO Rías Baixas. Its ALBARINO is one of v best.

Salceda, Bodegas Viña R Ala r res ★★ **73 75 78 80 81 82 83 84 85 86** Makes fruity light but well-balanced red wines.

Rioja Vintages

It used to be the custom to cross-blend vintages in Rioja to maintain a degree of consistency. Today at least 85% of each wine must be of the year on the label, although Rioja as a whole still shows less vintage variation than eg Bordeaux. The best vintages of the last 40 years have been: 52 55 ***64 68 70*** *73 76 78 80* ***81*** *82 83 85 86 87 88 89 and 90. (Those in bold type were outstanding.)*

Riojas are generally put on the market when they are ready to drink. The best reservas of the best vintages, however, have very long lives and improve with more bottle-age. The best 70s are still at their peak.

Sangre de Toro Brand name for a rich-flavoured red from TORRES.

Sangría Cold red wine cup traditionally made with citrus fruit, fizzy lemonade, ice and brandy. But too often repulsive commercial fizz.

Sanlúcar de Barrameda Centre of the Manzanilla district (see Sherry).

San Sadurní de Noya Cat w sp ★★→★★★ Town S of Barcelona, hollow with cellars where dozens of firms produce CAVA. Standards can be v high, though the flavour (of Parellada and other grapes) is quite different from that of champagne.

San Valero, Bodega Cooperativa Ara r p (w) res ★→★★ 85 86 87 90 Large CARINENA coop with some modern wines. Good red CRIANZA Monte Ducay; fresh Perçebal ROSADO with slight spritz; and good value young unoaked Don Mendo red.

Sarría, Bodegas de Nav r (p w) res ★★→★★★ **73 74 75 76 78 81 82 84 87** 88 89 Model estate BODEGA nr Pamplona: wines up to RIOJA standards.

Scala Dei, Cellers de Cat r w res ★★→★★★ **76 78 80 82 85** One of the few BODEGAS in tiny PRIORATO. Full-bodied reds (esp GRAN RESERVA), some oak-aged, and region's only white: Scala Dei Blanco. Less alcohol recently.

Scholtz, Hermanos And br ★★→★★★ Makers of the best MALAGA, including dry 10-yr-old AMONTILLADO, excellent Moscatel and traditional Dulce y Negro. Best of all is the dessert Solera Scholtz 1885.

Seco Dry.

Segura Viudas, Cavas Cat w sp ★★→★★★ CAVA of PENEDES (Freixenet-owned). Buy the Brut Vintage (83), Aria (88) or RESERVA Heredad.

Serra, Jaume Cat r w res ★★ **84 85 89** PENEDES firm making fruity refreshing whites and fruity well-balanced reds.

Sin Crianza See Crianza.

Sitges Cat w sw ★★ Coastal resort S of Barcelona formerly noted for its dessert wine made from Moscatel and Malvasia grapes. Only one maker, Celler Robert, survives.

Somontano Pyrenees foothills region. Best-known BODEGAS: the old French-established Lalanne (esp Viña San Marcos red from Moristel, Tempranillo and Cab S, white from Macabeo and Chard), Coop Somontano de Sobrarbe (esp Montesierra range and oak-aged Señorío de Lazán), and the new COVISÀ (Vínas del Vero).

Tarragona Cat r w br dr sw ★→★★★ (i) Table wines from the demarcated region; of little note. (ii) Dessert wines from the firm of DE MULLER.

Tinto Red.

Toro Cas-León r ★→★★ Demarcated region 150 miles NW of Madrid. Formerly made over-powerful (up to 16°) red wines, but now produces some tasty balanced reds. See Bodegas Fariña.

To decipher codes, please refer to symbols key at front of book, and to 'How to Read an Entry' on page 5.

Torremilanos Cas-León r res ★→★★ 76 79 81 82 83 85 86 87 88 Label of Bodegas López Peñalba, a fast-expanding family firm near Aranda de Duero. Their red Tinto Fino (Tempranillo) wines are lighter and more RIOJA-like than most. Also labelled 'Peñalba'.

Torres, Bodegas Cat r w p dr s/sw res ★★→★★★★ 64 70 71 73 74 75 76 77 78 79 80 81 82 83 84 85 86 87 88 89 World-famous family firm making most of the best table wines of PENEDES, and a flagship for the whole of Spain. Wines are flowery white Viña Sol, Green Label Fransola Sauv Bl and Parellada, Gran Viña Sol, MILMANDA oak-fermented Chard, semi-dry aromatic Esmeralda, Waltraud Ries, red Tres Torres and Gran Sangre de Toro, superlative Gran Coronas (Cab) RESERVAS, fresh and soft Las Torres Merlot and Santa Digna Pinot N. Mas Borras is a new 100% Pinot N. The family also has v'yds in Chile and California.

Utiel-Requeña Lev r p (w) Demarcated region W of Valencia. Sturdy reds and chewy vino de doble pasta for blending; also light fragrant rosé.

Valbuena Cas-León r ★★★ 75 76 77 78 79 80 82 83 84 85 Made with the same grapes as VEGA SICILIA but sold when either 3 or 5 yrs old. Best at about 10 yrs. Some prefer it to its elder brother.

Valdeorras Gal r w ★→★★ Demarcated region E of Orense. Dry and (at best) refreshing wines.

Valdepeñas Cas-La M r (w) ★→★★ Demarcated region nr the border of Andalucía. Mainly red wines, high in alcohol but surprisingly soft in flavour. Some superior wine (eg LOS LLANOS and FELIX SOLIS) is oak-matured.

Valencia Lev r w ★ Demarcated region exporting vast quantities of clean and drinkable table wine; also refreshing whites, esp Moscatel.

Vallformosa, Masia Cat r w p sp res ★★ 80 84 Good PENEDES wine; a fresh dry white Gran Blanc, good Vall Fort red and Vall RESERVAS.

Vega de la Reina Cas-León w r res ★★ 73 75 78 80 81 82 85 RUEDA BODEGA making complex old-style oaky reds with something of the quality of the famous VEGA SICILIA.

Vega Sicilia Cas-León r res ★★★★ 41 48 53 59 60 61 62 64 66 67 69 72 73 75 76 79 80 82 One of the v best Spanish wines, full-bodied, fruity, piquant, rare and fascinating. Up to 16% alcohol. See also VALBUENA.

Vendimia Vintage.

Verín Gal r ★ Town near N border of Portugal. Its wines are the strongest from Galicia, without a bubble, and with up to 14% alcohol.

Viña Literally, a vineyard. But wines such as Tondonia (LOPEZ DE HEREDIA) are not necessarily made with grapes from only the v'yd named.

Viña Pedrosa See Pérez Pascuas.

Viña Toña Cat w ★★→★★★ DYA Clean fresh and fruity white of Xarel-lo from small firm Celler R Balada. Justifiably high reputation in Spain

Vinícola de Castilla Cas-La M r p w ★★ 83 84 87 89 91 One of the largest firms in LA MANCHA. Red and white Castillo de Alhambra are palatable. Top wines: Cab S and Cencibel (Tempranillo), Señorío de Guadianeja GRAN RESERVAS.

Vinícola Navarra Nav r p w res ★★ 78 82 84 88 90 Old-established BODEGA, thoroughly traditional NAVARRA wines. The best is Castillo de Tiebas.

Vinival, Bodegas Lev r p w ★ Huge Valencian consortium marketing the most widely drunk wine in the region, Torres de Quart (rosé best).

Vino comun/corriente Ordinary wine.

Vino Joven See Joven.

Vitivino, Bodegas Lev r w ★★→★★★ 88 89 French J-L Gadeau has stirred JUMILLA with lively or meaty Altos de Pío from local Monastrell grapes.

Yecla Lev r w ★ Demarcated region N of Murcia. Its ailing cooperative, La Purisima, was once Spain's biggest. Best to avoid its wine.

Ygay See Marqués de Murrieta.

Yllera Cas-Léon r ★★ 86 88 Good value RIBERO DEL DUERO red from Los Curos (but bottled in Rueda so not DO).

Portugal

Portugal entries also cross-refer to Sherry, Port & Madeira, pages 134–140.

Abrigada, Quinta de Est r w res ★★ Family estate: characterful light whites and cherry-like PERIQUITA.

Adega A cellar or winery.

Alcobaça Est r w New IPR: strong reds and whites.

Alenquer Est r w Aromatic reds, strong whites from new IPR just N of Lisbon.

Alentejo r (w) ★→★★★ Vast tract of S Portugal with only sparse v'yds nr the Spanish border, but rapidly emerging potential for excellent wine. To date the great bulk of its wines has been coop-made. Estate wines from ROSADO FERNANDES, HERDADE DE MOUCHAO, QUINTA DO CARMO (now Rothschild-owned) and ESPORAO have potency and style. Best coops are at REDONDO, BORBA and REGUENGOS DE MONSARRAZ. Growing excitement here.

Algarve Alg r w ★ Demoted DO in the holiday area. With a few exceptions its wines are nothing to write home about.

Aliança, Caves B Lit r w sp res ★★→★★★ Large BAIRRADA-based firm making méthode traditionelle sparkling. Reds and whites incl good Bairrada wines and mature DAOS. Aliança Tinta Velha is the best-selling red in Portugal.

Almeirim Ribatejo r w Large new IPR east of ALENQUER.

Almodovar, Casa Agricola Alen w r res ★★ 84 86 87 The whites of this ADEGA at Vidigueira are better known, but its reds are worth trying.

Amarante Subregion in the VINHO VERDE area. Rather heavier and stronger wines than those from farther north.

Arrabida nr Lisbon r w New IPR W of SETUBAL. Reds mostly from Periquita (some Cab S allowed).

Arruda, Adega Cooperative de B Al r res ★ Vinho Tinto Arruda is a best buy, but avoid the reserva.

Aveleda, Quinta da Douro w ★★ DYA A first-class VINHO VERDE made on the Aveleda estate of the Guedes family of MATEUS fame. Sold dry in Portugal but sweetened for export.

Azeveda, Quinta de Min w ★★ DYA Superior VINHO VERDE from SOGRAPE. 100% Loureiro grapes.

Bacalhoa, Quinta da Est r res ★★★ 81 82 83 84 85 87 88 American-owned estate near SETUBAL, famous for harmonious fruity mid-weight Cab S vinified by JOAO PIRES.

Bairrada B Lit r w sp ★→★★★ 66 70 75 76 77 78 79 82 85 87 89 Demarcated region producing excellent red GARRAFEIRAS, esp Safeway 89. Also good sparkling by the méthode traditionelle. Now an export hit.

Barca Velha ('Ferreirinha') Trás-os-M r res ★★★★ 57 64 65 66 78 81 82 83 84 85 Perhaps Portugal's best red, made in v limited quantity in the high DOURO by the port firm of FERREIRA (now owned by Sogrape). Powerful resonant wine with deep bouquet, still unchallenged by younger rivals.

Barrocão, Cavas do B Lit r w res ★→★★★ Based in the BAIRRADA; blends good red DAOS and makes first-rate old Bairrada GARRAFEIRAS (60 64).

Basto A subregion of the VINHO VERDE area on the R Tamego, producing more astringent red wine than white.

Borba Alen r ★→★★ Small IPR area nr Evora, making some of the best wine from ALENTEJO.

Borba, Adega Cooperativa de Est r (w) res ★→★★ 82 84 87 88 89 Leading ALENTEJO coop modernized with stainless steel and oak by EC funding. Big fruity vinho de ano red and vg 82 reserva.

Borges & Irmão Merchants of port and table wines at Vila Nova de Gaia, incl GATAO and (better) Gamba VINHOS VERDES, sparkling Fita Azul.

Branco White.

Braga Subregion of the VINHO VERDE area, good red and white.

Buçaco B Al r w (p) res ★★★★ (r) 51 53 57 58 60 63 67 70 72 75 77, (w) 56 65 66 70 72 75 78 82 Legendary speciality of the Palace Hotel at Buçaco nr Coimbra, not seen elsewhere. At best incredible quality.

Bucelas Est w ★★★ 79 84 Tiny demarcated region just N of Lisbon. Caves VELHAS make aromatic wines with 11–12% alcohol. Reliable, not dramatic.

Camarate, Quinta de Est r ★★ 74 78 80 82 83 84 85 86 87 90 Notable red from FONSECA, S of Lisbon, incl detectable proportion of Cab S.

Campos da Silva Olivera, JC B Al r res ★★ 84 85 Small ADEGA with v fruity estate DAO, Sete Torres Reserva.

Carcavelos Est br sw ★★★ normally NV Minute demarcated region W of Lisbon. Excellent but rare sweet aperitif or dessert wines average 19% alcohol and resemble honeyed MADEIRA. For yrs the only producer was the Quinta do Barão; now JOAO PIRES has joined in.

Carmo, Quinta do Alen r w res ★★★ 86 87 88 89 Small and beautiful ALENTEJO ADEGA, bought in '92 by the Rothschilds of Lafite. 125 acres, plus cork forests. Ferments its wines in marble 'lagars'. Fresh dry white, but best is the fruity harmonious red.

Cartaxo Ribatejo r w ★ A district in the RIBATEJO N of Lisbon, now an IPR area making everyday wines popular in the capital.

Carvalho, Ribeiro & Ferreira B Al r w res ★★→★★★ Large merchants blending and bottling SERRADAYRES and excellent RIBATEJO GARRAFEIRAS.

Casa Ferreirinha Tras-os-M r res ★★★ The second wine to BARCA VELHA, made in less than ideal vintages.

Casa da Insua B Al r w ★★ One of the very few single-estate wines of the DAO area (though not DO), made with a proportion of Cab S for the proprietors by FONSECA.

Casa de Sezim Min w ★★★ DYA Top estate-bottled VINHO VERDE from a member of the new association of private producers, APEVV.

Casaleiro Trademark of Caves Dom Teodosio-João T Barbosa, who make a variety of standard wines: DAO, VINHO VERDE, etc.

Casal García Douro w ★★ DYA One of the biggest-selling VINHOS VERDES in Portugal, made at AVELEDA.

Casal Mendes Min w ★★ DYA The VINHO VERDE from Caves ALIANCA.

Castelo Rodrigo B Al r w Reds resembling DAO.

Cepa Velha Min w (r) ★★★ Brand name of Vinhos de Monção. Their Alvarinho is one of the best VINHOS VERDES.

Chamusca Ribatejo r w New IPR. Full fruity reds, strong whites; predominantly Periquita/Fernão Pires grapes respectively.

Chaves Trás-os-M r w New IPR. Sharp pale fizzy reds from granite soils. Rounder ones from schist.

Clarete Relatively light red wine.

Colares Est r ★★★ TOTB (the older the better) Small demarcated region on the sandy coast W of Lisbon. Its antique-style dark red wines, rigid with tannin, are from vines that have never suffered from phylloxera. Drink the oldest available: it needs at least 10 yrs (see Paulo da Silva).

Conde de Santar B Al r (w) res ★★→★★★ 70 73 78 85 86 Estate-grown DAO, later matured and sold by the port firm of CALEM. Reservas are fruity, full-bodied and exceptionally smooth.

Consumo (vinho) Ordinary wine.

Coruche Ribatejo r w Large new IPR of Sorraia river basin NE of Lisbon. Periquita and Fernão Pires grapes.

Corval, Quinta do Trás-os-M r ★★ Estate nr Pinhão: good CLARETES.

Côtto, Quinta do Trás-os-M r w res ★★★ 82 85 90 Pioneer table wines from port country; red Grande Escolha and Q do Côtto are dense fruity tannic wines that will repay long keeping. Also port.

Cova da Beira B Al r w New IPR on Spanish border for full-bodied reds, ageing well.

Dão B Al r w res ★★ 69 70 71 74 75 80 83 85 Demarcated region round the town of Viseu on the R Mondego. Produces some of Portugal's best-known, but often disappointing, table wines: solid reds of some subtlety with age; substantial dry whites. Most sold under brand names.

DOC (Denominacâo de Origem Controlada) Official wine region. There are 9 in Portugal, incl BAIRRADA, COLARES, DAO, DOURO, SETUBAL, VINHO VERDE.

Doce (vinho) Sweet (wine).

Douro The northern river whose valley produces port and some of Portugal's most exciting new table wines. See Barca Velha, Quinta do Côtto and others. Watch this space.

Encostas de Aire Est r w Fruity high-alcohol wines from large mid-Portugal IPR.

Encostas da Nave B Al r w New IPR. Fresh aromatic wines.

Esporão, Herdade do Alen w r ★★ 87 Owners Finagra SA spent US $10 million on their space-age winery, and planting 900 acres. Their light fresh Roupeiro white and 87 red, with a touch of Cab S, are pleasant but pricey.

Espumante Sparkling.

Esteva Trás-os-M r ★→★★ 87 DYA V drinkable young DOURO red from the port firm FERREIRA.

Evelita Trás-os-M r ★★ 75 79 Reliable middle-weight red made near VILA REAL by REAL COMPANHIA VINICOLA DO NORTE DE PORTUGAL (CVNE). Ages well.

Evora Alen r w Large new IPR south of Lisbon.

Thirty-one new Portuguese wine regions came into play in 1990. These 'IPRs' (Indicacões de Proveniência Regulamentada) are on a six-year probation for DOC status. In EC terminology they are VQPRDs. Either way they are worth watching.

Fonseca, JM da Est r w dr sw sp res ★★→★★★ Venerable firm in Azeitão nr Lisbon, with one of the longest and best ranges in Portugal, incl dry white PASMADOS, PORTALEGRE and QUINTA DE CAMARATE; red PERIQUITA, Pasmados, Quinta de Camarate, TERRAS ALTAS DAO; and famous dessert Moscatel de SETUBAL. Fonseca also owns ROSADO FERNANDES and makes the wines for CASA DA INSUA.

Fonseca Internacional, JM da Est p sp ★ Formerly part of the last, now owned by Grand Met. Produces LANCERS rosé and a surprisingly drinkable sparkling Lancers Brut made by a continuous process of Russian invention.

Gaeiras Est r ★★ Dry full-bodied well-balanced red made nr Obidos.

Garrafeira Label term. The 'private reserve' wine of a merchant, aged for a minimum of 2 yrs in cask and 1 in bottle, but often much longer. Usually their best, though traditionally often of indeterminate origin.

Gatão Min w ★★ DYA Standard VINHO VERDE from BORGES & IRMAO; fragrant but sweetened.

Gazela Min w ★★ DYA New VINHO VERDE made at Barcelos by SOGRAPE since the AVELEDA estate went to a different branch of the Guedes family.

Generoso Aperitif or dessert wine rich in alcohol.

Granja-Amareleja Alen r w New IPR on Spanish border nr EVORA.

Grão Vasco B Al r w res ★★ 70 73 75 78 80 81 82 83 85 87 89 One of the best brands of DAO, from a new high-tech ADEGA at Viseu. Fine red RESERVAS; fresh young white (DYA). Owned by SOGRAPE.

IPR Indicacões de Proveniência Regulamentada. See above.

Lafões B Al r w New IPR between DAO and VINHO VERDE.

Lagoa Alg r w New IPR in Algarve: strong whites and fruity reds.

Lagos Alg r w One of the many newly-established IPRs: red wines mostly from Periquita and Tinta Negra Mole grapes, whites from Boal Branco.

Lagosta Min w ★ DYA VINHO VERDE from the REAL COMPANHIA VINICOLA DO NORTE DE PORTUGAL.

Lancers Est p w sp ★ Sweet carbonated rosé and sparkling white extensively shipped to the US by FONSECA INTERNACIONAL.

Lima Subregion in N of VINHO VERDE area, for mainly astringent red wines.

Lourinhã Newly demarcated brandy-producing region.

Madeira br dr sw ★★→★★★★ Source of famous aperitif and dessert wines. See pages 134–140.

Maduro (vinho) A mature table wine – as opposed to a VINHO VERDE.

Mateus Rosé Trás-os-M p (w) ★ World's biggest-selling medium-sweet carbonated rosé, made by SOGRAPE at VILA REAL and Anadia in BAIRRADA.

Monção N subregion of the VINHO VERDE area on R Minho: producing the best of them from the Alvarinho grape.

Morgadio de Torre Min w ★★ DYA A top VINHO VERDE from SOGRAPE. Largely Alvarinho grapes.

Mouchão, Herdade de Alen r res ★★★ 74 82 Perhaps the best ALENTEJO estate, ruined in the '75 revolution; recently replanted.

Moura Alen r w New IPR: Periquita-based reds. Also white.

Obidos Est r w New IPR nr coast, S of ALCOBACA. Similar wines.

Pacheca, Quinta da Trás-os-M r w ★★ 82 Superior DOURO table wines, estate-grown -made and -bottled. Unfortunately not free of faults.

Palacio de Brejoeira Min w (r) ★★★ Outstanding estate-made VINHO VERDE from MONCAO, with astonishing fragrance and full fruity flavour.

Palmela Alen r w New IPR NE of SETUBAL. V'yds on sandy soils. Reds esp long-lived.

Pancas, Quinta de Est r res ★★ 87 Red to watch from Alenquer district N of Lisbon.

Pasmados Very tasty FONSECA red from the ALENTEJO.

Paulo da Silva, Antonio Bernardino Est r (w) res ★★→★★★ 68 70 74 77 79 80 83 84 85 His COLARES Chita is one of the very few of those classics still made (by the ADEGA Regional).

Penafiel Subregion in the S of the VINHO VERDE area.

Periquita Est r ★★ 71 74 77 78 80 82 84 85 86 87 88 One of Portugal's most enjoyable robust reds, made by FONSECA at Azeitão S of Lisbon. Periquita is a grape much grown in ALENTEJO.

Pinhel B Al w (r) sp ★ IPR region E of the DAO, making similar white, mostly sparkling.

Pires, Vinhos João Est r w sp res ★★→★★★ One of the best-equipped and best-run wineries in Portugal. Wines incl the delicious João Pires Branco (Moscato), Catarina containing Chard, dry white and red Santa Marta, red Santo Amaro made by macération carbonique, TINTO DE ANFORA, Quinta da BACALHOA, dessert SETUBAL, méthode traditionelle João Pires Bruto, and now CARCAVELOS.

Planalto Douro w ★★ Good white wine from SOGRAPE.

Planalto Mirandês Trás-os-M r w Large new IPR NE of DOURO. Port grapes in reds. Verdelho in whites.

Ponte de Lima, Cooperativa de Min r ★★ Maker of one of the best bone-dry red VINHOS VERDES, and first-rate dry and fruity white.

Porta dos Cavalheiros B Al ★★ 75 80 83 85 One of the best red DAOS, matured by Caves SAO JOAO in BAIRRADA.

Portalegre Est r w Important new IPR on Spanish border. Strong fragrant reds with potential to age. Alcoholic whites.

Portimao Alg r w New IPR. Dark reds from Tinta Negra Mole and Periquita grapes.

Quinta Estate.

Raposeira B Al w sp ★★ Well-known fizz made by the méthode traditionelle at Lamego. Ask for the Bruto. An outpost of Seagram.

Real Companhia Vinícola do Norte de Portugal Giant of the port trade (see page 138); also produces EVELITA, LAGOSTA, etc.

For key to grape variety abbreviations, see pages 6–9.

Redondo Alen r w Nr Spanish border. One of Portugal's best-kept secrets. Newly granted IPR status.

Reguengos de Monsarraz, Cooperativa de Alen r (w) res ★★ **82 83 86 87** Important coop making steadily better wines; the best of them red, esp Terras d'el Rei Reserva 86.

Ribatejo Region on R Tagus north of Lisbon. Several good GARRAFEIRAS etc.

Ribeirinho, Quinta de B Lit r sp ★★ **80 85** Luis Pato makes some of the best estate-grown BAIRRADA wines: fruity red and fresh méthode traditionelle sparkling.

Rosado Rosé.

Rosado Fernandes, José de Sousa Alen r res ★★ **71 75 79 83 86** Small firm recently acquired by FONSECA, making the most sophisticated of the full-bodied wines from the ALENTEJO, fermenting them in earthenware amforas and ageing them in oak.

Santarém Ribatejo r w New IPR. Reds and whites fruity and strong; reds will age.

São Claudio, Quinta de Min w ★★★ DYA Estate at Esposende: perhaps the best VINHO VERDE outside MONCAO.

São João, Caves B Lit r w sp res ★★→★★★ **75 76 78 80 82 83** One of the best firms in BAIRRADA, known for its fruity and full-bodied reds and PORTA DOS CAVALHEIROS DAOS. Also fizz.

Seco Dry.

Serradayres Est r (w) res ★ Blended RIBATEJO table wines from CARVALHO, RIBEIRO & FERREIRA. Usually sound and v drinkable; recently too tart.

Setúbal Est br (r w) sw (dr) ★★★ Small demarcated region S of the R Tagus, where FONSECA make a highly aromatic dessert Muscat, 6 and 20 yrs old.

Sogrape Sociedad Comercial dos Vinhos de Mesa de Portugal. Largest wine concern in the country, making VINHOS VERDES, DAO, MATEUS ROSE, VILA REAL red, etc, and now owners of FERREIRA port.

Solar dos Boucas VINHO VERDE estate acquired by port house QUINTA DO NOVAL. 70 acres. Its dry aromatic wine is a model.

Tavira Alg r w New Algarve IPR near Faro environs.

Terras Altas B Al r w res ★★ **75 76 78 79 80 82 83 84** 85 87 88 Good DAO wines made by FONSECA.

Tinto Red.

Tinto da Anfora Est r ★★ **78 80 81 82 84 85 86 87** Deservedly popular juicy and fruity red from JOAO PIRES. Repays at least 5 yrs in bottle.

Tomar Ribatejo r w New IPR for acidic whites, smooth reds.

Torres Vedras Est r w ★ Area N of Lisbon famous for Wellington's 'lines'. Major supplier of bulk wine; one of biggest coops in Portugal.

Valpaços Trás-os-M r New IPR. Similar wines to CHAVES (esp from schist soils).

Varosa B Al r w sp New IPR. Good base for sparkling wine. Also lightweight whites and reds (incl port grapes).

Velhas, Caves B Lit r w res ★★→★★★ Until very recently the only maker of BUCELAS; also good DAO and (80) Romeira GARRAFEIRAS.

Vidigueira Alen w r Famous for traditionally-made unmatured whites from volcanic soils. Newly awarded IPR status.

Vila Real Trás-os-M r ★→★★ Town in the demarcated DOURO region, now making some good reds.

Verde Green (see Vinhos Verdes).

Vinhos Verdes Min and Douro w ★→★★★ r ★ Demarcated region between R Douro and N frontier with Spain, producing 'green wines': wine made from barely ripe grapes and (originally) undergoing a special secondary fermentation to leave it with a slight sparkle. Today the fizz is usually just added CO_2. Ready for drinking in spring after harvest, it may be white or red. 'Green wine' is not an official term.

Sherry, Port & Madeira

The original authentic sherries of Spain, ports of Portugal and madeiras of Madeira are listed below. No other wines that use these names have a moral right to them; nor do any compare in quality and value for money with good examples of the originals.

The map on page 119 locates the port and sherry districts. Madeira is an island 400 miles out in the Atlantic from the coast of Morocco, a port of call for west-bound sailing ships: hence its historical market in North America.

In this section most of the entries are shippers' names followed by a brief account of their wines. The names of wine types are also included in the alphabetical listing.

Abad, Tomas Small sherry bodega owned by LUSTAU. Vg light FINO.

Almacenista Individual matured but unblended sherry; high quality, usually dark dry wines for connoisseurs. Often superb quality and value. See Lustau.

Amontillado In general use means medium sherry; technically means a FINO which has been aged in cask beyond its normal span to become darker, more powerful and pungent. The best are natural dry wines.

Amoroso Type of sweet sherry, v similar to a sweet OLOROSO.

Barbadillo, Antonio Much the largest SANLUCAR firm, with a range of 50-odd MANZANILLAS and sherries mostly excellent of their type, incl Sanlúcar FINO, superb SOLERA manzanilla PASADA, Fino de Balbaina, Principe AMONTILLADO. Also young Castillo de San Diego table wines.

Barbeito Shippers of good-quality madeira, one of the last independent family firms. Wines incl aperitif Island Dry, superior Crown range and rare vintage wines, eg MALMSEY 1901 and the latest, BUAL 1960.

Barros Almeida Large family-owned port house with several brands (including Feuerheerd, KOPKE): excellent 20-yr-old TAWNY and many COLHEITAS.

Bertola Sherry shippers, best known for their Bertola CREAM SHERRY.

Blandy Historic family firm of madeira shippers. Duke of Clarence MALMSEY is their most famous. 10-year-old reservas (VERDELHO, BUAL, Malmsey) are superior. Many glorious old vintages.

Blázquez Sherry bodega at JEREZ (owned by DOMECQ) with outstanding FINO, Carta Blanca, v old SOLERA OLOROSO Extra, and Carta Oro AMONTILLADO al natural (unsweetened).

Bobadilla Large JEREZ bodega, best known for v dry Victoria FINO and Bobadilla 103 brandy, esp among Spanish connoisseurs. Also excellent sherry vinegar.

Brown sherry British term for a style of inexpensive dark sweet sherry.

Bual One of the best grapes of madeira, making a soft smoky sweet wine, not usually as rich and sweet as MALMSEY.

Burdon English-founded sherry bodega owned by CABALLERO. Light FINO, Don Luis AMONTILLADO and raisiny Heavenly Cream are top lines.

Burmester Old, small, family-owned port house with fine soft sweet 20-yr-old TAWNY; also vg range of COLHEITAS. Vintages: **50 55 58 60 63 64 70** 77 80 84 85 89.

Caballero Important sherry shippers at PUERTO DE SANTA MARIA, best known for Pavon FINO, Mayoral Cream OLOROSO, excellent BURDON sherries and PONCHE orange liqueur.

Cálem Old family-run Portuguese house with fine reputation, esp for vintage wines. Owns the excellent Quinta da Foz (**80 82 84 87**). Vintages: **50** 55 58 **60 63** 66 **70 75 77** 80 82 83 **84** 85 86 87 88 89. Good light TAWNY; exceptional range of COLHEITAS: **48 50 52 57 60 62**.

Churchill The only recently founded port shipper, already respected for excellent vintages 82 and 85, also **83 84 86**. Also a vg CRUSTED. Quinta da Agua Alta is Churchill's single-QUINTA port: 87.

Cockburn British-owned port shippers with a range of good wines incl the v popular fruity Special Reserve. Fine vintage port from high v'yds can look deceptively light when young, but has great lasting power. Vintages: **55 60 61 63 67 70 75** 78 82 83 85 87.

Colheita Vintage-dated port of a single yr, but aged at least 7 winters in wood: in effect a vintage TAWNY. The bottling date is also shown on the label. Good examples from KOPKE.

Cortado See Palo Cortado.

Cossart Gordon Leading firm of madeira shippers founded 1745, best known for Good Company range but also producing 5-yr-old Reservas, old vintages (latest, 52) and SOLERAS (esp superb SERCIAL Duo Centenary).

Côtto, Quinta do Single-v'yd port from Miguel Champalimaud, best-known of a new wave of grower-bottlers up the DOURO. Vg vintage 82. See also in Portugal section.

Cream Sherry A style of amber sweet sherry made by sweetening a blend of well-aged OLOROSOS. It originated in Bristol.

Croft One of the oldest firms shipping vintage port: since 1673. Now owned by Grand Met Co. Well-balanced vintage wines tend to mature early (since 66). Vintages: **55 60 63 66 67 70 75 77 82** 85; and lighter vintage wines under the name of their Quinta da Roeda in several other years (**78 80 83** 87). Distinction is their most popular blend. MORGAN is a small separate company (see also Delaforce). Also now in the sherry business with Croft Original (PALE CREAM). Particular (medium), Delicado (FINO, also medium), and good PALO CORTADO.

Crusted Term for a vintage-style port, but usually blended from several vintages not one. Bottled young and bottle-aged, so it then forms a 'crust'. Needs decanting.

Delaforce Port shippers owned by CROFT, best known in Germany. His Eminence's Choice is an extremely pleasant TAWNY; VINTAGE CHARACTER is also good. Vintage wines are v fine, among the lighter kind: **55 58 60 63 66 70 74 75** 77 82 83 85; Quinta da Côrte in **78 80 84 87**.

Delgado Zuleta Old-established SANLUCAR firm best known for its marvellous La Goya MANZANILLA PASADA.

Diez-Merito SA Fast-growing JEREZ firm owned by Bodegas INTERNACIONALES specializing in 'own-brand' sherries. Owns Zoilo Ruiz-Mateos, formerly part of the ill-fated Rumasa empire. Its own FINO Imperial and OLOROSO Victoria Regina are excellent. DON ZOILO wines are superb.

Domecq Giant family-owned sherry bodegas at JEREZ, famous also for Fundador brandy. Double Century Original OLOROSO is their biggest brand, La Ina their excellent FINO. Other famous wines incl Celebration CREAM, Botaina (old AMONTILLADO) and the magnificent Rio Viejo (v dry amontillado) and Sibarita (PALO CORTADO). Recently: a range of wonderful old SOLERA sherries (Sibarita, Amontillado 51-1A and Venerable Oloroso). Now also in RIOJA.

Don Zoilo Luxury sherries, incl velvety FINO, sold by DIEZ-MERITO.

Dow Old name used on British and US markets by port shippers Silva & Cosens, well-known for relatively dry but splendid vintage wines, said to have a faint 'cedarwood' character. Also vg VINTAGE CHARACTER and Boardroom, a 15-yr-old TAWNY. Quinta do Bomfim is their single-QUINTA port. Vintages: **55 60 63 66 70 72 75 77** 80 83 85. Dow, GOULD CAMPBELL, GRAHAM, QUARLES HARRIS, SMITH WOODHOUSE and WARRE all belong to the Symington family.

Sherry, Port & Madeira entries also cross-refer to Spain and Portugal sections, respectively pages 119–128 and 129–133.

Dry Fly A household name in the UK, this crisp nutty AMONTILLADO is made in JEREZ for its British proprietors, Findlater Mackie Todd & Co.

Dry Sack See Williams & Humbert.

Duff Gordon Sherry shippers best known for their El Cid AMONTILLADO. Also good FINO Feria and Nina Dry OLOROSO. Owned by OSBORNE.

Duke of Wellington A luxury range of sherries from Bodegas INTERNACIONALES.

Eira Velha, Quinta da Small port estate with old-style vintage wines shipped by COCKBURN. Vintages: **72 78 80 82 85 87**.

Ferreira The biggest Portuguese-owned port growers and shippers (since 1751), recently bought by SOGRAPE (see Portugal). Well-known for old TAWNIES and juicily sweet, relatively light vintages: **60 63 66 70 75 77 78** 80 82 83 85 87. Also Dona Antónia Personal Reserve and splendidly rich tawny Duque de Bragança.

Urgent notice: sherry, port, madeira and food

By a quirk of fashion the wines of sherry, madeira and to some extent port are currently being left on the sidelines by a world increasingly hypnotized by a limited range of 'varietal' wines. Yet all three include wines with every quality of 'greatness', and far more gastronomic possibilities than are commonly realized. It is notorious that for the price of eg a bottle of top-class white burgundy you can buy three of the very finest fino sherry, which with many dishes (see Wine & Food) will make an equally exciting accompaniment. Mature madeiras give the most lingering farewell of any wine to a splendid dinner. Tawny port is a wine of many uses, especially wonderful at sea. Perhaps it is because the New World cannot rival these Old World classics that they are left out of the headlines.

Fino Term for the lightest and finest of sherries, completely dry, v pale and with great delicacy. Fino should always be drunk cool and fresh: it deteriorates rapidly once opened. TIO PEPE is the classic example.

Flor A floating yeast peculiar to FINO sherry and certain other wines that oxidize slowly and tastily under its influence.

Fonseca Guimaraens British-owned port shipper of stellar reputation, connected with TAYLOR'S. Robust deeply coloured vintage wine, among the v best. Vintages: Fonseca **70 75 77 80** 83 85 86 87 88; Fonseca Guimaraens 76 78. Quinta do Panascal 78 is a new single-QUINTA wine. Also delicious VINTAGE CHARACTER Bin 27.

Forrester Port shippers and owners of the famous Quinta da Boa Vista, now owned by Martini & Rossi. Their vintage wines tend to be round 'fat' and sweet, good for relatively early drinking. Baron de Forrester is vg TAWNY. Vintages: (Offley Forrester) 55 **60 62 63 66 67 70 72 75 77** 81 82 83 85 87 89.

Garvey Famous old sherry shippers at JEREZ. Their finest wines are deep-flavoured FINO San Patricio, Tio Guillermo Dry AMONTILLADO and Ochavico Dry OLOROSO. San Angelo Medium amontillado is the most popular. Also Bicentenary PALE CREAM.

Gonzalez Byass Enormous family-run firm shipping the world's most famous and one of the v best FINO sherries: TIO PEPE. Brands incl La Concha Medium AMONTILLADO, Elegante Dry fino, San Domingo PALE CREAM, Nectar CREAM and Alfonso Dry OLOROSO. Amontillado del Duque is on a higher plane, as are Matusalem and Apostoles: respectively sweet and dry old OLOROSOS of rare quality. Now linked with Grand Metropolitan.

Gould Campbell See Smith Woodhouse.

Graham Port shippers famous for some of the richest, sweetest and best of VINTAGE PORTS, largely from their own Quinta dos Malvedos. Also excellent brands, incl Six Grapes RUBY, LBV, and 10- and 20-yr-old TAWNIES. Vintages: **55 57 58 60 62 63 64 65 66 68 70 75 76 77 78 79** 80 82 83 84 85 86 87 88 89.

Guita, La Famous old SANLUCAR bodega (owned by Perez Marin) and its v fine MANZANILLA PASADA. Also vg vinegar.

Harvey's The largest sherry firm: owners of PALOMINO and DE TERRY and has links with BOBADILLA and GARVEY. World-famous Bristol shippers of Bristol Cream and Bristol Milk (sweet), Club AMONTILLADO and Bristol Dry (medium), Luncheon Dry and Bristol FINO (not v dry), and Tico, an odd sweet fino. More to the point is their very good '1796' range of high quality sherries and Adorno OLOROSO. Harvey's also control COCKBURN.

Henriques & Henriques Well-known independent madeira shippers of Funchal: wide range of rich and toothsome wines. Also a good dry aperitif, Ribeiro Seco; and v fine old reservas.

Hildalgo, Vinícola Old SANLUCAR family firm best known for vg pale MANZANILLA La Gitana, fine OLOROSO Seco and Jerez CORTADO.

Internacionales, Bodegas Once the pride of the now-defunct Rumasa company, incorporating such famous houses as BERTOLA, VARELA and DIEZ-MERITO, Internacionales is now the cornerstone of a new empire embracing PATERNINA and FRANCO-ESPANOLAS in RIOJA. Best-known sherries are the DUKE OF WELLINGTON range.

Jerez de la Frontera Centre of the sherry industry, between Cádiz and Seville in S Spain. The word 'sherry' is a corruption of the name, pronounced in Spanish 'hereth'. In French, Xérès.

Kopke The oldest port house, founded by a German in 1638. Fair quality vintage wines (**55 58 60 63 65 66 67 70 74 75 77 78 79 80 82 83 85 87 89**) and vg COLHEITAS.

Late-bottled vintage (LBV) Port of a single vintage kept in wood for twice as long as VINTAGE PORT (about 5 yrs), therefore lighter when bottled and ageing quicker. A real LBV will 'throw a crust' like vintage port. Few (eg WARRE, SMITH WOODHOUSE) qualify.

Leacock One of the oldest madeira shippers. Basic St John range is v fair; 10-yr-old Special Reserve MALMSEY and 13-yr-old BUAL are excellent.

Lomelino Tarquinio Madeira shippers once famous for their collection of antique wines. Standard range is Dom Henriques, top range is Imperial.

Lustau One of the largest family-owned sherry bodegas in JEREZ (now controlled by CABALLERO), making many wines for other shippers, but with a vg Dry Lustau range (esp FINO and OLOROSO) and Jerez Lustau PALO CORTADO. Pioneer shippers of excellent ALMACENISTA and 'landed age' wines; AMONTILLADOS and olorosos aged in elegant bottles before shipping. See also Abad.

Macharnudo One of the best parts of the sherry v'yds, N of JEREZ, famous for wines of the highest quality, both FINO and OLOROSO.

From January '93, madeiras labelled Sercial, Verdelho, Bual or Malmsey must be at least 85% from that grape variety. The majority made using the chameleon Tinta Negra Mole grape, which vinified similarly easily imitates each of these grape styles, may only be called seco (dry), meio seco (medium dry), meio doce (medium sweet) or doce (sweet) respectively. Meanwhile replanting is building up supplies of the (rare) classic varieties.

Madeira Wine Company In 1913 all the British madeira firms (26 in total) amalgamated to survive hard times. Remarkably, three generations later the wines, though cellared together, preserve their house styles.

Malmsey The sweetest form of madeira; dark amber, rich and honeyed yet with madeira's unique sharp tang.

Manzanilla Sherry, normally FINO, which has acquired a peculiar bracing salty character from being kept in bodegas at SANLUCAR DE BARRAMEDA, on the Guadalquivir estuary nr JEREZ.

Manzanilla Pasada A mature MANZANILLA half-way to an AMONTILLADO-style wine. At its best (eg LA GUITA) one of the most appetizing sherries.

Marqués del Real Tesoro Old sherry firm, famous for MANZANILLA and AMONTILLADO, bought by the enterprising José Estevez. Shrugging off the current slump in sales he has built a spanking new bodega – the first in years.

Martinez Gassiot Port firm, subsidiary of COCKBURN, known esp for excellent rich and pungent Directors 20-yr-old TAWNY, CRUSTED and LBV. Vintages: 55 60 63 67 70 75 82 83 85 87.

Medina A SANLUCAR family bodega doing well; linking with small companies to become a major exporter.

Morgan A subsidiary of CROFT port, best known in France.

Niepoort Small (Dutch) family-run port house with long record of fine vintages (**45 55 60 63 66 70 75 77 78** 80 81 83 84 85 87) and exceptional COLHEITAS.

Noval, Quinta do Great Portuguese port house making intensely fruity, structured and elegant vintage port; a few ungrafted vines still at the QUINTA make a small quantity of Nacional – extraordinarily dark, full, velvety and slow-maturing wine. Also vg 20-yr-old TAWNY. Vintages: **55 58 60 62 63 64 66 67 70 75 78** 80 82 83 84 85 87.

Offley Forrester See Forrester.

Oloroso Style of sherry, heavier and less brilliant than FINO when young, but maturing to greater richness and pungency. Naturally dry, but generally sweetened, for sale as CREAM.

Osborne Enormous Spanish firm with well-known brandy but also good sherries incl FINO QUINTA, Coquinero dry AMONTILLADO, 10 RF (or Reserva Familiale) OLOROSO. See also Duff Gordon.

Pale Cream Popular style of pale sherry made by sweetening FINO, pioneered by CROFT's Original.

Palo Cortado A style of sherry close to OLOROSO but with some of the character of an AMONTILLADO. Dry but rich and soft. Not often seen.

Palomino & Vergara Historic sherry shippers of JEREZ bought in '86 by HARVEY'S, best known for Palomino CREAM, Medium and Dry. Best wine: FINO Tio Mateo.

Pasada Style of FINO OR MANZANILLA which is close to AMONTILLADO: a stronger drier wine without FLOR character.

Poças Junior Family port firm specializing in TAWNIES and COLHEITAS.

Ponche An aromatic digestif made with old sherry and brandy, flavoured with herbs and orange, presented in eye-catching silvered bottles. See Caballero and de Soto.

Puerto de Santa María Second city and port of the sherry area, with important bodegas.

PX Short for Pedro Ximénez, the grape part-dried in the sun used in JEREZ for sweetening blends.

Quarles Harris One of the oldest port houses, since 1680, now owned by the Symingtons (see Dow). Small quantities of LBV, mellow and well-balanced. Vintages: **60 63 66 70 75 77** 78 80 83 85.

Quinta Portuguese for 'estate'. Also used to denote vintage ports which are usually, but not invariably, from the estate's v'yds, made in good but not exceptional vintages.

Rainwater A fairly light, not very sweet blend of madeira – traditionally popular in N America.

Ramos-Pinto Dynamic small port house specializing in single-QUINTA TAWNIES of style and elegance.

Real Companhia Vinícola do Norte de Portugal AKA Royal Oporto Wine Co and Real Companhia Velha; the largest port house, with a long political history. Many brands and several QUINTAS, incl Quinta dos Carvalhos which makes TAWNIES and COLHEITAS. Vintage wines generally dismal.

Rebello Valente Name used for the VINTAGE PORT of ROBERTSON. Light but elegant and well-balanced, maturing rather early. Vintages: **55 60 63 66 67 70 72 75 77** 80 83 85.

La Riva Distinguished firm of sherry shippers, now controlled by DOMECQ, making one of the best FINOS, Tres Palmas, among many good wines.

Rivero, JM The famous CZ brand of the oldest sherry house now belongs to Antonio Núñez, who makes Rivero sherries as well as his own.

Robertson Subsidiary of SANDEMAN, shipping REBELLO VALENTE VINTAGE, LBV, Robertson's Privateer Reserve, Game Bird TAWNY, 10-yr-old Pyramid and 20-yr-old Imperial. Vintages: **63 66 67 70 72 75** 77 80 83 85.

Rosa, Quinta de la Fine single-QUINTA port of the Bergqvist family at Pinhão. Recent return to traditional methods and stone lagares. Esp 85.

Rozes Port shippers controlled by Moët Hennessy. RUBY v popular in France; also TAWNY. Vintages: **63 67 77 78** 83 85 87.

Ruby Youngest (and cheapest) port style: simple, sweet and red. The best are vigorous and full of flavour; others can be merely strong and rather thin.

Rutherford & Miles Madeira shippers with one of the best known of all BUAL wines: Old Trinity House. Also Old Custom House SERCIAL and Old Artillery House MALMSEY. All are relatively rich in style.

Sanchez Romate Family firm in JEREZ since 1781. Best known in Spanish-speaking world, esp for brandy Cardinal Mendoza. Good sherry: FINO Cristal, OLOROSO Don Antonio, AMONTILLADO NPU ('Non Plus Ultra').

Passing the Port

Vintage port is almost as much a ritual as a drink. It always needs to be decanted with great care (since the method of making it leaves a heavy deposit in the bottle). The surest way of doing this is by filtering it through clean muslin or a coffee filter-paper into either a decanter or a well-rinsed bottle. All except very old ports can safely be decanted the day before drinking. A week may not be too long. At table the decanter is traditionally passed from guest to guest clockwise. Vintage port can be immensely long-lived. Particularly good vintages older than those mentioned in the text include 04 08 11 20 27 34 35 45 50.

Sandeman Giant of the port trade and a major figure in the sherry one, owned by Seagram. Founder's Reserve is their well-known VINTAGE CHARACTER; TAWNIES are much better. Vintage wines are at least adequate – some of the old vintages were superlative (**55 57 58 60 62 63 65 66 67 68 70 72 75** 77 78 **80** 82 85 88). Of the sherries, Medium Dry AMONTILLADO is best-seller, Don FINO is vg, and a new range of wonderful luxury dry old sherries incl Royal Ambrosante, Imperial Corregidor, Royal Esmerelda. Not to be missed.

Sanlúcar de Barrameda Seaside sherry-town (see Manzanilla).

Sercial Madeira grape making the driest of the island's wines – a good aperitif.

Shortridge Lawton MADEIRA shippers with v dry Reserva SERCIAL and v tangy 10-yr-old Special Reservas.

Smith Woodhouse Port firm founded in 1784, now owned by the Symington family (see Dow). Gould Campbell is a subsidiary. Relatively light and easy wines incl His Majesty's Choice 20-yr-old, Old Lodge TAWNY. Vintages (v fine): **60 70 75** 77 **80** 82 83 85 88.

Solera System used in making both sherry and (in modified form) madeira, also some port. It consists of topping up progressively more mature barrels with slightly younger wine of the same sort, the object being to attain continuity in the final wine. Most sherries when sold are blends of several solera wines.

Soto, José de Best known for inventing PONCHE, this family firm also makes a range of good sherries, esp Dry OLOROSO.

Tawny A style of port aged for many yrs in wood (in contrast to VINTAGE PORT, which is aged in bottle) until tawny in colour. Many of the best are 20-yrs-old. Low-price tawnies are blends of red and white ports. Taste the difference.

Taylor, Fladgate & Yeatman (Taylor's) Perhaps the best port shippers, esp for full rich long-lived VINTAGE wine and TAWNIES of stated age (40-yr-old, 20-yr-old, etc). Their VARGELLAS estate is said to give Taylor's its distinctive scent of violets. Vintages: 55 60 63 66 70 75 77 80 83 85. Quinta de Vargellas is shipped unblended in certain (lesser) vintages (67 72 74 76 78). Also now Terra Feita single-QUINTA wine (82). Their LBV is also better than most.

Terry, Fernando A de Magnificent bodega at PUERTO DE SANTA MARIA with an undistinguished range of sherries (but famous brandies), bought in '86 by HARVEY'S.

Tio Pepe The most famous of FINO sherries (see Gonzalez Byass).

Valdespino Famous family-owned bodega at JEREZ, owner of the Inocente v'yd and making the excellent aged FINO of that name. Tio Diego is their dry AMONTILLADO, Solera 1842 an OLOROSO, Del Carrascal their best amontillado. Matador is the name of their popular range.

Varela Sherry shippers best known for their Medium and CREAM.

Vargellas, Quinta de Hub of the Taylor's empire since 1893, giving its very finest ports. The label for in-between vintages. See Taylor Fladgate & Yeatman.

Verdelho Madeira grape for fairly dry but soft wine without the piquancy of SERCIAL. A pleasant aperitif. Some glorious old vintage wines.

Vesuvio, Quinta de Enormous 19th C FERREIRA estate in the high DOURO. Bought '89 by Symington family. 130 acres planted. Esp 88.

Vintage Character Somewhat misleading term used for a good quality, full and meaty port like a first-class RUBY, made by a version of the SOLERA system. Lacks the splendid 'nose' of VINTAGE PORT.

Vintage Port The best port of exceptional vintages is bottled after only 2 yrs in wood and matures very slowly for up to 20 or more in bottle. Always leaves a heavy deposit and therefore needs decanting.

Warre Probably the oldest of all British port shippers (since 1670), now owned by the Symington family (see Dow). Fine elegant long-maturing vintage wines, a good TAWNY (Nimrod), VINTAGE CHARACTER (Warrior), and excellent LBV. Their single-v'yd Quinta da Cavadinha is a new departure. Vintages: 55 58 60 63 66 70 75 77 80 83 85.

White Port Port made of white grapes, golden in colour. Formerly made sweet, now more often dry: a fair aperitif but a heavy one.

Williams & Humbert Famous first-class sherry bodega, recently bought by ANTONIO BARBADILLO. Dry Sack (medium AMONTILLADO) is its best-seller; Pando an excellent FINO; Canasta CREAM and Walnut BROWN are good in their class; Dos Cortados is its famous dry old OLOROSO.

Wisdom & Warter Not a magic formula for free wine, but an old bodega with good sherries, esp fine MANZANILLA La Guapa.

England

The English wine industry started again in the 1960s after a pause of some 400 years. Well over a million bottles a year are now being made from some 2,500 acres; almost all white and generally Germanic or similar to Alsace in style (some more Loire-like), many from new German varieties designed to ripen well in cool weather. Acidity is often high, which means that good examples have a built-in ability (and need) to age. Four years is a good age for many, and up to ten for some. The annual Gore-Browne Trophy and medals are awarded for the best. The English Vineyards Association (EVA) seal is worn by tested wines. Since 1991 non-hybrid English wines may be labelled as 'Quality Wine', taking them into the European Community quality bracket for the first time. Beware 'British Wine', which is neither British nor indeed wine, and has nothing to do with the following.

Adgestone nr Sandown (Isle of Wight) Prize-winning 8.5-acre v'yd on chalky hill site: Müller-T, Reichensteiner, Seyval Bl. First vintage: 70. Appley fragrant dryish wines age exceedingly well (eg 89).

Astley Stourport-on-Severn (Worcestershire) 4.5 acres producing good Kerner. ('Severn Vale' is sweet.)

Avalon Shepton Mallet (Somerset) Organically grown grapes. 2.3 acres.

Bardingley Staplehurst (Kent) 2.5-acres specializing in (Zweigelt) red, rosé.

Barkham Manor Vineyard Uckfield (Sussex) 34 acres of Müller-T, Kerner, etc, planted '85–'87. Also good Bacchus, Huxelrebe.

Barton Manor East Cowes (Isle of Wight) 10-acre v'yd producing consistently good aromatic medium-dry blend and sparkling. Now also Gewürz under plastic tunnels. Considerable recent investment.

Beaulieu nr Lymington (Hampshire) 4.6-acre v'yd, principally of Müller-T, est 1960 by Gore-Browne family on old monastic site.

Beenleigh Manor Totnes (Devon) 0.5 acres of trophy-winning Cab S and Merlot under polythene. Wine made at SHARPHAM.

Biddenden nr Tenterden (Kent) 20-acre mixed v'yd planted in '70: crisp medium-dry Müller-T and Ortega; also Pinot N rosé and a Reichensteiner sparkler. Makes wine for other growers, and good cider.

Bishops Waltham Bishops Waltham (Hampshire) 10.2 acres: Madeleine-Angevine, Reichensteiner and Schönburger.

Bookers Bolney (W Sussex) Müller-T; the sweet is better.

Boyton (Essex) Small 2-acre v'yd of Huxelrebe (90 is good) and Müller-T.

Boze Down nr Reading (Berkshire) Blends incl Chard are rather good.

Breaky Bottom nr Lewes (Sussex) Good dry wines, esp Seyval Bl, from 5.5-acre v'yd. Has achieved a semi-cult following.

Bruisyard nr Saxmundham (Suffolk) 10 acres of Müller-T. Making medium-dry wines since '76, now also sparkling wine.

Cane End Reading (Berkshire) 12 acres; wines made at CHILTERN VALLEY.

Carden Park nr Malpas (Cheshire) 9-acre v'yd in large 'leisure park' nr Welsh Marches. Good oak-aged Seyval Bl. New sparkling wines in '94.

Carr Taylor Vineyards nr Hastings (Sussex) 21 acres, planted '74. Gutenborner, Huxelrebe, Reichensteiner and Kerner. Also méthode traditionelle sparklers: Kerner-Reichenstiener (vintage and NV) and Pinot N rosé. Some lively intense and balanced wines.

Chiddingstone Edenbridge (Kent) 28-acre v'yd with stress on dry French-style wines. Some barrique-ageing.

Chilford Hundred Linton (nr Cambridge) 21 acres of Müller-T, Schönburger, Huxelrebe, Siegerrebe and Ortega making fairly dry wines since '74.

Chiltern Valley Wines Hambleden (Oxfordshire) 3 acres of own v'yds high up on the chalk, plus neighbouring growers': 4 white wines incl good Old Luxters Dry Reserve, rosé, and fine liquoreux eg sweet Noble Bacchus. Gold medal in '88. Impressive quality.

Cranmore Cranmore (Isle of Wight) 5-acre v'yd planted with Müller-T and Gutenborner.

Denbies Wine Estate Ranmore Common (Surrey) 250-acre venture using mix of German varieties and advice from Trier. England's biggest v'yd, with first harvest in '89. Good dry wine and Pinot N rosé.

Ditchling nr Hassocks (Sussex) 5-acre v'yd well-reputed for consistency. Good Müller-T.

Elham Valley nr Canterbury (Kent) 2-acre v'yd: Kerner, Madeleine-Angevine, good Seyval Bl, and medium-dry Müller-T (90 is a medal-winner).

Elmham Park nr East Dereham (Norfolk) 6-acre v'yd belonging to a wine merchant/fruit farmer. Müller-T, Madeleine-Angevine (best), etc, making Mosel-style light dry flowery wines. First vintage: 74. Also fine dry cider.

Fonthill Salisbury (Wiltshire) 9.5 acres; wines incl v pleasant Seyval, Dornfelder rosé.

Gifford's Hall Hartest (Suffolk) 12-acre v'yd now making good wine.

Halfpenny Green Stourbridge (W Midlands) 3 acres of vines. Emphasis on Huxelrebe, Reichensteiner and Seyval Bl.

Hambledon nr Petersfield (Hampshire) The first modern English v'yd, planted in '51 on a chalk slope with advice from Champagne. Grapes are Chard, Pinot N and Seyval Bl. Now 15.4 acres. Fairly dry wines.

Harden Farm Penshurst (Kent) 18 acres of Schönburger, Bacchus, Reichensteiner, Regner and Huxelrebe.

Headcorn (Kent) 5-acre medal-winning v'yd: Seyval Bl, Huxelrebe, etc.

Helions Vineyard Helion's Bumpstead (Essex) One acre, 50:50 Müller-T and Reichensteiner; vg dry wine (esp 90).

High Weald Winery Lenham (Kent) No vines, but an influential winemaker (proprietor Christopher Lindlar) for several growers.

Lamberhurst Priory nr Tunbridge Wells (Kent) England's leading winery, with 55 acres planted '72. Largely Müller-T, Seyval Bl and Reichensteiner. Approx half a million bottles; winemaking for several other v'yds, eg Horam Manor, 4.4 acres at Heathfield, Sussex. A regular prize-winner. Méthode traditionelle sparkling and 89 Schönburger are good news.

Leeford Vineyards nr Battle (Sussex) 35-acre v'yd; Saxon Valley label.

Loddiswell Kingsbridge (Devon) 6 acres plus one under plastic tunnels. Müller-T, Seyval Bl and Reichensteiner.

Manstree nr Exeter (Devon) Small v'yd, esp for sparkling wine: 'Essling' (90) is an award-winner.

Moorlynch nr Bridgewater (Somerset) 11 acres of an idyllic farm. Good wines.

New Hall nr Maldon (Essex) 87 acres of mixed farm planted with Huxelrebe, Müller-T and Pinot N. Experimental reds.

Nutbourne Manor nr Pulborough (Sussex) 12.5 acres: elegant and tasty Schönburger, Bacchus and Huxelrebe. Sussex Reserve is a new blend. Wines made by HIGH WEALD.

Penshurst nr Tunbridge Wells (Kent) 12 acres of the usual grape varieties, since '76.

Pilton Manor nr Shepton Mallet (Somerset) 12-acre hillside v'yd, chiefly Müller-T and Seyval Bl, planted '66.

Plumpton Agricultural College nr Lewes (Sussex) 2-acre experimental v'yd at college for winemakers.

Priory Vineyards Little Dunmow (Essex) Good wines from 10 acres.

Pulham nr Norwich (Norfolk) 12.6-acre v'yd planted '73; Müller-T, Auxerrois, Bacchus. Top wines using Magdalen label.

Queen Court Faversham (Kent) 7-acre brewery-owned v'yd of Müller-T.

Rock Lodge nr Haywards Heath (Sussex) 3-acre v'yd of Müller-T and Reichensteiner making dry white since '70; also méthode traditionelle sparklers and Late Harvest.

St-George's Waldron, Heathfield (E Sussex) 15 acres, planted '79. Müller-T etc and some Gewürz. Well-publicized; mostly farm-gate sales.

Sandhurst Cranbrook (Kent) Mixed farm with 16 acres of vines and 80 acres of hops, plus apple orchards, sheep, etc. Wines improving – worth watching.

Sedlescombe Robertsbridge (Sussex) 5.5 acres: claims to be England's first organic v'yd.

Sharpham Totnes (Devon) 5 acres of vines. Now has own winery run by Mark Sharman (see Beenleigh Manor).

Shawsgate Framlingham (Suffolk) 17 acres incl Chard. Wins awards.

Staple nr Canterbury (Kent) 7 acres, mainly Müller-T. Some Huxelrebe and Reichensteiner. Dry and fruity wines of fine quality.

Tenterden nr Tenterden (Kent) 17 acres, planted '77. Six wines from v dry to sweet, incl Müller-T, oak-aged Seyval Bl ('91 Gore-Browne Trophy winner), Gutenborner, rosé and sparkling.

Thames Valley Twyford (Berkshire) 17-acre v'yd of Müller-T, Pinot N, Schönburger, etc. Some serious red, oak-matured and Late Harvest wines: botrytis Clock Tower Selection won '92 Gore-Browne trophy.

Three Choirs nr Newent (Gloucestershire) Müller-T, Seyval Bl, Schönburger, Reichensteiner in expanded v'yds. Successful wines incl Bacchus Dry, Huxelrebe. Recently opened: a new £1 million winery.

Wickham nr Shedfield (Hampshire) 9.5-acre v'yd: incl Bacchus, Faberrebe, Schönburger, Seyval Bl.

Wootton nr Wells (Somerset) 6-acre v'yd of Schönburger, Müller-T, Seyval Bl, etc. Consistently good fresh fruity wines since '73.

The current trend towards 'low-alcohol' wines and beers, from which most alcohol has been removed by artificial means, should be a golden opportunity for wines that are naturally lower in alcohol than the 12 or 13 degrees expected in most table wines. Germany is the prime exponent; England is another. Their best wines, with plenty of fruity acidity, do not need high alcohol to make an impact. They are today's logical choice – at least at lunch-time.

Luxembourg

Luxembourg's 3,285 acres of vineyards are planted on limestone soils on the left bank of the Moselle. High-yielding Elbling and Rivaner (Müller-Thurgau) vines dominate, but there are also significant acreages of Riesling, Gewürztraminer and (usually best) Auxerrois, Pinot Blanc and Pinot Gris. These give light to medium-bodied (10.5–11.5°) dry Alsace-like wines.

The Vins Moselle cooperative produces and markets 70% of Luxembourg's wines, and the Domaine et Tradition estates association founded in 1988 is working to promote fine quality from noble grape varieties. The last five vintages in Luxembourg were all good, the 89, 90 and 92 outstanding.

Best producers: M Bastian, sparkling wine makers Aly Duhr et Fils, Caves Gales ('Clos des Rochers'), Clos Mon Vieux Moulin, Château de Schengen, Sunnen-Hoffmann.

Central & Southeast Europe

To say that parts of the region covered by this map are somewhat provisional these days is an understatement. But new regional autonomies and new statehoods are rapidly being followed by higher aspirations. So far Hungary and Czechoslovakia, and now Moldova, as well as Bulgaria, have taken the lead in what has become an area to follow with fascination.

In this section references are arranged country by country, all referring back to the map on this page. Labelling in all the countries involved, except Greece and Cyprus, is broadly based on the international pattern of place name plus grape variety. Main grape varieties are therefore included alongside areas and other terms in the alphabetical listings. Quality ratings are given where experience justifies more than a single everyday star.

Ukraine
TOKAY
MOLDAVIA
Moldova
TRANSYLVANIA
FOCSANI
Tirnave
Romania
BANAT
DEALUL MARE
DRAGASANI
DOBRUJA
Belgrade
Bucharest
R.Danube
Serbia
SVISHTOV
Varna
PAVLIKENI
SUKHINDOL
Black Sea
Sofia
Bulgaria
OVO
MISKET
R.Euros
Plovdiv
ASENOVGRAD
MELNIK
Istanbul
Macedonia
THRACE
Thessaloniki
Aegean Sea
Greece
Turkey
ATTICA
SAMOS
Athens
Patras
EPHALONIA
PELOPONNESE
SANTORINI
RHODES
CRETE

Austria

Austria has recently emerged as a vigorous and well-regulated producer of hearty white wines, including aromatic ones in the German style (more potent) and liquorous ones closer to Sauternes. Her red wines have yet to make an international reputation but this will come. New laws, passed in 1986 and revised for the 1991 vintage, include curbs on yields (Germany please copy) and impose higher levels of ripeness for each category than their German counterparts. Many regional names, introduced under the 1986 law, are still unfamiliar outside Austria. This is a country to explore.

Recent vintages

1992 Extremely hot summer may have led to acidity problems in some areas. Very good wines from the Wachau, Kamptal-Donauland and Styria. Good red wine year.

1991 Good to average quality along with a few vg wines from Burgenland.

1990 One of the best vintages of the last 50 yrs.

1989 Some weather problems reduced crop. Quality fair to good, best in Burgenland and Styria.

1988 Good quantity, some excellent wines.

1987 A third small harvest, but quality is reasonable.

1986 An outstanding vintage in most cases, though small.

1985 A small but excellent quality harvest.

Altsteirischer Mischsatz STYRIAN term for a GEMISCHTER SATZ.

Apetlon Burgenland w (r) s/sw sw ★→★★ SEEWINKEL village: good whites and some reds on sandy soil. Vg sweet wines, esp LENZ MOSER's Prädikat.

Ausbruch Term used for traditional, v sweet wines between Beerenauslese and Trockenbeerenauslese (see Germany) in richness but with the vinous quality and alcoholic strength of Sauternes.

Baden Vienna r w dr sw ★→★★★ Town and wine region S of VIENNA now incl in THERMENREGION.

Blauburger Middling-quality red grape. Best producer: W B S Retz.

Blauer Burgunder The Pinot N. Best from BURGENLAND, KAMPTAL-DONAULAND, THERMENREGION.

Blauer Portugieser With BLAUFRANKISCH, one of the two main red wine grapes of Austria: dark but rather characterless wine. The best is from Haugsdorf, WEINVIERTEL. Best grower: Lust. Used by WIENINGER in VIENNA to make a successful Beaujolais Nouveau-style wine.

Blaufränkisch Grape thriving in warm NEUSIEDLER SEE climate: potent reds, often barrique-aged; can be a little short and rarely age well. Once thought to be Gamay. 'Kékfrankos' in Hungary.

Bouvier Native Austrian grape giving soft low-acid but aromatic wine, esp for Beerenauslese and Trockenbeerenauslese.

Bründlmayer Large (123-acre) estate in KAMPTAL-DONAULAND. Excellent wines in Austrian and international styles. Notable Chard. Pleasant GRUNER V.

Burgenland r w dr sw ★→★★★ Region of 45,000 acres on the Hungarian border, with ideal conditions for sweet wines around the NEUSIEDLER SEE. Four regions: Neusiedlersee (E of the lake), Neusiedlersee-Hügelland (W shore and around EISENSTADT) and MITTEL- and SUDBURGENLAND (RUST and the SEEWINKEL). 'Noble rot' occurs regularly on both sides of the Neusiedler See (but not in Mittel- or Südburgenland) and AUSBRUCHE, Beerenauslesen, etc, are abundant. (See also Illmitz, Mörbisch, Rust, etc.)

Buschenschank Country cousin of Viennese HEURIGE.

Donauland-Carnuntum Unwieldy new name for the Danube (Donau) valley wine region incl KLOSTERNEUBURG.

Dürnstein w dr sw ★★→★★★ Wine centre of the WACHAU with famous ruined castle and the important FREIE WEINGARTNER coop. Some of Austria's best whites, esp RHEINRIESLING and GRUNER VELTLINER.

Eisenstadt Burgenland w (r) dr sw ★★→★★★ Capital of BURGENLAND, historic seat of ESTERHAZY family. Best growers: Barmherzigen Brüder, E Tinhof.

Esterházy Commercial operation of noble and historic family (patrons of Haydn): AUSBRUCH and other BURGENLAND wines can be superlative.

Falkenstein See Weinviertel.

Freie Weingärtner Important coop in DURNSTEIN in the WACHAU. Large quantities of excellent GRUNER VELTLINER and RIES (★★→★★★).

Gemischter Satz A blend of grapes. This is the wine of the HEURIGEN.

Gols Largest wine-producing commune in Austria, on the E side of the NEUSIEDLER SEE. Best producers: Heinrich, Nittnaus, Renner, Stiegelmar.

Grinzing Vienna w ★★ DYA Suburb of VIENNA, once famous for quality wines, now principally for often delicious lively HEURIGEN.

Grüner Veltliner Austria's most characteristic white grape (36%+ of white v'yds): at best spicy flowery racy vital wine. Far from retrenching, GV is the flavour of the decade.

Gumpoldskirchen Vienna w (r) dr sw ★★→★★★ Pretty resort S of VIENNA: characterful wines from ROTGIPFLER and ZIERFANDLER. See Thermenregion.

Heurige Means both 'new wine' and the tavern where it is drunk. Traditionally made from a mixture of grapes. See Gemischter Satz.

Hirtzberger, Franz Top WACHAU grower with 22 acres at Spitz. RIES (Hochrain, Singerriedl) and gutsy GRUNER VELTLINER.

Igler, Hans Coming name for reds (BLAUFRANKISCH, Cab, barrel-aged and blends) at Deutschkreuz in MITTELBURGENLAND.

Illmitz Seewinkel Sweet wine centre: Beerenauslese, Trockenbeerenauslese and 'Riedmandl' wines. Best producers: Kracher, Lang, Opitz.

Jamek, Josef The man who brought dry white wines to the WACHAU in the '50s. Controversial for his use of malolactic fermentation for RIES and GRUNER VELTLINER (★★→★★★).

Kahlenberg Vienna w ★★→★★★ Village and v'yd hill N of VIENNA, formerly celebrated for quality, now more famous for HEURIGEN.

Kamptal-Donauland w (r) dr sw ★→★★ Wine region around KREMS and the Kamp valley, a tributary of the Danube (Donau). Pleasant GRUNER VELTLINER and RIES. Best growers: BRUNDLMAYER, Dolle, Ehn, Hiedler, Jurtschitsch, MALAT-BRUNDLMAYER, Mantler, Nigl, SALOMON, Topf.

Klöch Styria w p (r) ★→★★★ The chief wine town of STYRIA, the SE province.

Klosterneuburg Donauland r w ★→★★★ District just N of VIENNA, with famous monastery, wine college and research station.

Kloster Und New wine college and tasting centre in restored Capuchin monastery at KREMS, run by ERICH SALOMON.

Kollwentz, Anton Innovative EISENSTADT winemaker (Weingut Römerhof). Good Sauv Bl, Welschriesling Eiswein, Cab, BLAUFRANKISCH, ZWEIGELT.

Krems Donauland w ★→★★★ Town and district just E of the WACHAU with good GRUNER VELTLINER and RHEINRIESLING, esp from Austria's biggest WINZERGENOSSENSCHAFT. Best growers: Aigner, Ditz, SALOMON, Weingut der Stadt Krems.

Langenlois Langenlois r w ★→★★ Chief town of the KAMPTAL with many modest and some vg wines, esp peppery GRUNER VELTLINER and RHEINRIESLING from loess and volcanic soils around Zöbing. Reds less interesting, but NB Pinot N and Merlot from BRUNDLMAYER.

Lenz Moser Major grower now in the 5th generation. Lenz Moser III invented a high vine system. His grandson, Lenz Moser V, makes good to excellent wine at Rohrendorf (nr KREMS), APETLON and elsewhere. Leases the Schlossweingut Malteser Ritterorden (formerly the estate of the Knights of Malta) at MAILBERG. Experiments with Cab S, Merlot and Pinot N. Took over SIEGENDORF in '88.

Mailberg Weinviertel r w ★★ Town of the WEINVIERTEL known for lively light wine (red and white) and the Malteser Ritterorden Bordeaux blends.

Malat-Bründlmayer, Gerald Major (50-acre) grower at Furth-Palt in KAMPTAL-DONAULAND. Successful 'international' wines: Chard, Pinot N, Cab S. Also méthode traditionelle sparkling.

Mayer, Franz ★→★★★ VIENNA's biggest grower, with 90 acres. HEURIGE wines but also serious RIES and Chard.

Mittelburgenland The best region for BLAUFRANKISCH and now a little Cab S. Best growers: Gesellmann, IGLER. See Burgenland.

Mörbisch Burgenland r w dr sw ★→★★★ Leading wine village of BURGENLAND. Good sweet wines. Reds and dry whites not inspiring. But NB oak-aged BLAUFRANKISCH from Schindler, the Burgermeister.

Morillon Name given to Chardonnay in STYRIA.

Müller-Thurgau Far less interesting than GRUNER VELTLINER; represents 10% of Austria's vines.

Muskat-Ottonel The strain of Muscat grape grown in E Europe, incl Austria. Can be dry and pungent. Also interesting Prädikat wines.

Neuburger Popular white grape: pleasant wine in KREMS and LANGENLOIS but soft and coarse in BURGENLAND. Excellent Prädikat wines.

Neusiedler See A shallow lake in flat sandy country on the Hungarian border. Autumn mists encourage botrytis in the wines of BURGENLAND. Under the new law it is the centre of 2 wine regions: see Burgenland.

Niederösterreich Lower Austria, ie the NE corner of the country, with 5 wine regions: DONAULAND-CARNUNTUM, KAMPTAL-DONAULAND, THERMEN-REGION, WACHAU, WEINVIERTEL.

Nikolaihof Estate in Mautern in the WACHAU with top RIES and GRUNER VELTLINER. Owns a small chunk of Austria's most famous v'yd: RIED Steiner Hund in KREMS-Stein.

Nüssdorf Vienna w ★★ Suburb of VIENNA with well-known HEURIGEN. RIED Nüssberg was a first-growth in Imperial times.

Oggau Burgenland w (r) sw ★★→★★★ One of the BURGENLAND wine centres, famous for dry whites and big reds. Best grower: Wilhelm Mad.

Pichler, Franz X Top WACHAU grower with 11 acres at Oberloiben nr DURNSTEIN. RIES, GRUNER VELTLINER and Sauv Bl.

Prager, Franz With JAMEK an innovator of dry white wine in the WACHAU.

Retz Weinviertel w (r) ★→★★ Wine centre of WEINVIERTEL, known for GRUNER V, etc. Its dry climate makes big reds, too. Best grower: W B S Retz.

Rhineriesling Austrian alias for German RIES.

Ried Single v'yd: when named on the label it is usually a good one.

Riesling When used alone is German Riesling. Welschriesling, which is almost always inferior, is labelled as such.

Rotgipfler Good and high-flavoured grape peculiar to GUMPOLDSKIRCHEN. Used with ZIERFANDLER to make powerful but lively whites.

Rust Burgenland w (r) dr sw ★→★★★ Most famous wine centre of BURGENLAND, justly famous since the 17th C for its AUSBRUCH, often made of mixed grapes. Increasing amounts of red wine now from wide range: BLAUFRANKISCH to Pinot N, Nebbiolo or even Syrah. Best producers: Schandl, Triebaumer (Paul and Ernst), Wenzel.

St-Laurent Traditional Austrian red grape believed to be related to Pinot Noir. Faintly Muscat-flavoured.

Salomon, Fritz ★★→★★★ Top grower of oak-aged RIES, WEISSBURGUNDER and Gewürz at Weinkelleri Undhof in the Danube valley nr KREMS. The estate is run by Erich S, a partner in the KLOSTER UND wine college.

Sattler, Willi Leading S STYRIAN grower at Gamlitz. Celebrated for Sauv Bl and MORILLON (alias Chard) – no longer unoaked.

Schilcher Pleasant sharp rosé, a speciality of W STYRIA. Best from Gundersdorf and Deutschlandsberg.

Schloss Grafenegg w dr sw ★★→★★★ Famous castle and estate of Metternich family nr KREMS. Gd standard whites; a few Auslesen; some dry (trocken).

Seewinkel 'Lake corner': the sandy district around the NEUSIEDLER SEE, famous for sweet wines.

Siegendorf, Klosterkeller First-class 60-acre BURGENLAND wine estate experimenting with Cab S and Merlot.

Sievering Vienna w ★★ Picturesque suburb of VIENNA with notable HEURIGEN.

Spätrot Another name for the ZIERFANDLER grape.

Spitzenwein Top wine – as opposed to TISCHWEIN (ordinary table wine).

Stift Monastery. These are still important in Austria's winemaking, combining tradition and high standards with modern resources.

Styria (Steiermark) Province in the SE, not famous for quality wine until v recently. Three wine regions: Süd (south, the best of the 3), Süd-Ost (southeast) and West-Steiermark. Sauv Bl, Chard (see Morillon) and Muskateller showing promise here. Top producers: Graf Stürgkh, Gross, Lackner-Tinnacher, Neumeister, Platzer, Polz, SATTLER, Tement.

Südburgenland Wine region in S of BURGENLAND, away from the lake. Some steep slopes. Grapes include Welschriesling and BLAUFRANKISCH.

Thallern Vienna w (r) dr sw ★★→★★★ Village near GUMPOLDSKIRCHEN and trade name of wines from STIFT Heiligenkreuz.

Thermenregion New name for region S of VIENNA, incl BADEN and GUMPOLDSKIRCHEN. Some good lively high-flavoured wines; whites best from ROTGIPFLER and ZIERFANDLER grapes. Reds best from BLAUER PORTUGIESER, Cab S, Pinot N, esp from Tattendorf and Teesdorf. Top producers: (whites) Biegler, Kurz, Schafler, Schellmann, Stadlmann; (reds) Fischer, Gisperg, Reinisch. See also Gumpoldskirchen.

Tischwein Everyday wine, as opposed to SPITZENWEIN.

Traiskirchen Vienna w (r) ★★ Village nr GUMPOLDSKIRCHEN with similar wine.

Veltliner See Grüner Veltliner.

Vienna (Wien) The capital city, with 1,750 acres of v'yds in its suburbs to supply its cafés and HEURIGEN. Best Growers: Breyer, MAYER, WIENINGER.

Vöslau Thermenregion r (w) ★ Spa town S of BADEN (and VIENNA) known for its reds. Best are Cab (NB Schlumberger), Pinot N, ZWEIGELT. Also light wines of BLAUER PORTUGIESER, etc.

Wachau Wine region on the S bank of the Danube round DURNSTEIN, with cliff-like slopes giving some of Austria's best whites, esp RIES and GRUNER VELTLINER. Best growers: Alzinger, HIRTZBERGER, JAMEK, Knoll, NIKOLAIHOF, PICHLER, PRAGER, Schmidl.

Weinviertel 'Wine quarter': name given to the huge and productive district between VIENNA and the Czech border. Mainly light acidic white wines. Formerly divided into Falkenstein-Matzen (E) and RETZ (W).

Weissburgunder Alias Pinot Bl. Increasingly used for solid, often dry wines, but also good in sweet Prädikaten.

Wieninger, Fritz Vienna producer. Esp for RIES, Chard, GRUNER VELTLINER, primeur BLAUER PORTUGIESER.

Winzergenossenschaft Growers' coop.

Zierfandler Flavourful white grape peculiar to BADEN. Blended with ROTGIPFLER.

Zweigelt Productive red grape, with care gives juicy cherry-scented wine.

Hungary

Hungary is the unquestioned regional leader in terms of tradition, although Austria is now ahead in quality. Magyar taste is for fiery, hearty, full-blooded wines, which their traditional grapes (mainly white) perfectly provide, but which are being superseded in many cases by 'safer' international varieties. Since the end of Communism several French, German and other concerns have bought land or entered into joint ventures, especially in Hungary's most famous region, Tokay. Expect to hear much more of this. Meanwhile visitors to the country will find plenty of original wines in the old style.

Alföld Hungary's Great Plain, producer of much everyday wine and some much better, esp at HAJOS, HELVECIA, KECSKEMET, KISKUNHALAS, Szeged.

Aszú Rotten: applied to v sweet wines esp TOKAY (Tokaji), where the aszú is late-picked and 'nobly rotten' as in Sauternes. (See page 51.) Used to designate both the sweet wine and the rotten berries.

Aszú Eszencia Tokaji br sw ★★★★ 57 63 The second highest quality of TOKAY commercially available: superb amber wine like a cross between Sauternes and fino sherry.

Badacsony Balaton w dr sw ★★→★★★ Famous 426-m hill on the N shore of LAKE BALATON whose basalt soil can give rich high-flavoured white wines, among Hungary's best.

Balaton Balaton r w dr sw ★→★★★ Hungary's inland sea and Europe's largest freshwater lake. Many good wines take its name. The ending 'i' (eg Balatoni, Egri) is the equivalent of -er in Londoner.

Balatonboglár Balaton r w p ★→★★ Progressive cellars with sound modern-style wines, esp whites. Also cuve close sparkling.

Balatonfüred Balaton w (r) dr sw ★★ Town on the N shore of LAKE BALATON, centre of the Balatonfüred-CSOPAK district. Softer, less fiery wines.

Bikavér Eger r ★ 'Bulls Blood': the historic name of the best-selling red wine of EGER: at best full-bodied and well-balanced, but dismally variable in its export version today. A three-variety blend (minimum), mostly KEKFRANKOS and Cab. Nowadays also made in SZEKSZARD.

Csopák Village next to BALATONFURED, with similar wines but drier whites, incl good Chard, Sauv Bl, SZURKEBARAT, etc.

Debrö Mátraalja w sw ★★ Town of the MATRAALJA famous for its mellow aromatic HARSLEVELU.

Eger Eger district r w dr sw ★→★★ Best-known red wine centre of N Hungary; a baroque city of cellars full of BIKAVER. Also fresh white LEANYKA (perhaps its best product today), OLASZRIZLING, Chard and Cab.

Eszencia The fabulous quintessence of TOKAY (Tokaji): intensely sweet wine from grapes wizened by botrytis. Formerly grape juice of v low, if any, alcoholic strength, reputed to have miraculous properties: this is now called NEKTAR. Today's Eszencia must attain 6% alcohol, which makes it, in reality, a super ASZU Eszencia.

Ezerjó The grape grown at MOR to make one of Hungary's best dry white wines; potentially distinguished, fragrant and fine.

Felsobabad Regional cellar S of Budapest with authentic (but in Hungary unauthorised) fragrant Pinot N.

Francois President French founded (1882). Sparkling wine producer at Budafok, nr Budapest. Vintage wine: President.

Furmint The classic grape of TOKAY (Tokaj), with great flavour and fire, also grown for table wine at LAKE BALATON and in SOMLO.

Gyöngyös Mátraalja w (r) ★★ Northern city of MATRAALJA offering real promise in dry whites of SZURKEBARAT, Chard, MUSKOTALY, Sauv Bl, etc. Recent investment by France and Australia.

Hajós Alföld r ★ Village in S Hungary known for good lively Cab S reds of medium body and ageing potential. Also gd (if unauthorised) Pinot N.

Hárslevelü The 'lime-leaved' grape used at DEBRO and as the second main grape of TOKAY. Gentle mellow wine.

Helvécia (Kecskemet) Historic ALFOLD cellars. V'yds ungrafted: phylloxera cannot negotiate sandy soil. Whites and rosés modernist; reds trad.

Hungarovin Wine traders and producers with huge cellars at Budafok near Budapest, selling mainly 'western varietals' and making cuve close, transfer and méthode traditionelle sparkling.

Izsak Major sparkling wine producer; the majority by cuve close.

Kadarka The commonest red grape of Hungary, grown in vast quantities for light everyday wine on the plains in the south; capable of ample flavour and interesting maturity (eg at SZEKSZARD and VILLANY).

Kecskemet Major town of the ALFOLD. Much everyday wine, some better.

Kékfrankos Hungarian for Blaufränkisch; reputedly related to Gamay. Makes good light and full-bodied reds in many areas, esp at SOPRON on the Austrian border, and is used in BIKAVER at EGER.

Kéknyelü High-flavoured white grape making the best and 'stiffest' wine of MT BADACSONY. It should be fiery and spicy stuff.

Kiskunhalas Huge-scale plains winery, good esp for KADARKA.

Különleges Minöség Special quality: highest official quality grading.

Leányka or Király Old Hungarian white grape also grown in Transylvania. Makes admirable aromatic faintly Muscat dry wine in many areas. Kiral ('Royal') Leányka is supposedly superior.

Mátraalja Wine district in the foothills of the Mátra range in N Hungary, incl DEBRO, GYONGYOS and NAGYREDE.

Mecsekalja District in S Hungary, known for the good whites of PECS.

Minöségi Bor Quality wine. Hungary's appellation contrôlée.

Mór N Hungary w ★★→★★★ Town famous for its fresh dry EZERJO. Now also Ries, Sauv Bl.

Muskotály Makes light, though long-lived, Muscat wine at TOKAY (Tokaji) and EGER. Very occasionally makes ASZU at Tokay.

Nagyburgundi Literally 'great burgundy' – an indigenous grape and not Pinot N as sometimes thought. Makes sound solid wine in S Hungary, esp around VILLANY and SZEKSZARD.

Nagyrede Mátraalja Foothill winery. Competent and modern.

Nektar New legal term for the unfermented juice formerly called ESZENCIA.

OBI Official laboratory based in Budapest, responsible for labelling, quality control and export licence.

Olaszrizling Hungarian name for the Italian Riesling or Welschriesling.

Oporto Red grape increasingly used for soft jammy wines to drink young.

Pécs Mecsek w (r) ★→★★ Major wine city of S Hungary. Good source of OLASZRIZLING, Pinot Bl, etc.

Pezsgö Sparkling wine, mostly transfer method, can often be v palatable.

Pinot Noir Normally means NAGYBURGUNDI. But see Felsobabad.

Puttonyos The measure of sweetness in TOKAY (Tokaji). A 7-gal container from which ASZU is added to SZAMORODNI. One 'putt' makes it sweetish; 6 v sweet indeed. Each putt is a 20–25 kilo hod of ASZU grapes added to 136 litres of base wine. The minimum now made is 3 putts, the maximum 6. Tokay of 4 putts is often best-balanced.

Siklos Southern district known for its white wines.

Somló N Hungary w ★★ Isolated small v'yd district N of BALATON: white wines (formerly of high repute) from FURMINT and ancient Juhfark grapes.

Sopron W Hungary r ★★ Little enclave S of the Neusiedler See (see Austria). Light KEKFRANKOS reds and some Austrian-style sweet wines.

Szamorodni Word meaning 'as it comes'; used to describe TOKAY without the addition of ASZU grapes. Can be dry or (fairly) sweet, depending upon proportion of aszú grapes naturally present. Sold as an aperitif.

Szekszárd r ★★ District in south-central Hungary. KADARKA red wine which needs age (say 3–4 yrs). Also good organic wines and (now) BIKAVER.

Szürkebarát Literally means 'grey friar': Pinot Gr, which makes rich (not necessarily sweet) wine in the BADACSONY v'yds and elsewhere.

Tokay (Tokaji) Tokaji w dr sw ★★→★★★★ The ASZU is Hungary's famous strong sweet wine, comparable to a maderized Sauternes, from hills in the NE close to the Soviet border. See Aszú, Eszencia, Furmint, Puttonyos, Szamorodni. Also dry table wine of character.

Villány Siklos r p (w) ★★ Southernmost town of Hungary and well-known centre of red wine production. Villányi Burgundi is largely KEKFRANKOS and can be good. Cabs S and F are v promising. See also Nagyburgundi.

Villány-Siklós Wine region named after the two towns.

Zweigelt Indigenous (S) red grape: deep-coloured spicy flavoursome wine.

Bulgaria

In little more than a decade Bulgaria has become one of the world's top four wine exporters and the second-largest exporter of bottled wines after France, trading 85% of its production. Enormous new vineyards and industrial-sized wineries have overwhelmed an old, if embattled, wine tradition. The formerly state-run and state-subsidized wineries learnt almost everything from the New World and offer Cabernet, Chardonnay and other varieties at bargain prices. Controlled appellation ('Controliran') wines, introduced in 1985, have been joined by wood-aged 'Reserve' bottlings.

A drop in sales to the USSR in recent years has led to renewed emphasis on quality wines, somewhat higher prices and a ban on planting outside the 27 Controliran regions. The next stage is research and investment to upgrade both vineyards and equipment.

In 1990 the organizing monopoly, Vinprom, was disbanded to give wineries autonomy (30 at first; the number continues to increase, as does privatization). A brisk air of competition is now provoking even greater efforts towards quality.

Asenovgrad Main MAVRUD-producing cellar on the outskirts of PLOVDIV – new stainless steel being introduced. Mavrud and CAB can last well.

Boyar, Domaine Bulgaria's first independent wine merchants for almost 50 yrs: based in Sofia, set up '91, now marketing in the UK.

Burgas Black Sea resort and source of easy whites, incl a MUSCAT blend.

Cabernet The Bordeaux grape is highly successful in Bulgaria. Dark vigorous fruity and well-balanced wine drinks well young, but top qualities mature well for a surprisingly long time.

Chardonnay Rather less successful. V dry but full-flavoured wine, improves with a yr in bottle. Some recent oak-aged examples are promising.

Damianitza MELNIK winery with gd Strambolovo MERLOT and Melnik CAB.

Dimiat The common native white grape, grown in the E towards the coast. Agreeable dry white without memorable character.

Euxinograd (Château) Ageing cellar on the coast, part of the ex-King's palace. Wines reserved for State functions and top restaurants.

Gamza Good red grape, the Kadarka of Hungary. Aged wines, esp from LOVICO SUHINDOL, can be delicious.

Han Krum The most modern makers of white wine, esp oak-aged CHARD, nr VARNA in the east. Also lighter Chard and SAUV BL.

Haskovo Southern region, principal source of MERLOT for export.

Iskra Sparkling wine, normally sweet but fair quality. Red, white or rosé.

Karlovo Town famous for its 'Valley of Roses' and pleasant white MISKET.

Khan Krum See Han Krum.

Korten Subregion of SLIVEN. Korten CAB is firmer than most.

Lovico Suhindol Neighbour of PAVLIKENI, site of Bulgaria's first coop (1909). Good for GAMZA, CAB, MERLOT, PAMID and blends. First to declare independence after state monopoly's collapse in '90. Privatized in '92. Now Bulgaria's most important winery.

Mavrud Grape variety and darkly plummy red from S Bulgaria, esp ASENOVGRAD. Can mature 20 yrs. Considered the country's best.

Melnik City of the extreme southeast and its highly prized grape. Dense red wine that locals say can be carried in a handkerchief. Needs at least 5 yrs and lasts for 15. Also CAB, ripe and age-worthy.

Merlot Soft red grape variety grown mainly in HASKOVO in the south.

Misket Indigenous Bulgarian grape: mildly aromatic wines, often used to fatten up white blends.

Muscat Ottonel Normal Muscat grape, grown in E Bulgaria for medium-sweet fruity whites.

Novi Pazar Controlled appellation CHARD winery nr VARNA with finer wines.

Novo Selo Controliran red GAMZA from the north.

Oriachovitza Major southern area for Controliran CAB-MERLOT. Rich savoury red best at 4–5 yrs. Recent RESERVE Cab releases have been good, esp **84, 86**.

Pamid The light soft everyday red of the southwest and northwest.

Pavlikeni Northern wine town with a prestigious estate specializing in GAMZA and CAB of high quality. Also light 'Country wine' blend of MERLOT and Gamza.

Petrich Warm SW region for soft fragrant MELNIK, also blended with CAB.

Pleven Northern cellar important for PAMID, GAMZA and CAB. Also Bulgaria's wine research station.

Plovdiv Southern wine town and region, source of good CAB. Winemaking mostly at ASENOVGRAD.

Preslav Bulgaria's largest white wine cellar, in NE region. Esp for SAUV BL and RESERVE CHARD. Also makes rather good brandy.

Provadya Another centre for good white wines, esp dry CHARD.

Reserve Used on labels of selected and oak-aged wines.

Riesling (In Bulgaria) normally refers to Italian Riesling (Welschriesling). Some Rhine Riesling is grown: now made into Germanic-style white.

Rkatziteli One of Russia's favourite white grapes for strong sweet wine. Produces bulk dry or medium whites in NE Bulgaria.

Russe Northeastern wine town on the Danube. Some fresh high-tech whites: Welschriesling-MISKET blends, straight medium-dry Welschriesling, CHARD, MUSCAT and gd Aligoté. Now also reds, esp Controliran Yantra Valley CAB S.

Sakar Southeastern region for quality MERLOT, some of Bulgaria's best.

Sauvignon Blanc Grown in E Bulgaria, recently released for export.

Silvaner Some pleasant dry Silvaner is exported as 'Klosterkeller'.

Sliven Southern region, esp for CAB S. Also MERLOT and Pinot N (Merlot is blended with Pinot N in a 'Country Wine'). Also Silvaner, MISKET and CHARDONNAY.

Sonnenkuste Brand of medium-sweet white sold in Germany.

Stara Zagora S region producing CAB and MERLOT to RESERVE quality.

Suhindol See Lovico Suhindol.

Sungarlare E town giving its name to a dry Controliran MISKET; also CHARD.

Svishtov CAB-producing winery by the Danube in the north. A front-runner in Bulgaria's controlled appellation wines.

Tamianka Sweet white wine based on aromatic grape also of this name; the same as Romania's Tamiîoasa .

Targovichte Independent white wine cellar near Schumen. Concentrates on medium and sweet wines.

Tirnovo Strong sweet dessert red wine.

Varna Major coastal appellation for CHARD (buttery and unoaked), SAUV BL. Also Aligoté, Ugni Bl.

Former Czechoslovakia

Re-established January '93 as the Czech (Moravia and Bohemia) and Slovak republics. While there is little or no tradition of exporting from this mainly white wine producing region, there are good wines to be had. Labels will say whether they are blended or single varietal but origin and grapes are not always indicated. All are worth trying for value.

Moravia Favourite wines in Prague: variety and value. V'yds situated along Danube tributaries. Many wines from Austrian border: similar grapes, Grüner Veltliner, Müller-T, Sauv Bl, Traminer, St-Laurent, Pinot N, Blauer Portugieser, etc; and similar wines, eg from Satov (modern, mostly white, grapes from local farms and coops), Znojmo (long-established, ideal limestone soil). Other regions: Jaroslavice (wood-matured reds), Prímetice (full aromatic whites), Mikulov (white, red, dry and sweet traditional-method sparkling; bottles from France), Blatnice, Hustopece, Saldorf and Velké Pavlovice.

Bohemia Winemaking since 9th C. Same latitude and similar wines to eastern Germany. Best: N of Prague, in Elbe valley, and (best known) nr Melník (King Karel IV bought in Burgundian vines in 15th C; today Ries, Rulander and Traminer predominate). 'Bohemia Sekt' is growing, eg from Stary Plzenec: tank-fermented (mostly), some oak used, with grapes from Slovakia and Moravia too; French advice.

Slovakia Warmest climatic conditions and most of former Czechoslovakia's wine. Best in E, neighbouring Hungarian Tokay v'yds. Slovenia uses Hungarian varieties and makes good Tokay too. Key districts: Malokarpatská Oblast (largest region, in foothills of Little Carpathians, incl Rulander, Ries, Traminer, Limberger, etc), Malá Trna, Nové Mesto, Skalice (small, mainly reds), and (in Tatra foothills) Bratislava, Pezinok, Modra.

The Former Yugoslav States

Before its disintegration in 1991 Yugoslavia was well-established as a supplier of wines of international calibre, if not generally of exciting quality. Current political disarray makes commercial contacts difficult except in Slovenia, whose 'Riesling' was the pioneer export, since followed by Cabernet, Pinot Blanc, Traminer and others. All regions except the central Bosnian highlands make wine, almost entirely in giant cooperatives. The Dalmatian (Croatian) coast and Macedonia have good indigenous wines whose roots go deep into the ancient world.

In this edition the wines of Serbia, Bosnia-Herzegovina and Macedonia are omitted.

Slovenia

Beli Pinot The Pinot Bl, a popular grape variety.

Cvicek Traditional pale red or dark rosé of the Sava Valley.

Grasevina Slovenian for Italian RIESLING (also called Welschriesling, LASKI RIZLING, etc). The normal Riesling of the region.

Jerusalem Slovenia's most famous v'yd, at LJUTOMER. Its best wines are late-picked RAJNSKI RIZLING, LASKI RIZLING.

Kraski Means grown on the coastal limestone or Karst.

Laski Rizling Yet another name for Italian RIES. Makes best-known Slovenian wine, though not its best-quality. Top export brand: 'Cloburg' from the Podravski region

Ljutomer (or Lutomer) -Ormoz Slovenia's best-known and probably best white wine district, in the northeast, famous for its LASKI RIZLING: at its best, rich and satisfying wine. Export qualities are variable.

Malvasia Ancient white grape giving luscious wine.

Maribor Important centre in the northeast. White wines, mainly from VINAG, incl LASKI RIZLING, RIES, Sauv Bl, Pinot Bl, Traminer.

Merlot Grown in Slovenia with reasonable results. Comparable with neighbouring NE Italian.

Radgonska Ranina Ranina is Austria's Bouvier grape. Radgona is nr MARIBOR. Wine is sweet. Trade name is Tigrovo Mljeko (Tiger's Milk).

Rajnski (or Renski) Rizling The Rhine RIESLING: rare in these regions, but grown a little in LJUTOMER-ORMOZ.

Refosco Italian grape grown in the east and in ISTRIA (Croatia) as TERAN.

Riesling Used without qualification formerly meant Italian Riesling. Now legally limited to real Rhine Riesling.

Sipon Name for Furmint of Hungary.

Slamnak A late-harvest LJUTOMER estate RIES.

Tigrovo Mljeko See Radgonska Ranina.

Tocai The Pinot Gr, making rather heavy white wine.

Vinag Huge production cellars at MARIBOR. Top wine: Cloburg LASKI RIZLING.

Croatia

Babic Standard red of DALMATIA, ages better than ordinary PLAVAC.

Banat Partly in Romania: up-to-date wineries making adequate RIES.

Bogdanusa Local white grape of the DALMATIAN islands, esp Hvar and Brac. Pleasant refreshing faintly fragrant wine.

Burgundac Bijeli Chard, grown in SLAVONIA.

Dalmaciajavino Important coop based at Split and selling a full range of DALMATIAN coastal and island wines.

Dalmatia The coast of Croatia, from Rijeka to Dubrovnik. Has a remarkable variety of characterful wines, most of them potent.

Dingac Heavy sweetish red from the local PLAVAC grape, speciality of the mid-DALMATIAN coast.

Faros Substantial age-worthy PLAVAC red from the island of Hvar.

Grk White grape, speciality of the island of Korcula, giving strong, even sherry-like wine, and also a lighter pale one.

Istria Peninsula in the N Adriatic, Porec- its centre, with a variety of pleasant wines, the MERLOT as good as any.

Marastina Strong dry white of the DALMATIAN islands, best from Cara Smokvica on Hvar.

Opol Pleasantly light pale red made of PLAVAC grapes around Split and Sibenik in DALMATIA.

Plavac Mali Native red grape of DALMATIA; wine of body and strength, can age well. See Dingac, Opol, Postup, etc. Ordinary reds are often called Plavac. There is also a white, Plavac Beli.

Portugizac Austria's Blauer Portugieser: plain red wine.

Posip Pleasant white of the DALMATIAN islands, notably Korcula.

Postup Sweet and heavy DALMATIAN red from the Peljesac peninsula nr Korcula. Highly esteemed locally.

Slavonia N Croatia, on the Hungarian border between Slovenia and Serbia. A big producer of standard wines, mainly white, incl most of the former 'Yugoslav Riesling'.

Teran Stout dark red of ISTRIA. See Refosco (Slovenia).

Vugava Rare white variety of Vis in DALMATIA. Linked (at least in legend) with the Viognier of the Rhône Valley.

Romania

Romania has a long winemaking tradition and good potential for quality, wasted during decades of supplying the Soviet Union with cheap sweet wine. The present political situation sadly allows little progress. Quantity is still the goal. But with cleaner winemaking, earlier bottling and carbonic maceration, there is certainly the potential to rival the success of Bulgaria.

Alba Iulia Town in the TIRNAVE area of Transylvania, known for off-dry whites from Italian RIES, FETEASCA and MUSKAT-OTTONEL.

Aligoté The junior white burgundy grape makes pleasantly fresh white.

Babeasca Traditional red grape of the FOCSANI area: agreeably sharp wine tasting slightly of cloves.

Banat Plain on border with Serbia. Workaday Italian RIES, light red CADARCA.

Cabernet Increasingly grown, particularly at DEALUL MARE, to make dark intense wines, though often too sweet for Western palates.

Cadarca Romanian spelling of the Hungarian Kadarka.
Chardonnay Used at MURFATLAR to make sweet dessert wine.
Cotesti Part of the FOCSANI area making reds of PINOT N, Merlot, etc, and dry whites claimed to resemble Alsace wines.
Cotnari Romania's most famous historical wine but very rarely seen: light dessert wine from MOLDAVIA. Rather like v delicate Tokay.
Dealul Mare Important up-to-date v'yd area in the SE Carpathian foothills. Red wines from CAB, Merlot, PINOT N, etc. Whites from TAMIIOASA, etc.
Dobruja Black Sea region round the port of Costanta. See Murfatlar.
Dragasani Region on the R Olt south of the Carpathian Mts. Both traditional and 'modern' grapes. Good MUSKAT-OTTONEL.
Feteasca Romanian white grape with spicy, faintly Muscat aroma. Two types: F Alba (same as Hungary's Leányka; considered more ordinary, but good base for sparkling wine) and F Royale (F Alba x Furmint cross).
Feteasca Neagra Red Feteasca. Light wines, made coarse by clumsiness.
Focsani Important eastern region incl COTESTI, NICORESTI and ODOBESTI.
Grasa A form of the Hungarian Furmint grape grown in Romania and used in, among other wines, COTNARI.
Jidvei Winery in the cool Carpathians (TIRNAVE) among Romania's N-most v'yds. Good whites: FETEASCA, Furmint, RIES, SAUV BL.
Moldavia The northeast province. Temperate, with good v'yd potential.
Murfatlar Big modern v'yds nr the Black Sea, specializing in sweet wines incl CHARD. Now also dry reds and whites.
Muskat-Ottonel The E European Muscat, a speciality of Romania.
Nicoresti Eastern area of FOCSANI, best known for its red BABEASCA.
Odobesti The central part of FOCSANI; white wines of FETEASCA, RIES, etc.
Oltenia Wine regions including DRAGASANI. Sometimes also a brand name.
Perla The speciality of TIRNAVE: a pleasant blended semi-sweet white of Italian RIES, FETEASCA and MUSKAT-OTTONEL.
Pinot Noir Grown in the south: can surprise with taste and character.
Pitesti Principal town of the Arges region south of the Carpathian Mts. Traditionally whites from FETEASCA, TAMIIOASA, RIES.
Premiat Reliable range of higher quality wines for export.
Riesling Italian Riesling. Very widely planted. No exceptional wines.
Sadova Town in the SEGARCEA area exporting a sweetish rosé.
Sauvignon Blanc Romania's tastiest white, esp blended with FETEASCA.
Segarcea Southern wine area near the Danube. Rather sweet CAB.
Tamîoasa Traditional white grape known as 'frankincense' for its exotic scent and flavour. Pungent sweet wines often have botrytis.
Tîrnave Important Transylvanian wine region (Romania's coolest), known for its PERLA. Well-situated for dry wines, eg JIDVEI's.
Trakia Export brand. Better judged for Western palates than most.
Valea Calugareasca 'The Valley of the Monks', part of DEALUL MARE with a well-known, switched-on research station – currently proposing new AC-style rules. CAB (esp Special Reserve 85), Merlot and PINOT N are admirable, as are Italian RIES, Pinot Gr.

Greece

Since Greece's entry into the EC its antique wine industry has started moving into higher gear. Much Greek wine is still fairly primitive, but a new system of appellations is in place and the past five years have seen substantial investment in equipment and expertise. Modern, well-made but still authentic Greek wines are worth tasting.

Achaia-Clauss Well-known wine merchant with cellars at PATRAS, N PELOPONNESE. Makers of DEMESTICA, etc.
Agiorgitiko Widely planted red-wine grape in the NEMEA region.

Agioritikos Country wine appellation of gd medium dry white and rosé from Agio Oros or Mount Athos the monastic peninsula in Halkidiki. Source of Cab and other grapes for TSANTALI.

Attica Region round Athens, the chief source of RETSINA.

Autocratorikos New sparkling medium-dry white from TSANTALI.

Botrys Old-established Athenian wine and spirits company.

Boutari Merchants and makers with high standards in MACEDONIAN and other wines, esp NAOUSSA and SANTORINI. Grand Réserve is the best wine (84).

Cair Label of the RHODES coop. Makes Greece's only classic sparkling wine.

Calliga Modern winery with 800 acres on CEPHALONIA. ROBOLA white and Monte Nero reds from indigenous grapes are adequately made.

Cambas, Andrew Important wine-growers and merchants in ATTICA.

Carras, John Estate at Sithonia, Chalkidiki, N Greece, producing interesting red and white wines under the names Château Carras (**75 79 81 83 84 85**), Porto Carras and COTES DE MELITON. Ch Carras is a Bordeaux-style barrel-aged red, worth 10–20 yrs in bottle.

Castel Danielis One of the best brands of dry red wine, from ACHAIA-CLAUSS.

Cava Legal term for blended aged red and white.

Cephalonia (Kephalonia) Ionian (western) island with good white ROBOLA and red Thymiatiko. See Calliga.

Corfu Adriatic island with wines scarcely worthy of it. Ropa is the traditional red.

Côtes de Meliton Appellation of the CARRAS estate applying to red and white wines, incl Château Carras.

Courtakis, D Athenian merchant with mild RETSINA and good dark NEMEA.

Crete Island with the name for some of Greece's good red wine. Appellations are: Archanes, Daphnes, Peza and Sitia. Cretan white can also be suprisingly good.

Demestica A reliable brand of dry red and white from ACHAIA-CLAUSS.

Emery Maker of good CAVA Emery red and vg Villare white on RHODES.

Gamalafka Speciality of Mykonos. Alarmingly like sherry vinegar.

Gentilini New ('84) up-market white from CEPHALONIA, a ROBOLA blend, soft and appealing. Now a v promising oak-aged version. To watch.

Goumenissa (Appellation) Good quality oak-aged mid-weight red from western MACEDONIA. Look for BOUTARI.

Hatzimichali Small Atalanti estate and its wines. The whites are Greek grape-based; the reds incl Cab S.

Ilios Very drinkable standard RHODES wine.

Kokkineli The rosé version of RETSINA: like the white. Drink cold.

Kouros Highly rated white from Kourtakis of ATTICA; also red.

Kretikos White wine made by BOUTARI from CRETAN varieties.

Lac des Roches Sound blended white from BOUTARI.

Limnos (Appellation) N Aegean island with sweet golden Muscat wine.

Lindos Name for the higher quality of RHODES wine, whether from Lindos itself or not. Acceptable, no more.

Macedonia Quality wine region in the north, for NAOUSSA, etc.

Malvasia The famous grape is said to originate from Monemvasia in the S PELOPONNESE. See Rhodes.

Mantinia (Appellation) A fresh white from the PELOPONNESE, by CAMBAS.

Mavro Black – the word for dark (often sweet) red wine.

Mavrodaphne (Appellation) Literally 'black laurel': dark sweet concentrated red, a speciality of the PATRAS region, N PELOPONNESE.

Mavroudi Red wine of Delphi and N shore of Gulf of Corinth: dark, plummy.

Metsovo Town in Epirus (north) producing Cab blend called Katoi.

Minos Popular CRETAN brand; the Castello red is best.

Naoussa (Appellation) Above average strong dry red from MACEDONIA in the north, esp from BOUTARI and TSANTALI.

Nemea (Appellation) Town in the E PELOPONNESE famous for its lion (a victim of Hercules) and its fittingly forceful MAVRO.

Patras (Appellation) White wine and wine town on the Gulf of Corinth.

Pegasus, Château NAOUSSA estate for superior red (esp **81 86 88**).

Peloponnese The southern landmass of mainland Greece, with half of the country's v'yds, incl NEMEA and PATRAS.

Retsina White wine with Aleppo pine resin added, tasting of turpentine and oddly appropriate with Greek food. The speciality of ATTICA. Much modern retsina is made disappointingly mild.

Rhodes Easternmost Greek island. Chevalier de Rhodes is a pleasant red. See also Cair, Emery, Ilios.

Robola (Appellation) The dry white of CEPHALONIA, island off the Gulf of Corinth. Can be a pleasant soft wine of some character.

Samos (Appellation) Island off the Turkish coast with an ancient reputation for its sweet pale golden Muscat. Best are (fortified) Anthemis and (natural) Nectar.

Santorini Dramatic volcanic island north of CRETE, making sweet Vinsanto from sun-dried grapes, and dry white Thira. Santino and Atlantis are dry reds. Unrealized potential here.

Semeli, Château Estate nr Athens making good white and red, incl Cab S.

Strofilia Brand name for the wines of a small 'boutique' winery estate at Anavissos. Good whites, and reds incl Cab S.

Tsantali Producers at Agios Pavlos with a wide range of country and appellation wines, incl MACEDONIAN and wine from the monks of Mt Athos, NEMEA, NAOUSSA and Muscat from SAMOS and LIMNOS. CAVA is a blend.

Vaeni Promising red from NAOUSSA producers' coop.

Xynomavro The best of many indigenous Greek red grapes, basis for NAOUSSA and other northern wines.

Zitsa (Appellation) Region of 6 villages in mountainous N Epirius. Delicate Debina (grape) white, still or fizzy.

Cyprus

Cyprus exports 75% of its production, mostly strong wines of reasonable quality, especially low-price Cyprus 'sherry'; though old Commandaria, a treacly dessert wine, is the island's finest product. Until recently only two local grapes were grown. Now a dozen other native varieties are on trial, and the international standards are inevitably being planted. The island has never had phylloxera.

Afames Village at the foot of Mt Olympus, giving its name to dry tangy red (MAVRO) wine from SODAP.

Alkion A new smooth light dry white from KEO (XYNISTERI from Limassol).

Aphrodite Consistent medium-dry XYNISTERI white from KEO, named after the Greek goddess of love.

Arsinöe Dry white wine from SODAP, named after an unfortunate female whom Aphrodite turned to stone.

Bellapais Fizzy medium-sweet white from KEO, named after the famous abbey nr Kyrenia. Essential refreshment for holidaymakers.

Commandaria Good quality brown dessert wine made since ancient times in the hills north of LIMASSOL, named after a crusading order of knights. The best (as old as 100 yrs) is superb, of incredible sweetness. Most is just standard Communion wine.

Domaine d'Ahera Modern-style lighter estate red from KEO. (Grenache and local Lefkas grapes.)

Emva Brand name of well-made fine, medium and cream SHERRIES.

Etko See Haggipavlu.

Haggipavlu Well-known wine merchant at LIMASSOL. Trades as Etko.

Keo The biggest and most go-ahead firm at LIMASSOL. Standard Keo Dry White and Dry Red are vg value. See also Othello and Aphrodite.

Khalokhorio Principal COMMANDARIA village, growing only XYNISTERI.

Kokkineli Rosé: the name is related to 'cochineal'.

Kolossi Crusaders' castle nr Limassol giving its name to red and white table wines from SODAP.

Laona The largest of the small independent regional wineries at Arsos. Good range of wines incl a 'nouveau' and an oak-aged red.

Limassol 'The Bordeaux of Cyprus'. Southern wine port and its region.

Loel Major producer, with Amathus and Kykko brands, Command Cyprus SHERRY and good Negro red.

Mavro The black grape of Cyprus (and Greece) and its dark wine. Opthalmo is another, lighter and sharper.

Monte Roya Modern regional winery at Chryssoroyiatissa Monastery.

Mosaic KEO's brand of Cyprus SHERRIES. Includes a fine dry wine.

Muscat All major firms produce pleasant low-price 15° Muscats.

Othello A good standard dry red (MAVRO and Opthalmo grapes from PITSILIA). Solid satisfying wine from KEO.

Palomino Soft dry white made of this (SHERRY) grape by LOEL. V drinkable ice-cold.

Pitsilia Region south of Mt Olympus producing the best white and COMMANDARIA wines.

Rosella Brand of light dry fragrant rosé from KEO. Opthalmo grapes from PITSILIA.

St Panteleimon Brand of medium-sweet white from KEO.

Semeli Good traditional red from HAGGIPAVLU.

Sherry Cyprus makes a full range of sherry-style wines, the best (particularly the dry) of fair quality.

SODAP Major wine coop at LIMASSOL.

Thisbe A fruity medium-dry light wine from KEO (XYNISTERI grapes from LIMASSOL).

Xynisteri The native white grape of Cyprus.

Zoopiyi Principal COMMANDARIA village, growing MAVRO grapes.

Asia & North Africa

Algeria As a combined result of Islam and the EC the once massive vineyards of Algeria have dwindled in the last decade from 860,000 acres to under 200,000. Red, rosé and white wines of some quality are still made in the coastal hills of Tlemcen, Mascara, Haut-Dahra, Zaccar, Tessala, Médéa and Ain-Berrem. Sidi Brahim is a drinkable red brand. Most goes for blending.

China Germans and Russians started making wine on the Shantung (now Shandong) peninsula in the early 1900s. Since 1980 a modern industry, initiated by Rémy Martin, has produced the adequate white Dynasty and Tsingtao wines; and new more sophisticated plantings of better varieties in Shandong and Tianjin, further north, promise more interest in the future. Basic table wines are made of the local Dragon Eye and Muscat Hamburg grapes (especially in Tianjin). In Quingdao, Welschriesling has been followed by Chardonnay, and the Hua Dong winery started experimental plantings of a number of different varieties incl Cabernet in 1985. As of 1992 Rémy Martin are making 'Imperial Court', China's first méthode traditionelle sparkling wine, near Shanghai. After trials with 23 varieties, Chardonnay, Pinots Noir and Meunier and Ugni Blanc are proving best suited.

India In 1985 a Franco-Indian firm launched a Chardonnay-based sparkling wine, Omar Khayyam, made at Narayangoan, near Poona, southeast of Bombay. Plans are to export up to 2 million bottles and to add still wines of Chardonnay and Cabernet. Omar Khayyam sets an astonishing standard. Slightly drier Princess Jaulke follows, made with Thompson Seedless grapes and advice from Charbaut et Fils of Champagne.

Japan Japan has a small wine industry in Yamanashi Prefecture, west of Tokyo. Most of the production here is blended with imports from South America, Eastern Europe, etc. Premium wines of Sémillon, Chardonnay, Cabernet and the local white grape, Koshu, are light but can be good, though expensive. The main producers are Mann's, Mercian and Suntory. Château Lumière and Château Mercian lead the way with high quality Chardonnay, Cabernet, etc. The most interesting (and expensive) are Suntory's Sauternes-like Château Lion and Mercian's Kikyogahara Merlot and Cabernet of extraordinary denseness and quality. Regrettably, Japanese labelling laws have been so lax that misrepresentation of imported wines as 'Japanese' has in the past been the rule rather than the exception. A new law stipulates that if the percentage of imported bulk wine in the bottle is above 50% it must be indicated (the larger percentage should be written before the smaller).

Lebanon The small Lebanese wine industry, based on Ksara in the Bekaa valley northeast of Beirut, continues against all odds to make red wine of real vigour and quality. Château Musar (★★★) produces splendid matured reds, largely of Cabernet Sauvignon; a full-blooded white, surprisingly capable of ageing 10–15 yrs; and recently a lighter red, 'Tradition', which is 75% Cinsaut, 25% Cabernet Sauvignon.

Morocco Morocco today makes North Africa's best wine (85% of it red), from vineyards along the Atlantic coast (Rabat to Casablanca, light fruity), and around Meknes and Fez (solid full-bodied), also further east around Berkane (tangy earthy) and in the Gharb and Doukkalas regions. In 10 years they have declined in area from 190,000 to 35,000 acres. The main producers are Chaudsoleil, Meknes Vins and Sincomar. Tarik and Toulal are two drinkable reds. Vin Gris is the best bet for hot-day refreshment.

Tunisia Tunisia now has 22,000 acres of vines (compared with 120,000 10 years ago). Her speciality is sweet Muscat, but reasonable reds and rosés come from Cap Bon, Carthage and Mornag.

Turkey Most of Turkey's 1.5 million acres of vineyards produce table grapes. But her wines, from Thrace, Anatolia and the Aegean, are remarkably good. Indigenous varieties such as Narince (for white) and Bogazkere (for red) are used along with Riesling, Sémillon, Pinot Noir and Gamay. Trakya (Thrace) white and Buzbag (Anatolian) red are the well-known standards of Tekel, the State producer. Doluca, Karmen, Kavaklidere and Taskobirlik are private firms of good quality. Doluca's Villa Neva red from Thrace is very well made. But Buzbag is perhaps Turkey's best and most original wine.

The Former Soviet Union

Over 3 million acres of v'yds make the republics of the former USSR collectively the world's fourth-biggest wine producer. Ukraine (incl Crimea) is the largest, followed by Moldova, the Russian Republic and Georgia. The Soviet consumer has a sweet tooth, for both table and dessert wines, but drier wines and European varieties are increasingly planted as wineries become export-conscious. Clearly the unfolding republics will give some exciting wines in the future.

Ukraine and Crimea Crimea produces first-class dessert wines. Sotheby's auction house disclosed as much in '90, with sales of old wines from the Tsar's Crimean cellars at Massandra (Muscats, and port- and madeira-like wines of v high quality). Also Novasvit and Grand Duchess méthode traditionelle (the latter from Odessa Winery founded by Louis Roederer in 1896). Ukraine is good for Aligoté and Artemosk sparkling; mostly Romanian varieties.

Moldova With the most temperate climate and now the most modern outlook, Moldova has high potential. Former Moscow-bottling was disastrous. Grapes incl Cab, Pinot N, Merlot, Saperavi (fruity), Ries, Pinot Gr, Aligoté, Rkatsiteli. The 63 Negru de Purkar released in '92 gave a startling glimpse of Moldova's potential, reinforced by following vintages (with 4 yrs oak, and v best from Cab S-Saperavi-Rara Negre blends (as 63), acidic). Purkar may be the best winery. Krikova is also good: esp Kodru 'Claret' blend, Krasny Reserve Pinot N-Merlot-Malbec. Abrodsov is méthode traditionelle sparkling. Investment from Germany, Italy, UK, enables local clean bottling. (NB Moldavia is neighbouring Romanian region.)

The Russian Republic Makes fair Ries (Anapa, Arbau, Beshtau) and sweet sparkling Tsimlanskoye 'Champanski'. Also Chard, Sauv Bl, Welschriesling (heavy, often oxidized).

Georgia Uses antique methods to make extremely tannic (heavily barrel-aged) wines for local drinking, slightly newer techniques for export blends (Mukuzani, Tsinandali); Georgians are disinclined to modernize. Kakhetià, E Georgia, is famed for v tannic red and white. Imeteria (west) makes milder, highly original wines. Sparkling is v cheap, drinkable. When equipment (incl bottles and stoppers) and techniques improve Georgia will be an export hit. Vg potential.

Israel

Israeli wine, since the industry was re-established by a Rothschild in the 1880s, has been primarily of kosher interest until recently, when Cabernet Sauvignon, Riesling, Sauvignon Blanc, Sémillon, Petite Sirah and Grenache of fair quality have been introduced. Three-quarters of Israel's annual 15-million-bottle production is white.

Ashkelon Family-owned firm making red and white wines. Labels are Segal's and Ben-Ami.

Barkan Fruity and simple wines: white and red.

Baron Small family grower best known for Muscat. Also some Cab S.

Carmel Israel's largest coop, est 1882, with two newly modernized wineries. Top wines are Rothschild series, esp Cab S and Emerald Ries. Also good Sauv Bl, Chard and Dry Muscat.

Eliaz Medium-sized winery producing light-style red and white wines.

Gamla & Golan Mainly Cab S, produced by YARDEN.

Yarden Young ('83) modern sophisticated winery in the Golan Heights, involving Californian oenologists and setting highest standards for Israel. Over 20 wines: top is full-bodied oaky Galil Cab S (85); good Merlot, crisp Sauv Bl and Chard; recently some sparkling.

North America
California

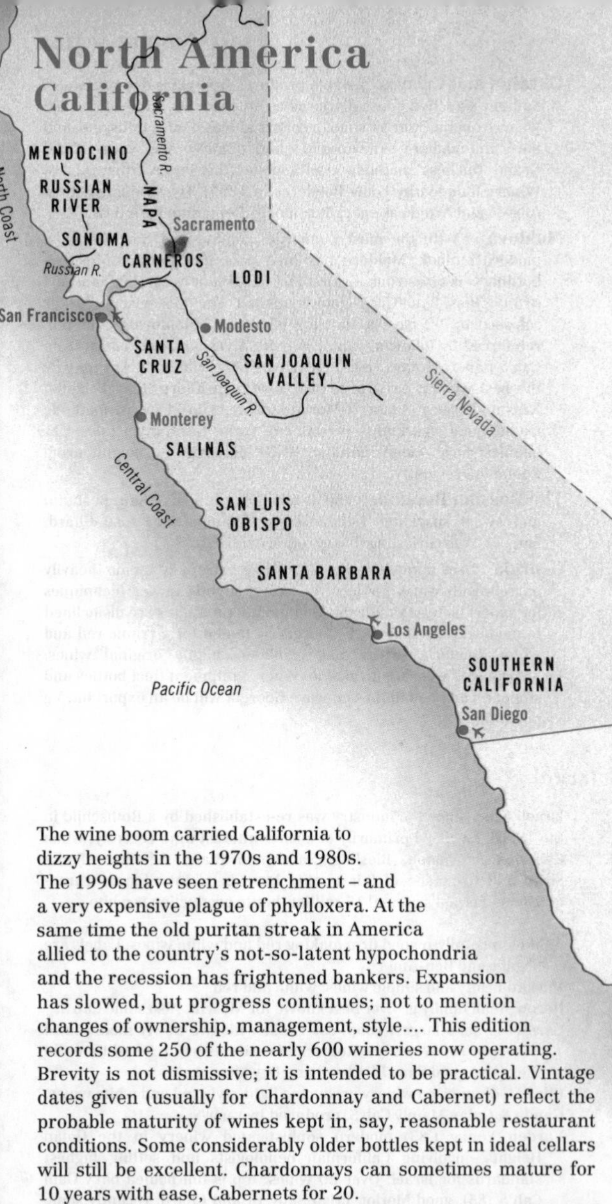

The wine boom carried California to dizzy heights in the 1970s and 1980s. The 1990s have seen retrenchment – and a very expensive plague of phylloxera. At the same time the old puritan streak in America allied to the country's not-so-latent hypochondria and the recession has frightened bankers. Expansion has slowed, but progress continues; not to mention changes of ownership, management, style.... This edition records some 250 of the nearly 600 wineries now operating. Brevity is not dismissive; it is intended to be practical. Vintage dates given (usually for Chardonnay and Cabernet) reflect the probable maturity of wines kept in, say, reasonable restaurant conditions. Some considerably older bottles kept in ideal cellars will still be excellent. Chardonnays can sometimes mature for 10 years with ease, Cabernets for 20.

Appellation areas (AVAs) are an important recent fact of life: they are being registered thick and fast; the current total is over 50, with five in the Napa Valley alone and four more proposed. It is still too soon to use them as a guide to style. Listed below are the broad regions usually referred to. But grape varieties combined with brand names are still the key to California wine.

Principal vineyard areas

Central Coast

A long sweep of coast with increasing though scattered wine activity, from San Francisco Bay south to Santa Barbara.

Hecker Pass Pass through the SANTA CRUZ MTS S of San Francisco Bay with a cluster of small old-style wineries.

Livermore Valley E of San Francisco Bay long famous for white wines but now largely built-over.

Monterey See Salinas Valley.

Salinas Valley/Monterey The Salinas Valley runs inland SE from Monterey. After frenzied expansion in the '70s, many vines were removed. What are left make wines of great character. Currently refining its internal divisions: Arroyo Seco AVA (esp Chard and Ries), Santa Lucia Highlands AVA (Chard, has hopes for Pinot N), San Lucas AVA (steady commercial wines), and coastal Carmel Valley (tiny, sometimes impressive Cab and Chard).

San Luis Obispo Edna Valley just S of San Luis Obispo (1,000 acres) and more scattered v'yds nr Paso Robles (5,000 acres).

Santa Barbara Santa Maria Valley is dominant, esp for vg Chardonnay and distinctive Pinot N. The smaller Santa Ynez Valley also has cool foggy conditions: good for Burgundian varieties at seaward end, Bordeaux' varieties in warmer inland areas.

Santa Cruz Mts Wineries (though few v'yds) are scattered round the Santa Cruz Mts S of San Francisco Bay, from Saratoga down to HECKER PASS.

Temecula (Rancho California) New small area in S California, 25 miles inland, halfway between San Diego and Riverside.

North Coast

Encompasses Lake, Menodocino, Napa and Somoma counties, all north of San Francisco.

Alexander Valley/Russian River (Sonoma) Top quality area from Alexander Valley (N of Napa Valley) towards the sea (Russian River). Incl Dry Creek Valley.

Carneros, Los Important cool region N of San Francisco Bay, shared between NAPA and SONOMA counties.

Lake Clear Lake AVA: warm climate, most impressive for Sauv Bl, good for Cab S. Small Guenoc Valley AVA similar.

Mendocino Northernmost coastal wine country; a varied climate coolest in Anderson Valley nr the coast, warm around Ukiah inland.

Napa The Napa Valley, N of San Francisco Bay. The oldest and most-honoured of California wine valleys busily fragmenting itself: Stag's Leap AVA (Cab), CARNEROS AVA (shared with SONOMA, good Chard, Pinot N and sparkling), Mt Veeder (Cab), Howell Mountain AVA (Cab, Zinfandel, Chard), Atlas Peak AVA (Sangiovese) and likely AVAs on the valley floor, Rutherford and Oakville.

Russian River See Alexander Valley.

Sonoma County N of San Francisco Bay, between rival NAPA and the sea. California's most divided wine area. Includes historic Sonoma Valley AVA ('Valley of the Moon', versatile, partly in CARNEROS, see Napa); far west, Russian River Valley AVA (increasinlgly devoted to Chard, Pinot N, sparkling, encompassing Chalk Hill and Sonoma-Green Valley AVAs); warmer inland, Alexander, Dry Creek and Knights Valley AVAs (Cab S, Zin, increasingly Rhône types).

The Interior

Amador County in the SIERRA FOOTHILLS E of Sacramento. Grows vg Zinfandel, esp in Shenandoah Valley AVA.

Lodi Town and district at the N end of the SAN JOAQUIN VALLEY, its hot climate modified by a westerly air-stream.

San Joaquin Valley The great central valley of California, fertile and hot, the source of most of the jug and dessert wines in the State. (Incl LODI AVA and the Clarksburg AVA on the Sacramento River delta.)

Sierra Foothills Encompasses AMADOR (Shenandoah Valley, Fiddletown AVAs), El Dorado (AVA of the same name), Calaveras counties, among others. Zin is the universal grape.

Recent vintages

The Californian climate is far from being as consistent as its reputation. Although, on the whole, grapes ripen regularly, they are subject to spring frosts in many areas, sometimes a wet harvest-time and too often drought.

Wines from the San Joaquin Valley tend to be most consistent year by year. The vintage date on these, where there is one, is more important for telling the age of the wine than its character.

Vineyards in the Central Coast region are widely scattered; there is little pattern. The Napa and Sonoma valleys are the areas where comment can usefully be made on the last dozen or more vintages of the top varietal wines: Cabernet Sauvignon and Chardonnay.

Chardonnay

NB These ageing assessments are based on well-balanced wines with fruit flavours dominant. Very rich and oaky examples tend to be v short-lived: 2 yrs at most. Marker wines for good ageing qualities incl eg Chappellet, Clos du Bois-Calcaire, Dehlinger, Freemark Abbey, Matanzas Creek, Shafer, Silverado, Simi, Sonoma-Cutrer, Trefethen.

1992 A comfortable growing year; good at least, maybe better than that.
1991 Abundant but delayed harvest may lack acid balance. Looking like wines for the near term; charming more than sturdy.
1990 Healthy and trouble-free. Coming along as an irreproachable vintage but not a grand one.
1989 Ups and downs after rainy harvest, but the ups reach some of the decade's highest peaks.
1988 Big soft quick-developers. Many lack focus. Drink up soonish.
1987 Ideal weather; vg wines for this year.
1986 Many solid and worthy. Nothing to wait for.
1985 Big crop, good acidity, excellent and maturing well. Mostly ready.
1983 Good once, but only the very best carry on.
1982 Cool harvest; the best wines were lean and tart and have aged well.
1981 Good if not too strong. Drink up.

Cabernet Sauvignon

NB As with Chardonnays, over-rich and over-oaky wines usually collapse quickly. The markers for the assessments below are not Reserves, but fine standard Cabernets from eg Beaulieu, Beringer-Knights Valley, Caymus, Chappellet, Clos du Val, Fetzer-Barrel Select, Freemark Abbey, Hafner, Jordan, Laurel Glen, Louis Martini-Monte Rosso, Parducci, Raymond, Shafer, Silverado-Alexander Valley Vineyards.

1992 The early book says these will develop quickly and well.
1991 Long cool summer, ideal autumn. Winemakers continue to be optimistic.
1990 Early wines are surprisingly soft, round, approachable, and just a little lacking in flavour. However, long autumn left the window wide open for every style. Big wines may be very fine.
1989 Many beautifully dark, flavoury wines with solid structure for ageing; some got caught in rains.
1988 Most are more charming than solid. Can be drunk.
1987 Evolving as perhaps the best of the decade overall.
1986 Quickly approachable vintage. Baby fat is now fleshy.
1985 Lean, firm to hard, deep-flavoured. Slow-maturing but impressive.
1984 Showy early: ripe and fragrant. Possibly best now and 3 more years.
1983 Several awkward hard wines. The best have depth but need time to reveal it.
1982 Epitome of a charming vintage, good now and (for the best) a while longer.
1981 Promptly picked examples have substance and depth. Probably at peak.
1980 High reputation but merely good and solid. Over-tannic. Ready to drink.
1979 Apparently lightish, but the best keep going sturdily.
1978 Excellent. Generally ready, and many fading.
1977 Attractive wines now mainly crumbling.
1976 Drought made v concentrated wines. Good ones are v ripe and potent now.
1975 Delicate, charming; mature.
1973 Big crop of good wines. Drink up.
1970 One of the best ever. Mature.

California wineries

Acacia Napa ★★★ (Chard) 85 86 87 88 89 90 91 (Pinot N) 83 84 85 86 87 88 89 90 Specialist in single-v'yd CARNEROS Chard (Marina) and Pinot (Lund, St-Clair, Madonna): depth, durability. Owned by CHALONE. 25,000 cases.

Adelaida Cellars San Luis Obispo ★★ Soft Chard and supple Cab from Paso Robles. 4,500 cases.

Alderbrook Sonoma ★★ (Chard) 87 88 89 90 Indelibly flavoured, age-worthy Dry Creek Sém, crisp Chard, Sauv Bl. 20,000 cases.

Alexander Valley Vineyards Sonoma ★★→★★★ (Chard) 90 91 (Cab S) 75 78 81 82 83 84 85 86 87 88 89 90 91 Long-lived, richly varietal Cab leads list; Chard has regained form after brief lapse. Also dark sturdy Pinot N, mild Ries. 60,000 cases.

Almaden San Joaquin ★ Famous pioneer name, now a Heublein-owned everyday brand, operated from Madera. 1^+ million cases.

S Anderson Vineyard Napa ★★→★★★ (Chard) 87 88 89 90 Robust Chard and robuster classic sparkling. 15,000 cases.

Arrowood Sonoma ★★→★★★ (Chard) 88 89 90 91 (Cab S) 85 86 87 88 Long-time CHATEAU ST JEAN winemaker Dick A makes leaner wines on his own behalf. 8,000 cases going to 15,000.

Atlas Peak Napa Huge international investment in E hills. Sangiovese-Cab 'Consenso' extremely promising.

Au Bon Climat Sta Barbara ★★→★★★ (Chard) 86 87 88 89 90 91 Ultra-toasty Chard; well-wooded Pinot N. Dynamic experimental little winery also produces QUPE and VITA NOVA wines in Sta Maria Valley. 5,000 cases.

Beaucannon Napa ★★ Owners of Bordeaux' Ch Lebegue turning out consistently supple stylish Cab S, Merlot, Chard from own 250 acres.

Beaulieu Vineyard Napa ★★★ (Cab S) 70 74 79 78 80 81 82 83 84 85 86 87 Long-time growers and makers of justly famous age-worthy Georges Delatour Private Reserve Cab S. Also vg Rutherford Cab, approachable Beautour Cab and crackerjack dry oak-free Sauv Bl. $400,000^+$ cases.

Bel Arbors Oddly spelt second label of FETZER.

Belvedere Sonoma ★★ Bold Chard, Cab S and Zin from individual v'yds are top of line; Grove Street series is value. 250,000 cases.

Benziger See Glen Ellen.

Beringer Napa ★★→★★★ (Chard) 83 88 89 90 91 (Cab S) 77 78 79 80 81 82 83 84 85 86 87 88 89 90 Century-old winery restored to front rank. Reserve Chard and esp Reserve Cab S outstanding. Solid Fumé Bl, Zin, Knights Valley Cab. 1.4 million cases. Everyday label: Napa Ridge.

Black Mountain Sonoma ★★ Chard, Sauv Bl, Zin. 20,000 cases. Second label: J W Morris.

Boeger El Dorado ★★ Steady SIERRA FOOTHILLS Cab S, Merlot, Zin, Sauv Bl.

Bonny Doon Sta Cruz Mts ★★→★★★ (Chard) 87 88 90 91 Rabid francophile led charge towards Rhône varieties: esp red Cigare Volant (Grenache-Mourvèdre), white Cuvée des Philosophes (Marsanne-Roussanne) and Le Sophiste. Now trying Italian. Never a dull moment. 8,000 cases.

Bouchaine Napa ★★ (Chard) 87 88 89 90 (Pinot N) 88 89 90 91 Specialist in well-wooded CARNEROS Chard, Pinot, so far vg bone-dry Gewürz (88 89).

Brander Vineyard Sta Barbara ★★ Impressive intense Sauv (90) from Sta Ynez V. Good Cab F-S Bouchet (84 85 86 87), 87 Merlot. 8,000 cases.

Bronco Wine Company High-capacity winery. Owns LAURIER, GRAND CRU and part of Montpellier. C C Vineyard and J F J Cellars are labels for generic and varietal wines.

Bruce, David Sta Cruz Mts ★★ (Chard) 88 89 90 91 Long-time source of heavyweight Chard now moderated. Good Pinot (esp 87). 32,000 cases.

To decipher codes, please refer to symbols key at front of book, and to 'How to Read an Entry' on page 5.

Buehler Napa ★★ (Cab S) 85 86 87 88 89 90 Impressive 20,000-case E hills estate has turned sharp corner: recent Cabs, Zins to watch. Vg Pinot Bl.

Buena Vista Sonoma ★★ (Chard) 87 88 89 90 91 (Cab S) 83 84 85 86 87 88 89 90 Pioneer name now German-owned and an utterly reliable source of taste-like-the-grapes Chard, Sauv Bl, Cab S, Merlot, Gewürz, Ries, mainly from own 1,100-acre v'yd in CARNEROS. 110,000 cases.

Burgess Cellars Napa ★★ (Chard) 87 88 89 90 91 (Cab S) 80 81 82 83 84 85 86 87 88 90 (Zin) 82 83 85 86 87 Emphasis on dark weighty well-oaked reds. 30,000 cases.

BV Abbreviation of BEAULIEU VINEYARD used on its labels.

Davis Bynum Sonoma ★★ (Chard) 86 87 88 89 90 91 (Cab S) 83 84 85 86 87 90 (Pinot N) 84 86 87 88 89 90 Reliable, sometimes stylish wines go beyond special selection Chard, Cab S to include correct Pinot N, enticing dry Gewürz. 28,000 cases.

Byron Vineyards Sta Barbara ★★★ (Chard) 87 88 89 90 91 (Pinot N) 84 85 86 87 88 89 90 ROBERT MONDAVI-owned source of tasty polished Pinot N and vg Chard from estate v'yds. Also some Cab S, Sauv Bl from nearby.

Cain Cellars Napa ★★ (Cain Five) 84 85 86 87 88 Emphasis is on Cain Five, blended from Cab family varieties grown in estate v'yd on Spring Mt. Also Cab S, Chard. 30,000 cases.

Cakebread Napa ★★★ (Chard) 87 88 89 90 91 (Cab S) 81 82 83 84 85 86 87 88 90 Bold style rules in memorable Sauv Bl as well as excellent Chard and Cab. 40,000 cases.

Calera San Benito ★★★ (Chard) 87 88 89 90 91 (Pinot N) 80 81 82 84 85 86 87 88 89 90 Dark, often tannic, heady estate Pinot Ns are much in fashion; each named after a section of the hilly chalky v'yd (Jensen, Selleck, Reed). Also smoky well-knit Chard; now Viognier. 10,000 cases.

Callaway S California ★★ (Chard) 87 88 89 90 91 Mild easy whites incl lees-aged Chard, oak-aged Fumé. 150,000 cases. Reds coming.

Cambria Sta Barbara Affiliate of KENDALL-JACKSON produces extra-smoky rather sweet Chard and well-oaked Pinot N from own grapes. 18,000 cases and growing fast.

Carey Cellars Sta Barbara ★★ (Chard) 87 88 89 90 91 (Cab S) 85 86 87 88 89 90 Since acquisition by FIRESTONE, an impressive little (mainly estate) winery. Vg Chard, Merlot, Sauv Bl.

Carmenet Sonoma ★★→★★★ (Cab S blend) 83 84 85 86 87 88 89 90 CHALONE-owned mountain v'yd and winery above SONOMA town produces classy plummy full Cab-based blend. Also Edna Valley white based on Sauv Bl. 27,000 cases.

Carneros Creek Napa ★★★ (Chard) 87 88 89 90 91 (Pinot N) 81 82 83 84 85 86 87 88 89 90 Resolute explorer of climates and clones in CARNEROS focuses on Pinot N. Well-oaked Reserve, lightheartedly fruity Fleur and reliable estate bottlings. Also deftly oaked Chard. 25,000 cases.

Caymus Napa ★★★→★★★★ (Cab S) 75 76 77 78 79 80 81 82 83 84 85 86 87 88 89 90 Dark firm herbaceous estate Cab S is the celebrated core; weightier, more oaky Reserve and slightly lighter Napa Valley cover the flanks. Also dark Zin, ultra-ripe Pinot N. 35,000 cases. Good value second label: Liberty School.

Chalk Hill Sonoma ★★ In hills nr Windsor, revitalized winemaking leading to oakier Chard, Sauv Bl, Cab S from large estate v'yd. 65,000 cases.

Chalone Monterey ★★★★ (Chard) 81 83 84 85 86 87 88 89 90 91 (Pinot N) 80 81 82 86 87 88 90 Unique hilltop estate high in the Gavilan Mts; source of smoky woody flinty slow-ageing Chard and (latterly) dark tannic Pinot N, both meant to imitate burgundies. Also Pinot Bl and Chenin Bl styled after Chard. 25,000 cases. Company also owns ACACIA, CARMENET, EDNA VALLEY, Gavilan. Links with (Lafite) Rothschilds.

Chappellet Napa ★★★ (Chard) 82 83 84 85 86 87 88 89 90 91 (Cab S) 74 75 76 77 78 79 80 81 82 83 84 85 86 87 88 89 90 Beautiful amphitheatrical hillside v'yd yields lean racy Cab S, understated Chard and California's best dry Chenin Bl – all long-lived. 30,000 cases.

Chateau De Baun Sonoma ★★ Newcomer doing well by Chard and Pinot N from RUSSIAN RIVER estate v'yd.

Chateau Montelena Napa ★★★ (Chard) **85 86 87 88 89 90 91** (Cab S) **75 76 77 78 79 80 81 82 83 84 85 86 87 88 90** Understated firm age-worthy Chard and epically tannic Cab S. 28,000 cases.

Château Potelle Napa French-owned new producer of balanced quietly impressive NAPA Chard, also Cab S and Mt Veeder Zin. 22,000 cases.

Chateau St Jean Sonoma ★★★ (Chard) **88 89 90 91** Intensely flavoured, richly textured, individual-v'yd Chards (Robert Young, Belle Terre, McCrea), Fumé Bls (Petite Etoile), and sweet botrytised Ries and Traminers (Robert Young, Belle Terre). Just starting with reds (Cab S, Pinot N) again. Idiosyncratic classic sparkling from separate winery. Owned by Suntory. 150,000 cases.

Château Souverain Sonoma ★★ (Chard) **86 87 88 89 90 91** (Cab S) **84 85 86 87 88 90** Reliable accessible wines. Price-worthy Reserve Chard, Cab S and Dry Creek Zin, all distinctive, not overdone. 150,000 cases.

Château Woltner Napa ★★★ (Chard) **87 88 89 90 91** Ex-owners of Ch la Mission Haut Brion now encamped on NAPA hillside making 4,000 cases. Overpriced Chards from 3 separate blocks of their v'yd.

Chimney Rock Napa ★★ (Cab S) **85 86 87 88 89 90** Chard and recently impressive Cab S from Stag's Leap district. 12,000 cases.

Christian Brothers Madera (San Joaquin Valley) ★★ Since '89 acquisition by Heublein, settling in at the low end of price scale. Sound wines. Volume in flux.

Cline Cellars Carneros (Sonoma) 'Rhône Ranger' offers Mourvèdre etc. 5,000 cases.

Clos du Bois Sonoma ★★→★★★ (Chard) **85 86 87 88 89 90 91** (Cab S) **79 80 81 82 83 84 85 86 87 88 89 90** Sizeable Allied-Hiram Walker firm at Healdsburg has consistent Cab S, Chard, Gewürz. Single-v'yd Chard (Calcaire, Flintwood), Cab S (Briarcrest), Cab S blend (Marlstone), from ALEXANDER, Dry Creek valleys, can be memorable. 320,000 cases.

Clos Pegase Napa ★★→★★★ (Chard) **87 88 89 90 91** (Cab S) **86 87 88 90** Post-modernist winery-cum-museum (or vice versa) with ever-improving, deftly understated wines. 40,000 cases.

Clos du Val Napa ★★★ (Chard) **87 88 89 90 91** (Cab S) **72 73 75 78 79 80 81 82 83 84 85 86 87 88 89 90 91** French-run. Supple polished Cab S, Merlot, bold Zin from Stag's Leap district; improving Chard, Pinot N from CARNEROS. Joli Val is label for non-estate wines (Chard, Cab, Sém). 55,000 cases.

Concannon Livermore ★★ WENTE BROS now own this historically famous source of Sauv Bl. Also Chard, Cab S. 85,000 cases.

Conn Creek Napa ★★→★★★ (Chard) **87 88 89 90 91** (Cab S) **80 81 82 83 84 85 86 87 88 89 90** Best known for supple, almost juicy Cab. Chard gaining reputation. Owned by Château Ste Michelle (Washington). 30,000 cases.

Cooks 'Cooks Champagne', see Guild.

Corbett Canyon San Luis Obispo ★★ (Chard) **87 88 90 91** (Pinot N Res) **84 85 86 87 88 89 90** Recently memorable Reserve Pinot N is best. Reserve lots small; good value Coastal Classics line abundant. 100,000+ cases.

Corison Napa Valley ★★★ Long-time CHAPPELLET winemaker on her own making supple flavoury Cab S of promise as ager.

Culbertson Temecula ★★ Sparkling wine specialist blends local and STA BARBARA grapes with medal-winning results. Recently some table wines too. 40,000 cases.

Cuvaison Napa ★★★ (Chard) **86 87 88 89 90 91** (Cab S) **84 85 86 87 88 90** Lean crisp CARNEROS Chard is steadily in the top rank. Dark ripe Merlot and up-valley Cab S are following suit. 65,000 cases. Pinot N to come.

Dehlinger Sonoma ★★→★★★ (Chard) **87 88 89 90 91** (Pinot N) **80 81 82 83 84 85 86 87 88 89 90** Firm fruit-filled Chard and dark full complex Pinot N from Russian River estate. Both long-lived. 9,000 cases.

DeLoach Vineyards Sonoma ★★★ (Chard) **85 86 87 88 89 90 91** (Pinot N) **79 80 81 84 85 86 87 88 89 90** Unctuous super-fruity Chard and dark slow-ageing Pinot N are best known. Bold, often heady Zin (and uncommonly fine white Zin) should be. Also solid Gewürz, Sauv Bl. 70,000 cases.

deLorimier Sonoma ★★ Still settling into style, but estate ALEXANDER VALLEY Chard, Sauv-Sém and Cab family blends show promise. 5,000 cases.

Diamond Creek Napa ★★★ (Cab S) **75 76 77 78 79 80 81 82 83 84 85 86 87 89 90** Austere long-ageing Cabs from hilly v'yd nr Calistoga go by names of v'yd blocks, eg Gravelly Meadow, Volcanic Hill. 3,000 cases.

Domaine Carneros Napa (★★★) Showy US outpost of Taittinger in CARNEROS exaggerates austere style of its parent in Champagne. 25,000 cases+.

Domaine Chandon Napa ★★→★★★ Californian outpost of Moët & Chandon is most broadly known for reliable Brut and Blanc de Noirs; most praised for Reserve, locally available Club Cuvée and luxury cuvée Etoile. Shadow Creek is second (non-Napa) label. 500,000 cases.

Domaine Napa Napa ★★→★★★ (Chard) **87 88 89 90 91** (Cab S) **85 86 87 88 90** French owner/grower and NZ winemaker collaborate on consistently supple well-balanced Chard, Cab S, Sauv Bl. 10,000 cases.

Dominus Napa (★★★★) 83 **84 85** 86 **87 88 89 90** Partnership of Christian Moueix of Pomerol and inheritors of INGLENOOK make increasingly intense, massively tannic Cab-based blend. Little of it is even nearly mature. 89 looks magnificent.

Dry Creek Vineyard Sonoma ★★ Unimpeachable source of dry tasty whites, esp Chard and Fumé Bl, but also Chenin Bl. Cab S and Zin rather underrated. David Stare label for somewhat weighty reserve Cab blend, Sauv blend, and Chard. 80,000 cases.

Duckhorn Vineyards Napa (Merlot) **82 83 84 85** 86 **87** 89 **90** (Cab) **81 82 83 84** 85 86 **87** 88 **90** Known for dark tannic almost plummy-ripe reds, eg single-v'yd Merlot (Three Palms, Vine Hill). Also Sauv. 18,000 cases.

Dunn Vineyards Napa (★★★) (Cab S) **80 81 82** 83 **84 85 86 87 88 89 90** On his own, ex-CAYMUS winemaker Randall Dunn makes dark tannic austere Cabs from Howell Mountain, slightly milder ones from the valley floor. 4,000 cases.

Durney Vineyard Monterey ★★ (Cab S) **79 80 81 82 83 84 85 86 87** 90 Estate in Carmel Valley. Dark robust Cab. Chard joining list. 15,000 cases.

Eberle Winery San Luis Obispo ★★ Oaky fat supple Chard and Cab from Paso Robles. 12,000 cases.

Edna Valley Vineyard San Luis Obispo ★★→★★★ (Chard) **86 87 88 89 90 91** Characterful Chard from a joint venture of local grower and CHALONE. Pinot N starts well but fades quickly in most vintages. 48,000 cases.

Estancia See Franciscan.

Etude Napa ★★→★★★ Winemaker-owned label of Tony Soter (long-time CHAPPELLET, now respected consultant). Front-rank CARNEROS Pinot N (85 86 87 88 89), excellent Cab; both burnished and supple. 4,000 cases.

Far Niente Napa ★★ (Chard) **87 88 89 90 91** (Cab S) **84 85 86 87** 88 89 90 V oaky Chard, more restrained Cab at high prices. 36,000 cases.

Ferrari-Carano Sonoma ★★★ (Chard) **87 88 89 90 91** (Cab S) **86 87 88 90** Stylish Chard (Reserve seriously over-oaky), Fumé Bl and, more recently, Merlot and Cab S from 1,000 still-developing acres in ALEXANDER, Dry Creek and Knights valleys. 50,000 cases.

Fetzer Mendocino ★★→★★★ (Chard) **87 88 89 90 91** (Cab S) **79 80 81 82 83 84 85** 86 87 88 90 Rapidly expanding winery with always reliable (Sun Dial Chard, Valley Oaks Fumé), sometimes memorable (Barrel Select Chard, Cab S and Reserve Zin) range. Bel Arbors is good value second label. 1.5 million cases. Sold to Brown-Forman Distillers.

Ficklin San Joaquin ★★★ First in California to use Douro grapes. Still California's best 'port', Tinta. Sometimes vintages. 10,000 cases.

Field Stone Sonoma ★★ Sturdy, increasingly steady; esp for Petite Sirah. Also Cab. 12,000 cases.

Firestone Sta Barbara ★★★ (Chard) 87 88 89 90 91 (Merlot) 84 85 86 87 88 89 Increasingly fine Chard overshadows but does not outshine delicious Ries. Merlot is good; Cab one of STA BARBARA's best; Sauv Bl and Gewürz also vg. 75,000 cases. Also owns nearby CAREY.

Fisher Sonoma ★★ Mountain estate for often fine Chard; NAPA grapes dominate steady Cab. 10,000 cases.

Flora Springs Wine Co Napa ★★★ (Chard) 87 88 89 90 91 (Cab S) 84 85 86 87 88 89 90 Old stone cellar. Fine Sauv Bl became Soliloquy, to parallel flavoury Cab and luxury Cab blend Trilogy. Now both are top-line Flora Springs. Regular bottlings called Floréal. Good Chard. 18,000 cases.

Fogarty, Thomas Sta Cruz Mts ★★ Fine Gewürz form Ventana sets the pace; whole line is well made.

Folie à Deux Napa ★★ Impeccable Chards; unexpectedly fine Chenin Bl. Cab a recent addition. 8,000 cases.

Foppiano Sonoma ★★ Long-established wine family annually turns out fine reds, esp transcendent Petite Sirah. Reserve label for Chard, Cab (fine 85 87) is Fox Mountain; good value second label is Riverside Farms. About 50,000 cases.

Forman Napa ★★★ The winemaker who brought STERLING its first fame in the '60s now makes excellent Cab, Chard on his own. 15,000 cases.

Foxen Sta Barbara ★★ Tiny producer of memorable Pinot N, Cab S, Chard and others from Sta Maria grapes.

Franciscan Vineyard Napa ★★ (Chard) 87 88 89 90 91 (Cab S) 79 80 81 82 83 84 85 86 87 88 89 90 Substantial v'yd at Oakville producing increasingly stylish Chard, Cab and Cab blend MERITAGE. Sister label Estancia goes on good value Sauv Bl and MONTEREY Chard. Third label, Pinnacles, is for Monterey grapes. 100,000+ cases.

Franzia San Joaquin ★ Penny-saver everyday wines under Franzia and other labels; varietals under William Bates brand. All say 'Made and bottled in Ripon'. 5 million cases.

Freemark Abbey Napa ★★★→★★★★ (Chard) 85 86 87 88 89 90 91 (Cab S) 70–80 81 82 83 84 85 86 87 88 90 Inexhaustible stylish Cabs (esp single-v'yd Bosché, Sycamore) of great depth. Almost-bold Chards, incl single-v'yd Carpy. Late harvest Ries Edelwein always among finest.

Fritz, J Sonoma ★★ Splendid Dry Creek Zin, fine Russian River Chard from 12,000-case winery deserving of greater fame.

Frog's Leap Napa ★★ Small winery charming as its name (and T-shirts). Good for rich flavoured Zin (81 85 86 87 88 89 90), solid Cab (82 83 84 85 86 87 88 89 90). Chard, Sauv worth second looks too. 16,000 cases.

Gainey Vineyard, The Sta Barbara ★★ Chard, Cab and recent Sauv Bl and Merlot. Pinot N from Benedict v'yd. Also good Ries. 12,000 cases.

Gallo, E & J San Joaquin ★→★★ (Cab S) 80 81 82 (Zin) 81 84 The world's biggest winery: pioneer in quantity and quality. Family-owned. Hearty 'Burgundy' and 'Chablis Blanc' set national standards. Wide acclaim won for vintage Cab. Varietals from huge SONOMA v'yds aimed up-mkt. Also André fizz, etc. 40 million+ cases. 'Super-premium' wines coming.

Gan Eden Sonoma (★★) Kosher producer of serious Chard and Cab won wide critical acclaim for early vintages. 25,000 cases.

Gary Farrell Sonoma (★★→★★★) Winemaker's label for excellent well-oaked full-flavoured Pinot Ns (Howard Allen Ranch, RUSSIAN RIVER VALLEY). Also vg Chards and Sauv Bl.

Geyser Peak Sonoma ★→★★ Since brief marriage with Penfolds of Australia, extensive v'yds of Henry Trione in ALEXANDER and RUSSIAN RIVER valleys (lovely grapes) make oaky Aussie-style wine. 500,000 cases.

Giumarra San Joaquin ★ Penny-saver everyday wines. 500,000+ cases.

Glen Ellen Sonoma ★★→★★★ Fast-growing family winery puts its best efforts into excellent Benziger of Glen Ellen Chard, Cab, Sauv Bl, etc from SONOMA grapes; works hard on value-for-money but misnamed Proprietor's Reserve line of easy quaffers. Also M G Vallejo, priced one step up from Prop Reserve. 3.5 million cases.

Gloria Ferrer Sonoma ★★ Substantial classic sparkling winery of Spain's Freixenet has scored well, esp for Cuvée Royale and Cuvée Carneros. 65,000 cases.

Green and Red Napa ★★ Tiny winery. Vigorous Italianate Zin. 2,000 cases.

Greenwood Ridge Mendocino ★★ Established specialist in Anderson Valley Ries now offers attention-getting Cab (83 84), Sauv Bl (88), Zin. 3,000 cases. Now vg Chard and Pinot N from MENDOCINO.

Grgich Hills Cellars Napa ★★★ (Chard) 85 86 88 89 90 91 (Cab S) 81 82 83 84 85 86 87 90 Winemaker Grgich and grower Hills join forces on a stern Chard, impressively rich Cab, Sauv Bl, and – too little noticed – Spätlese-sweet Ries. Also plummy thick SONOMA Zin. 40,000 cases.

Groth Vineyards Napa ★★★ (Chard) 87 88 89 90 91 (Cab S) 82 83 84 85 86 87 88 89 90 Estate at Oakville challenges leaders with polished refined Cab (and weightier woodier Reserve). Also vg Chard. 30,000 cases.

Guenoc Vineyards Lake County ★★ Ambitious winery/v'yd venture just N of NAPA county line. NB for Zin (81 84 85 88), Petite Sirah, other reds. Chard coming nicely. Property once belonged to Lillie Langtry, hence Reserve Langtry label for MERITAGES and Domaine Breton for second label varietals. 75,000 cases.

Guild San Joaquin ★ Ex-coop owned by Canandaigua of New York. B Cribari is top table wine, Cooks American Champagne a runaway success among tank-fermented sparklers. Also owns Dunnewood V'yds (ex-Cresta Blanca) in Mendocino and Dunnewood. 3 million cases?

Gundlach-Bundschu Sonoma ★★→★★★ (Chard) 87 88 89 90 91 (Cab S) 78 79 80 81 82 83 84 85 86 87 88 89 90 Pioneer name solidly revived by newest generation. Rhinefarm Vineyard on label signals worthy-to-fine Gewürz, Cab, Chard. 50,000 cases.

Hagafen Napa ★★ First and perhaps still finest of the serious kosher producers. Cab, Chard, Johannisberg Ries. 6,000 cases.

Handley Cellars Mendocino ★★ (Chard) 87 88 89 90 91 Winemaker-owned small producer of refined Chard and Gewürz (90), classic sparkling and refreshing Brightlighter (Gewürz-based). 12,000 cases.

Hanzell Sonoma ★★★ (Chard) 87 88 89 90 91 (Pinot N) 84 85 86 87 88 89 90 The late founder revolutionized California Chards, Pinot Ns in late '60s. Two owners later Hanzell remains a throwback source of its original ripe full-flavoured style. 2,000 cases.

Haywood Vineyard Sonoma ★★ Source of intense Zin and conventional Chard under Racke ownership. 34,000 cases before sale. Vintner Select is bought-in wine.

Heitz Napa ★★★★ (Cab S) 61–80 81 82 83 84 85 86 87 88 89 90 An individualist winemaker has set lofty standards for his peers with his dark deep emphatic Cabs, esp Martha's Vineyard but also Bella Oaks and Napa Valley. Other wines eccentric or worse. 40,000 cases.

Hess Collection, The Napa ★★→★★★★ (Chard) 88 89 90 91 (Cab S) 85 86 87 88 89 A Swiss art collector's winery-cum-museum in former Mont La Salle winery of CHRISTIAN BROTHERS. Steadily improving Cab, Chard. Hess Selection label is vg value. 15,000 cases, aiming for 50.

Hill Winery, William Napa ★★★ (Chard) 89 90 91 (Cab S) 80 81 82 83 84 85 86 87 88 89 90 V'yds high in Mayacamas Mts yield steady Chard; ever more stylish Cabs. 12,000 cases. Same owners as CALLAWAY, CLOS DU BOIS.

Hop Kiln Sonoma ★★ Good source of bold-as-brass Petite Sirah and Zin. Even Gewürz is full-flavoured and large-scale. 10,000 cases.

Husch Vineyards Mendocino ★★ Reliable Chard, Sauv Bl, Cab; sometimes outstanding Pinot N and Gewürz from Anderson Valley. 15,000 cases.

Inglenook Napa ★★→★★★ (Chard) 87 88 89 90 91 (Cab S) 80 81 82 83 84 85 86 87 88 89 90 Great old NAPA winery, now owned by Grand Met, regained much of its earlier footing, esp with supple Cab, heartier Cask (Reserve) Cab and thoroughly tannic Reunion Cab. Also Merlot, Gravion (Sauv Bl-Sém) and Reserve Chard. But currently on hold with no winemaking facilities. 110,000 cases.

Iron Horse Vineyards Sonoma ★★★ (Chard) **87 88 89 90 91** (Cab S) **80 81 83 84 85 86 87** 88 89 90 Substantial RUSSIAN RIVER property concentrates increasingly on v successful classic sparkling with real finesse, but continues with Chard and Pinot N from same estate v'yd. Cab, Sauv Bl from affiliated ALEXANDER VALLEY v'yd can be memorable. Joint venture coming up with Laurent-Perrier. 40,000 cases.

Jekel Vineyards Monterey ★★ (Chard) **85 86 87 88 89 90 91** (Cab S) **78 79 80 81 82 83 84 85 86 87 88 89 90** Jekel's ripe juicy Ries is most successful wine from SALINAS v'yds. Also good Chard, intensely regional (fruit-flavoured) Cab. Financial complications here. 60,000 cases.

Jepson Vineyards Mendocino ★★ Chard, Sauv Bl, classic sparkling, and pot-still brandy from estate in Ukiah area. 30,000 cases.

Johnson-Turnbull Napa ★★ (Cab S) **80 81 82 83 84 85 86 87** 88 90 Rich full minty Cabs from estate facing the ROBERT MONDAVI winery; Chard from SONOMA grapes. 10,000 cases.

Jordan Sonoma ★★★ (Chard) **88 89 90 91** (Cab S) **78 79 80 81 82 83 84 85 86 87** 88 90 Extravagant ALEXANDER VALLEY estate models its Cab on supplest Bordeaux. But it lasts. (Chard is less successful.) Separate classic sparkling called simply 'J' is deft fresh luxurious. 75,000 cases.

Karly Amador ★★ Among the more ambitious sources of SIERRA FOOTHILLS Zin. 12,000 cases.

Keenan Winery, Robert Napa ★★ (Chard) **88 89 90 91** (Cab S) **82 83 84 85 86 87** 90 Winery on Spring Mountain has veered away from overweight heavily oaked to more restrained Cab, Merlot, Chard. 12,000 cases.

Kendall-Jackson Lake County ★★ (Chard) **87 88 89 90 91** (Cab S) **80 81 82 83 84 85 86** 87 88 89 90 Dynamic maker of popular slightly sweet Chards and Sauv Bls; v oaky Cab. Hard-to-get single-v'yd Zins (labelled Ciapusci, DePratt, Mariah) can be memorable, as can Syrah (Durrell). 500,000 cases. See also Cambria.

Kenwood Vineyards Sonoma ★★→★★★ (Chard) **87 88 89 90 91** (Cab S) **78 79 80 81 82 83 84 85 86 87** 88 90 Substantial producer of vg winning Sauv Bl and Zin, solid Chard (incl single-v'yd Beltane) and Cab S (single-v'yd Jack London can challenge the best). 150,000 cases.

Kistler Vineyards Sonoma (Chard) **87 88 89 90 91** Chards much in the smoky buttery style. Pinot N and Cab more recent. 9,000 cases.

Konocti Cellars Lake County ★★ Excellent value Sauv Bl, Chard, Cab from small coop. Recent MERITAGES (red, white) show promise. 40,000 cases.

Korbel Sonoma ★★ Long-established classic sparkling specialists who place extra emphasis on fruit flavours, lots of fizz. Natural, Brut and Blanc de Blancs are best. 1.5 million cases.

Krug, Charles Napa ★★ (Chard) **87 88 89 90 91** (Cab S) **78 79 80 81 82 83 84 85 86 87** 88 90 Historically important winery with generally sound wines. Cabs at head of list. CK-Mondavi is jug brand. 200,000 cases.

Kunde Estate Sonoma ★★ Long-time growers turned winemakers ('88). Gd (Chard) to brilliant (Sauv) early results. Cab, Merlot: similar promise.

La Crema Sonoma (Chard) **87 88 89 90 91** (Pinot N) **80 81 82 83 84 85 86 87 88 89** 90 RUSSIAN RIVER grapes dominate in deftly oaked Chard and often deep-flavoured Pinot N. 80,000 cases.

Lakespring Napa ★★ Merlot, Cab, Chard, Sauv. 18,000 cases. Edging up.

Landmark Sonoma (Chard) **83 84 85 86 87 88 89 90 91** Ever steadier Chard-only producer offers 3 (SONOMA COUNTY, basic; Sonoma Valley Two Williams; ALEXANDER VALLEY Damaris). 15,000 cases.

Laurel Glen Sonoma ★★★ (Cab S) **81 82 83 84 85 86** 87 88 90 Fine, distinctly regional Cab from steep v'yd in Sonoma Mountain AVA. 5,000 cases.

Laurier Sonoma ★★★ (Chard) **87** (Cab S) **78 79 80 81 82 83 84 85 86** Lovely wines formerly; but now only a label owned by the Franzias Bronco Wine Co. Currently only Chard. Await developments.

Lazy Creek Mendocino ★★ 'Retirement hobby' of a long-time restaurant waiter is yielding serious Anderson Valley Gewürz and Chard. Also Pinot N. 2,000 cases.

Leeward Winery Ventura (Chard) 87 88 89 Ultra-toasty Central Coast Chards are the mainstay. 18,000 cases.

Lohr, J Central Coast ** Wide range of steady varietals from wineries in Sta Clara, SAN LUIS OBISPO, v'yds in NAPA and Clarksburg. 200,000 cases.

Long Vineyards Napa ** (Chard) 87 88 89 90 91 (Cab S) 79 80 81 82 83 84 85 86 87 90 Tiny neighbour of CHAPPELLET: lush Chard, flavoury Cab S.

Lyeth Vineyard Sonoma ** Former winery, now a brand owned by J C Boisset (Burgundy). Christophe is more modest label for bought wines.

Lytton Springs Sonoma ** Now RIDGE-owned: ink-dark hard heady Zins.

MacRostie Sonoma ** Veteran winemaker producing reliably silky subtle CARNEROS Chards.

Madrona El Dorado ** Loftiest v'yds in SIERRA FOOTHILLS good for steady Chard (among others). 10,000 cases.

Maison Deutz San Luis Obispo *** Californian arm of Champagne Wm Deutz shows a firm sense of style, using grapes from v'yds nr STA BARBARA county line. 25,000 cases.

Mark West Vineyards Sonoma ** (Chard) 87 88 89 90 91 (Pinot N) 80 81 82 83 84 85 86 87 88 90 V satisfactory Gewürz from v'yd in coolest part of RUSSIAN RIVER. Also sturdy to rustic Chard, Pinot N and, at times, classic Blanc de Noirs sparkling. 22,000 cases. Now owned by Marion Wine Group, with Marion label for less expensive wines.

Markham Napa **→*** (Chard) 87 88 89 90 91 (Cab S) 80 81 82 83 84 85 86 87 88 90 Japanese-owned. Recently good to excellent. 20,000 cases.

Martin Bros San Luis Obispo ** (Chard) 87 88 89 90 Fine dry Chenin Bl, good oaked Chard. Family winery aims to establish Paso Robles as California's Piedmont with Nebbiolo.

Martini, Louis M Napa **→*** (Chard) 87 88 89 90 91 (Cab S) 51 52 55 59 60–80 81 82 83 84 85 86 87 88 89 90 Family-owned winery with high standards at every level, esp v'yd Cab (Monte Rosso), Merlot (Los Vinedos del Rio), Pinot N (La Loma). Emerging source of crisp RUSSIAN RIVER/CARNEROS Chard. Second label Glen Oaks. 235,000 cases.

Masson Vineyards Monterey *→** Chard, Ries, Cab, Pinot N on a big scale.

Matanzas Creek Sonoma *** (Chard) 85 86 87 88 89 90 91 (Merlot) 85 86 87 88 89 90 Fine ripe fruity Chard, Sauv; renowned Merlot.

Maurice Car'rie Temecula ** Setting standards for its region with reliable approachable Chard, Sauv Bl and others.

Mayacamas Napa *** (Chard) 85 86 87 88 89 91 (Cab S) 70 73 74 75 76 78 79 80 81 82 83 84 85 86 87 88 89 90 Vg small v'yd with rich Chard and firm (but no longer steel-hard) Cab. Some Sauv Bl, Zin. 5,000 cases.

McDowell Valley Vineyards Mendocino ** Obligatory Chard, Cab, but owners' hearts are with Rhône varieties, esp Syrah from ancient vines and Grenache (labelled Les Vieux Cépages). 100,000 cases.

Meridian San Luis Obispo **→*** Nestlé-owned latecomer property. Impressive STA BARBARA Chard (88 89 90 91), Pinot N (88) and Paso Robles Syrah (88), Cab. 300,000 cases.

Meritage Trademarked name for reds or whites using Bordeaux grape varieties. Little followed; may soon expire.

Merry Vintners Sonoma (**) Winemaker-owned producer of well-oaked regular and Reserve Chards. Branching into Pinot N.

Milano Mendocino ** Chard. 10,000 cases.

Mill Creek Sonoma ** Cab, Merlot, Chard, Sauv Bl. 15,000 cases.

Mirassou Central Coast ** Fifth-generation grower in Sta Clara, pioneer in MONTEREY (SALINAS VALLEY). Cab, Chard, Sauv Bl, Gewürz, Pinot N and v pleasant classic sparkling. 350,000 cases.

Mondavi, Robert Napa **→**** (Chard) 88 89 90 91 (Cab) 74 75 76 77 78 79 80 81 82 83 84 85 86 87 88 90 Winery with brilliant quarter-century record of innovation in styles, equipment, technique. Famous successes: Cab, Sauv (sold as Fumé Bl), Chard, even Pinot N. 'Reserves' are marvels, regularly among NAPA's best. 500,000 cases. Less pricey California appellation varietals: Mondavi-Woodbridge. See also Opus One.

Monterey Peninsula Monterey ** Small winery in MONTEREY town: chunky long-living reds, esp Zin, Cab, from SALINAS grapes and others.

Monterey Vineyard, The Monterey ** Seagram-owned label for Chard, Pinot N, Cab: Classic and more costly Limited Release. 550,000 cases.

Monteviña Amador ** (Cab S) **80 81 82 83 84 85 86 87 88 89 90** (Zin) **80 81 82 83 84 85 86 87 88** Major force in revitalizing hearty-style SIERRA FOOTHILL Zins. Now, under ownership of SUTTER HOME, turning also to a major exploration of Italian varieties. 50,000 cases.

Mont St John Napa ** Old NAPA wine family makes good value Pinot N, Chard from own CARNEROS v'yd; buys in for solid Cab. 20,000 cases.

Monticello Cellars Napa **→*** (Chard) **85 86 87 88 89** 90 91 (Cab S) **80 81 82 83 84 85 86** 87 88 89 90 Ultra-modern winery nr Napa City. Outstanding Gewürz (now v limited) first caught the eye. Refined Jefferson Ranch, darkly tannic Corley Reserve Cabs, sternly oaky Chard now the major effort. Dom Montreaux is classic sparkling. 25,000 cases.

Morgan Monterey **→*** (Chard) **87 88 89 90 91** Winemaker-owner: steady local Chard, fine ALEXANDER V Sauv. Also vg Pinot. 20,000 cases.

Mount Eden Vineyards Sta Cruz Mts ** (Chard) **87 88 89 90 91** Expensive big-scale Chard from old Martin Ray v'yds and gentler one from MONTEREY. Also Pinot N, Cab. 4,000 cases.

Mount Veeder Napa ** (Cab S) **75 76 78 80 81 82 83 84** 85 86 87 88 89 90 Once oaky Chards and austere Cabs are gentler and better balanced since acquired by FRANCISCAN. Now MERITAGE (88). About 8,000 cases.

Mumm Napa Valley *** G H Mumm-Seagram joint venture out of the box fast with fine vintages (**85 86**) and NV Brut. Also distinctive single-v'yd Winery Lake 'cuvée'. 125,000 cases.

Nalle Sonoma **→*** (Zin) **84 85 86 87 88 89 90 91** Winemaker-owned Dry Creek cellar gets to the very heart of Zin. Wonderfully berryish young; that and more with age. Now also a trickle of Cab. 2,500 cases.

Navarro Vineyards Mendocino **→*** (Chard) **87 88 89 90 91** Firm fine Chard, outstanding dry Gewürz and Ries from cool Anderson Valley. Pinot N begins to find a footing. 12,000 cases.

Newton Vineyards Napa *** (Chard) **88 89 90 91** (Cab S) **81 82 83 84 85 86** 87 88 90 Luxurious estate growing more so; formerly ponderous style now reined back to the merely opulent for Chard, Cab, Merlot.

Niebaum Collection Napa **→*** Heublein-owned label: small lots from some of highest quality v'yds they acquired with BEAULIEU and INGLENOOK. V superior Chards (Reference, Laird, Bayview), Sém (Chevrier), good Cabs from winemaker Judy Matulich-Weitz. 20,000 cases.

Opus One Napa **** (Cab S) **78 79 80 81 82 83 84 85 86** 87 88 89 90 Joint venture of R MONDAVI and Baronne Philippine de Rothschild. Spectacular new winery opened '92. Wines are showpieces too. 10,000 cases.

Parducci Mendocino ** (Chard) **88 89 90 91** (Cab S) **78 80 81 82 83 84 85 86 87 88 89 90** Long-est v'yds and winery ever reliable for Cab, Cab-Merlot, Zin, Barbera. No-oak Chard, off-dry Sauv. 350,000 cases.

Pecota, Robert Napa ** Cab, Sauv Bl, Chard, Gamay. 18,000 cases.

Pedroncelli Sonoma ** (Chard) **87 88 89 90 91** (Cab S) **81 82 83 84 85 86 87 88 89 90 91** Old family firm with above-average sturdy vinous Cab, Zin (esp Reserves). Chard, Sauv Bl growing stylish. 125,000 cases.

Pepi, Robert Napa **→*** (Chard) **86 87 88 89 90 91** (Cab S) **82 83 84 85** 86 87 88 90 Originally Sauv Bl specialist; now thoughtfully restrained Chard, Cab, winning Sangiovese Grosso (Colline di Sasso 89).

Phelps, Joseph Napa *** (Chard) **85 86 87 88 89 90 91** (Cab S) **74 75 76 77 78 79 80 81 82 83 84 85** 86 87 88 89 90 Deluxe winery and beautiful v'yd with impeccable standards. Vg Chard, Cabs (esp Backus Vineyard), pioneer Syrah and splendid late-harvest Ries, Gewürz. Reserve red Insignia can be over-tannic at times. 60,000 cases.

For key to grape variety abbreviations, see pages 6–9.

Philippine Baronne P de Rothschild's new brand. (See also Opus One.)

Philips, R H Yolo ** Large producer worth seeking out esp for some of California's most stylish tributes to the Rhône.

Pine Ridge Napa **→*** (Chard) **87 88 89 90 91** (Cab S) **79 80 81 82 83 84 85 86 87 88 89 90** Winery nr Stag's Leap makes consistently well-oaked Chard, Cab (several) and Merlot. 50,000 cases.

Piper Sonoma Sonoma *** Venture of Piper-Heidsieck: mostly RUSSIAN RIVER grapes. Vg classic sparklers esp gd with bottle-age. 125,000 cases.

Preston Sonoma *** (Cab S) **83 84 85 86 87** 88 89 90 Small winery with excellent Dry Creek Valley v'yd esp for Zin, Cab, Petite Sirah-Syrah blend. Also Sauv Bl. 25,000 cases.

Quady Winery San Joaquin ** Imaginative dessert wines from Madera incl port-like Starboard, celebrated orangey 'Muscat Essencia', dark Muscat Elysium and, latest, Moscato d'Asti-like Electra. 15,000 cases.

Quail Ridge Napa ** (Chard) **87 88 89 90 91** Specialist in barrel-fermented Chard. Also Cab. Recently added vg Sauv Bl and Merlot. Owned by Heublein. 15,000 cases.

Quivira Sonoma ** Melony Sauv Bl and intensely berryish Zin lead the list. Cabernet Cuvée is a MERITAGE-like blend. 12,000 cases.

Qupé Sta Barbara **→*** Never-a-dull-moment cellar-mate of AU BON CLIMAT. Marsanne, Pinot Bl, Syrah are worth trying.

Rafanelli, A Sonoma ** (Zin) **80 81 82 83 84 85 86 87 88 89 90** Hearty, somewhat rustic Dry Creek Zin; Cab of striking intensity. 6,000 cases.

Rancho Sisquoc Sta Barbara ** Highly personal little winery shows vivid quality of Sta Maria Valley grapes, incl Ries, Chard, even Silvaner.

Ravenswood Sonoma ** Best known for dark, sturdy Zins. 15,000 cases.

Raymond Vineyards and Cellar Napa *** (Chard) **85 86 87 88 89 90 91** (Cab S) **74 75 77 78 79 80 81 82 83 84 85 86 87** 88 89 90 Old NAPA wine family now with Japanese partners. Emphatically fruity Chard and Sauv Bl; dark sturdy keeper Cabs, esp Reserve. 110,000 cases.

Ridge Sta Cruz Mts **** (Cab S) **78 80 81 82** 83 84 85 86 87 88 Winery of highest repute among connoisseurs draws from NAPA, SONOMA, SAN LUIS OBISPO and its own mountain v'yd for concentrated v tannic Cabs and Zins, needing long maturing in bottle. Most notable efforts from single v'yds, esp Monte Bello, York Creek (Spring Mt) Cabs, Geyserville, Dusi Zins. Now also extremely smoky Chard. 40,000 cases.

Rochioli, J Sonoma ** Owners of v'yd famed for Pinot N now making vg example of their own. Also fine Sauv Bl.

Roederer Estate Mendocino *** Anderson V branch of Champagne house (est '88). Resonant Roederer style apparent. Potentially 90,000 cases.

Rombauer Vineyards Napa ** Well-oaked Chard, dark Cab (esp Reserve-style 'Meilleur du Chai'). 15,000 cases.

Roudon-Smith Sta Cruz Mts ** Chard, Cab. 10,000 cases.

Round Hill Napa ** Formerly diverse range now narrowed to Cab, Chard, Merlot, Sauv Bl, but in 3 price ranges: bargain California, regular Round Hill, separate top-of-the-line Rutherford Ranch. 350,000 cases.

Rutherford Hill Napa **→*** (Chard) **87 88 89 90 91** (Cab S) **80 81 82 83 84 85 86 87 88 89 90** Larger stable-mate of FREEMARK ABBEY. Good with several flavoury Chards (Jaeger, XVS), sturdy Cabs (XVS) and Merlots. Merlot to be future main line: 80% of production. 100,000 cases.

Rutherford Ranch See Round Hill.

Rutherford Vintners Napa ** (Chard) **87 88 89 90 91** (Cab S) **77 78 79 80 81 82 83 84 85 86 87 88 90** Subtle but eminently age-worthy Cabs are the main event; Château Rutherford is Reserve lot. 12,000 cases.

St Andrews Napa ** (Chard) **85 86 87 88 89 90 91** (Cab S) **83 84** 85 86 87 88 90 Steadily excellent Chard estate on Silverado Trail nr Napa City. Is abandoning Cab S. Recently acquired by CLOS DU VAL. 15,000 cases.

St Clement Napa **→*** (Chard) **87 88 89 90** (Cab S) **78 80 81 82 83 84** 85 86 87 88 89 90 Distinctive Sauv Bl worth ageing. Austere Chard, sturdy Cab and Merlot. Japanese-owned. 15,000 cases.

St Francis Sonoma ** (Chard) 85 86 88 89 90 91 Gaining speed after slow start. Firm v tasty Sonoma Valley estate Chard (esp 90). Steady Merlot. Also Gewürz, Cab. 34,000 cases.

St Supery Napa ** French-owned, supplied by 500-acre estate v'yd in Pope Valley. Good Sauv Bl, accessible Cab. Also Chard – and now Merlot. 25,000 cases, able to expand tenfold.

Saintsbury Napa *** (Chard) 81 83 84 85 86 87 88 89 90 91 (Pinot N) 84 85 86 87 88 89 90 CARNEROS' finest (and slowest-ageing) Pinot N. Lighter Pinot N Garnet and oaky Chard also vg. 35,000 cases.

Sanford Sta Barbara *** (Chard) 85 86 87 88 89 90 91 (Pinot N) 81 84 85 86 87 88 89 90 91 Specialist in clean-fruity intense age-worthy Pinot N (esp Barrel Select). Exceptionally bold Chard; firmly regional Sauv Bl and a little Pinot N 'Gris'. 30,000 cases.

Santa Barbara Winery Sta Barbara ** (Chard) 85 86 87 88 89 90 91 (Pinot) 85 86 87 88 89 90 Former jug-wine producer, now among regional leaders, esp for Reserve Chard. Also Pinot N, Zin, Cab. 28,000 cases.

Santa Cruz Mountain V'yd Sta Cruz Mts ** Huge tannic heady Pinot N and Cab dominate. 2,500 cases.

Santa Ynez Valley Winery Sta Barbara ** Sauv Bl, Chard and Merlot. 20,000 cases.

Santino Amador ** Stylish SIERRA FOOTHILLS Zins (Fiddletown, Grand Père); also crackerjack white Zin. Italian varieties too. 30,000 cases.

Scharffenberger Mendocino ** First to try MENDOCINO for serious classic sparkling. Now Clicquot-owned and doing well. 25,000 cases.

Schramsberg Napa **** Dedicated specialist: California's best sparkling. Historic caves. Reserve splendid; Bl de Noir outstanding, deserves 2–10 yrs'. Luxury 'cuvée' J Schram from '92 is America's Krug. 50,000 cases.

Schug Cellars Sonoma (Chard) 87 88 89 90 91 German-born and trained owner-winemaker developing refined Chard and Pinot N from CARNEROS. Relocated from NAPA to CARNEROS in '91. 10,000 cases.

Sebastiani Sonoma ** Substantial old family firm works on several different market levels: SONOMA appellations at top (esp Reserve), North Coast varietals in middle, August Sebastiani Country wines in jugs. Also Vendange penny-saver label. 4 million cases.

Seghesio Sonoma ** (Chard) 87 88 89 90 91 (Pinot N) 86 87 88 89 90 Long-time jug-wine producer recently turned to bottling its own wines with striking results. Vg Chard, Pinot N; often exceptional Zins (esp Dry Creek, ALEXANDER VALLEY Reserves). 85,000 cases.

Sequoia Grove Napa **→*** (Chard) 87 88 89 90 91 (Cab) 83 84 85 86 87 88 90 Vg Chards age well. ALEXANDER VALLEY and NAPA Cabs: dark firm.

Shadow Creek See Domaine Chandon.

Shafer Vineyards Napa **→*** (Chard) 87 88 89 90 91 (Cab S) 77 78 79 80 81 82 83 84 85 86 87 88 89 90 Polished Chard (new 80 acres of Chard in CARNEROS), stylish Cab (esp Hillside Select) and Merlot from v'yd and 16,000-case cellar in Stag's Leap district.

Shaw Vineyards and Winery, Charles F Napa ** (Chard) 87 88 89 90 91 Founded as Gamay specialist; has added fine Sauv Bl and increasingly stylish Chard. But future uncertain. 40,000 cases.

Sierra Vista El Dorado ** Steady Chard, Cab S, Zin, Syrah from SIERRA FOOTHILLS grapes. 6,000 cases.

Silver Oak Napa **→*** (Cab S) 78 79 80 81 82 83 84 85 86 87 88 90 Cabs, thoroughly American-oaked, incl pricey Bonny's V'yd. 24,000 cases.

Silverado Vineyards Napa *** (Chard) 85 86 87 88 89 90 91 (Cab S) 81 82 83 84 85 86 87 88 89 90 Showy hilltop Stag's Leap district winery. Cab, Chard, Sauv Bl all consistently refined; Cabs from '81 on ageing well.

Simi Alexander Valley *** (Chard) 83 85 86 87 88 89 90 91 (Cab S) 81 82 83 84 85 86 87 88 90 Restored historic winery has flowered under expert direction of Zelma Long. Wonderfully long-lived Chard, Sauv Bl. Fruity Chenin Bl and Cab rosé for summer fests. Vg Cab recently austere. New Sauv Bl-Sém Sendal. 130,000 cases.

Smith & Hook Monterey ★★ (Cab S) 80 81 82 83 84 85 86 87 88 89 90 Specialist in dark intensely regional Cabs – so herbaceous you can taste dill. Also Merlots. Lone Oak is second label for Cab, Chard. 10,000 cases.

Smith-Madrone Napa ★★ Soft round but durable Spring Mt Ries. Also Cab. Chard. 6,000 cases.

Sonoma-Cutrer Vineyards Sonoma ★★★→★★★★ (Chard) 82 83 84 85 86 87 88 89 90 91 Ultimate specialist in Chard. Advanced techniques display characters of individual v'yds, as in Burgundy. So far Les Pierres is No 1 ager; Russian River Ranches is quickly accessible. 75,000 cases.

Spotteswoode Napa ★★★→★★★★ (Cab S) 82 83 84 85 86 87 88 89 90 Seductive resonant Cab from tiny estate v'yd right in St Helena town. Also supple polished Sauv Bl. 3,500 cases.

Stag's Leap Wine Cellars Napa ★★★→★★★★ (Chard) 85 86 87 88 89 90 91 (Cab S) 78 79 80 81 82 83 84 85 86 87 88 89 90 Celebrated v'yd and cellar for Cabs (NAPA, Stag's Leap V'yd, and recently controversial top-of-line Cask 23). Also vg Chard, Ries, improving Sauv Bl. 40,000 cases.

Sterling Napa ★★★ (Chard) 87 88 89 90 91 (Cab S) 82 83 84 85 86 87 88 90 Proficient (also scenic) winery owned by Seagram. Strong tart Sauv Bl and Chards. Burly Cab, Reserve (Cab-based) and Three Palms (Merlot-based). Winery Lake V'yd Pinot N still promises more than it performs. Vg Merlot. 150,000 cases.

Stonegate Napa ★★ Estate Chard, Sauv Bl, Cab, Merlot. 15,000 cases.

Stony Hill Napa ★★★ (Chard) 81 83 84 85 86 87 88 89 90 91 Hilly v'yd/winery for many of California's v best whites over past 30 yrs. Founder Fred McCrea died in '77, widow Eleanor in '91; son Peter carries on powerful tradition. Chard less steely, more fleshy than before. Oak-tinged Ries and Gewürz understated but age-worthy. 4,000 cases.

Stratford Napa ★★ Merchant label for reliable Cab, Merlot and Chard. 20,000 cases.

Strong Vineyard, Rodney Sonoma ★★ (Chard) 85 86 87 88 89 90 91 (Cab S) 81 83 84 85 86 87 88 90 Formerly SONOMA V'yds, draws mostly on RUSSIAN RIVER VALLEY for steady Chards (esp Chalk Hill V'yd) and Pinot N; ALEXANDER VALLEY for Cabs (esp single-v'yd Alexander's Crown) and Sauv Bl. 375,000 cases.

Sutter Home Napa ★★ (Zin) 78 80 81 82 83 84 85 86 87 88 89 90 Best known for sweet white Zin; most admired for sometimes heady Amador Zin. Starting with bargain-priced Cab, Chard. 3 million cases.

Swan, Joseph Sonoma ★★ (Pinot N) 85 86 (Zin) 74 76 77 78 79 80 81 82 83 84 85 86 Ultra-bold style for Zins and Pinot Ns of late Joe Swan continues under direction of his son-in-law. 2,000 cases.

Swanson Napa ★★→★★★ Estimable age-worthy Chards lead list; vigorously pursuing Italian, Rhône red varieties.

Taft Street Sonoma ★★ After muddling along, has hit an impressive stride with good value RUSSIAN RIVER Chards, good Sauv Bl. 18,000 cases.

Trefethen Napa ★★→★★★ (Chard) 83 84 85 86 87 88 90 91 (Cab S) 74 75 76 77 78 79 80 81 82 83 84 85 86 87 88 90 Respected family-owned winery in NAPA'S finest old wooden building. Vg dry Ries, tense Chard for ageing (late-released Library wines show how well). Cab shows increasing depths. Value in low-priced blends: Eshcol Red, White.

Tudal Napa ★★ (Cab S) 79 80 81 82 83 84 85 86 87 88 89 90 Tiny estate winery N of St Helena; steady source of dark firm ageable Cabs.

Tulocay Napa ★★ (Chard) 87 88 89 90 91 (Pinot N) 84 85 86 87 88 89 90 Tiny winery at Napa City. Chard and esp Pinot N can be really accomplished. Cab S is also worth attention. 2,400 cases.

Ventana Monterey ★★ (Chard) 87 88 89 90 91 '78 winery on large v'yd keeps shuffling its range, but Chards (fruity Gold Stripe, oakier Cristal) remain on top, with Sauv Bl increasingly notable. 42,000 cases.

Viader Napa Argentine Delia Viader fled to California to do her own thing: fine Cab-based blend from estate in hills above St Helena.

Viansa Sonoma ★★ Reliable source of Napa-Sonoma Chard, Sauv Bl and Cab is turning attention to Sangiovese. No 91 wine made.

Vichon Winery Napa ★★→★★★ (Chard) 87 88 89 90 91 (Cab S) 81 82 83 84 85 86 87 88 89 90 MONDAVI-owned. Subtle agreeable Chevrignon (Sauv Bl-Sém) equally worthy Cab. Stern oaky Chard. 50,000 cases.

Villa Mt Eden Napa ★★ (Chard) 87 88 89 90 91 (Cab S) 80 83 84 85 86 87 88 90 Rich, nearly plummy Cab made the name of this small Oakville estate. Bought by Château Ste Michelle group (see Washington) and improving strongly. Two lines: Grand Reserve and Cellar Select. 24,000 cases and expanding.

Vita Nova Sta Barbara Label from stable of AU BON CLIMAT. To watch.

Weibel Alameda and Mendocino ★→★★ Mainly tank-made sparklers; also range of accessible table wines for current drinking. 7,500 cases.

Wente Bros Livermore and Monterey ★→★★ Historic specialists in whites, esp LIVERMORE Sauv, Sém. MONTEREY sweet Ries can be exceptional. Of growing importance for classic sparkling. 300,000 cases.

Whitehall Lane Napa ★★ Recent Japanese purchase. Obligatory Chard, Cab, weighty Merlot, and some fresh lively Pinot N (81 82 83 84 85 86 87 90). 20,000 cases.

White Oak Sonoma ★★ (Chard) 87 88 89 90 91 Source of underrated, vibrantly fruity ALEXANDER VALLEY Chards and Sauv Bls. 11,000 cases.

Wild Horse Winery San Luis Obispo ★★→★★★ (Pinot N) 85 86 87 88 89 90 Reaches into STA BARBARA for impressive Pinot N. Also Chard, Cab. 15,000 cases.

Williams & Selyem Sonoma ★★★→★★★★ (Pinot N) 85 86 87 88 89 90 Intense smoky pricey Pinot N of emphatic character, esp Rochioli and Allen v'yds.

William Wheeler Sonoma ★★ (Chard) 87 88 89 90 91 (Cab S) 82 83 84 85 86 87 88 90 Historic emphasis on emphatically dark, tannic Cab and lively Sauv from Dry Creek. Since French (J C Boisset's) acquisition, also affable Rhône-type RS Reserve. 19,000 cases. Also vinifies LYETH.

Zaca Mesa Sta Barbara ★★ (Chard) 87 88 89 90 91 (Pinot N) 84 85 86 87 88 89 90 Deliberately down-sized from 80– to 35,000 cases and refocused on buttery Chard, well-wooded Pinot N. Increased emphasis on Syrah.

ZD Napa ★★→★★★ (Chard) 87 88 89 90 91 (Pinot N) 84 85 86 87 88 89 90 Lusty Chard well marked by American oak is the ZD signature wine. Pinot N is often finer. 18,000 cases.

The Pacific Northwest

This region occupies the same latitudes on the Pacific Coast as France does on the Atlantic. As in California, the modern wine industry dates back to the early '60s. Each of the northwestern States (Oregon, Washington, Idaho) has developed a distinct identity, with wine of similar quality to that of north California.

Oregon's vines (about 5,000 acres) lie mainly in the cool temperate Willamette and warmer Umpqua valleys between the Coast and Cascade Ranges, in climates not unlike those of France, leading to delicate flavours.

Washington's vineyards (about 11,000 acres) are mostly east of the Cascades in a drier, more severe climate tempered by the Yakima and Columbia rivers, and Idaho's are east of Oregon along the Snake River. Both are regions with warm days and cold nights which preserve acidity and intensify flavours.

In Oregon most of the 70-odd wineries are small and highly individual; and vintages are as uneven as in Burgundy, whose Pinot Noir is this state's most celebrated grape. A rare succession of good vintages for Pinot Noir, '88, '89 and '90, have also yielded notable Chardonnay and Pinot Gris.

The Washington industry, with about 90 wineries, is remarkably consistent over a wide range. Cabernet and Merlot grow excellently, as well as all the classic white varieties. A run of fine vintages, '88, '89, '90, '91, has coincided with maturing winemaking talent. Despite small harvests in 1990 and 1991, most wines remain excellent bargains.

Oregon

Adelsheim Vineyard Willamette Valley Nicely oaked Pinot N, Chard often best early. Pinot Gr fresher.

Alpine Vineyards Willamette Valley Small estate winery with high spots, incl Pinot N, Ries.

Amity Willamette Valley Distinctive Pinot N, several styles, good Gewürz and some good Chard.

Argyle Willamette Valley Since '87, Australia's NW outpost, led by Brian Croser. Dry Ries, Chard and vg sparkling.

Bethel Heights Willamette Valley Deftly made, thoughtfully styled Chard and Pinot N from estate nr Salem have won consistent praise.

Bridgeview Vineyards Rogue Valley Starting to command attention, esp for whites: good Gewürz, also Chard and Pinot N.

Cameron Willamette Valley Neighbour of KNUDSEN-ERATH attracting attention for Pinot N.

Château Benoit Willamette Valley Most consistent successes have been Müller-T and Ries. A recent entrant into sparkling wines.

Drouhin Willamette Valley Bold enterprise of one of Beaune's great names. Fine 89 Pinot N.

Elk Cove Vineyards Willamette Valley Pinot N from small estate has been somewhat erratic, steadier now and can rival the best. Also fresh Ries, well-oaked Chard and Pinot Gr.

Eyrie Vineyards, The Willamette Valley Pioneer ('65) winery with Burgundian convictions. Oregon's most famous and consistently good Pinot N and v oaky Chard. Also Pinots Gr (irreplaceable with salmon) and Meunier, and dry Muscat.

Knudsen-Erath Willamette Valley Oregon's second-largest winery, established itself with good value Pinot N and Chard, less consistent in recent vintages.

Montinore Willamette Valley Ambitious winery with, for Oregon, huge 465-acre v'yd nr Forest Grove.

Oak Knoll Willamette Valley Started with fruit wines but has turned into one of Oregon's larger and more skilful Pinot N producers.

Ponzi Willamette Valley Small winery almost in Portland,well-known for Ries. Also Pinot Gr, Chard and delicate Pinot N.

Rex Hill Willamette Valley Well-financed assault on top levels of Pinot N (quality, price): some success, esp from single v'yds. Also Chard, Ries.

Shafer Vineyard Cellars Willamette Valley Meticulous small producer of frequently good Pinot N, sometimes excellent, delicate Chard.

Sokol Blosser Willamette Valley One of the larger Oregon wineries; aims at popular taste with easy, accessible Chard, Ries and Pinot N. Also Sauv Bl, Merlot (seldom grown in Oregon).

Tualatin Vineyards Willamette Valley Substantial estate winery: Chard, Pinot N (and white from Pinot N), Gewürz of ever more personal style.

Tyee Willamette Valley Recent arrival. Early vintages of Gewürz, Chard, Pinot N are well made.

Yamhill Valley Willamette Valley Young estate near college town of McMinnville focuses on Chard and Pinot N.

Washington/Idaho

Arbor Crest Spokane (Washington) Expanding winery has had ups and downs. Ups are Chard and Sauv Bl.

Barnard Griffin Prosser (Washington) Small producer of well-made Merlot, Chard and Sauv Bl.

Château Ste Chapelle Caldwell (Idaho, nr Boise) Top-drawer winemaking keeps intensely flavoured, impeccably balanced Chard, Ries from Washington and local v'yds nr forefront in NW. Reds on the rise.

Château Ste Michelle Ubiquitous in Washington Regional giant growing ever larger. Owners had Château Ste M and COLUMBIA CREST at 750,000 cases before '91 acquisition of Snoqualmie, then the state's second-largest producer. Major v'yd holdings, first-rate equipment and skilful winemakers keep Chard, Sém, Sauv Bl, Ries, Cab and Merlot in the front ranks. First serious efforts at sparkling are attractive.

Chinook Wines Yakima Valley (Washington) Owner-winemaker Kay Simon buying in Yakima Valley grapes for sturdy Chard, Sauv Bl and Merlot.

Columbia Crest Columbia Valley (Washington) CHATEAU STE MICHELLE label for well-made accessible wines priced one cut lower, most of them from big River Run v'yd.

Columbia Winery Woodinville (Washington) A pioneer ('62, as Associated Vintners): still a leader. Balanced stylish understated single-v'yd wines, esp Merlot (Milestone), Cabs (Otis, Red Willow), Syrah (Red Willow). Oak-fermented Woodburne Chard, elegant Pinot, fruity Sém impressive.

Covey Run Yakima Valley (Washington) Mostly estate wines. Intriguing Aligoté and Caille de Fumé; intense, often heady Merlot and Cab.

Gordon Brothers Columbia Valley (Washington) Tiny but promising cellar for Chard, Merlot and Cab.

Hedges Cellars Puget Sound (Washington) Esp for Washington's first (vg) Cab S-Merlot blend. Began as negociant label, now with own v'yd.

Hogue Cellars Yakima Valley (Washington) Leader in the region, best known at start for off-dry whites (esp Ries, Chenin Bl, Sauv Bl), but more recently memorable for stylish balanced Chard, Merlot, Cab.

Kiona Vineyards Yakima Valley (Washington) Good v'yd for substantial Cabs and (Austrian) Lembergers; fruity Chard and Ries.

Latah Creek Spokane (Washington) Small cellar, mainly for off-dry Chenin Bl, Ries. Erratic, esp with drier oak-aged types.

Leonetti Walla Walla (Washington) Harmonious though individualistic Cab and fine big-scale Merlot.

Neuharth W Washington Olympic Peninsula winery uses Yakima Valley grapes for supple balanced Cab (Chard fair, though not equal to reds).

Preston Wine Cellars Columbia Valley (Washington) Early winery with wide range of wines. Some eccentric, some sound and conventional.

Quilceda Creek Vintners Puget Sound (Washington) Ripe well-oaked Cab S from Columbia Valley grapes is the speciality.

Salishan Vancouver (Washington) Promising Pinot N from nr Willamette V.

Silver Lake nr Seattle (Washington) Fine regular and reserve Chard and Sauv Bl; promising Cab, Merlot.

Staton Hills Yakima Valley (Washington) Recently reliable, s'times excellent Cab; still gd off-dry white (Ries, Chenin, Gewürz). Also sparkling.

Stewart Vineyards Yakima Valley (Washington) Estate v'yds well-suited to whites, esp Chard and Ries. Latterly some promising Cabs.

Paul Thomas Bellevue (Washington) Started as (still is in part) a fruit winery; now: full-flavoured Chard, Sauv, Chenin Bl. Reds show promise.

Washington Hills Cellars Yakima Valley (Washington) Newly est. Winemaker Brian Carter making solid attractive Sém, Fumé Bl and Cab.

Waterbrook Walla Walla (Washington) Young winery gaining ground on leaders with esp Cab, Merlot, Sauv Bl.

Woodward Canyon Walla Walla (Washington) Small cellar with well-oaked ultra-bold Cab and buttery Chard.

The Eastern States & Canada

Producers in New York and other eastern states, as well as Ohio and Ontario, traditionally made wine from hardy native grapes, varieties of Vitis labrusca whose wine has strong 'foxy' flavour off-putting to non-initiates. To escape the labrusca flavour, growers then turned to more nuanced French-American hybrids. Today fashion has largely bypassed these, although Seyval Blanc and Vidal keeps their fans. Eastern growers plant European varieties. Success is mixed, but progress, from Virginia to British Columbia, is fast.

Allegro Established Pennsylvania producer of noteworthy Chard, Cab, late-harvest Seyval Blanc.

Aurora (Aurore) One of the best white French-American hybrids, the most widely planted in New York. Good for sparkling.

Baco Noir One of the better red French-American hybrids. High acidity but clean dark wine that usually needs ageing.

Banfi V'yd at Old Brookville, LONG ISLAND, with good Chards.

Bedell LONG ISLAND winery known for first-class Merlot.

Bridgehampton LONG ISLAND (S Fork) estate. Variable Chard.

Brights Canada's biggest producer, in Ontario. Wine from Canadian and foreign grapes. Sawmill Creek label incl worthy Chard, Fumé Bl, BACO NOIR, Merlot-Baco Noir blend. Also in British Columbia.

Canandaigua Wine Co Major producer (the third largest in the US, behind Gallo and Heublein) of labrusca, dessert and sparkling wines. Bought WIDMER'S in '86. Also in California.

Catawba Old native American grape, perhaps the second most widely grown. Pale red and 'foxy' flavoured. Appears in crowd-pleasing, dry, off-dry and sweet styles.

Cave Spring Ontario boutique: sophisticated Chard and Ries.

Cayuga White hybrid created at Cornell Univ. Delicate fruity off-dry wine.

Chaddsford Pennsylvania producer since '82; esp for burgundy-style Chard.

Chambourcin Red grape of French origin; under-appreciated Bordeaux-like reds and agreeable rosé.

Château des Charmes Small Ontario winery. Good Chard, Aligoté, Cab.

Chautauqua See Lake Erie.

Chelois Popular red hybrid. Dry medium-bodied burgundy-style wine.

Clinton Vineyards Hudson River winery known for clean dry Seyval Bl and spirited Seyval sparkling.

Concord Labrusca variety, by far the most widely planted grape in New York. Heavy 'foxy' sweet red wines, but mostly grape juice and jelly. Long a staple of kosher wines.

Debonné Vineyards Popular Ohio estate: hybrids, eg CHAMBOURCIN and VIDAL; and vinifera, eg Chard, Ries.

De Chaunac French-American hybrid found in New York and Canada. Too often the usually full dark wine can be disagreeable.

Delaware Old pink American grape. Makes charming floral slightly 'foxy' dry and off-dry white still wines. Also used for sparkling.

Finger Lakes Beautiful historic upstate NY cool-climate region, source of most of the state's best wines, and the seat of its 'vinifera revolution'.

Firelands Ohio estate on Isle St George in LAKE ERIE, growing Chard and Cab. Owned by Meier's Wine Cellars, Ohio's biggest producer.

Frank, Dr Konstantin (Vinifera Wine Cellars) Small but influential winery. The late Dr F was a pioneer in growing European vines in the FINGER LAKES. Wines good, if uneven. Vg new Chateau Frank sparkling.

Gehringer Bros Okanagan Valley, BC. Good Ries, Ehrenfelser, Müller-T.

Glenora Wine Cellars Established FINGER LAKES producer of outstanding sparkling wine and good Chard.

Gray Monk US's N'most v'yd (Okanagen Valley, BC). Good Kerner, Gewürz.

Gristina Promising young winery on LONG ISLAND's North Fork.

Hargrave Vineyard Pioneering, well-established winery on North Fork of LONG ISLAND. Good Cab and Chard.

Hillebrand Estates Aggressive Ontario producer attracting attention with Chard, VIDAL ICE WINE and Ries.

Hunt Country Vineyards FINGER LAKES winery; makes friendly white blends and Vignoles (see Ravat).

Ice wine Wine made from frozen grapes. See Eiswein, page 103.

Inniskillin Top Ontario winery at Niagara-on-the-Lake. Skilful burgundy-style Chard, Pinot N; Ries, notable VIDAL ICE WINE. Good MARECHAL FOCH.

Johnson Estate Solid old down-home property in LAKE ERIE-CHAUTAUQUA region. Reds and whites from American and hybrid grapes.

Knapp Versatile FINGER LAKES winery. Tasty Cab, Ries, Bl de Bls sparkling.

Lake Erie The biggest grape-growing district in the east; 25,000 acres along the shore of Lake Erie, incl portions of New York, Pennsylvania and Ohio. 90% is CONCORD, most heavily in CHAUTAUQUA County.

Lamoreaux Landing New FINGER LAKES house: promising Chard and Ries.

Lenz Classy winery on N Fork of LONG ISLAND. Good Chard, Gewürz, Merlot.

Long Island The most talked about new wine region E of the Rockies. Still defining itself. Most of its 15 wineries are on the North Fork. Best varieties: Chard, Cab, Merlot. A long growing season.

Maréchal Foch Workmanlike red French hybrid. Depending on vinification, yields boldly flavoured or nouveau-style wines.

Millbrook The No 1 Hudson River region winery. Money-no-object viticulture has lifted Millbrook into New York's firmament. Chards are splendid, Cab F can be delicious.

Niagara Quintessential labrusca greenish-white grape, sometimes called 'white Concord'. Makes lovely aromatic sweet wine and wants to be gobbled right off the vine.

Okanagan Valley The (dry) seat oif wine-growing in British Columbia.

Palmer Superior LONG ISLAND producer becoming a byword in the rough-and-tumble metropolitan market. Good Chard and Cab.

Pindar Vineyards Huge 245-acre mini-Gallo winery on North Fork, LONG ISLAND. Wide range of popular varietals, incl Chard, Merlot, and an esp good Bordeaux-type red blend, Mythology.

Ravat (Vignoles) French-American white hybrid of intense flavour and high acidity, often made in yummy 'late harvest' style.

Rivendell Hudson River producer now a hot property winning countless awards for Chard, Seyval Bl and proprietary blends.

Sakonnet Largest New England winery, based in Little Compton, Rhode Island. Its regional reputation, resting on Chard, VIDAL and dry Gewürz, has blossomed since '85.

Summerhill Enter British Columbia with a bang. Heavy investment; charming results in sparkling Riesling.

Swedish Hill Creditable Ries from FINGER LAKES. Also Chancellor and late-harvest Vignoles.

Treleaven Promising FINGER LAKES winery. Good Ries and Chard.

Vidal Mainstay French-American hybrid: full-bodied personable dry whites.

Vineland Estates Good Ontario producer whose VIDAL ICE WINE, dry and semi-dry Ries and Ries Ice Wine are admired.

Wagner Vineyards Jewel of a winery in the FINGER LAKES – arguably New York's best – for succulent barrel-fermented Chard, dry and sweet Ries, RAVAT ICE WINE, NIAGARA and good Pinot N.

Widmer's Big FINGER LAKES winery specializing in native American wines, esp a fine sparkling NIAGARA. Also Manischewitz kosher wines.

Wiemer, Hermann J Creative, German-born FINGER LAKES winemaker. Interesting Ries incl vg sparkling and 'late harvest' versions.

Woodbury The top LAKE ERIE-CHAUTAUQUA winery. Good Chard and sparkling.

Virginia

Virginia's significant modern wine-growing, which began in 1972, is coming into its own. Whites, especially Chardonnay, lead the way. With 43 wineries producing good Chardonnay, Riesling, Cabernet Sauvignon, Cabernet Franc and Merlot from 1,300 acres of grapes, Virginia is one of the more versatile new wine states. The most important producers include Prince Michel Vineyards (the largest), Barboursville Vineyards, as well as Ingleside Plantation Vineyards, Linden Vineyards, Naked Mountain Vineyard, Meredyth Vineyards, Montdomaine Cellars, Oasis Vineyard (for its 'Champagne') Piedmont Vineyards, Rapidan River Vineyards and the Williamsburg Winery.

Missouri

A blossoming wine industry, with 29 producers, some of whom make good Seyvals, Vidals and dessert Vignoles. The best estate is Stone Hill, in Hermann, founded in 1847, which makes a sumptuous red from an American grape known as Norton (or Cynthiana). Hermannhof, in the same town (founded 1852), is drawing notice for the same varieties. Mount Pleasant, in Augusta, makes a rich 'port' and a nice sparkler. Names to watch: Augusta Winery, Blumenhof, Les Bourgeois, Montelle, Röbller, St James.

Maryland

Catoctin, a boutique winery with mountain vineyards, is building a reputation for solid, modestly priced Cabernet Sauvignons and Chardonnays. The state's best-known producer is Boordy Vineyards, which gets good marks for Seyval, Vidal and Cabernet Sauvignon.

The Southwest

Texas

In the past few years a brand-new Texan wine industry has sprung noisily to life. It already seems past the experimental stage, with 450 growers and 25 wineries now active. Texan wines have begun to show some form. Principal wineries are:

Bell Mountain Vineyards Hill-county winery at Fredericksberg. 52 acres. Erratic but known for Cab S.

Cap Rock 120 acres nr Lubbock since '90. Chard, Chenin Bl, Sauv Bl and sparkling all promising.

Cordier Estates (Ste-Genevieve Vineyards) Much the largest producer, leasing 1,000 acres for Sauv Bl. Links with Cordier of Bordeaux.

Fall Creek Vineyards Hill-county estate with 65 acres, making fine Sauv Bl and Chard. Also Cab S.

Leftwich Small production of good Chard from v'yds at Lubbock; winery nr Austin.

Llano Estacado Pioneer nr Lubbock with 220 acres (210 leased). Known for Chard and Cab S.

Pheasant Ridge Lubbock estate founded '78. Now 36 acres. Esp for reds.

South America

Argentina

Argentina has the world's fifth-largest wine production, most of it uncritically consumed within S America. But things are stirring. The country's crop of gold medals at Vinexpo Bordeaux '89 surprised everyone. Quality vineyards (all irrigated) are concentrated in Mendoza province in the Andean foothills at about 2,000 feet. San Rafael, 140 miles south of Mendoza city, is slightly cooler. Salta to the north and Rio Negro, south, also produce interesting wines. Modernization is now rapid; exports increasing, while the domestic market begins to demand higher standards.

Bianchi, Bodegas Well-known premium wine producer at San Rafael owned by Seagram. Don Valentin Cab and Bianchi Borgoña are best-sellers. 'Particular' is their top Cab.

Canale, Bodegas The Premier Rio Negro winery: Cab and Sém both won Bordeaux gold medals.

Crillon, Bodegas Owned by Seagram, only for tank-method sparkling.

Esmeralda Producers of a good Cab and Chard, St Felician, at Mendoza.

Etchart Salta winery. Typical aromatic but dry Torrontes white (gold medal at Bordeaux, '87); sound range of reds in Salta and Mendoza.

Flichman, Bodegas Old Mendoza firm now owned by a bank. Top Caballero de la Cepa white and red, plus Syrah, Merlot and sparkling.

Goyenechea, Bodegas Basque family firm in San Rafael making old-style wines, including Aberdeen Angus red.

Lopez, Bodegas Family firm best known for their Château Montchenot red and white and Château Vieux Cab.

Luigi Bosca, Bodegas Small Mendoza winery with excellent Malbec, Cab S and Syrah; also interesting Chard, Sauv Bl and Ries.

Martins Recent notable Merlot and Malbec from Mendoza.

Nacari, Bodegas Small La Rioja cooperative. Its Torrontes white won a gold medal and Oscar at Vinexpo, Bordeaux '87.

Norton, Bodegas Old firm, originally English, now Austrian-owned. Reds (esp Malbec) are best. Perdriel is premium brand. Also good sparkling.

Orfila, José Long-established bodega at St Martin, Mendoza. Top wines: Cautivo Cab and white Extra Dry (Pinot Bl). Now making sparkling wine in France for local sale.

Peñaflor Argentina's biggest wine co, reputedly the world's third largest. Bulk wines, but also some of Argentina's finest: TRAPICHE (esp Medalla), Andean V'yds, Fond de Cave (Chard, Cab). Exported 'Sherry': Tio Quinto.

Perez Cuesta Small new winery with outstanding reds, esp Syrah (Gold Medal at Vinexpo '91) and Malbec.

H Piper Sparkling wine made under licence from Piper-Heidsieck.

Proviar, Bodega Producers of Baron B and M Chandon sparkling wine under Moët & Chandon supervision. Also still reds and whites including vg Castel Chandon, less exciting Kleinburg, Wunderwein (whites), smooth Comte de Valmont, Beltour and Clos du Moulin reds.

Rural, Bodegas La ('San Filipe') Family-run winery at Coquimbito (Mendoza) making some of Argentina's best Ries and Gewürz whites and some good reds. Also a charming wine museum.

Santa Ana, Bodegas Old-established family firm at Guaymallen, Mendoza. Wide range incl good Syrah Val Semina and sparkling 'Villeneuve'.

San Telmo Modern winery with a Californian air and outstanding fresh full-flavoured Chard, Merlot, Cab and esp Malbec.

Suter, Bodegas Swiss-founded firm owned by Seagram making best-selling Etiquetta Marron white and good classic 'JS' red.

Toso, Pascual Old Mendoza winery at San José, making one of Argentina's best reds, Cabernet Toso. Also Ries and sparkling wines (incl one méthode traditionelle).

Trapiche Premium label of PENAFLOR and a spearhead of technical advance. Single-grape wine range incls Merlot, Malbec, Cab S, Pinot N, Chard and Torrontes. Also 'Oak Cask' selection.

Weinert, Bodegas Small winery. Tough old-fashioned reds led by good Cab-Merlot-Malbec Cavas de Weinert and promising Sauv Bl.

Chile

Conditions are ideal for wine-growing in central Chile, the Maipo Valley near Santiago, and for 150 miles south. But the country's potential has only started to emerge in the past seven years. So far wines are good – not yet fine. Irrigation is universal. Chilean Cabernets have led the way with original flavours, rapidly gaining in quality. Other varieties, especially Sauvignon Blanc and Chardonnay, now show equal promise. Stainless steel and new oak have bought international standards. A new region (Casablanca), between Santiago and Valparaiso on the coast, is proving especially good for Chardonnay. Top wineries, including most of those following, are members of the Asociación de Exportadores y Embotelladores de Vinos AG. Many long-time growers are no longer supplying large bodegas but branching out, even exporting, alone.

Bisquertt Colchagua winery (1,056 acres) for generations owned by family of same name. Began exporting in '91.

Caliterra Former venture of ERRAZURIZ and Franciscan of California. Now solely owned by Errazuriz. Good value Chard, Cab.

Canepa, José Chile's most modern big bodega, of Italian origin, handling wine from several areas. Vg frank and fruity Cab from Lontüé, Curico, and 100 miles south; recently particularly good Chard (some oak-aged), RIES and Sauv Bl. Top wines from Domaine Caperana.

Carta Vieja 770 acres in Maule. Del Pedregal family-owned for 6 generations.

Casablanca Second bodega of VINA SANTA CAROLINA. For premium wines.

Concha y Toro Biggest, most outward-looking wine firm, with several bodegas and v'yds all over Chile incl 2,500 acres in the Maipo Valley. Remarkable dark deep Cab, Merlot, Petit Verdot. Brands are Marqués de Casa Concha, Casillero del Diablo. Chard and Sauv Bl now well est. New top wine: Don Melchor Cab. Banfi (USA) are minority shareholders.

Cousiño Macul Distinguished and beautiful old estate nr Santiago. V dry Sém and Chard. Don Luis light red, Don Matias dark and tannic, are good Cabs. Antiguas Reservas is top export Cab.

Domaine Oriental French-owned modern winery in Maule Valley, Talca.

Domaine Rabat Since 1927 in Maipo and Colchagua; offers Cab, Chard, Sauv Bl. Different labels from each estate incl Dom Rabat, Santa Adela.

Echeverria Grower from Curicó now producing good Sauv Bl.

Errazuriz Historic firm in Aconcagua Valley, N of Santiago, modernized and making v rich full-bodied wines, esp Cab Don Maximiano.

Exposicion Label of Talca Coop. Growers cover 1,625 v'yd acres.

Lomas de Cauquenes Cooperative formed by Cauquenes growers after 1939 earthquake. Grapes from 650 acres.

Montes 250-acre estate at Curico emerging as a leader with good fresh Sauv Bl; Chard and Fumé Bl aged in American oak; light Merlot, good Montes Cab S and excellent Montes Alpha (89) from French oak. Nogales and Villa Montes are unoaked less expensive wines.

Robles, Los Label of coop of Curico. Wines incl Cab and Merlot.

Saint Morillon Lontüé bodega with Sauv Bl, Chard, Cab, Cab Reserva. Now favouring Valdivieso label incl popular sparkling wine. Owned by Mitjan.

San Pedro Long established at Lontüé, Curico; now under Spanish control. One of the biggest exporters: range is good to vg. Gato Negro and Gato Blanco are top sellers. Castillo de Molina is top. Santa Helena is assoc.

Santa Ema 550-acre Maipo estate belonging to Pavone family since 1955. Esp Cab, Merlot, Sauv Bl and Chard.

Santa Emiliana Co-owned with CONCHA Y TORO. Second label popular in Canada and USA, Walnut Crest.

Santa Ines Family winery in Isla de Maipo. Labels: De Martino, Santa Ines.

Santa Monica Rancagua winery; best label is Tierra del Sol.

Segu-Olle Linares estate owned by two Catalan families. Label: Caliboro.

Tarapaca Ex Zavala Producer rated in Chile for red wines.

Torreon de Paredes Recent family-owned bodega (253 acres). Modern; no expense spared. Good Reserva Cab.

Torres, Miguel Enterprise of Catalan family firm (see Spain) at Lontüé sets a modern pace. Good Sauv Bl (Bellaterra is oak-aged) and Chard, vg Ries. Cab is made more 'elegantly' than other Chileans.

Undurraga Famous family business; one of first to export to the USA. Old and modern style wines: good clean Sauv Bl, oaky yellow Viejo Roble.

Vascos, Los Family estate in Colchagua Province. 400 acres. Some of Chile's best Cab (Bordeaux- and California-influenced). Also stylish Sauv-Sém. Made headlines in '88 by link with Lafite-Rothschild (50% owners). Wines from '87 have been excellent.

Villard Recent venture of Frenchman Thierry Villard.

Viña Carmen A second bodega of SANTA RITA.

Viña Porta Newly created winery in Rancagua. Cabs look promising.

Viña Portal del Alto Small bodega with excellent Cab-Merlot blend.

Viña Santa Carolina Architecturally splendid old Santiago bodega with old-style 'Reserva de Familia'.

Viña Santa Rita Long-established bodega in the Maipo Valley S of Santiago. Medalla Real Cab and Reserva are best-sellers abroad.

Vinicola Montealegre CANEPA'S 2nd bodega. Labels: Rowan Brook, Peteroa.

Brazil

European grape variety plantings are transforming Brazilian wines. International investments, esp in Rio Grande do Sul and Santana do Liuramento, esp from France (eg Moët & Chandon), are significant. Exports are beginning.

Mexico

The oldest American wine industry has upgraded quality. Good in Baja California (85% of total) and at Aguascalientes. Some of the better Baja C producers: L A Cetto (in Valle de Guadaloupe, the largest, esp for Cab S and Syrah), Bodegas Santo Tomas (since 1888, Mexico's oldest), Monte Xanic (with Napa-award winning Cabernet), Bodegas San Antonio, and Cavas de Valmar.

Peru

Viña Tacama near Ica exports some very promising wines, especially the Gran Vino Blanco white. But serious phylloxera.

Uruguay

Winemaking since 1700s, influenced along the way by France, Spain, Germany and Italy. Great efforts are currently being made, with French advice and grape varieties, to improve wine from the 30,000 acres of warm, humid vineyards. At present it is of local and tourist interest only. 50% is planted with hybrids.

Australia

Australia's wine industry is now the most dynamic, creative and self-critical in the world. Not only are all importing countries aware of the quality and value for money of its wines, but other producing countries, even France, are reflecting its influence. Yet it is little more than 20 years since new technology made top quality Australian table wines possible. Old-style wines were burly Shiraz reds, or Sémillon or Riesling whites, grown in warm regions. A progressive shift to cooler areas, to new wood fermentation and ageing, with Cabernet, Chardonnay, Pinot Noir and Sauvignon Blanc at the forefront, has seen a radical change in style which still seems to gather pace. Nonetheless flavour and strength continue to be Australian hallmarks and the best wines still have great character and the ability to age splendidly.

Exports have been the great success story over the last seven years, increasing from eight million to 100 million litres. But it is not easy to keep tabs on individual wines. There are now almost 700 wineries in commercial production. Labels are becoming less garrulous (but less informative) as Australian consumers become more sophisticated. Such information as they give can be relied on, while prizes in shows (which are highly competitive) mean a great deal. In a country lacking any formal grades of quality the buyer needs all the help he or she can get.

Wine areas

The vintages here are those rated as good or excellent for the reds of the areas in question. Excellent recent vintages are marked by an accent.

Adelaide Hills (S Aus) 84' 85 86' 88 90 91' Spearheaded by PETALUMA: 22 wineries at v cool, 450-metre sites in the Mt Lofty ranges.

Adelaide Plains (S Aus) 82 84' 86' 87 88' 90 91 Small area immediately N of Adelaide, formerly known as Angle Vale. Wineries incl Lauriston, Minton Grove, PRIMO ESTATE.

Barossa (S Aus) 66 76 80 82 84' 86' 87 88 90' 91 Australia's most important winery (though not v'yd) area, processing grapes from diverse sources (local, to MURRAY VALLEY; high quality cool regions: from adjacent hills, to COONAWARRA far to the south) to make correspondingly diverse wines.

Bendigo/Ballarat (Vic) 73 75 80' 82' 84 87 88 89 91' 92' Wide-spread small v'yds, some of extreme quality, recreating the glories of the last century. 19 wineries incl BALGOWNIE, CHATEAU LE AMON, HEATHCOTE and Passing Clouds.

Canberra District (ACT) 18 wineries now sell 'cellar door' to local and tourist trade. Quality is variable, as is style.

Clare Watervale (S Aus) 71' 75' 80' 82 84' 85 86' 89 90 91 Small, high quality area 90 miles N of Adelaide, best for Ries; also Shiraz and Cab. 23 wineries spill over into new adjacent subdistrict, Polish Hill River.

Coonawarra (S Aus) 66 71 76' 79 80' 82' 84' 86' 87 88 90' 91 Southernmost and finest v'yd of state: most of Australia's best Cab, successful Chard and Shiraz. New arrivals incl Balnaves, PARKER ESTATE, Penley Estate.

Geelong (Vic) 80' 82' 84 85 86 88 90 91 92' Once famous area destroyed by phylloxera, re-established mid-'60s. V cool dry climate: firm table wines from vg grapes. Names incl BANNOCKBURN, IDYLL, SCOTCHMAN'S HILL.

Goulburn Valley (Vic) 68 71' 76 80' 82 85 86 88 90 91' 92' A mixture of v old (eg CHATEAU TAHBILK) and relatively new (eg MITCHELTON) wineries in a temperate region; full-flavoured table wines.

Granite Belt (Qld) 85 87' 88 90 91 Rapidly developing, high altitude and (relatively) cool region just N of NSW border, with 15 wineries: spicy Shiraz and rich Sém-Chard are district specialities.

Great Western (Vic) 78 80' 82' 84' 85 86 88 90 91' 92' Temperate region in central W of state. High quality table and sparkling wines. Now 9 wineries, 7 of recent origin.

Hunter Valley (NSW) 66' 67 73 75' 79' 83 85 86' 87 91' The great name in NSW. Broad soft earthy Shiraz reds and Sém whites that live for 30 yrs. Cab not important; Chard increasingly so.

Margaret River (W Aus) 73' 76 79' 81 82' 85' 86' 87 90 91 92' Temperate coastal area producing superbly elegant wines 174 miles S of Perth. 30 operating wineries; others planned.

Mornington Peninsula (Vic) 84' 86' 87 88 90 91 92' Exciting wines in new cool coastal area 25 miles S of Melbourne. 400 acres. 28 commercial wineries on dolls-house scale incl DROMANA, ELGEE PARK, Merricks.

Mount Barker/Frankland River (W Aus) 80 81' 83 85 86 87 89 90 92' Promising, new, far-flung, cool area in extreme S of state; GOUNDREY and PLANTAGENET are the two biggest and best wineries.

Mudgee (NSW) 74 75 78 79 83 84' 86 87 90 91 Small isolated area 168 miles NW of Sydney. Big reds of colour and flavour, full Chards; from (23 wineries).

Murray Valley (S Aus, Vic & NSW) vintages not normally important Key irrigated v'yds nr Mildara, Swan Hill (Vic and NSW), Berri, Loxton, Morgan, Renmark and Waikerie (S Aus). Principally 'cask' table wines. 40% of total Australian wine production.

NE Victoria 66' 70' 71' 75' 80' 82' 86' 87 88 90 92' Historic area incl Corowa, Rutherglen, Wangaratta. Generally heavy reds and magnificent sweet dessert wines. 25 wineries.

Padthaway (S Aus) 80 82' 84 85 86' 87 88 90' 91 Large v'yd area (no wineries) developed by big companies as an overspill of COONAWARRA. Cool climate; some good Pinot N reds, excellent Chard (esp LINDEMANS and HARDY'S), also Chard-Pinot N sparkling wines.

Perth Hills (W Aus) Fledgling area 19 miles E of Perth with 11 wineries and a larger number of growers on mild hillside sites.

Pyrenees (Vic) 82 84 85 86 87 88 90 91' 92' Central Vic region with 8 wineries: rich minty reds and some interesting whites, esp Fumé Bl.

For key to grape variety abbreviations, see pages 6–9.

Riverina (NSW) NV Large-volume producer centred around Griffith; good quality 'cask' wines (esp white), great sweet botrytised Sém.

Southern Vales (S Aus) 71' 77 80' 82' 84 85 86' 87 88 90 91' Covers energetic McLaren Vale/REYNELLA regions on S outskirts of Adelaide. Big reds now being rapidly improved; promising Chard.

Swan Valley (W Aus) 75' 78' 81' 82' 84' 85' 86 88 89' 90 91' The birthplace of wine in the west, on the N outskirts of Perth. Hot climate makes strong low-acid table wines, but good dessert wines. Declining in importance viticulturally.

Tasmania 82' 84' 86 87 88' 90 91' 38 v'yds now offer wine for commercial sale, producing over 700,000 litres. Great potential for Chard, Pinot N and Ries in cool climate.

Upper Hunter (NSW) 75' 79' 80' 81' 83' 85' 86' 87 90 91' Est early '60s; irrigated vines producing mainly white wines, lighter and quicker-developing than Lower Hunter Valley whites. Often good value.

Yarra Valley ('Lilydale') 76 78' 80' 81 82 84' 85 86' 88' 90' 91' 92' Historic wine area nr Melbourne, now being rapidly redeveloped by enthusiasts: 33 small wineries. Growing emphasis on v successful Pinot N. A superb v'yd area; noble varieties only; almost 2,000 acres.

Wineries

Alkoomi (Mount Barker) ★★→★★★ 20-year veteran producing 15,000 cases of fine steely Ries and potent long-lived reds incl rare Malbec.

Allandale (Hunter Valley) ★→★★ Small winery without v'yds, buying selected local grapes. Quality variable; can be good, esp Chard.

Allanmere (Hunter Valley) ★★→★★★ Small winery run by expatriate English doctor, making excellent Sém, Chard and smooth reds.

All Saints (NE Vic) ★→★★ Once famous old family winery bought in '92 by BROWN BROTHERS.

Angove's (Riverland, S Aus) ★→★★ Long-est MURRAY VALLEY family business in Adelaide and Renmark. Notable value in Cab and whites, esp Chard.

Arrowfield (Upper Hunter) ★★ Large irrigated v'yd. Light Cab, succulent Reserve Chard; also wooded Sém. Majority owned by Japanese co.

Bailey's (NE Vic) ★★→★★★★ Rich old-fashioned reds of great character, esp Bundarra Hermitage, and magnificent dessert Muscat and 'Tokay'. Now part of ROTHBURY group.

Balgownie (Bendigo/Ballarat) ★★★ Fine reds, particularly straight Cab. Also occasional exceptional Chard. Now owned by MILDARA.

Bannockburn (Geelong) ★★★ Intense complex Chard and Pinot N using Burgundian techniques.

Basedow (Barossa Valley) ★★→★★★ Smallish winery buying grapes for reliably good range of red and white; Sém 'White Burgundy' esp good.

Berri-Renmano Coop (Riverland, S Aus) ★→★★ See Renmano.

Best's (Great Western) ★★→★★★ Conservative old family winery in GREAT WESTERN with good mid-weight reds, and Chard not half bad.

Blass, Wolf (Bilyara) (Barossa) ★★★ The ebullient German winemaker merged his business with MILDARA in late '91. Dazzling labels, extraordinary wine-show successes, mastery of blending varieties and areas, and lashings of new oak all continue, though the signs are that less extreme sensations are on the way.

Botobolar (Mudgee) ★★ Marvellously eccentric little organic winery. Gill Wahlquist exports successfully to the UK.

Bowen Estate (Coonawarra) ★★★ Small winery; intense but not heavy Cab and spicy Shiraz.

Brand (Coonawarra) ★★→★★★ Family estate now half owned by McWILLIAMS. Fine bold and stylish Chard, Cab and Shiraz under Laira label. A few quality blemishes in late '70s/early '80s now rectified.

Bridgewater Mill (Adelaide Hills) ★★★ Second label of PETALUMA; suave wines, Sauv Bl and Shiraz best.

Brokenwood (Hunter Valley) ★★★ Exciting quality of Cab and Shiraz since '73 – Graveyard Shiraz is outstanding. New winery in '83 added high quality Chard and Sém.

Brown Brothers (Milawa, Vic) ★→★★★ Old family firm with new ideas, wide and reliable range of rather delicate single-grape wines, many from cool mountain districts. Chard, Ries and dry white Muscat continually outstanding. See also All Saints.

Buring, Leo (Barossa) ★★→★★★ 'Chateau Leonay', old white-wine specialists, now owned by LINDEMANS. Steady Reserve Bin Ries is great with age.

Campbells of Rutherglen (NE Vic)★★ Smooth ripe reds and good dessert wines, the latter in youthful fruity style.

Cape Clairault (Margaret River) ★★ Progressive producer of Sém, Sauv Bl and Cab, in reasonable quantities, with good progress in quality.

Cape Mentelle (Margaret River) ★★→★★★★ Idiosyncratic robust Cab departs from district style and can be magnificent; also Zinfandel and v popular Sém. David Hohnen also founded Cloudy Bay, NZ. Both were bought in '90 by Veuve Clicquot.

Capel Vale (SW W Aus) ★★★ Outstanding range of whites, incl Ries and Gewürz. Also vg Cab.

Cassegrain (Hastings Valley, NSW) ★★→★★★ New winery on NSW coast, taking grapes both from local plantings and from HUNTER VALLEY.

Chambers' Rosewood (NE Vic) ★★→★★★ Good cheap table and great dessert wines, esp 'Tokay'.

Chapel Hill (McLaren Vale, S Aus) ★★→★★★★ Once tiny, now booming producer of extra-rich fruity-oaky Chard, Shiraz and Cab, all big show successes.

Chateau Le Amon (Bendigo) ★★★ V stylish minty Cab and peppery Shiraz.

Chateau Francois (Hunter Valley) ★★ Idiosyncratic operation of former Fisheries Director: clean reds, soft whites and great olives.

Chateau Hornsby (Alice Springs, N Territory) ★→★★ A charming aberration and magnet for tourists to Ayer's Rock.

Chateau Rémy (Great Western/Avoca) ★★ Owned by Rémy Martin. Sparkling based on Chard and Pinot N is much improved. Also good Blue Pyrenees Cab S.

Chateau Reynella (S Vales) ★→★★★ Histoic winery serving as HQ for BRL Hardy group. Pleasant table wines, superb vintage Port.

Chateau Tahbilk (Goulburn Valley) ★★→★★★ Beautiful and historic family estate making long-lived Cab, Shiraz, Ries and Marsanne. Private Bins are outstanding; value for money ditto. Sadly, Eric Purbrick died in '91. His grandson presses on.

Chateau Yaldara (Barossa) ★→★★ Busy producer of plethora of brands incl Acacia Hill, Lakewood, Robert Thumm and Chateau Yaldara; oaky, slightly sweet and cheap.

Coldstream Hills (Yarra Valley) ★★★→★★★★ Well-known winery, built in '87 by wine critic James Halliday. International acclaim for prize-winning Pinot, vg Chard (esp Reserve wines), delicate Cab and Merlot.

Conti, Paul (Swan Valley) ★★ Elegant 'Hermitage', also fine Chard and other whites.

Coriole (S Vales) ★★→★★★ Shiraz (esp Lloyd Reserve) from old estate vines; nicely balanced by oak is best, others solid.

Craigmoor (Mudgee) ★★ Oldest district winery, now part of ORLANDO group. Good Chard and Sém (the two are also blended), and Cab-Shiraz.

Croser (Adelaide Hills) ★★★→★★★★ Now Australia's top sparkling Chard-Pinot N blend. Offshoot of PETALUMA with Bollinger as partner. Lean, fine, with splendid backbone from Pinot N.

Cullens Willyabrup (Margaret River) ★★★ Mother-daughter team pioneered the region with butch but kindly Cab-Merlot, substantial but subtle Sauv Bl and bold Chard: all real characters.

Dalwhinnie (Pyrenees) ★★→★★★★ 3,500-case producer of concentrated rich Chard, Shiraz and Cab S, arguably the best in PYRENEES.

d'Arenberg (S Vales) ★→★★ Old-style family outfit making strapping rustic reds and Ries.

De Bortoli (Griffith, NSW) ★→★★★ Irrigation-area winery. Standard reds and whites but magnificent sweet botrytised Sauternes-style Sém. See also next entry.

De Bortoli (Yarra Valley) ★★→★★★ Formerly Ch Yarrinya: bought by De Bortoli and now YARRA's largest producer. Main label good to adequate; second label, Windy Peak, vg value.

Delatite (Central Vic) ★★★ Rosalind Ritchie makes appropriately willowy and feminine Ries, Gewürz, Pinot N and Cab from this v cool mountainside v'yd.

Diamond Valley (Yarra Valley) ★★→★★★ Producer of outstanding Pinot N in significant quantities; other wines good rather than great.

Domaine Chandon (Yarra Valley) ★★★ The showpiece of the YARRA VALLEY. Sparkling wine from grapes grown in all the cooler parts of Australia, with strong direction from owner Moët & Chandon. Immediate success in UK under Green Point label.

Drayton's Bellevue (Hunter Valley) ★★ Traditional 'Hermitage' and Sém, occasionally good Chard; recent quality improvements after a lapse.

Dromana Estate (Mornington Peninsula) ★★★ Largest and best producer in district. Great skill in making light but fragrant Cab, Pinot N and Chard. Second label: Schinus Molle.

Eaglehawk (Clare) ★→★★★ Formerly Quelltaler. Once known for Granfiesta 'Sherry'. Recently good Ries and Sém. Owned by MILDARA BLASS.

Elgee Park (Mornington Pensinsula) ★★ Region's longest-established v'yd producing good Cab-Merlot, Chard, Ries and a hatful of Viognier.

Evans and Tate (Swan Valley) ★★→★★★ Fine elegant Sém, Chard, Cab, Merlot from MARGARET RIVER, Redbrook. SWAN VALLEY Gnangara v'yds give useful Cab-Shiraz.

Evans Family (Hunter Valley) ★★★ Excellent Chard from small v'yd owned by family of Len Evans and made at ROTHBURY ESTATE. Fermented in new oak. Repays cellaring.

Freycinet (Tasmania) ★★→★★★ East coast winery producing voluptuous rich Pinot N, good Chard and Cab.

Forest Hills (Mount Barker) ★★→★★★ Pioneer v'yd in region, now in common ownership with VASSE FELIX. Ries and Chard can be and usually are excellent.

Geoff Merrill (S Vales) ★→★★★ Ebullient maker of Geoff Merrill, Mount Hurtle and Cockatoo Ridge wines, sometimes elegant, sometimes a little thin.

Giaconda (Central Vic) ★★★ Very small but ultra-fashionable winery nr Beechworth, producing eagerly sought Chard and Pinot N.

Goundrey Wines (Great Southern, W Aust) ★★★ Recent expansion and quality upgrade. Now in first rank: esp good Cab and wooded whites.

Grange See Penfolds.

Grant Burge Wines (Barossa) ★★→★★★ Rapidly expanding output of silky-smooth reds and whites from the best grapes of Burge's v'yd holdings. Burge was founder of KRONDORF.

Green Point See Domaine Chandon.

Hanging Rock (Macedon, Vic) ★→★★★ Eclectic range incl budget Picnic White and Red; huge Heathcote Shiraz; complex sparkling.

Hardy's (S Vales, Barossa, Keppoch, etc) ★→★★★ Historic company using and blending wines from several areas. Best are 'Collection' series and (Australia's greatest) 'Vintage Ports'. Hardy's bought HOUGHTON and REYNELLA and, most recently, STANLEY. Reynella's beautifully-restored buildings are now group headquarters. '92 merger with BERRI-RENMANO and public ownership (BRC Hardy) makes this Australia's second largest wine co.

Heathcote (Bendigo) ★★ Stylish producer of eclectic range showing abundant flavour and technical skill. But tends to syrupy Chard.

Heemskerk (Tasmania) ★★★ Most successful commercial operation in TASMANIA: herby Cab, promising Chard, also Pinot N and Ries. Recent partnership with Louis Roederer produced Jansz sparkling wine.

Heggies (Adelaide Hills) ★★ V'yd at 500m in E Barossa Ranges owned by S SMITH & SONS; separately marketed: excellent Ries and Botrytis Ries.

Henschke (Barossa) ★★★→★★★★ Family business, perhaps Australia's best, known for delectable Shiraz (esp Hill of Grace), vg Cab and red blends. New high-country v'yds on ADELAIDE HILLS add excitement.

Hill-Smith Estate (Adelaide Hills) ★★ Another separate brand of S SMITH & SONS; Sauv Bl and Cab-Shiraz can be outstanding value.

Hollick (Coonawarra) ★★★ Hollick family plus former TOLLANA winemaker: good Chard, Ries; much-followed reds, Whilga and Ravenswood.

Houghton (Swan Valley) ★→★★★ The most famous old winery of WA. Soft ripe 'White Burgundy' is their top wine; a national classic. Also excellent Cab, Verdelho etc. See Hardy's.

Huntington Estate (Mudgee) ★★→★★★ Small winery; the best in MUDGEE. Fine Cabs, clean Sém and Chard. Invariably under-priced.

Idyll (Geelong) ★★ Small winery making Gewürz and Cab in v individual style. Also 'Blush' rosé. A pioneer exporter.

Jeffrey Grosset (Clare) ★★→★★★ Exceedingly elegant Ries, Chard and Cab made in consistent style by fastidious winemaker.

Jim Barry Wines (Clare) ★★→★★★ Hard-working family firm now doing esp well with Ries; The Armagh is a spectacular (and expensive) pretender to the throne of GRANGE Hermitage.

Kaiser Stuhl (Barossa) ★→★★ Now part of PENFOLDS; a huge winery taking fruit from diverse sources. Diminishing importance as a brand.

Katnook Estate (Coonawarra) ★★★ Excellent pricey Cab and Chard; also Sauv Bl, Pinot N, Ries.

Krondorf Wines (Barossa) ★★→★★★ Part of MILDARA BLASS group with niche market brands: Show Reserve wines are best.

Lake's Folly (Hunter Valley) ★★★★ The work of an inspired surgeon from Sydney. Cab is v fine and complex. Chard exciting and age-worthy.

Lark Hill (Canberra District) ★★→★★★ Best and most consistent CANBERRA producer, making esp attractive Ries.

Leasingham (Clare) ★→★★★ Important medium-sized quality winery purchased by HARDY'S in '87. Good Ries, Sém, Chard and Cab-Malbec blends under Domaine label.

Leconfield (Coonawarra) ★★→★★★ COONAWARRA Cab of great style. Ries and Chard improving under former TYRRELL winemaker.

Leeuwin Estate (Margaret River) ★★→★★★★ Leading W Australia estate, lavishly equipped, producing superb (and v expensive) Chard; developing fine Pinot N, vg Ries, Sauv Bl and Cab.

Lehmann Wines, Peter (Barossa) ★★→★★★ Defender of the BAROSSA faith, Lehmann makes vast quantities of wine (some sold in bulk), with vg 'special cuvées' under own label. Under financial duress in '93, alas.

Lindemans (orig Hunter, now everywhere) ★→★★★ One of the oldest firms, now a giant owned by PENFOLDS. Owns BURING in BAROSSA, Rouge Homme in COONAWARRA, and important v'yds at PADTHAWAY. Outstanding Chard and Coonawarra reds. Pioneer of new styles, yet still makes fat, old-style 'Hunters'. Bin-number Classics can be v good. The dominant performer at wine shows.

Little's (Hunter Valley) ★★ Popular little winery with wide range of wines; energetic exporters.

McWilliams (Hunter Valley & Riverina) ★→★★★ Famous family of HUNTER winemakers at Mount Pleasant: 'Hermitage' and Sém – 'Elizabeth' is the only bottle-aged Sém (6 yrs) sold and is vg value. Also pioneers in RIVERINA with noble varieties, incl Cab and sweet white Lexia. Quality showing marked improvement.

Marsh Estate (Hunter Valley) ★★→★★★ Substantial producer of good Sém, Shiraz and Cab of growing quality.

Mildara (Coonawarra & Murray Valley) ★→★★★ 'Sherry' and brandy specialists at Mildara on Murray River, also make fine Cab and Ries at COONAWARRA. Now also own BALGOWNIE, BLASS, KRONDORF and YELLOWGLEN.

Miramar (Mudgee) ★★→★★★ Some of MUDGEE's best whites, esp Chard.

Mitchells (Clare) ★★★ Small family winery, excellent Ries and Cab.

Mitchelton (Goulburn Valley) ★★→★★★ Big, modern winery. A wide range incl a vg wood-matured Marsanne, Shiraz, Cab from COONAWARRA and classic Ries from Goulburn Valley is one of Australia's v best. Second label, Thomas Mitchell, is esp good value.

Montrose (Mudgee) ★★→★★★ Reliable, underrated producer of vg Chard, and Cab blends. Now part of the ORLANDO group.

Moondah Brook Estate (Gingin, WA) ★★ HOUGHTON v'yd 80 kms NW of Perth: v smooth flavourful Chard, Chenin Bl, Verdelho and Cab.

Moorilla Estate (Tasmania) ★★★ Senior winery on outskirts of Hobart on Derwent River: vg Ries, Traminer and Chard; Pinot N disappointing.

Morris (NE Vic) ★★→★★★★ Old winery at Rutherglen: Australia's greatest dessert Muscats and 'Tokays'; also recently vg low-price table wines.

Moss Wood (Margaret River) ★★★★ To many the best MARGARET RIVER winery (with only 29 acres). Sém, Cab, Pinot N, Chard, all with rich fruit flavours, not unlike top-class California wines.

Mountadam (Barossa) ★★★ High Eden winery of David and Adam Wynn. Chard is rich voluptuous long. Other labels incl David Wynn, Eden Ridge.

Mount Langi Ghiran (Great Western) ★★→★★★ Producer of superb rich peppery Rhône-like Shiraz, vg Cab and less exhilarating Ries.

Mount Avoca (Pyrenees) ★→★★ Solid alcoholic and at times distinctly rustic wines with considerable impact; the best age well.

Mount Helen (Strathbogie Ranges, Vic) ★→★★★ The high-altitude v'yd owned by TISDALL with its own brand; complex high-flavoured wines which only occasionally reach their full potential.

Mount Mary (Yarra Valley) ★★★ Dr John Middleton is a perfectionist making tiny amounts of suave Chard, vivid Pinot N, and (best of all) Cab S-Cab F-Merlot. All age well.

Murray Robson Wines (Hunter Valley) ★★ The reincarnation of Murray Robson in a winery nr ROTHBURY.

Orlando (Gramp's) (Barossa) ★★→★★★ Great pioneering company, bought by management in '88 but now owned by Pernod Ricard of France. Full range from best-selling Jacob's Creek 'Claret' to excellent Jacaranda Ridge Cab from COONAWARRA. See also Wyndham Estate.

Parker Estate (Coonawarra) ★★★ New estate making exceptional Cab, esp Terra Rossa First Growth.

Penfolds (orig Adelaide, now everywhere) ★→★★★★ Ubiquitous excellent co in BAROSSA, COONAWARRA, CLARE, RIVERINA, etc. Bought LINDEMANS in '90. Its Grange Hermitage (78 80 82') is deservedly ★★★★. Bin 707 Cab not far behind. Other bin-numbered wines (eg Cab-Shiraz 389) can be outstanding. Consistently Australia's best red-wine co. Grandfather 'Port' can be excellent. In late '90 Penfolds/Lindemans group was taken over by South Australian Brewing Co, already owner of SEPPELT.

Penley Estate (Coonawarra) ★★→★★★ High profile, no-expense-spared newcomer: rich, textured, fruit and oak Cab; also Shiraz-Cab, Chard.

Petaluma (Adelaide Hills) ★★★★ A rocket-like '80s success with COONAWARRA Cab, ADELAIDE HILLS Chard, CLARE Ries; all processed at winery in Adelaide Hills. Reds have become richer from 84 on, 88 and 90 are outstanding. Also: BRIDGEWATER MILL. Now owns TIM KNAPPSTEIN wines. See also Croser.

Petersons (Hunter Valley) ★★→★★★ For a time the most promising small HUNTER winery for exceptional Chard and vg Sém; recently wobbly.

Piper's Brook (Tasmania) ★★★ Cool-area pioneer with vg Ries and Pinot N, excellent Chard from the Tamar Valley nr Launceston. Lovely labels.

Pirramimma (S Vales) ★→★★ Big supply of good standard; reds best.

Plantagenet (Mount Barker) ★★→★★★ The region's largest producer: wide range of varieties, esp rich Chard, Shiraz and vibrant potent Cab.

Primo Estate (Adelaide Plains) ★★ Successes incl vg botrytised Ries.

Quelltaler See Eaglehawk.

Redman (Coonawarra) ★→★★ The most famous old name in COONAWARRA; makes two wines: 'Claret' and Cab. Recent quality disappointing.

Renmano (Murray Valley) ★→★★ Huge coop now part of BRC group (see Hardy's). 'Chairman's Selections' value. Exceedingly voluptuous Chard.

Reynella (S Vales) ★★→★★★ Historic red wine specialists S of Adelaide. Rich Cab (partly COONAWARRA), 'Claret' and fine 'Port'. See Hardy's.

Reynold's Yarraman Estate (Upper Hunter Valley) ★★ Former stone prison building promises well as winery of former HOUGHTON and WYNDHAM winemaker John Reynold.

Rockford (Barossa) ★★→★★★ Small producer, wide range of thoroughly individual wines, often made from v old, low-yielding v'yds.

Rosemount (Upper Hunter & Coonawarra) ★→★★★ Rich unctuous HUNTER 'Show' Chard is an international smash. This and COONAWARRA Cab lead the wide range.

Rothbury Estate (Hunter Valley) ★★★→★★★★ A true estate with over 500 acres of v'yd. Now a public listed company under chairmanship of Len Evans. Traditional HUNTER Shiraz and Séms to keep for ever. Rich buttery Cowra Chard is vg and good value too. HUNTER Chard now barrel-fermented. New: Chard and Sauv Bl v'yds in Marlborough, NZ. Also owns BAILEY'S and ST HUBERTS.

Rouge Homme (Coonawarra) ★★ Separately branded and promoted arm of LINDEMANS with keenly priced Chard and Cab-Shiraz leaders.

Rymill Riddoch Run (Coonawarra) ★★→★★★ Descendants of John Riddoch carrying on the good work of the founder of COONAWARRA. Strong dense Shiraz and Cab esp noteworthy.

St Hallett (Barossa) ★★★ Rejuvenated winery. 100 yr-old vines give splendid Old Block Shiraz. Rest of range is smooth and stylish.

St Huberts (Yarra Valley) ★★→★★★ Acquired by ROTHBURY late '92; accent on rich buttery Chard and smooth 'berry' Cab. Second label is Rowan.

St Leonards (NE Vic) ★★ Excellent varieties sold only 'cellar door' and by mailing list, incl exotics, eg Orange Muscat.

Saltram (Barossa) ★→★★★ Seagram-owned winery making wines of variable quality. Pinnacle Selection are best; also Mamre Brook.

Sandalford (Swan Valley) ★→★★ Fine old winery with contrasting styles of red and white single-grape wines from SWAN and MARGARET RIVER areas. Wonderful old fortified Verdelho.

Saxonvale (Hunter Valley) ★★ Medium-sized operation: good early-maturing Sém and Chard. Also good soft Cab and Shiraz. Owned by WYNDHAM.

Schinus Molle See Dromana Estate.

Scotchman's Hill (Geelong) ★★ Newcomer making significant quantities of v stylish Pinot N, good Chard and Cab F at modest prices.

Seaview (S Vales) ★★ Brand name owned by PENFOLDS; scarcely used.

Seppelt (Barossa, Great Western, Keppoch, etc) ★→★★★ Far-flung producers of Australia's most popular sparkling wine (Great Western Brut); also good dessert and some vg private bin wines, incl Chard from GREAT WESTERN and Drumborg (Vic), PADTHAWAY and BAROSSA (S Aus). Top sparkling is highly regarded 'Salinger'. Now linked with PENFOLDS/LINDEMANS/BURING, etc, to form Australia's biggest wine co.

Seville Estate (Yarra Valley) ★★→★★★ Tiny winery with Chard, v late-picked Ries, Shiraz, Pinot N and vg Cab.

Shaw & Smith (S Vales) ★★★ Trendy new venture of flying winemaker Martin Shaw and Australia's first MW Michael Hill-Smith. Crisp Sauv Bl and complex barrel-fermented Chard are the two wines.

S Smith & Sons (alias Yalumba) (Barossa) ★→★★★ Big old family firm with considerable verve, using computers, juice evaluation, etc, to produce full spectrum of high-quality wines, incl HILL-SMITH ESTATE. HEGGIES V'yd is best. Angas Brut, a good value sparkling wine, and Oxford Landing Chard are now world brands.

Stanley Bottled under Stanley-Leasingham label. See Leasingham.

Stanton & Killeen (NE Vic) ★★ Small old family firm. Rich Muscats, also strong Moodemere reds.

Stoniers Merricks (Mornington Peninsula) ★★★ Seriously challenging DROMANA ESTATE for pride of place on the Peninsula. Chard, Pinot N are consistently vg; also Cab.

Taltarni (Great Western/Avoca) ★★★ Dominique Portet, brother of Bernard (Clos du Val, Napa), son of André (ex-Ch Lafite), produces huge but balanced reds for long ageing, good Sauv and adequate sparkling.

Tarrawarra (Yarra Valley) ★★★ Multi-million dollar investment: limited quantities of idiosyncratic expensive Chard, robust long-lived Pinot N.

Taylors Wines (Clare) ★→★★ Large unit: range of inexpensive table wines.

Terrace Vale (Hunter Valley) ★★ Small syndicate-owned winery with French winemaker. Good Sém and Chard.

Tim Knappstein Wines (Clare) ★★★ Tim K, an exceptionally gifted winemaker, makes Ries, Fumé Bl, Gewürz and Cab. See Petaluma.

Tisdall Wines (Goulburn Valley) ★★→★★★ Large winery at Echuca making local (Rosbercon) wines and finer ones from central Victorian ranges (Mt Helen Cab, Chard, and Ries).

Tollana (Barossa) ★★→★★★ Old company once famous for brandy. Has latterly made some fine Cab and Ries. Acquired by PENFOLDS in '87.

Tolley Pedare (Barossa) Century-old family-run winery crushing 3,000 tonnes. Gewürz consistently among best in Australia; wooded Sém, Chard and Cab honest and reliable.

Tulloch (Hunter Valley) ★→★★ An old name at Pokolbin for dry reds, Chard, Verdelho. Now part of PENFOLDS group but a shadow of its former self.

Tyrrell (Hunter Valley) ★★→★★★ Some of the best traditional HUNTER wines, 'Hermitage' and Sém. Pioneered Chard with his big rich Vat 47. Also delicate Pinot.

Vasse Felix (Margaret River) ★★→★★★ With CULLENS, pioneer of the MARGARET RIVER. Elegant Cabs, notable for mid-weight balance, bought by the late Robert Holmes à Court in '87.

Virgin Hills (Bendigo/Ballarat) ★★★★ Tiny supplies of one blended red (Cab-Shiraz-Malbec) of legendary style and balance.

Westfield (Swan Valley) ★→★★ John Kosovich's Cab, Chard and Verdelho show particular finesse for a hot climate. Also good 'Port'.

Wirra Wirra (S Vales) ★★→★★★ Under PETALUMA influence: high quality, beautifully-packaged whites and reds have made a big impact.

Woodleys (Barossa) ★★ Well-known for low-price Queen Adelaide label. Acquired by SEPPELT in '85.

Wyndham Estate (Branxton, NSW) ★→★★ Aggressive large HUNTER and MUDGEE group with brands: CRAIGMOOR, Hollydene, Hunter Estate, MONTROSE, Richmond Grove and SAXONVALE. Acquired by ORLANDO in '90.

Wynns (Coonawarra) ★★→★★★ Since its acquisition by PENFOLDS in '85 has produced even better wines: Ries, Chard, Shiraz and Cab – all very good, esp John Riddoch Cab.

Yalumba See S Smith & Sons.

Yarra Burn (Yarra Valley) ★★ Makes Sém, Sauv-Bl, Chard, sparkling Pinot N, Pinot N and Cab; has found the going tough, but perseveres.

Yarra Ridge (Yarra Valley) ★★→★★★ Expanding young winery, v successful Chard, Cab, Sauv, Pinot, all with flavour and finesse at modest prices.

Yarra Yering (Yarra Valley) ★★★→★★★★ The best-known Lilydale boutique winery. Esp racy powerful Pinot N, deep herby Cab (Dry Red No 1) and Shiraz (Dry Red No 2).

Yellowglen (Bendigo/Ballarat) ★→★★ High-flying sparkling winemaker owned by MILDARA. Sales are more impressive than quality.

Yeringberg (Yarra Valley) ★★★ Dreamlike historic estate still in the hands of the founding family, now again producing v high quality Chard, Cab, Pinot N, in minute quantities.

New Zealand

Over the last decade New Zealand has made an international impact with white table wines of startling quality, well able to compete with those of Australia or California. In 1982 it exported 12,000 cases; in 1992 some 403,000. It is now regarded as the top cool-climate region among the world's newer wine countries.

In recent years new vineyard areas have opened up in Martinborough (North Island, north of the capital city Wellington), Canterbury and Central Otago (South Island).

White grapes predominate. Formerly dominant Müller-Thurgau is being rapidly overtaken by varieties in demand overseas: in 1993 Chardonnay supplanted it as number one. Next in line are Sauvignon Blanc, Cabernet Sauvignon and Pinot Noir respectively, with Riesling gaining prestige.

Intensity of fruit flavours and crisp acidity are the hallmarks of New Zealand's wines. No region on earth can match the pungency of its best Sauvignon Blanc. Barrel fermentation and/or ageing add to their complexity and interest. Marlborough also makes very fine sweet Rieslings with botrytis. 1989 was perhaps the first vintage to produce really worthy reds. The principal areas and producers follow.

Allan Scott (Blenheim) Est '90. Chard, Ries and good Sauv Bl (first good vintage 92). Neighbour of famous CLOUDY BAY.

Ata Rangi (Martinborough) Est '80 primarily for reds; now also excellent Chard. Pinot N outstanding and Cab-Merlot-Petit Syrah (Célèbre).

Auckland Largest city in NZ. Location of head offices of major wineries, with a large number of medium and small wineries in outskirts.

Babich (Henderson, nr Auckland) Large old Dalmatian family firm, highly respected in NZ for consistent quality and value. Also uses MARLBOROUGH, GISBORNE and HAWKES BAY grapes. Good Chards (esp Irongate, Stopbank), Sauv Bl (92 is an excellent value big medal-winner), Sém-Chard, Gewürz, Cab S and Cab-Merlot. Pinot N still not so good.

Brajkovich See Kumeu River.

Brookfields (Hawkes Bay) One of the area's top v'yds: Chard, Sauv Bl, Cab S, Cab-Merlot (outstanding).

Cellier Le Brun (Renwick, nr Blenheim) Small winery est by son of Champagne family: some of NZ's best traditional method sparkling incl vintage, NV, rosé (vg 89 90), Bl de Blancs (90 exceptional).

Cloudy Bay (Blenheim) Offshoot of W Australia's Cape Mentelle, both bought in '90 by Veuve Clicquot. Top name for Sauv Bl, Chard. Richly subtle excellent Cab-Merlot 89 shows reds' high promise. New release (92) Pelorus méthode traditionelle showing good potential.

Collard (Henderson, nr Auckland) Small family winery using grapes from four main areas: top-award Chard from each. Also Sauv (esp Rothesay), Chenin, Ries, Cab-Merlot, Sém. Consistent gd quality (esp HAWKES BAY).

Cooks (Hawkes Bay) Large co merged with CORBANS and McWilliams in '85. Good steady Chard (esp Winemakers Reserve). Also Cab-Merlot and late-harvest Sauv Bl-Sém.

Coopers Creek (Huapai Valley, NW of Auckland) Small winery augmenting own grapes with GISBORNE, HAWKES BAY and MARLBOROUGH fruit. Exporting good Chard, Sauv Bl, Ries, dry and late-harvest. Also Cab S-Merlot and popular blends: Coopers Dry (white), Coopers Red.

Corbans (Henderson, nr Auckland) Old-established firm with winery at MARLBOROUGH. Now incorporates COOKS, McWilliams and (new premium brand) STONELEIGH. Marlb'h gives vg Sauv, Chard, Ries, Cab. Corbans is sound wide range. Additional premium wines: Robard & Butler label.

Delegat's (Henderson, nr Auckland) Medium-sized family winery. Grapes from GISBORNE and HAWKES BAY: gd Chard, Sauv Bl, Proprietor's Reserve Cabs, Merlots (89 90), impressive 'Auslese' Ries. Also Chard and Sauv from MARLBOROUGH sold under successful export brand Oyster Bay.

De Redcliffe (Mangatawhiri, SE of Auckland) Small progressive winery and resort 'Hotel du Vin'; good Chard, Ries, Sauv Bl, Sém, Cab-Merlot.

Deutz (Auckland) The Champagne firm in a pioneer joint venture with MONTANA. Sparkling results.

Esk Valley (Bayview, Hawkes Bay) Former large family co, now merged with VILLA MARIA/VIDAL. Small range incl vg dry Chenin, and some of NZ's best reds, esp 90 Merlot and Merlot-Cab F, also Cab-Merlot Private Bin.

Giesen Estate (Burnham, S of Christchurch, and Canterbury, S Island) German family winery: good Chards (Reserve School Road), Sauv, botrytised Ries, Cab-Merlot from own and some MARLBOROUGH grapes.

Gisborne Site of 3 large wineries, CORBANS, MONTANA and PENFOLDS, and centre of large viticultural area incl MATAWHERO and Tolaga Bay. Good area for Müller-T, Chard, Sém and Gewürz.

Goldwater (Waiheke Island in Hauraki Gulf, nr Auckland) Small v'yd at sea edge, known best for Cab-Merlot; also MARLBOROUGH Chard – esp outstanding own-grown 92 Delamore.

Grove Mill (Blenheim) Excellent new winery bursting onto the scene with 89 Chard; Lansdowne in '90 even better and 91 promising. Vg Cab S-Merlot, Cab-Pinotage. Also Gewürz, Sauv Bl, botrytis Sauv Bl, Ries.

Hawkes Bay Large viticultural region on E coast of North Island, S of GISBORNE. Known for high quality grapes, esp Chard and Cab S.

Highfield Estate (Marlborough) Grape-grower turned winemaker, producing Sauv Bl, Chard, Ries, Merlot.

Hunters (Marlborough) Small progressive winery using only MARLBOROUGH grapes. Already highly reputed for outstanding Sauv Bl (oaky 'Fumé' style), and Chard. Ries since '89. Also Cab S.

Jackson Estate (Blenheim) Large private v'yd. First vintage 91: impressive Sauv (91 92), also Chard, Ries (sweet botrytis version one of NZ's best).

Kumeu River (Kumeu, NW of Auckland) Establishing reputation for Fumé-style Sauv, Chard, Cab-Merlot and light fruity Cab F under Brajkovich family crest label.

Landfall Wines (Gisborne) New winery with medal-winning Chard (Revington Vineyard, 89 90). Also vg Gewürz, Sauv Bl.

Lincoln Vineyards (Henderson, nr Auckland) Medium-sized family winery; esp for Chard, Chenin Bl and Cab. 88, 90 show real promise.

Marlborough Leading export (and now NZ's largest) wine region, at N end of South Island on stony plain formed by Wairau River. Well-suited to white varieties Chard, Sauv Bl and Ries, but also good Cab S and promising Pinot N. Potential here for vg sparkling.

Martinborough New smallish appellation in S Wairarapa (N of Wellington, North Island). Stony soils, similar to MARLBOROUGH.

Martinborough Vineyards (Martinborough) Largest of area's small estates. Awards already for Chard, 'Fumé' Sauv Bl, Pinot N, 89 91.

Matawhero (nr Gisborne) Small winery with est name for Gewürz, concentrated and aromatic Chard, also Sauv Bl and Sauv Bl-Sém.

Matua Valley (NW of Auckland) Medium-sized family winery. Pioneer with new varieties. Own grapes supplemented by fruit from HAWKES BAY, GISBORNE and MARLBOROUGH. Well-known: Judd Chard (Gisborne), intense unwooded Sauv Bl (Shingle Peak) and oaky Reserve, unique Pinot N-Bl, good Cab S, Merlot, Ries, Gewürz and late-harvest Muscat.

McDonald (Hawkes Bay) MONTANA's new venture. Philosophy: premium wine from new v'yds. Wines now called Church Road. Great potential.

Merlen Wines (Marlborough) German-born winemaker Almuth Lorenz is producing excellent Chard and Ries (90 91) with long life ahead.

Mills Reef (Bay of Plenty) Small-scale producer of top quality and v attractive Chard, Sauv Bl, Ries and Gewürz.

Millton (nr Gisborne) Small organic producer. Good Sauv Bl-Sém blend, Chard (Clos de Ste-Anne 89 outstanding) and Ries (dry and late harvest, vg 91). Splendid barrel-fermented Chenin Bl (87 90) like fine Anjou.

Mission (Greenmeadows, Hawkes Bay) Oldest continuing wine establishment in NZ, French mission-founded and still run by Society of Mary. Good Sém-Sauv Bl and Cab-Merlot; Reserve Cab-S is best wine by far.

Montana (Auckland and Hawkes Bay) NZ's largest wine enterprise: wineries in GISBORNE, MARLBOROUGH; incorporating Penfolds label (in NZ only). Pioneer v'yds in Marlborough, also uses Gisborne and HAWKES BAY grapes. Marlb'h labels incl Sauv Bl and Chard (vg and outstanding Show Reserves), Ries, Cab S, Pinot N. Gisborne Chard also big-selling and sound. Original Lindauer sparkling joined by excellent cuvée DEUTZ.

Morton Estate (Katikati, nr Tauranga, North Island) Expanding winery: excellent Chard (range is best black label, white then yellow labels). Also Fumé Bl, Gewürz, Ries and good méthode traditionelle (89 90 91).

Nautilus (nr Auckland) Owned by Australia's Yalumba, this young winery produces a vg Chard from MARLBOROUGH and Sauv Bl from HAWKES BAY.

Neudorf (Nelson) Charming small-scale winery: meaty highly-scented Chard (89 90 91), good Ries, Sauv Bl and Pinot N.

Ngatarawa (nr Hastings, Hawkes Bay) Boutique winery in old stables of est HAWKES BAY family. Good Glazebrook label Chard, Sauv, Cab-Merlot.

Nobilo (Huapai Valley, NW of Auckland) NZ's largest family winery: own plus GISBORNE, HAWKES BAY, MARLBOROUGH, MARTINBOROUGH fruit. Gd Chard (esp Marlb'h), pungent Sauv, Sém; long renowned for age-worthy reds. Assoc label: Classic Hills. Concept One is Huapai Cab-Pinotage.

Palliser Estate (Martinborough) New ambitious winery: first vintage 89. Good Chard, Sauv Bl, Ries; also v rich intense Pinot N.

Pask, C J (Hawkes Bay) Rising star of the area; outstanding Chard and Sauv Bl since 91. Also good Cab S, Pinot N.

Robard & Butler See Corbans.

Rongapai (Waikato, S of Auckland) German-influenced winery renowned for botrytised Chard and Ries.

St Nesbit (Karaka, S of Auckland) Expanding boutique winery for well-made barrique-matured red blend Cab S-Cab F-Merlot (vg 91).

Savidge Estate (Gisborne) Past grape suppliers, now successfully marketing own Chard, Chenin Bl, Sauv Bl and red.

Selak's (Kumeu, NW of Auckland) Small family firm with good export reputation for fresh sharpish Sauv Bl, Sauv Bl-Sém blend (in 'Fumé' style), Chard, Cab S. (Founders is label for top Chard and Cab wines.)

Stoneleigh See Corbans.

Stonyridge (Waiheke Island, nr Auckland) Boutique winery concentrating on two reds in Bordeaux style: Larose exceptional (**87 92**), Airfield vg.

Te Kairanga (Martinborough) Largest winery in region, with underground facilities. Chard, Sauv Bl, Pinot N, Cab S.

Te Mata (Havelock North, Hawkes Bay) Restored winery producing good Chard (esp Elston) and Sauv Bl from nearby v'yds, plus excellent 'Coleraine' Cab-Merlot (91 92) from proprietor's home v'yd.

Vavasour (Awatere Valley, nr Blenheim) First vintage 89. 91 Chards reaching top quality; Dashwood label Chard also good. Vg Fumé Bl, Sauv Bl; also Cab-Merlot, Cab S-Cab Fr.

Vidal (Hastings, Hawkes Bay) Atmospheric old winery, merged with VILLA MARIA. Top HAWKES BAY Chards (**90 91**). Vg Cab S, Cab S-Merlot, Fumé Bl.

Villa Maria (Mangere, S Auckland) Large co incl VIDAL and ESK VALLEY. Ihumatao (nr Auckland airport), GISBORNE, HAWKES BAY grapes. Esp oak-fermented Chard, Sauv (and wooded 'Fumé'), Gewürz, Cab, Cab-Merlot.

Waipara Springs (N Canterbury) Recent producer of model Sauv Bl, Chard and Pinot N (90 91 good). To follow.

Wairau River (Marlborough) Small winery, full-flavoured Sauv and Chard.

Weingut Seifried (Upper Moutere, nr Nelson) Small winery started by Austrian immigrant. Esp Chard, Sauv, Ries (dry, late-harvest), Pinot.

South Africa

Quality in South Africa's table wines began around 1975 when vineyard owners started to add to their plantings of Cabernet Sauvignon, already successful, the greater challenges of Chardonnay, Sauvignon Blanc and even Pinot Noir. New laws in 1973 defining Wines of Origin encouraged new small estates. The success of small new wineries in the 1980s has encouraged others to buy oak barrels from France. Cellarmasters are now showing more care in harvesting and cellar treatment and standards are rising steadily.

Recommended vintages refer to the wine preceding them in brackets.

Allesverloren r ★→★★ (Cab S) **86 87** 89 **91** Old 395-acre family estate, best known for 'Port'. Also hefty well-oaked but not always long-lived CAB and Shiraz from hot wheatlands district of Malmesbury.

Alphen ★ Gilbeys brand name for wines from STELLENBOSCH area.

Alto r ★★→★★★ (Cab S) **86 87 89** High 247-acre mountain v'yds S of STELLENBOSCH, facing the Atlantic. Solid CAB; and Cab blended with Merlot and Shiraz. Best since mid-'80s (with new French oak).

Altydgedacht r w ★→★★ (Cab S) **85 86 87** 88 89 Durbanville estate, best for CAB; also gutsy Tintoretto blend of Barbera and Shiraz.

Avontuur r w ★★ (r) **87** 89 90 91 200-acre ST'BOSCH v'yd, bottling since '87. Soft Bordeaux-style blend, Avon Rouge; CAB, Merlot, promising CHARD.

Backsberg r w ★★→★★★ (red) **84 88 87** 89 **91** (Chard) **86 88 89 90** Frequently prize-winning 395-acre estate at PAARL. Pioneered oak-fermented CHARD in mid-'80s with US advice. Delicious Bordeaux blend Klein Babylonstoren is best; also vg oaked SAUV BL John Martin. Proprietor Sydney Back still going strong.

Bellingham r w ★ Big-selling brand of DGB. Sound reds, popular whites, esp sweet soft CAPE RIES-based Johannisberger (exported as Cape Gold).

Bergkelder Big STELLENBOSCH co, member of Oude Meester group, making/distributing many brands (FLEUR DU CAP, GRUNBERGER), 18 estate wines. First to use French oak (now 10,000 barrels), top for fine oaked reds.

Bertrams r ★★→★★★ **84 88 87** 89 **91** Gilbeys brand of good to vg varietals, esp Shiraz, PINOTAGE. Also Robert Fuller Reserve Bordeaux-style blend.

Beyerskloof r ★★★ (Cab S) **89 90 91** New small STELLENBOSCH property, devoted to vg tannic deep-flavoured CAB S.

Blaauwklippen r w ★★→★★★ (red) **84 86 87** 88 90 91 STELLENBOSCH winery making among the Cape's best bold reds, esp CAB Reserve. Also S Africa's top Zin; patchy but improving CHARD; good off-dry RIES.

Bloemendal r w ★→★★ (Cab S) 88 89 91 (Chard) **90 91 92** Young sea-cooled estate at Durbanville. Fragrant light CAB; soft elegant CHARD.

Boberg Controlled region for fortified wines comprising PAARL and TULBAGH.

Bon Courage w sw ★→★★ ROBERTSON estate; vg dessert whites, incl GEWURZ, botrytis RIES, respectable CHARD.

Boplaas r w ★★ V'yds in dry hot Karoo. Earthy deep 'Vintage Reserve Port' best since '87, fortified Muscadels. Links with Grahams in Portugal.

Boschendal w sp ★★→★★★ (Chard) 89 91 617-acre estate nr Franschhoek in PAARL area. Good CHARD and méthode traditionelle; also Cape's first 'blush' off-dry Blanc de Noirs. Owned by Anglo-American Corp.

Bouchard-Finlayson r w (★★★) First French-Cape partnership, between Paul Bouchard of Bouchard Ainé in Burgundy and Peter Finlayson at Hermanus, Walker Bay. Maiden release 91 promising, esp PINOT N.

Breede River Valley Fortified and white wine region E of Drakenstein Mts.

Buitenverwachting r w sp ★★★ (Chard) 89 90 91 Exceptional, German-financed, recently replanted CONSTANTIA v'yds. Vg SAUV (plain, oaked Bl Fumé), CHARD, Bordeaux blend (88 89), Merlot. Lively clean méthode traditionelle (Pinots Gr and Bl). Restaurant worthy of a Michelin star.

Cabernet Sauvignon The great Bordeaux grape, most successful in COASTAL REGION. Range of styles: sturdy long-lived to elegant fruity. More use of new French oak since '82 is making great improvements. Best recent vintages: **82 84 86 87 89 91**.

Cape Independent Winemakers Guild Young group of winemakers in the vanguard of quality without direct links to major wholesalers. Holds an annual auction of progressive-style wines.

Cape Riesling See Riesling.

Cathedral Cellars See KWV.

Cavendish Cape ★★ Range of remarkably good 'Sherries' from the KWV.

Chardonnay Classic white variety, fairly new in S Africa due to official restrictions. Recent release of good vines resulted in leap in quality and number. Great expectations. Now over 100 Chard labels; a decade ago, 3. Best vintage so far is **89**; **91** also vg and 93 good.

Chateau Libertas ★ Big-selling CAB S brand made by SFW.

Chenin Blanc Work-horse grape of the Cape; one vine in three. Adaptable, sometimes vg. KWV makes good value example. See also Steen.

Cinsaut The principal bulk-producing French red grape in S Africa; formerly known as Hermitage. V seldom seen with varietal label.

Claridge r w ★★→★★★ (red) 91 (Chard) **91 92** Good barrel-fermented CHARD and CAB-Merlot from small new winery at Wellington nr PAARL.

Clos Malverne r ★★ 89 90 91 Small STELLENBOSCH winery. Individual dense CAB S, PINOTAGE from own v'yds and purchased grapes.

Coastal Region Demarcated wine region, incl CONSTANTIA, Durbanville, PAARL, STELLENBOSCH, SWARTLAND, TULBAGH.

Colombard French white grape, as popular in Cape as in California. Crisp lively flowery, usually short-lived wine; often in blends, or for brandy.

Constantia Once the world's most famous sweet Muscat-based wine (both red and white), from the Cape.

Delaire Vineyards r w ★★ (Chard) **89 91** (red) 90 91 Full-flavoured CHARD, Bordeaux blend named Barrique, and elegant off-dry RHINE RIES, from young winery at Helshoogte Pass above STELLENBOSCH.

Delheim r w dr sw ★★→★★★ (red) 86 87 88 89 91 Big winery with high mountain v'yds at Driesprong nr STELLENBOSCH. Elegant barrel-aged CAB S-Merlot-Cab F blend, Grand Reserve. Good value Cab, PINOTAGE, Shiraz; variable PINOT N; improving CHARD and SAUV BL. Sweet wines incl GEWURZ and outstanding botrytis STEEN.

De Wetshof w sw ★★→★★★ (Chard) 87 88 89 91 Pioneering ROBERTSON estate with powerful CHARD and fresh dry RHINE RIES. Also dessert GEWURZ, Rhine Ries under Danie de Wet label.

Douglas Green ★→★★ Cape Town merchants, marketing range of sound wines incl 'Sherries' and 'Ports' mostly from KWV.

Drostdy ★ Good range of 'Sherries' from BERGKELDER.

Drostyhof r w ★ Well-priced range incl CHARD made at TULBAGH cellars.

Edelkeur ★★★★ Excellent intensely sweet white made with nobly rotten grapes (see page 51) by NEDERBURG.

Eikendal Vineyards r w ★★→★★ (red) 87 88 90 91 (Chard) **91** 92 93 Swiss-owned 100-acres v'yds and winery in STELLENBOSCH. Vg CHARD; CAB S-Merlot blend Classique. Fresh whites incl semi-sweet CHENIN BL.

Estate wine Official term for wines grown and made on registered estates, but which may be bottled elsewhere. V'yds need not be contiguous or even nearby provided they enjoy similar 'ecological conditions'.

Fairview Estate r w dr sw ★★→★★★ (red) 88 90 91 (Chard) **90 91** 92 Enterprising PAARL estate with wide range. Best are Reserve Merlot, PINOTAGE, Bordeaux blend Charles Gerard Reserve. Also lively Gamay, good CHARD, plus sweet CHENIN BL.

To decipher codes, please refer to symbols key at front of book, and to 'How to Read an Entry' on page 5.

Fleur du Cap r w sw ★★→★★★ (red) 86 87 88 90 91 Good value range from BERGKELDER at STELLENBOSCH, esp excellent CAB S in good yrs since '86. Also Merlot, improving CHARD, fine GEWURZ and botrytis CHENIN BL.

Gewürztraminer The famous spicy grape of Alsace, best at NEDERBURG and SIMONSIG. Naturally low acidity makes it difficult to handle at the Cape.

Glen Carlou r w ★★→★★★ (red) 89 90 91 (Chard) 90 91 92 PAARL property: excellent Bordeaux blends Grande Classique and Les Trois, and Merlot; also fine CHARD.

Graça ★ Huge-selling slightly fizzy white blend in Portuguese-style bottle.

Graham Beck Winery w sp ★★ Avant-garde ROBERTSON winery (57 acres); first méthode traditionelle Brut Royale NV and CHARD well-received.

Grand Cru (or Premier Grand Cru) Term for a totally dry white, with no quality implications. Generally to be avoided.

Groot Constantia r w ★★→★★★ Historic gov't-owned estate nr Cape Town. Superlative Muscat in early 19th C. Renaissance in progress; so far fine CAB (esp blend Gouverneur's Reserve), Shiraz, whites, dessert Muscat.

Grünberger ★ BERGKELDER brand using STEEN to make range of dry and semi-sweet white wines.

Hamilton Russell Vineyards r w ★★★→★★★★ (Pinot N) 85 86 87 89 90 91 (Chard) 86 87 89 90 91 The Cape's top PINOT N 'Burgundy' v'yds and cellar. Small yields, French-inspired vinification in cool, most southerly region of Walker Bay. Many awards. Priciest wines in S Africa.

Hanepoot Local name for the sweet Muscat of Alexandria grape.

Hartenberg r w ★★ STELLENBOSCH estate, recently modernized; rich well-aged Shiraz.

Kanonkop r ★★★→★★★★ (red) 84 86 89 90 91 Outstanding estate in N STELLENBOSCH. Individual powerful CAB S and Bordeaux-style blend Paul Sauer. Benchmark PINOTAGE, barrel-finished since '89 with dramatic improvement.

Klein Constantia r w sw ★★★→★★★★ (red) 86 87 88 89 (Chard) 90 91 A new Cape star: old subdivision of famous Groot Constantia neighbour. Emphatic CHARD, SAUV BL, and fine powerful CAB S, Bordeaux-style blend Marlbrook first released in '88, also Shiraz. A Muscat Frontignan 86, Vin de Constance, revives an 18th-C Constantia legend. Revamped since early '80s. Frequent national champions.

KWV The Kooperatieve Wijnbouwers Vereniging, S Africa's national wine coop created in 1917 to absorb surpluses: vast premises in PAARL, a range of good wines, esp Cathedral Cellars reds, RIES, 'Sherries', sweet dessert wines. In '92 gave up widely criticized powers to control national production with quotas, freeing growers to plant v'yds at will.

Laborie r w ★→★★ KWV-owned showpiece estate in PAARL district. Blended white and red.

La Bri ★★ Whites made in Franschhoek coop cellar from SAUV BL, RHINE RIES and Sém. Sauvage de la Bri is best.

La Motte r w ★★★ (red) 86 87 88 89 91 Lavish new Rupert family estate nr Franschhoek. Lean but stylish, intensely flavoured reds: CAB S, Shiraz, Merlot, Bordeaux-style blend Millennium. Racy SAUV BL.

Landgoed Afrikaans for 'estate': a word that appears on official seals and frequently on ESTATE WINE labels.

Landskroon r w ★→★★ Family estate owned by Paul and Hugo de Villiers. Good dry reds, esp Shiraz, CAB S, Cab F.

Late Harvest Term for a mildly sweet wine. 'Special Late Harvest' must be naturally sweet (no added concentrate). 'Noble Late Harvest' is the highest dessert wine quality level.

Le Bonheur r w ★★★ (red) 84 86 87 STELLENBOSCH estate often producing classic tannic minerally CAB, big-bodied SAUV BL.

Lemberg w ★★ Tiny estate in TULBAGH, making full-bodied wood-aged Hárslevelü and SAUV BL labelled Aimée.

Leroux, JC ★★ Old brand revived as BERGKELDER's sparkling wine house. SAUV BL (charmat) and PINOT N (méthode traditionelle). Also CHARD.

Lievland r w ★★→★★★ (red) 87 89 90 STELLENBOSCH estate making top Cape Shiraz and vg CAB S, Merlot. Also range of whites incl intense RIES, off-dry and promising Sauternes-style dessert wine.

L'Ormarins r w sw ★★★ (red) 84 86 87 89 (Chard) 89 90 One of two Rupert family estates nr Franschhoek. CAB S and vg claret-style Optima. Fresh lemony CHARD, forward oak-aged SAUV BL, and outstanding GEWURZ-Bukketraube botrytis dessert wine.

Louisvale w ★★ (Chard) 90 91 92 STELLENBOSCH winery. Attractive CHARD only.

Meerlust r w ★★★ (red) 84 86 87 89 Old family estate S of STELLENBOSCH; the Cape's only Italian winemaker (Giorgio Dalla Cia). Outstanding Rubicon (Médoc-style blend), Merlot, PINOT N. CHARD still in pipeline.

Middelvlei r ★★→★★★ (red) 89 STELLENBOSCH estate making good PINOTAGE and CAB. Marketed by BERGKELDER.

Monis ★→★★ Well-known wine concern of PAARL, with fine 'Vintage Port'.

Morgenhof r w dr s/sw ★ Fresh start at this expensively refurbished STELLENBOSCH estate. New French owner and change of winemaker (from '92). Range of improving reds; dry and semi-sweet whites; 'Port'.

Mulderbosch Vineyards w ★★→★★★ Enthusiastic reception for new penetrating impressive SAUV BL from mountain v'yds nr STELLENBOSCH, one oak-fermented, the other fresh, bold.

Muratie Ancient estate in STELLENBOSCH, best known for its 'Port'. Recently sold; bright future expected.

Nederburg r w p dr sw s/sw sp ★★→★★★★ (red) 82 84 86 87 89 91 (Chard) 89 90 91 Probably S Africa's best-known label, from large modern PAARL winery (650,000 cases pa, some 50 wines). Bicentenary in '92. Own grapes and suppliers'. Sound CAB, Shiraz, CHARD, RIES, blends in regular range. Limited Vintages, Private Bins often outstanding. '80s pioneer of botrytis dessert wines (CHENIN BL, GEWURZ, SAUV, Muscat, even Chard). Stages Cape's biggest annual wine event, the Nederburg Auction.

Neethlingshof r w sw ★★→★★★ (red) 87 89 90 91 (Chard) 91 Rising estate, replanted with classic varieties, cellar revamped at huge cost since '85 by German investor. Run jointly with nearby replanted Stellenzicht v'yds for 250,000-case pa production. Vg CAB S, Merlot, CHARD joining fresh SAUV BL, excellent GEWURZ and blush Blanc de Noir. National Champion dessert botrytis from RIES, Sauv Bl.

Neil Ellis Wines r w ★★★ (red) 86 87 89 91 (Chard) 89 91 92 Good wines from Devon Valley nr STELLENBOSCH (16 widely spread coastal v'yds). Spicy structured CAB S; excellent Whitehall SAUV BL; full bold CHARD.

Nuy Cooperative Winery r w dr sw sp ★★ Small Worcester Coop, frequent local-award winner. Outstanding dessert wines, traditional fortified Muscadels, regularly excellent Cape COLOMBARD. Good S African RIES.

Oak Valley Wines ★ New export brand, blend of good coop cellar wines from STELLENBOSCH, incl CAB-Shiraz, SAUV BL-CHENIN BL blends.

Overgaauw r w ★★ (red) 84 86 87 89 90 91 Old family estate W of STELLENBOSCH; CHARD, CAB S, Merlot, and Bordeaux-style blend Tria Corda. Also 'Port' from 5 Portuguese varieties.

Paarl Town 30 miles NE of Cape Town, and the surrounding demarcated district, among the best in the country, particularly for 'Sherry'.

Paul Cluver w ★★ New label launched '92. Good SAUV BL, RHINE RIES: grapes from cool upland Elgin Coastal region. Wines made by NEDERBURG.

Pierre Jourdan sp ★★★ Fine NV méthode traditionelle made at Clos Cabriere estate, Franschhoek. Most notable: Brut Sauvage and Cuve Belle Rose (pure PINOT N).

Pinotage S African red grape, a cross between PINOT N and CINSAUT, useful for high yields and hardiness. The results can be delicious but, more often, overstated flamboyant esters dominate. Recent experiments and barrel-ageing show potential for finesse.

Pinot Noir Like counterparts in California and Australia, Cape producers struggle for fine, burgundy-like complexity. They are getting closer. Best are BLAAUWKLIPPEN, HAMILTON RUSSELL, MEERLUST, RUSTENBERG.

Plaisir de Merle New SFW-owned cellar nr PAARL producing its first reds from own v'yds in '93, with advice from Château Margaux.

Pongracz ★★ Successful good value méthode traditionelle from PINOT N and CHARD, produced by the BERGKELDER, named after the exiled Hungarian ampelographer who upgraded many Cape v'yds.

Premier Grand Cru See Grand Cru.

Rhebokskloof r w ★→★★ (red) 90 (Chard) 92 200-acre estate behind PAARL mountain, with a sound, small range. Most promising is CAB. Has the Cape's first American winemaker.

Rhine Riesling Produces full-flavoured dry and off-dry wines but reaches perfection when lusciously sweet as 'Noble LATE HARVEST'. Generally needs 2 yrs or more of bottle-age. Also called Weisser Ries.

Riesling S African Ries (actually Crouchen Bl) is v different from RHINE RIES, providing neutral easy-drinking wines. Known locally as Cape Ries.

Rietvallei w sw ★★ ROBERTSON estate: excellent fortified Muscadel. Also CHARD.

Robertson Demarcated district E of, and inland from, the Cape. Mainly dessert wines (notably Muscat), with white table wines on the increase. Few reds. Incl Bonnievale. Irrigated v'yds.

Roodeberg ★ Sound red from the KWV: blend of PINOTAGE, Shiraz, Tinta Barocca, CAB S in about equal parts.

Rooiberg Cooperative Winery ★ Successful big-selling ROBERTSON range of 33 labels. Good CHENIN BL, COLOMBARD.

Rozendal r ★★★ (red) **83 84 86 87 89 91** Small STELLENBOSCH v'yd cellar, making excellent CAB-Merlot blend.

Ruiterbosch ★★ Individual wines from outside traditional Cape vine area nr Mossel Bay on Indian Ocean. Striking SAUV BL and RHINE RIES. Made at BOPLAAS cellars, Calitzdorp.

Rustenberg r w ★★★→★★★★ (red except Pinot N) **80 82 84 86 87 88 89 91** (Chard) **86 87 89 90 91** The most beautiful old STELLENBOSCH estate, founded 300 yrs ago, making wine for last 100. Grand fine reds, esp Rustenberg Gold CAB and Médoc-style blend. Also lighter Cab-CINSAUT-Merlot. Variable PINOT, best recent 88. Individual charming CHARD. Formerly sold whites under sister estate's name, Schoongezicht.

Rust en Vrede r ★★→★★★ (red) **86 87 89** Well-known estate just E of STELLENBOSCH: red only. Gd CAB, Shiraz, vg Bordeaux-style blend Rust en Vrede.

Sauvignon Blanc Adapting well to warm conditions. Widely grown and marketed in both wooded and unwooded styles. Also v sweet.

Simonsig r w sp sw ★★→★★★ (red) **84 86 87 89 90 91** (Chard) **88 89 90 91** Malan family STELLENBOSCH estate with a wide range, starring vg CAB, CHARD, PINOTAGE, GEWURZ (dessert-style). First release in '92 of widely acclaimed Cab-Merlot blend Tiara. Also popular wood-matured dry white Vin Fumé and first Cape méthode traditionelle.

Simonsvlei r w p sw sp ★ One of S Africa's best-known coop cellars, just outside PAARL. A prize-winner with PINOTAGE.

Spier r w ★ Five-farm estate W of STELLENBOSCH. PINOTAGE probably best.

Steen S Africa's commonest white grape, said to be a clone of CHENIN BL. It gives strong tasty lively wine, sweet or dry: short-lived if dry; lasts better when off-dry or sweet. Normally better than S African RIES.

Stein Name often used for commercial blends of semi-sweet white wine. Not necessarily to be despised.

Stellenbosch Town and demarcated district 30 miles E of Cape Town (oldest town in S Africa), extending to the ocean at False Bay. Heart of the wine industry, with all 3 of the largest companies. Most top estates, esp for red wine, are in the mountain foothills.

Stellenbosch Farmers' Winery (SFW) The world's fifth largest winery, and S Africa's biggest, after KWV, marketing equivalent of 14 million cases pa. Several ranges incl NEDERBURG; top is ZONNEBLOEM. Wide selection of mid- and low-price wines.

Stellenryck Collection r w ★★★ Top quality BERGKELDER range. RHINE RIES, Fumé Blanc, CAB among S Africa's best.

Swartland Cooperative r w dr s/sw sw sp ★ Vast range of big-selling low-price wines, chiefly white CHENIN BL and dry, off-dry or sweet, but (recently) penetrating, SAUV BL, also big no-nonsense PINOTAGE. From dry wheatland area, among Cape's hottest.

Talana Hill r w ★★ (red) 88 89 (Chard) 89 90 91 New STELLENBOSCH winery: good CHARD and Bordeaux-style blend Royale.

Tassenberg ★ Popular PINOTAGE-based blend by SFW, known fondly as 'Tassies'. Traditional student party and braaivleis (barbecue) wine. Oom Tas, a dry Muscat, is white equivalent.

Thelema r w ★★★ (Cab S) 89 90 91 (Chard) 88 89 90 91 Outstanding new v'yds and winery at Helshoogte, above STELLENBOSCH. Impressive minty CAB, excellent CHARD, and both oaked and unoaked SAUV BL.

Theuniskraal w ★ TULBAGH estate: whites incl S Afrian RIES, GEWURZ.

Tulbagh Demarcated district N of PAARL best known for the white wines of THEUNISKRAAL and TWEE JONGEGEZELLEN and the dessert wines from DROSTDY. See also Boberg.

Twee Jongegezellen w sp ★★ Old TULBAGH estate, helped pioneer cold fermentation in '60s, night harvesting in '80s; still in Krone family, the 18th-C founder. Esp whites, best known: popular dry TJ89 (mélange of a dozen varieties), Schanderl off-dry Muscat-GEWURZ. Recently méthode traditionelle Cuvée Krone Borealis Brut (CHARD, PINOT N).

Uiterwyk r w ★ Old estate W of STELLENBOSCH. CAB, Merlot, pleasant whites.

Uitkyk r w ★★ (red) 86 87 89 Old estate (400 acres) W of STELLENBOSCH famous for Carlonet (big gutsy CAB) and Carlsheim (SAUV BL) white. Recently added Pinot Gr, CHARD.

Van Loveren r w sw sp ★★ Go-ahead ROBERTSON estate: big range of whites incl muscular CHARD and scarcer varieties eg Fernão Pires, Hárslevlü.

Vergelegen w ★★ One of Cape's oldest wine farms, at Somerset West, founded in 1700. Long neglected, now spectacularly restored: new vines and octagonal sunken hilltop cellar. Les Enfants series marked '92 re-launch with wine from bought-in grapes; good CHARD, SAUV BL.

Vergenoegd r w sw ★ Old family estate in S STELLENBOSCH supplying high-quality 'Sherry' to KWV and bottling CAB S, Shiraz.

Villiera r w ★★★ PAARL estate with popular NV méthode traditionelle 'Tradition'. First-rate SAUV BL. good RHINE RIES. Fine Bordeaux-style blend CAB-Merlot 'Cru Monro'. Recently exceptional Merlot.

Vriesenhof r w ★★→★★★ (Cab S) 82 84 86 88 89 (Chard) 88 89 91 Highly rated slow-developing CAB S and Bordeaux blend Kalista. Since '88, excellent CHARD. Also Pinot Bl.

Warwick r w ★★→★★★ (red) 86 87 89 91 STELLENBOSCH estate, run by one of Cape's few female winemakers. CAB and vg Médoc-style blend Trilogy.

Weisser Riesling See Rhine Riesling.

Welgemeend r ★★→★★★ (red) 86 87 89 Boutique PAARL estate: Médoc-style blends, delicate CAB and Amadé, a Grenache-Shiraz-PINOTAGE blend.

Weltevrede w dr sw ★→★★ (Chard) 89 90 Progressive ROBERTSON estate. Blended, white and fortified wines; vg CHARD.

Wine of Origin The Cape's appellation contrôlée, but without French crop yield restrictions. Demarcated regions are described on these pages.

Woolworths Wines Best S African supermarket wines, many specially blended. Top are CHARDS, young reds incl Merlot, Bordeaux-style blends.

Worcester Demarcated wine district round BREEDE and Hex river valleys, E of PAARL. Many coop cellars. Mainly dessert wines, brandy, dry whites.

Zandvliet r ★→★★ (Shiraz) 86 87 89 Estate in the ROBERTSON area making fine light Shiraz and more recently a CAB S.

Zandwijk r w New estate in PAARL district producing quality kosher wine.

Zevenwacht r w ★★→★★★ (Cab S) 84 86 87 89 Large STELLENBOSCH estate. Wines only available via shareholders and restaurants. Impressive CAB.

Zonnebloem r w ★★ (Cab S) 82 84 86 87 89 (Chard) 90 91 Good quality range from SFW incl CAB S, Merlot, Bordeaux-style blend Laureat launched '92 , Shiraz, PINOTAGE, SAUV BL, CHARD.

A little learning...

The jargon of laboratory analysis is increasingly seen on the back-labels of New World wines. It is creeping menacingly into newspapers and magazines. What does it mean? This hard-edged wine-talk is very briefly explained below.

The most frequent technical references are to the ripeness of grapes at picking; the resultant alcohol and sugar content of the wine; various measures of its acidity; the amount of sulphur dioxide used as a preservative; and occasionally the amount of 'dry extract' – the sum of all the things that give wine its character.

The **sugar** in wine is mainly glucose and fructose, with traces of arabinose, xylose and other sugars that are not fermentable by yeast, but can be attacked by bacteria. Each country has its own system for measuring the sugar content or ripeness of grapes, known in English as the '**must weight**'. The chart below relates the three principal ones (German, French and American) to each other, to specific gravity, and to the potential alcohol of the wine if all the sugar is fermented.

Sugar to alcohol: potential strength

Specific Gravity	°Oechsle	Baumé	Brix	% Potential Alcohol v/v
1.065	65	8.8	15.8	8.1
1.070	70	9.4	17.0	8.8
1.075	75	10.1	18.1	9.4
1.080	80	10.7	19.3	10.0
1.085	85	11.3	20.4	10.6
1.090	90	11.9	21.5	12.1
1.095	95	12.5	22.5	11.9
1.100	100	13.1	23.7	13.6
1.105	105	13.7	24.8	13.1
1.110	110	14.3	25.8	15.1
1.115	115	14.9	26.9	14.4
1.120	120	15.5	28.0	16.4

Residual sugar is the sugar left after fermentation has finished or been artificially stopped, measured in grams per litre.

Alcohol content (mainly ethyl alcohol) is expressed in percent by volume of the total liquid. (Also known as 'degrees'.)

Acidity is both fixed and volatile. **Fixed acidity** consists principally of tartaric, malic and citric acids which are all found in the grape, and lactic and succinic acids which are produced during fermentation. **Volatile acidity** consists mainly of acetic acid, which is rapidly formed by bacteria in the presence of oxygen. A small amount of volatile acidity is inevitable and even attractive. With a larger amount the wine becomes 'pricked' – starts to turn to vinegar.

Total acidity is fixed and volatile acidity combined. As a rule of thumb for a well-balanced wine it should be in the region of one gram per thousand for each 10°Oechsle (see above).

pH is a measure of the strength of the acidity, rather than its volume. The lower the figure the more acid. Wine normally ranges in pH from 2.8 to 3.8. Winemakers in hot climates can have problems getting the pH low enough. Lower pH gives better colour, helps prevent bacterial spoilage and allows more of the SO_2 to be free and active as a preservative.

Sulphur dioxide (SO_2) is added to prevent oxidation and other accidents in winemaking. Some of it combines with sugars etc and is known as '**bound**'. Only the '**free**' SO_2 that remains in the wine is effective as a preservative. **Total SO_2** is controlled by law according to the level of residual sugar: the more sugar, the more SO_2 needed.

A few words about words

In the shorthand essential for this little book (and sometimes in bigger books as well) wines are often described by adjectives that can seem irrelevant, inane – or just silly. What do 'fat', 'round', 'full', 'lean' and so on mean when used about wine? Some of the more irritatingly vague are expanded in this list:

Attack The first impression of the wine in your mouth. It should 'strike' positively, if not necessarily with force. Without attack it is feeble or too bland.

Attractive Means 'I like it, anyway'. A slight put-down for expensive wines; encouragement for juniors. At least refreshing.

Balance See Well-balanced.

Big Concerns the whole flavour, including the alcohol content. Sometimes implies clumsiness, the opposite of elegance. Generally positive, but big is easy in California and less usual in, say, Bordeaux. So the context matters.

Charming Rather patronizing when said of wines that should have more impressive qualities. Implies lightness and possibly slight sweetness. A standard comment regarding Loire wines.

Crisp With pronounced but pleasing acidity; fresh and eager.

Deep/depth This wine is worth tasting with attention. There is more to it than the first impression; it fills your mouth with developing flavours as though it had an extra dimension. (Deep colour simply means hard to see through.) All really fine wines have depth.

Easy Used in the sense of 'easy come, easy go'. An easy wine makes no demand on your palate (or intellect). The implication is that it drinks smoothly, doesn't need maturing, and all you remember is a pleasant drink.

Elegant A professional taster's favourite term when he or she is stuck to describe a wine whose proportions (of strength, flavour, aroma), whose attack, middle and finish, whose texture and whose overall qualities call for comparison with other forms of natural beauty.

Fat With flavour and texture that fills your mouth, but without aggression. Obviously inappropriate in eg a light Moselle, but what you pay your money for in Sauternes.

Finish See Length.

Firm Flavour that strikes the palate fairly hard, with fairly high acidity or tannic astringency giving the impression that the wine is in youthful vigour and will age to gentler things. An excellent quality with high-flavoured foods, and almost always positive.

Flesh Refers to both substance and texture. A fleshy wine is fatter than a 'meaty' wine, more unctuous if less vigorous. The term is often used of good Pomerols, whose texture is notably smooth.

Flowery Often used as though synonymous with fruity, but really means floral, like the fragrance of flowers. Roses, violets, etc are sometimes specified.

Fresh Implies a good degree of fruity acidity, even a little nip of sharpness, as well as the zip and zing of youth. All young whites should be fresh: the alternative is flatness, staleness. . . ugh.

Fruity Used for almost any quality, but really refers to the body and richness of wine made from good ripe grapes. A fruity aroma is not the same as a flavoury one. Fruitiness usually implies at least a slight degree of sweetness. Attempts at specifying *which* fruit the wine resembles can be helpful. Eg grapefruit, lemon, plum, lychee. On the other hand writers' imaginations freqently run riot, flinging basketfuls of fruit and flowers at wines which could well be more modestly described.

Full Interchangeable with full-bodied. Lots of 'vinosity' or wineyness: the mouth-filling flavours of alcohol and 'extract' (all the flavouring components) combined.

Hollow Lacking a satisfying middle flavour. Something seems to be missing between first flavour and last. A characteristic of wines from greedy proprietors who let their vines produce too many grapes. A very hollow wine is 'empty'.

Lean More flesh would be an improvement. Lack of mouth-filling flavours; often astringent as well. Occasionally a term of appreciation of a distinct and enjoyable style.

Length The flavours and aromas that linger after swallowing. In principle the greater the length the better the wine. One second of flavour after swallowing = one 'caudalie'. Ten caudalies is good; 20 terrific.

Light With relatively little alcohol and body, as in most German wines. A very desirable quality in the right wines.

Meaty Savoury in effect with enough substance to chew. The inference is lean meat; leaner than in 'fleshy'.

Oaky Smelling or tasting of fresh-sawn oak, eg a new barrel. Appropriate in a fine wine destined for ageing in bottle, but currently often wildly overdone by winemakers to persuade a gullible public that a simple wine is something more grandiose. Over-oaky wines are both boring and tiring to drink.

Plump The diminutive of fat, implying a degree of charm as well.

Rich Not necessarily sweet, but giving an opulent impression.

Robust In good heart, vigorous, and on a fairly big scale.

Rough Flavour and texture give no pleasure. Acidity and/or tannin are dominant and coarse.

Round Almost the same as fat, but with more approval.

Structure The 'plan' of the flavour, as it were. Without structure wine is bland, dull, and won't last.

Stylish Style is bold and definite; wears its cap on its ear.

Supple Often used of young red wines which might be expected to be more aggressive. More lively than an 'easy' wine, with implications of good quality.

Well-balanced Contains all the desirable elements (acid, alcohol, flavours, etc) in appropriate and pleasing proportions.

Masters of Wine

The Institute of Masters of Wine was founded in London in 1953 to provide an exacting standard of qualification for the British wine trade. A small minority pass its very stiff examinations, even after rigorous training, both theoretical and practical. (They must be able to identify wines 'blind', know how they are made, and also know the relevant EC and Customs regulations.) In all, only 162 people have qualified to become Masters of Wine. Twenty-three 'Masters' are women.

In 1988 the Institute, aided by a grant from the Madame Bollinger Foundation, opened its examinations for the first time to non-British candidates. The first to pass was a New Zealander. 'Master of Wine' (MW) should eventually become the equivalent of a Bachelor of Arts degree in the worldwide wine trade.

What to drink in an ideal world

Wines at their peak in 1994

Red Bordeaux
Top growths of 87, 84, 83, 81, 79, 78, 76, 75, 70, 66, 62, 61, 59
Other crus classés of 87, 86 (St-Emilion/Pomerol), 85, 83, 82 (St-Emilion/Pomerol), 81, 79, 78, 75, 70, 66, 61
Petits châteaux of 90, 89, 88, 86, 85, 83, 82

Red Burgundy
Top growths of 87, 86, 85, 82, 80, 79, 78, 76, 72, 71, 69, 66, 64
Premiers Crus of 89, 88, 87, 86, 85, 83, 78, 76, 71
Village wines of 91, 90, 89, 88, 85

White Burgundy
Top growths of 89, 88, 87, 86, 85, 83, 82, 79, 78...
Premiers Crus of 91, 90, 89, 88, 86, 85, 83, 78...
Village wines of 92, 91, 90, 89, 88, 86, 85

Champagne
Top wines of 85, 83, 82, 81, 79, 78, 76, 75...

Sauternes
Top growths of 85, 84, 83, 82, 81, 79, 78, 76, 75, 71, 70, 67...
Other wines of 89, 88, 86, 85, 83, 82, 81, 79, 76, 75...

Sweet Loire wines
Top growths (Anjou/Vouvray) of 88, 86, 85, 78, 76, 75, 71, 64...

Alsace
Grands Crus and late-harvest wines of 89, 88, 86, 85, 83, 81, 78, 76...
Standard wines of 92, 91, 90, 89, 88, 85, 83...

Rhône reds
Hermitage/top northern Rhône reds of 88, 86, 85, 83, 82, 79, 78, 71, 70, 69...
Châteauneuf-du-Pape of 91, 89, 88, 86, 85, 83, 82, 81

German wines
Great sweet wines of 86, 85, 83, 76, 75, 71, 67...
Auslesen of 88, 86, 85, 83, 79, 76, 75, 71...
Spätlesen of 91, 89, 88, 86, 85, 83, 79, 76...
Kabinett and QbA wines of 91, 90, 89, 88, 85, 83...

Italian wines
Top Tuscan reds 88, 86, 85, 82, 79, 78, 71
Top Piedmont reds 87, 86, 85, 83, 82, 79, 78, 74, 71...

California wines
Top Cabernets/Zinfandels of 88, 86, 85, 84, 82, 81, 80, 79, 78, 77, 76, 75, 74, 70
Most Cabernets etc of 89, 88, 87, 86, 85...
Top Chardonnays of 90, 89, 88, 87, 86, 85, 83, 82, 81, 79...
Most Chardonnays of 92, 91, 90, 89, 88...

Australian wines
Top Cabernets and Shiraz of 89, 88, 86, 84, 82, 80, 79, 75, 71...
Most Cabernets etc of 90, 89, 88, 87, 86...
Top Chardonnays of 91, 90, 89, 88, 87, 86
Most Chardonnays of 92, 91...
Top Sémillons and Rieslings of 91, 90, 88, 86, 82, 79...

Vintage Port
83, 82, 80, 75, 70, 66, 63, 60, 55, 48, 45...

QUICK REFERENCE VINTAGE CHARTS

These charts give a picture of the range of qualities made in the principal areas (every year has its relative successes and failures) and a guide to whether the wine is ready to drink or should be kept.

I	drink now		—	needs keeping
/	can be drunk with pleasure now, but the better wines will continue to improve		⊼	avoid
		0	no good	10 the best

FRANCE

	RED BORDEAUX		WHITE BORDEAUX		ALSACE
	MEDOC/GRAVES	POM/ ST-EM	SAUTERNES & SW	GRAVES & DRY	
92	3–7 ∠	3–6 I/	3–6 —	4–7 I/	7–9 I/—
91	4–8 ∠	2–4 I/	2–5 /	6–9 I/—	5–8 I/—
90	7–10 ∠	8–10 ∠	7–9 ∠	7–8 I/	7–9 I/—
89	7–9 ∠	7–9 ∠	7–9 ∠	6–8 I/	7–10 I/
88	7–9 ∠	7–10 ∠	6–10 I/—	7–9 I/	8–10 I/
87	3–6 I	3–6 I	2–5 ⊼	7–10 I/	7–8 I
86	6–9 I/—	5–7 I/—	7–10 I/—	7–9 I	7–8 I
85	6–8 I/—	7–9 I/	6–8 I/	5–8 I	7–10 I/
84	3–6 I	2–5 I	4–6 I	5–7 ⊼	4–6 I
83	6–9 I/	6–9 I/	6–10 I/—	7–9 I	8–10 I
82	8–10 I/—	7–9 I/—	3–7 I/	7–8 I	6–8 I
81	5–8 I/	6–9 I/	5–8 I/	7–8 I	7–8 I
80	4–7 I	3–5 I	5–9 I	5–7 I	3–5 ⊼
79	5–8 I	5–7 I	6–8 I/	4–6 ⊼	7–8 I
78	6–9 I	6–8 I	4–6 I	7–9 I	6–8 I
77	3–5 ⊼	2–5 ⊼	2–4 ⊼	6–7 ⊼	
76	6–8 I	7–8 I	7–9 I/	4–8 ⊼	
75	4–8 I	5–9 I	8–10 I/	8–10 I	

	BURGUNDY			RHONE	
	COTE D'OR RED	COTE D'OR WHITE	CHABLIS	RHONE (N)	RHONE (S)
92	4–7 ∠	6–8 ∠	5–8 I/	4–8 ∠	3–6 ∠
91	5–7 ∠	4–7 I/	4–6 I/	6–9 I/—	4–7 I/
90	7–10 —	7–9 I/—	6–9 I/—	6–9 ∠	7–9 ∠
89	6–9 I/—	6–9 I/	7–10 I/	6–8 ∠	6–8 ∠
88	7–10 I/—	7–9 I/	7–9 I/	7–9 I/—	5–8 I/—
87	6–8 I/	4–7 I/	5–7 I	3–6 I/	3–5 I
86	5–8 I/	7–10 I/	7–9 I	5–8 I/	4–7 I/
85	7–10 I/—	5–8 I/	6–9 I	6–8 I/	6–9 I/—
84	3–6 ⊼	4–7 ⊼	4–7 ⊼	5–7 I	4–6 I
83	5–9 I/	6–9 I	7–9 I	7–10 I/	7–9 I
82	4–7 I	6–8 I	6–7 I	5–8 I	5–8 I/
81	3–6 ⊼	4–8 I	6–9 I	5–7 I	4–7 I
80	4–7 I	4–6 ⊼	5–7 ⊼	6–8 I	5–8 I

Beaujolais 92 was very good, 91 superb, the fourth very good vintage in a row. **Mâcon-Villages** (white) 92, 91 and 90 are good now. **Loire** (Sweet Anjou and Touraine) best recent vintages: 90, 89, 88, 85, 84, 83, 82, 79, 78, 76. **Upper Loire** (Sancerre and Pouilly Fumé): 90, 89, 88 are good now. **Muscadet** DYA.

	GERMANY		ITALY	USA	
	RHINE	MOSELLE	TUSCAN REDS	CALIFORNIA CABS	CALIFORNIA CHARDS
92	5–9 I/—	5–9 I/—	3–6 I/	6–9 —	6–8 I/
91	5–7 I/—	5–7 I/—	4–6 I/	8–10 —	5–7 I/
90	8–10 I/—	8–10 I/—	7–10 ∠	7–9 ∠	6–9 I/
89	7–10 I/—	8–10 I/—	5–8 I/	6–9 ∠	5–8 I/
88	6–8 I/	7–9 I/—	6–9 I/	6–8 I/	6–8 I/
87	4–7 I	5–7 I	4–7 I	7–10 I/—	7–9 I/
86	4–8 I	5–8 I	5–8 I/	5–8 I/	6–8 I
85	6–8 I/	6–9 I/	7–10 I/—	7–9 I/—	7–9 I
84	4–6 ⊼	4–6 ⊼	0–4 ⊼	5–7 I	4–6 ⊼
83	6–9 I	7–10 I/	5–7 I	4–8 I/	4–7 I
82	4–6 ⊼	4–7 ⊼	5–8 I/	5–8 I/	5–6 I
81	5–8 ⊼	4–8 ⊼	4–7 I	4–7 I	6–8 ⊼
80	4–7 ⊼	3–7 ⊼	6–7 I	5–7 I	5–7 ⊼